PHL

54060000107606

WITHDRAWN

THE
PAUL HAMLYN
LIBRARY

———◆———

DONATED BY
THE PAUL HAMLYN
FOUNDATION
TO THE
BRITISH MUSEUM

———◆———

opened December 2000

D1348886

Parchments of Gender

Parchments of Gender

Deciphering the Bodies of Antiquity

Edited by
MARIA WYKE

CLARENDON PRESS · OXFORD
1998

Oxford University Press, Great Clarendon Street, Oxford OX2 6DP
Oxford New York
Athens Auckland Bangkok Bogotá Buenos Aires Calcutta
Cape Town Chennai Dar es Salaam Delhi Florence Hong Kong Istanbul
Karachi Kuala Lumpur Madrid Melbourne Mexico City Mumbai
Nairobi Paris São Paolo Singapore Taipei Tokyo Toronto Warsaw
and associated companies in
Berlin Ibadan

Oxford is a registered trade mark of Oxford University Press

Published in the United States
by Oxford University Press Inc., New York

© Oxford University Press 1998
The moral rights of the author have been asserted

All rights reserved. No part of this publication may be reproduced,
stored in a retrieval system, or transmitted, in any form or by any means,
without the prior permission in writing of Oxford University Press.
Within the UK, exceptions are allowed in respect of any fair dealing for the
purpose of research or private study, or criticism or review, as permitted
under the Copyright, Designs and Patents Act, 1988, or in the case of
reprographic reproduction in accordance with the terms of the licences
issued by the Copyright Licensing Agency. Enquiries concerning
reproduction outside these terms and in other countries should be
sent to the Rights Department, Oxford University Press,
at the address above

British Library Cataloguing in Publication Data
Data available

Library of Congress Cataloging in Publication Data
Parchments of gender : deciphering the bodies of antiquity
edited by Maria Wyke.
Includes bibliographical references and index.
1. Body, Human—Social aspects—Mediterranean Region. 2. Body, Human—Symbolic
aspects—Mediterranean Region. 3. Sex role—Mediterranean Region—History. 4. Body,
Human, in literature. 5. Social history—To 500. 6. Mediterranean Region—Social life
and customs. I. Wyke, Maria.
GT497.M44P37   1998   306.4—dc21   98-8002
ISBN 0-19-815080-6

1 3 5 7 9 10 8 6 4 2

Typeset by Best-set Typesetter Ltd., Hong Kong
Printed in Great Britain on acid-free paper by
Bookcraft (Bath) Ltd., Midsomer Norton

306 . 4 WYK
WITHDRAWN
THE
BRITISH
MUSEUM
THE PAUL HAMLYN LIBRARY

Contents

Contents

List of Illustrations

Notes on Contributors

CYNTHIA M. BAKER is Assistant Professor of Judaism and Christianity in Late Antiquity in the Near Eastern Studies Department at Cornell University, Ithaca, NY. She has taught in both the Religion Department and the Women's Studies Program at Duke University and is the author of a number of articles on gender and space in Jewish antiquity.

MARY BEARD teaches Classics at the University of Cambridge and is a Fellow of Newnham College. She is preparing (with John Henderson) a book on Seneca's *Apocolocyntosis*.

JON L. BERQUIST is Editor at Chalice Press in St Louis, Mo. Formerly he was Associate Professor of Old Testament Studies and Associate Dean at Phillips Graduate Seminary, Tulsa, Okla. He is the author of *Judaism in Persia's Shadow: A Social and Historical Approach* (1995). His current research includes body and family rhetoric in ancient Judaism and Christianity.

SARAH CURRIE was a Fellow of the Pembroke Center for Teaching and Research on Women, Brown University, during their 1994–5 seminar series on 'A Question of Violence'.

EMMA DENCH is Course Director for Classics at Birkbeck College, University of London. She is the author of *From Barbarians to New Men: Greek, Roman, and Modern Perceptions of Peoples from the Central Apennines* (1995). She is currently working on concepts of identity in ancient Italy in the Julio-Claudian period.

CAROL DOUGHERTY is Associate Professor of Greek and Latin at Wellesley College. Her primary interests are oral poetics, ethnography, literature, and cultural studies of archaic and classical Greece. She is the author of *The Poetics of Colonization: From City to Text in Archaic Greece* (1993) and co-editor of *Cultural Poetics in Archaic Greece: Cult, Performance, Politics* (1993).

HELENE P. FOLEY is Olin Professor of Classics at Barnard College, Columbia University. She is the editor of *Reflections of Women in*

Antiquity (1981), author and editor of *The Homeric Hymn to Demeter* (1994), co-author of *Women in the Classical World: Image and Text* (1994), and author of *Ritual Irony: Poetry and Sacrifice in Euripides* (1985), as well as articles on Greek literature and women in antiquity.

ERIK GUNDERSON is Assistant Professor of Classics at Ohio State University. In 1996 he completed his doctoral thesis on rhetorical theories of performance in the Roman world. His main research interests include problems in the construction of masculine identity at Rome; to this end he has worked on Roman spectacles, rhetoric, elegy, and philosophy as venues for male self-constitution.

EDITH HALL is Fellow in Classics at Somerville College, Oxford. She previously taught Classics at the Universities of Reading and Cambridge. She is the author of *Inventing the Barbarians: Greek Self-Definition through Tragedy* (1989) and the editor of *Aeschylus' Persians: Translated with Introduction and Commentary* (1996).

ANN ELLIS HANSON is a MacArthur Fellow and at present teaches in the Department of Classical Studies, University of Michigan. She is the author of some sixty articles in the fields of papyrology and Greek and Roman medicine, and edits both *the Society for Ancient Medicine Review* and the *American Studies in Papyrology* monograph series. She is currently preparing a new critical edition of Hippocrates, *Diseases of Women I and II*, and is editing papyrus texts from Roman Egypt.

JOHN HENDERSON teaches Classics at the University of Cambridge and is a Fellow of King's College. Among his books is (with Mary Beard) *Classics: A Very Short Introduction* (1995).

MARIA WYKE is Senior Lecturer in Classics at the University of Reading. She has published widely on gender and the representation of women in ancient Rome, co-edited a volume of essays on *Women in Ancient Societies: 'An Illusion of the Night'* (1994), and is author of *Projecting the Past: Ancient Rome, Cinema and History* (1997). As a companion to this volume, she has also edited a Special Issue for the journal *Gender and History* on 'Gender and the Body in the Ancient Mediterranean' (1997).

Introduction

MARIA WYKE

THE central and unifying theme of this collection is the ancient body's relation to gender, for the bodies and genders of antiquity still matter. Ancient bodies continue to be appropriated as sites on which to negotiate modern sexualities and genders, their somatic metaphors can still activate the gendered rhetoric and practices of (for example) modern warfare, and their analysis now occupies a prominent place in current academic debates about sexuality, gender, and the body.[1]

Thanks to Michel Foucault's three-volume *History of Sexuality* (whose last two volumes on ancient sexualities were published in English translation in 1985 and 1986), antiquity has gained a significant purchase on the historiography of sexuality. For Foucault, a proper understanding of sexuality as a culturally constructed discursive apparatus necessitated a return to the texts of antiquity in order to study the formation of the desiring subject in the cultures of Greece, Rome, and early Christianity. The seeming alterity of our distant past became an instrument with which to challenge contemporary belief in the existence of biologically determined, historically unchanging sexual behaviours and identities. The publication of Foucault's work immediately led to an outburst of interest in ancient sexual systems among scholars of antiquity, and to a substantial increase in the audience for such scholarship.[2] Recognizing the insufficiency of Foucault's understanding of ancient sexualities (such

---

[1] For the following discussion of scholarship on sexuality, gender, and the body in antiquity see also M. Wyke (ed.), *Gender and the Body in Mediterranean Antiquity*, *Gender and History*, Special Issue 9.3 (Blackwell, Oxford, 1997).

[2] In 1990 alone, three book-length essay collections and one special issue of a non-classical journal were published on the subject of ancient sexuality: John J. Winkler, *The Constraints of Desire: The Anthropology of Sex and Gender in Ancient Greece* (Routledge, London, 1990); David Halperin, *One Hundred Years of Homosexuality* (Routledge, London, 1990); David Halperin, John J. Winkler, and Froma Zeitlin (eds.), *Before Sexuality: The Construction of Erotic Experience in the Ancient Greek World* (Princeton University Press, Princeton, 1990); *differences*, 2.1 (1990), guest edited by David Konstan and Martha Nussbaum under the title 'Sexuality in Greek and Roman Society'.

as his notorious elision of female desire), such scholarship in turn has
been fed by, or interlocked with, a more broadly based analysis of gender
in antiquity. Anthologies now regularly appear in which the ancient
sexual subject is conceived as necessarily enmeshed in larger discourses
of female–male relations, and its study as requiring confrontation with
the total interdependence of gender identities and the centrality of hier-
archically organized gender distinctions to all ancient intellectual and
social systems.[3]

Along with sexuality and gender, the body has also become a central
analytical tool in the study of subject formation. In the first volume of
History of Sexuality, Foucault wrote that, ever since the seventeenth
century, there has been an increasing intensification in the West of the
body as an object of knowledge and an element in relations of power.
Following on and expanding from Foucault's concern with discourses of
sexuality and the body, a continually expanding corpus of critical literature has theorized and historicized the body as a cultural construct, from,
for example, the sociological publications on the body of *Theory, Culture
and Society* to Judith Butler's concerns with the discursive control over
bodies and sexualities in *Bodies that Matter: On the Discursive Limits of
'Sex'* (1993).[4] Such studies disclose that the surface of the body is a crucial
site for the display of difference (including gender difference), its examination and physical transformation or containment fundamental to a
particular society's practices of power. Just as Foucault, in his later volumes of *History of Sexuality*, recognized the crucial role of the cultural
discourses of Greece, Rome, and early Christianity in the formation of
sexuality, so more recent scholars have recognized the fundamental contribution of antiquity to the cultural formation of the body as a concept
and a set of practices in the West and, consequently, its historically

---

[3] Anthologies whose essays are frequently cited in this volume include: Amy Richlin
(ed.), *Pornography and Representation in Greece and Rome* (Oxford University Press,
Oxford, 1992); Nancy S. Rabinowitz and Amy Richlin (eds.), *Feminist Theory and the
Classics: Thinking Gender* (Routledge, New York, 1993); Léonie Archer, Susan Fischler, and
Maria Wyke (eds.), *Women in Ancient Societies: 'An Illusion of the Night'* (Macmillan,
Basingstoke, 1994); Richard Hawley and Barbara Levick (eds.), *Women in Antiquity: New
Assessments* (Routledge, London, 1995).

[4] The following are examples of the most recent theoretical works on the body on which
this volume itself draws: Mike Featherstone, Mike Hepworth, and Bryan S. Turner (eds.),
The Body: Social Process and Cultural Theory (SAGE, London, 1991); Sue Scott and David
Morgan (eds.), *Body Matters: Essays on the Sociology of the Body* (Falmer, London, 1993);
Chris Shilling, *The Body and Social Theory* (SAGE, London, 1993); Judith Butler, *Bodies that
Matter: On the Discursive Limits of 'Sex'* (Routledge, New York, 1993).

constituted bodies have regularly appeared in research on antiquity from the late 1980s.[5]

The body/gender axis of *Parchments of Gender: Deciphering the Bodies of Antiquity* thus brings together several central trends in current scholarship on the cultural construction of ancient subjects. In fact this volume originates from an overwhelming response to a call for papers to appear in a special issue of the journal *Gender and History* that was originally distributed by Edith Hall (for whose substantial work on the initial stages of this project I would like to express my great thanks). The disparate essays collected here, as those in its sister volume *Gender and the Body in the Ancient Mediterranean* (*Gender and History*, 9.3 (1997)), converge on a coherent account of ancient bodies as peculiarly privileged sites for the production, display, and regimentation of gender identity and gender differentials, and as a visible material locus for gender's complex interactions with other claims to identity in the communities of the ancient world from fifth-century BCE Athens to third-century CE Roman Galilee. Layered in history, the ancient body is not given naturally but culturally.[6] It is not a raw material upon which a conscious agent acts, but a semiotic system which its bearer can never fully master. Ancient bodies are, therefore, 'parchments of gender': textual skins on which gender is inscribed and on which can be traced other interconnected matrices of knowledge and power that give those bodies their seemingly legible contours. But already read, reread, and contested in antiquity, these parchments are for us now cracked and obscured and thus require the most careful transcription.

---

[5] See, for example, Aline Rousselle, *Porneia: On Desire and the Body in Antiquity*, trans. Felicia Pheasant (Basil Blackwell, Oxford, 1988); Peter Brown, *The Body and Society: Men, Women and Sexual Renunciation in Early Christianity* (Columbia University Press, New York, 1988); Page DuBois, *Sowing the Body: Psychoanalysis and Ancient Representations of Women* (University of Chicago Press, Chicago, 1988). More recent works engaged with ancient bodies which are cited in this volume include: Catharine Edwards, *The Politics of Immorality in Ancient Rome* (Cambridge University Press, Cambridge, 1993); Lesley Dean-Jones, *Women's Bodies in Classical Greek Science* (Clarendon Press, Oxford, 1994); Tamsyn Barton, *Power and Knowledge: Astrology, Physiognomics, and Medicine under the Roman Empire* (University of Michigan Press, Ann Arbor, 1994); Maud Gleason, *Making Men: Sophists and Self-Presentation in Ancient Rome* (Princeton University Press, Princeton, 1995); N. B. Kampen (ed.), *Sexuality in Greek Art* (Cambridge University Press, Cambridge, 1996). As this volume goes to press, I am also aware of at least two new anthologies on ancient bodies which are due to appear: James I. Porter (ed.), *Constructions of the Classical Body*, and Dominic Montserrat (ed.), *Changing Bodies, Changing Meanings: Studies on the Human Body in Antiquity*. I am grateful to them both for showing me drafts of their introductions prior to publication.

[6] See the introduction to Porter, *Constructions of the Classical Body*.

Despite the diversity of evidentiary sources and methodologies here deployed, the essays in *Parchments of Gender* collectively present a coherent problematic of antiquity's gendered bodies and persistently interrogate readings of them both then and now. Frequently overlapping in the regions, periods, and cultures placed under scrutiny, the essays work collaboratively to position the bodies of ancient Mediterranean societies as texts in a developing tradition of corporeal knowledge (whether medical, religious, philosophical, ethnographic, historical, rhetorical, poetic, artistic, and so on). All the contributions examine in various ways the intertextuality of ancient bodies, cataloguing metaphors for and of the body (woman's body as house, open quiver, ploughed furrow; man's body as beast, speech, warfare; the sickness of the body politic; the decoration of prose styles) which bind it to gender and other modes of cultural production. Such somatic discourses are defined as a practice of description, inscription, discipline, and instruction designed to place boundaries around sexual and gendered subjects and to control them. They constitute a taxonomy of gender requiring constant iteration through the technologies of performance, spectatorship, self-examination, display, or concealment in order to sustain their claims to authority.

The explorations of corporeal expressions of sexuality and erotic desire contained in this volume work to destabilize any simple binary division between masculinity and femininity and its association with hierarchical oppositions between domination and submission, penetration and receptivity, mind and body. Through their careful readings of ancient bodies, the contributors disclose that while femininity can appear as highly embodied, excessively sexual, and in need of control, it can also be invasive and even (in the case of Sapphic homoeroticism or imperial apotheosis) transcendently disembodied. Masculinity can appear as penetrable, unstable, highly embodied, and disturbingly hypersexual. The discourses of the ancient body here outlined also offer a visibly gendered physiognomy of social and political life. Women's bodies appear frequently as alienated, bodies for others, that are incapable of holding power or capable of threatening social order, contained, isolated, denigrated, even assaulted, yet none the less cherished, and displayed as integral to the health of the body politic. The male body is permanently troubled. Only constant self-scrutiny and control can attempt to ward off threats to the stability of masculine identity, to citizenship, the state, and military superiority posed by the fearful (yet simultaneously appealing) feminine Other.

Somatics push to the surface cracks and fractures in the contours of gender. Tension, contradiction, change, and failure are themes which recur throughout this volume's readings of ancient bodies. Excess and loss, abnormality and disease, poisoning and annihilation work to collapse the seeming order of ancient bodies and genders, and the ideal fixity of their boundaries.[7] While some contributors sketch out an ancient search for transcendence of the troublesome temporality of the body and the limitations of gender in memory, philosophic inquiry, song, ritual, or monumental sculpture, attention is also paid (particularly in the opening and concluding essays) to the importance of the emotional experience and the worldly consequences of antiquity's embodiment of gender. For antiquity's fragmentary, contradictory, but authoritative 'parchments of gender' have been taken up into the canons of later centuries as discourses through which to configure the genders, sexualities, politics, and ethnicities of later cultures and to construct the pleasures and the suffering of modern gendered bodies.

The arrangement of the essays in *Parchments of Gender* has been designed to provide a loose structure and sense of chronological progression, accumulating layers of history and transformation onto the gendered bodies of antiquity. However, the essays do not, nor are they meant to, constitute rigid distinctions of place, time, or topic nor do they pretend to construct some authentic evolutionary tale of the ancient gendered body through the ages, however superficially satisfying such a grand, linear narrative might seem. Several of the chapters, in fact, explicitly demonstrate the exchanges, transformations, or contradictions operating within and between ancient Mediterranean societies regarding the embodiment of gender. Instead *Parchments of Gender* offers diverse transcriptions of antiquity's gendered bodies, a far more fragmentary, contextual, and multi-layered enterprise. For, as the contributors suggest, the gendered bodies of antiquity are always multivalent, always undergoing change, and always in a state of permanent contradiction. In that, precisely, lies their fascination.[8]

We are very familiar with the idea that, in the tragic performances of fifth-century BCE Athens, male actors frequently costumed themselves in the 'bodies' of women. The almost exclusively male audience was then licensed to explore emotions such as grief and lamentation (conventionally disparaged as feminine) by watching their fellow-citizens 'playing

---

[7] On the significance of ancient bodies' lack of fixity, see Montserrat, *Changing Bodies, Changing Meanings*.

[8] See also Wyke, *Gender and the Body*.

the other'. In the opening essay of this volume, however, Edith Hall argues provocatively that this does not constitute the total emotional experience undergone by the male spectators of fifth-century tragedy. For satyr dramas regularly served as conclusions to such tragic performances in which a hypersexual, aggressive masculinity was paraded in the exaggeratedly phallic bodies of the satyric chorus. Through the collation and careful exploration of the surviving fragments of this neglected genre, Edith Hall suggests that the comic embodiment of a violent male eroticism may have functioned socially in the culture of the Athenian polis as a 'corrective' gendered contrast to tragedy's emphasis on the destructive *eros* of women. As she puts it incisively, Athenian male citizens left the theatre not crying but laughing, their confidence reaffirmed in a masculine collective identity, based on the body, in libidinal awareness, and in violence against women.

Greek lyric poetry and philosophy have also frequently provided a focal point for analyses of ancient genders, sexualities, and erotic desires. Conventionally, in such studies, women have been found to be equated with the body, nature, emotion, and the particular, men with mind, culture, reason, and the universal in a hierarchical organization of relations between the sexes. Through close comparative readings of the representations of female and male homerotic desire in the fragments of Sappho's lyric poetry and in Plato's philosophic dialogues, Helene Foley's essay works to destabilize such simple binary oppositions between femininity and masculinity. In contrast to Hall's depiction of the corporeal excess of satyric male *eros* in Athenian theatre, Foley demonstrates that in these texts *both* masculine and feminine erotics are represented as not exclusively about bodies. She thus counters a tendency in recent feminist criticism that pits Sappho as the paradigmatic celebrant of the materiality of the body against Plato's philosophic aim to transcend it. In both the cases of Sappho and Plato, she argues, their writings depict a radical withdrawal from the standard male pederastic relation with its emphases on erotic hierarchies of dominance and submission, self-control and citizenly behaviour, and its link to the political reproduction of the polis and its governing class.

After Foley's exploration of the poetic and philosophical transcendence of the body, Ann Hanson returns us to medical constructions of gender on and in the bodies of women. For example, was the uterus (and, by extension, its possessor) a dangerous, roaming animal to be tamed, as some early medical treatises suggest? Investigating the Hippocratic collections of recipes and therapies for gynaecological disorders dated to the late fifth and early fourth centuries BCE, Hanson observes that (prior to systematic dissection which would disclose the muscles and ligaments of the uterus) the collection cannot completely demystify uterine disorders, but the therapies they assemble from earlier sources are none the less modulated by an increasingly sophisticated medical knowledge of the gendered body. Causes and cures are outlined in terms of mechanical principles whereby woman's fundamental anatomical distinction is the soft and spongy texture of her flesh, her physiology dominated by a superabundance of blood, and her treatment for disease dictated by the logical principle that opposites cure opposites. Hanson thus pinpoints the beginnings of an epistemic shift in the medical construction of gender on women's bodies.

The next two essays are concerned with the impact of Greek conceptions of the gendered body on other communities in the ancient Mediterranean and tie new embodiments of gender to issues of ethnic identity, power, and the integrity of the body politic. The rhetoric of the Book of Sirach, a religious text depicting and prescribing the quotidian activity of the body and family life in the Jewish community of Palestine in the early Hellenistic period *c*.200–175 BCE, is infused with violence against its daughters' bodies. The text, as it is interpreted by Jon Berquist, faces the craven sexual seductiveness of an object the culture values economically and symbolically but proclaims it as forbidden to the father's own desire. Sirach's body rhetoric constructs a network of hierarchical social relations which controls the troubling daughter by keeping her ostensibly pristine and virginal in the house of her ever vigilant father. But why was such concern with the Jewish daughter and her dangerously sexual body not expressed in earlier wisdom literature? For Berquist, the father's power operates on the materiality of his daughter's body in parallel with effects in the social body. The narrator isolates himself and his daughter from the new Hellenized culture of an increasingly urbanized Palestine in which the sexual purity of young women's bodies has become a central issue alongside the purity of Jewish identity itself.

Emma Dench demonstrates further the close interconnection between questions of gender, bodily representation, ethnic identity, and military supremacy in Hellenistic and Roman Italy from the fourth to the first centuries BCE. From the Athenian polis of the fifth and fourth centuries BCE, she argues, first the peoples of Hellenistic and then of Roman Italy appropriated and redeployed the embodied and engendered rhetoric of barbarism in ethnocentric attempts to project the relative political positions of themselves and others in the world. Most frequently images of indigenous masculine austerity and self-control were set against and over the feminine decadence of the barbaric Other and read into and from bodies in terms of clothing, gesture, sexual behaviour, and appetite. By the end of the Roman Republic the application of such categories had become immensely complex and prone to slippage. For both Augustus and his marble city, 'masculine' austerity could now also mark a lack of cultural sophistication, while 'feminine' extravagance and consumption could advertise absolute power and limitless empire. In either case, these two competing modes of celebrating military success and superiority—austerity and decadence—were sited problematically on gendered bodies.

The troubled male body forms the subject of the next two essays as that body is manifested in two Roman texts of the late first century CE. Sarah Currie challenges the current critical tendency to explore the formation of gender through the body (outlined above) and, instead, considers how gender could invade bodies and threaten their subjectivity. Poisons disturb the Italian garden which Pliny the Elder attempts to craft in his *Historia naturalis*, published towards the end of the first century CE, because they are seemingly inseparable from life-giving herbal therapies. While the gynaecological treatises of the *Hippocratic Corpus* (as discussed in Hanson's earlier essay) reassuringly catalogue recipes and therapies for disorders of the female body, Pliny's text is beset by deception and death-dealing. When they intrude into his *Historia naturalis*, poisons disrupt the relation between bodies and subjects. They inhabit bodies and annihilate the supposedly fixed boundaries of the self. The practice of poisoning, furthermore, is here associated with women and becomes accordingly a threat peculiar to men. Poison invades, occupies, and feminizes male bodies, disturbing and then destroying their integrity. Through her investigation of the feminized activity of poisoning, Currie subverts any view of the ancient male body as a stable locus for the inscription of gender.

A new vision of the male body is laid out in Roman texts on the use of the orator's body and voice, such as Quintilian's *Institutio oratoria* (which was published within twenty years of Pliny's *Historia naturalis*). Drawing on Michel Foucault's *Discipline and Punish* and the *History of Sexuality*, Erik Gunderson suggests that discussions of oratorical performance constitute a new textural site for the elaboration of a technology of the Roman body. Roman rhetorical theorists such as Quintilian seek to secure a distinct social meaning for the orator's body as exclusively good and virile, as the body of a 'real' man—that is, an enfranchised adult, a masterful husband, a protective soldier. Quintilian's text produces a description of the male body, even creates a body, that requires of the orator a new self-reflexive operation of corporeal surveillance, and his handbook becomes a necessary prop because the orator's body is always on the verge of failing, of threatening to collapse into illegitimate effeminacy and thus ruin its bearer. Such readings of the orator's body have important worldly consequences because illegitimate bodies fall short of the status required to receive a hearing in the political space of Rome. As with Currie, Gunderson thus exposes the male body as one constantly vulnerable to gender troubles.

The essay by Mary Beard and John Henderson picks up on a number of earlier themes in this volume. It now deals with the body of the emperor, *the* man among Romans (after Gunderson), it investigates the problematics of representing absolute power (after Dench), and it explores the vocabulary of transcendence, of flight from the body into immortality (after Foley). The objects of their analysis are a set of official visual representations of imperial ascension into heaven, of the emperor's journey from man to god, on coins, cameos, and public commemorative sculpture. How does gender make a difference to the creation and representation of the new deity? For the additional conveyance of the emperor's wife to heaven posed considerable iconographic problems. Beard and Henderson argue that the visual construction of a divine Romanity was precariously realized through foreign schemata that placed the militant masculinity of the emperor at risk. Focusing in on the joint apotheosis of Antoninus Pius and his wife Faustina which was depicted on a column erected in 161 CE, they chart a shift from the militaristic triumphalism of a divine Roman masculinity to a Hellenizing cosmopolitanism of philosophized marital concordance. Torn between an insistence on the literal transport of bodies and sublation beyond carnal representation, coded in terms of gender norms, the result can be viewed as either powerful image-theatre or bathos.

Rounding off these modern rereadings of the ancient inscription of gender on the body, Cynthia Baker returns us to the Jewish communities of the ancient Mediterranean in the third century CE. She investigates the 'architectural' construction of the body of the Jewish wife in the culture of Roman Palestine, some 500 years after Sirach had required the containment of Jewish daughters in their fathers' house (as discussed in the earlier essay by Berquist). Why do the authoritative rabbinic texts of the period regularly deploy 'house' as a form of homology for the body of the Jewish wife? According to Baker, such a metaphoric physiology effectively prescribes the wife's role as caretaker of her body, cleaning it and setting it in order in service to the master of that 'house'. She argues further that the architecture of domestic housing in third-century Palestine operates as a discursive system of social practices that were also actively involved in the constitution of the wifely body as an invisible domain to be inhabited only by her husband. In clear contrast to the technologies of rhetorical theory which placed the Roman orator's body on constant display, open to the gaze of all (and most especially himself), the architectural mediation of social intercourse in Palestinian dwellings refuses surveillance and interrupts the gaze. Such 'anopticism' thus effectively constructs the Jewish wife's subjectivity through her bodily disappearance.

The two essays which conclude *Parchments of Gender* mark a significant break from the rest of the volume, for they explore the hegemonic force of or rhetorical appeal to the gendered bodies of antiquity in the popular culture and political discourse of the late twentieth century. New formations of ancient bodies continue to flourish in modern appropriations of them and their investigation opens the way to an analysis of the present. In my own essay, I consider the representation of the militant, martyred body of the Roman soldier Sebastian in British cinema of the 1970s, interpreting the production and reception of Derek Jarman's *Sebastiane* as a site for a hotly contested debate about British masculinity and homosexual desire in the aftermath of gay liberation. On what basis could Jarman's film appropriate from Christian hagiography the suffering body of St Sebastian as a visual emblem of homosexual identity and desire? I argue that play with the signs of gender could mark visual representations of the piercing of Sebastian as the delineation of a once forbidden sexual act. A youthful, beautiful Sebastian embodies a passive feminine role joyously receptive to his muscular, masculine penetrators. Furthermore, in the context of debates since the late 1970s on the value of sado-masochistic rituals of sexual pleasure, the narrative of Jarman's film can be reread as a challenge to the fixity of modern gender categorizations which have been conventionally deployed to denigrate homosexual identity. The suffering body of the Roman martyr is thus appropriated to heroize a passivity traditionally marked as feminine and to call into question modern taxonomies of gender and male *eros*. The male body of antiquity is here no longer assailed by gender troubles but rather revels in them.

Carol Dougherty concludes this volume appropriately with an appeal for a better understanding of the dynamic relationship between the past and present embodiment of gender, arguing that reflection on the one enriches our understanding of the other. She discloses how representations of rape in the mythology of ancient Greece and Rome interact with the real mass rapes of women which have taken place as recently as the spring of 1992 in the former Yugoslavia. She first looks to antiquity to restore a symbolic significance to rape as a weapon of modern, ethnic warfare. In the rhetoric of Greek and Roman conquest, she finds that women's bodies can stand in for a territory and its occupants. Rape there powerfully and persuasively represents military and political domination as erotic conquest; the aggressive penetration of a gendered body enacts the violent possession of a land. While Dougherty then finds such symbolism resurfacing in first-hand testimonies from Bosnian women about their own brutal experiences of wartime rape, she also observes that such chilling testimony reflects back on our understanding of such foundational myths as the rape of the Sabine women. In the light of the Bosnian war, we should consider that such ancient narratives of rape may incorporate not just metaphor but also textual indices of real violence enacted against women's bodies in pursuit of political conquest in the ancient Mediterranean. We may agree that ancient bodies are discursive constructs, 'parchments of gender', but the experiences that followed from such constructs could be brutally real.

1

Ithyphallic Males Behaving Badly; or, Satyr Drama as Gendered Tragic Ending

EDITH HALL

WHILE historians of European culture are familiar with ancient Greek tragedy and comedy, they are unlikely to be well acquainted with the third ancient theatrical genre, satyr drama. Hundreds of satyr plays were produced, yet only Euripides' *Cyclops* survives in its entirety, together with a substantial part of Sophocles' *Trackers* (*Ichneutae*).[1] One of the few certainties about this enigmatic genre is that its gender orientation was more profoundly male than that of tragedy and comedy. Like them it was produced by male poets and performed by male actors, in front of an almost exclusively male audience. Yet unlike the choruses of tragedy and comedy, which could represent either females or males, the chorus of satyr drama by convention consisted of male satyrs with conspicuous phalluses.[2]

Satyr plays served as the conclusions to performances of tragedy, in which the Athenian audience had often been identifying with female

[1] All citations of fragmentary satyr plays, except those by Euripides, are from the four completed volumes of *Tragicorum Graecorum Fragmenta*, ed. B. Snell and S. Radt (Vandenhoeck & Ruprecht, Göttingen, 1977–86). Euripidean fragments are cited from A. Nauck, *Tragicorum Graecorum Fragmenta*, 2nd edn., with supplement by B. Snell (Teubner, Hildesheim, 1964).

[2] The plural noun 'satyrs' (*saturoi*) was completely interchangeable with the term 'satyr drama' ('*saturikon* [or *silenikon*] *drama*'): see Ar. *Thesm.* 157, and Aristotle's pupil Chamaeleon's treatise on satyr drama, a companion piece to his *On Comedy*, which was entitled *On Satyrs* (*peri Saturon*): see F. Wehrli (ed.), *Die Schule des Aristoteles*, vol. ix, 2nd edn. (Schwabe & Co. Verlag, Basel, 1969), 60 and 85; F. Brommer, *Satyroi* (K. Triltsch, Würzburg, 1937), 4; G. M. Hedreen, *Silens in Attic Black-Figure Vase-Painting* (University of Michigan Press, Ann Arbor, 1992), 10 n. 1. This strongly supports the view that the presence of the satyr chorus was an invariable element of the genre. The case for satyr-free satyr drama has nevertheless occasionally been made since P. Décharme, 'Le Drame satyrique sans satyres', *REG* 12 (1889), 290–9. Yet the title of the Aeschylean *Nurses* (*Trophoi*) *of Dionysos* is irrelevant, for the satyrs will have been the nurses in that play, as they almost certainly were in Sophocles' *Dionysiskos*. The other alleged evidence for female choruses more likely suggests satyric transvestism: see below, n. 37.

characters and reacting with emotions socially constructed as 'feminine'. This chapter argues that one function of satyr drama was to reaffirm in its audience at the end of the tragic productions a masculine collective consciousness based in libidinal awareness.

In Sophocles' *Trackers* the nymph Cyllene says to the satyrs, 'You always did behave like a baby. You're a full-grown man with a beard. But you are as saucy as a goat among the thistles. It's time that bald skull stopped fluttering with ecstasy' (fr. 314. 366–8).[3] The satyrs, like their divine master Dionysos, confound many of the polarities by which the Greeks organized their conceptual grasp of the world.[4] They are almost human, yet both slightly bestial and marginally divine. They are childlike and yet their bald heads suggest that they are simultaneously old. They live in the untamed wild and yet in myth are involved in the invention of technology and the arts of civilization. They are innocent yet knowing, often stupid yet capable of cunning. They are pugnacious yet timorous and oddly charming. The single social and psychological boundary they emphatically do not confuse or challenge is that between male and female. They are culturally and behaviourally masculine and *homosocial*, by which I mean that they are represented as preferring to live with members of their own sex, and to share with them in performing exclusively masculine activities (for example, hunting and athletics). The satyrs are also by biology exaggeratedly male. Their extreme male libidinousness is visually signified by their state of almost invariable erection, represented in the theatre by the actors' costumes (see Fig. 1.1). When Cyllene says that the satyrs' bald heads are fluttering with ecstasy, a sexual double entendre is almost certainly intended, for the satyrs' rounded, naked bald heads, often pictorially represented thrusting forwards, offer a visual duplicate of their phallus-tip: punning on the similiarities between the Greek words for 'phallus' (*phallos* and *phales*) and for 'bald' (*phalakros*) came easily to the writers of satyr plays. The satyrs' hairiness and other enlarged bodily extremities—they have tails, upwardly pointing animal ears, and sometimes hoofed feet—complete the picture of a hyperbolic maleness, a caricatured male animality.

Satyrs are attested in ancient art and literature from archaic Greek

[3] Translated by D. L. Page, *Greek Literary Papyri*, vol. i (Harvard University Press, Cambridge, Mass., 1952), 51.

[4] On Dionysos' capacity for dissolving polarities see C. P. Segal, 'The Menace of Dionysos: Sex Roles and Reversals in Euripides' *Bacchae*', *Arethusa*, 11 (1978), 185–202, repr. in J. Peradotto and J. P. Sullivan, *Women in the Ancient World* (University of New York Press, Albany, 1984), 195–212.

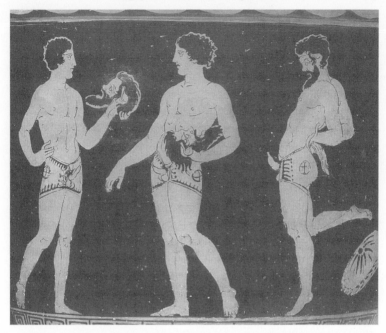

FIG. 1.1 Three chorus-men dress for a satyr play.

epic until the later Roman Empire, and their reputation as 'good-for-nothings' is already established in their earliest literary manifestation (Hesiod fr. 123. 2). But thereafter their identity is fundamentally defined by their sexual appetite:[5] all satyrs are potential rapists. In satyr drama they are obsessed with their genitals. In *Trackers* their father Silenus rebukes them for being just 'bodies and tongues and phalluses' (*phaletes*, *Ichn.* fr. 314. 150–1). A medicinal herb which enhanced sexual desire and performance in men was even named after them (Hesychius, s.v. *saturion*).

The satyrs' lust is often directed at their mythical female companions, the nymphs or maenads: the earliest mention of the silens (equivalents of the satyrs), in the *Homeric Hymn to Aphrodite* (262–3), depicts them making love to nymphs. Centuries later the satyr which Sulla's army

[5] See the hilariously thorough documentation by François Lissarrague, 'The Sexual Life of Satyrs', in D. M. Halperin, J. J. Winkler, and F. I. Zeitlin (eds.), *Before Sexuality* (Princeton University Press, Princeton, 1990), 53–81.

allegedly captured was found asleep in a grove of the nymphs (Plutarch, *Vit. Sull.* 27). When the satyrs' desires are directed at humans they become more frightening. According to the ancient sources, some people believed that satyrs really might assault women, at least in remote parts of the world. In the second century CE, for example, the Greek traveller Pausanias tells the story of the Carian Euphemos, whose ship was driven to islands inhabited by satyrs. The satyrs ran down to the ship and grabbed at the women passengers; the frightened sailors tossed them a barbarian woman, 'and she was raped by the satyrs not only in the usual place but all over her body' (1. 23. 7). Similarly, Philostratus, the biographer of the mystic and philosopher Apollonius, records that when Apollonius was dining in an Ethiopian village in the first century CE, he was surprised by the cry of the village women. The men grabbed clubs and stones and shouted for their friends as if they had caught an adulterer. It transpired that the village had for nine months been visited by 'the apparition of a satyr', which 'was mad for women and had already killed the two it apparently desired most' (Philost. *Vit. Apoll.* 6. 27).

The satyrs' literary heyday was the fifth century BCE, coincident with Athens' greatness as a democratic imperial power. During this period hundreds of satyr plays were performed after tragedies in the theatre of Dionysos at Athens. In satyr plays mythical heroic characters like those of tragedy (for example, Odysseus and Heracles) humorously interact with a chorus invariably consisting of priapic satyrs, and with the satyrs' father Silenus. The subject-matter is heroic myth. Favoured plot motifs are servitude and escape, drinking, eating, sex, hunting, and athletics. Athletics in particular opened up possibilities for raucous fun with the infibulation and associated practices which athletes used for controlling their penises during competitions: in Aeschylus' *Theoroi* Dionysos comments that the satyrs have prepared for competing in the athletics events at the Isthmian games by bobbing their ithyphalloi so that they now look like mouse tails (fr. 78a. 29). The temporal location of satyr drama is early mythical time, for it often portrays the infancy of gods and heroes or the invention of technologies such as wine or musical instruments. While both tragedy and comedy choose the civic settings of public spaces or citizens' homes, satyr drama usually reflects the imagined life of the pre-urban (even palaeolithic) male by locating itself outside mountain caves or on remote seashores.[6] Sophocles' *Trackers*, for example, is set on

---

[6] The Roman architect Vitruvius recommends that the scenery for satyr drama be decorated 'with trees, caves, mountains and other things associated with the countryside' (5. 6. 9).

Mount Cyllene in Arcadia. It portrays the enslaved satyrs tracking the stolen cattle of Apollo, arriving at the cave where the nymph Cyllene is nursing the newborn Hermes, and their response to the baby's invention of the lyre.

Satyr drama was performed by the same actors and chorus-members as the foregoing tragedies, and shared with tragedy most of its conventions (its heroes' costumes, metrical structures, and avoidance of audience address). The men who played the satyrs had previously dressed as the women, men, or supernatural females (e.g. the Oceanids in *Prometheus Bound*) who constituted the choruses of all extant tragedies. Yet the genre's jocularity, and its obsession with bodily functions, betray a closer affinity of ethos with comedy than with tragedy.[7] In Euripides' *Cyclops* cooking, eating, farting, and belching were central jokes (see e.g. 325–8, 523), and in Aeschylus' satyric *Lycurgus* the titular mythical king staggered around, drunk on beer (fr. 124). Satyr drama was also rowdier than tragedy: satyrs danced and pranced continuously, and used more meaningless 'shouting noises' (*epiphthegmata*)[8]—the satyrs in Sophocles' *Trackers*, for example, yell to the audience 'u u, ps ps, a a' (fr. 314. 176). The peripatetic critic Demetrius after all defined satyr drama as *tragoidia paizousa*, 'tragedy at play' (*de Eloc.* 169).

Euripides' *Cyclops* offers insights into the homosocial and sexually focused world of the satyr. It takes the incident of Odysseus' escape from the one-eyed giant Polyphemus from *Odyssey* 9 and introduces into the plot a chorus of satyrs who have been shipwrecked on Sicily and are currently the Cyclops's slaves. After drinking wine Polyphemus seizes Silenus, whom he mistakes for Ganymede, the Trojan boy Zeus loved. He staggers into his cave to rape the ageing satyr, thus allowing Odysseus and the others to blind him and subsequently escape. Polyphemus' sexual preferences, as he states, are homoerotic (583–4). He prefers this 'Ganymede' to the other satyrs, whom in his alcoholic confusion he identifies with the (female) Graces. *Cyclops* thus dramatizes a boisterous all-male plot involving drinking and morally uncomplicated violence enacted against a villain who also happens to be a homosexual rapist. But there are hints, even in this exclusively male world, of the satyrs' notion of the function of the female sex. Before Odysseus' arrival Silenus

---

[7] See B. Seidensticker, 'Das Satyrspiel', in G. A. Seeck (ed.), *Das griechische Drama* (Wissenschaftliche Buchgesellschaft, Darmstadt, 1979), 247.

[8] R. Browning (ed.), 'A Byzantine Treatise on Tragedy', in L. Varcl and R. F. Willetts (eds.), *Geras: Studies Presented to George Thomson* (Charles University, Prague, 1963), 67–81, at 70 par. 9.

laments the absence of wine on the island: he longs to drink in order
to get an erection, for it is a satyric topos that drink enhances
ithyphallicism.[9] In Nemesianus' *Eclogue* 3. 18–65, whose inspiration was
probably Sophocles' satyric *Dionysiskos*, the satyrs yearn sexually for
nymphs after drinking the newly invented wine. In *Cyclops* Silenus also
fantasizes about what he would do if there were any females available: he
wants to pull at breasts, and to handle 'depilated meadows' (169–71). By
this he means that he wants to fondle female genitals, for the 'meadow'
is a euphemism for the female pubic area. Satyrs enact Silenus' fantasy by
fingering the genitals of sleeping females in illustrations on several
vases.[10]

In *Cyclops* the satyric chorus' expressed views on women are confined
to their desire for Helen of Troy. In tragedy the people of both Troy and
Greece blame Helen for the Trojan War and would like to see her killed
(e.g. Eur. *Tro.* 874–9). But the satyrs of *Cyclops* have a different punishment in mind when they ask Odysseus what the Greeks did with her
(179–87):

So when you caught that young woman, didn't you all 'knock her through' one
after the other, since she takes pleasure in sexual intercourse with many men?
The traitress! When she glimpsed the man [Paris], with his embroidered baggy
trousers around his two legs and a golden chain around the middle of his neck,
she got so excited that she left Menelaus, the best of fellows. Would that the race
of women did not exist—except for a few for me![11]

Three aspects of the presentation of the satyrs' lechery here deserve
attention. First, sexual double entendre is a preferred mode of satyric
discourse, for the 'neck' (*auchen*) can in Greek imply an erect penis.[12]
Seaford therefore suggests that here the pair of baggy trousers is a euphemism for the scrotum.[13] Helen is imagined by the satyrs as becoming
excited by eyeing Paris' private parts. Secondly, multiple rape is the
satyrs' fantasy. All satyrs would obviously want to rape Helen. They may
actually have attempted to 'gangbang' her in Sophocles' *Marriage of
Helen* (see Aristides 2. 399). But they conceive rape as a *collective* activity.
The Cyclops' uncontrolled sexuality is portrayed as the impulse of an

---

[9] See Richard Seaford (ed.), *Euripides' Cyclops* (Clarendon Press, Oxford, 1984), 135, for
further examples.

[10] J. D. Beazley, *Attic Red-Figure Vase-Painters*, 2nd edn. (Clarendon Press, Oxford,
1963), 371. 14, 462. 43.

[11] My translation.

[12] J. Henderson, *The Maculate Muse: Obscene Language in Attic Comedy* (Yale University
Press, New Haven, 1975), 114 and 171.

[13] Seaford, *Euripides' Cyclops*, 139; see also Henderson, *The Maculate Muse*, 27.

autarkic, tyrannical individual who in threatening Silenus threatens the whole community of satyrs. In contrast the satyrs' eroticism, however rampant, is presented as fun rather than as dangerous partly because it is unindividuated, even egalitarian. Thirdly, the dream of a world without the 'race' of women is a misogynist commonplace, expressed by men in Euripides' own tragedies (see *Hipp.* 618–24). But the satyrs, as exponents of 'tragedy at play', typically undercut the seriousness of the rhetoric appropriated from tragedy with a comic clause exempting themselves from any ban on females.

Throughout tragedy's heyday in the fifth century BCE, satyr plays were an intrinsic part of the theatrical experience of watching tragic performances. At this time most tragedies were first performed at the City Dionysia, the largest annual Athenian festival of Dionysos, according to a regular formula of three-plus-one: three tragic poets competed against one another over three days with a programme of four plays each, three tragedies plus a satyr drama, performed in that order sequentially.

We do not know how the tragic competition came to be formulated as a contest between groups comprising three tragedies plus a satyr play. Aristotle may be correct in stating that tragedy developed out of a chronologically anterior satyr drama (*Poetics* 4. 1449^{a}19–24): alternatively, truth may lie behind Horace's view that satyr plays were added to the drama competitions after tragedy had become established in them (*AP* 220–1). But regardless of the evolutionary process, in the fifth century satyr drama was treated as an intrinsic part of the tragic performances, as fundamentally inseparable from the foregoing tragedies. Pat Easterling suggests that it is helpful to recall the tradition that the dramatist Ion of Chios criticized Pericles on the ground that virtue, like a complete 'tragic production' (*tragike didaskalia*), needed a satyric element (Plut. *Pericles* 5).[14] The three-plus-one formula did not last for ever. At some point in the fourth century, before 341 BCE, the programme was altered so that only a single satyr play preceded the entire drama festival.[15] Satyr plays are subsequently attested in various performance

[14] See P. E. Easterling, 'A Show for Dionysos', in P. E. Easterling (ed.), *The Cambridge Companion to Greek Tragedy* (Cambridge University Press, Cambridge, 1997), 36–53.
[15] See N. E. Collinge, 'Some Reflections on Satyr-Plays', *PCPS* 185 (1958–9), 28–35, at 28; A. W. Pickard-Cambridge, *The Dramatic Festivals of Athens*, 3rd edn., revised with a supplement by J. Gould and D. M. Lewis (Clarendon Press, Oxford, 1988), 79. The apparent exclusion of satyr plays from the contest when tragedies were introduced at the smaller Lenaea festival in the 430s BCE may have prefigured the 4th-century abandonment of the three-plus-one model. Perhaps that is also how we should see Euripides' pro-satyric experiment with *Alcestis*, whose performance was also in the 430s.

contexts until the second century CE,[16] including Python's fourth-
century *Agen*, in which Alexander the Great's administrator Harpalus
apparently attempted a necromancy to summon from the underworld
his dead *hetaira* Pythionike.[17] But the current argument is concerned
solely with the fifth-century satyr play's function as the final component
of a composite performance of four dramas.

In earlier tragedy, particularly in Aeschylus, the satyr drama was sometimes connected in subject-matter with the tragedies which had preceded
it, forming what the later Alexandrian scholars called a *tetralogy*. To close
the *Oresteia* tetralogy, for example, the satyric *Proteus* treated Menelaus'
journey home from Troy. The first preceding tragedy, *Agamemnon*, had
dramatized his brother's homecoming in a more sombre manner. Other
Aeschylean tetralogies included the *Oedipodeia* (the satyr drama was
Sphinx), the *Danaids*, and the *Lycurgeia*. But Aeschylus also sometimes
presented four plays without any obvious connection in subject-matter,
for example the group *Phineus*, *Persae*, *Glaukos Potnieus*, and the satyric
Prometheus Firekindler.[18] Little illumination, however, is to be gained
from exploring connected tetralogies, since neither *Cyclops* nor any of
the more substantial fragments is known to have been part of any extant
tragike didaskalia.[19]

Since the satyr play functioned for decades as the conclusion to and
culmination of tragic performances at the City Dionysia, it must have
been perceived in that context to be aesthetically, psychologically, emotionally, and socially appropriate, even indispensable. The two genres
were fundamentally and dialectically interdependent.[20] Discussions of
the relationship between them goes back even beyond Demetrius (see
above), but none, apparently, has explored the gender dynamics of this
interface.

In the Renaissance (besides regularly being confused with satire),
satyr drama was viewed as a genre intermediate between tragedy and
comedy, and 'imitated' in the form of pastoral tragicomedy. *Cyclops*,
indeed, played an important role in the discussion of mixed genres in

---

[16] See Seidensticker, 'Das Satyrspiel', 228–31.
[17] See B. Snell, *Scenes from Greek Drama* (University of California Press, Berkeley and
Los Angeles, 1964), 99–138.
[18] On possible links between these plays see Edith Hall (ed.), *Aeschylus' Persians* (Aris &
Phillips, Warminster, 1996), 10–11.
[19] On the exiguous remains of Aeschylus' *Amymone* (which was the last play of the
Danaids tetralogy) see below.
[20] The first scholar to perceive the dialectical interdependence of the two genres was
F. Brommer, *Das Satyrspiele* (De Gruyter, Berlin, 1959), 5: 'The satyr play in its heyday
is unthinkable without tragedy, but so is tragedy unthinkable without satyr drama.'

general.[21] Satyr drama was first properly understood by Isaac Casaubon in 1605, but his treatise still bears traces of this 'mixed' or 'middle' genre theory.[22] In the nineteenth century three new concepts entered the critical discourse: first, the notion of tragic 'burlesque' (or 'travesty' or 'parody'). Secondly, A. W. Schlegel's famous lectures introduced the functionalist idea of satyr drama as providing psychological 'release', 'relaxation', or 'resolution' of tragic conflict.[23] Thirdly, aesthetic disapproval was expressed as commentators began to see satyr drama as a regrettably primitive 'after-piece' of no intrinsic merit or pertinence to the foregoing tragedies: 'the practice of terminating a trilogy with a satyric play . . . may seem questionable to modern taste, and can hardly be defended upon artistic grounds.'[24] Throughout our own century many have continued to draw on the 'parody', 'release', and 'inferior after-piece' paradigms. The last two are fused, for example, in the introduction to a Penguin translation of *Cyclops* and *Trackers* published in 1957:

Thus we have the unique example of a primitive drama continuing to exist side by side with the highest literary achievement; of the greatest dramatists writing what are almost folk-plays as well as their great tragedies . . . It is almost as if Shakespeare had written a *Punch and Judy* to be presented as an after-piece to *Romeo and Juliet* . . . By the time of Sophocles and Euripides the most obvious function of the satyr play was to supply a release from the tragic tension of the preceding plays.[25]

More adventurous conceptions of the genre have appeared, but gender has never figured prominently in their formulation: satyr drama has been thought to offer the tragic playwrights a chance to abandon heroics and write more realistically,[26] or to make explicit references to contemporary politics.[27] Luigi Campo's triple division of satyr dramas into those with

---

[21] B. M. T. Herrick, *Tragicomedy* (University of Illinois Press, Urbana, Ill., 1955), 7–14.

[22] *De Satyrica Graecorum poesi, & Romanorum satira libri duo* (Paris, 1605, repr. in facsimile with an introduction by P. E. Medine, Delmar, New York, 1973), 130–1: 'A satyr play is a dramatic poem, connected with tragedy, with a chorus composed of satyrs. It represents a notable action pertaining to illustrious persons, which is partly serious and partly humorous, with a jocular style and for the most part a happy outcome.'

[23] A. W. Schlegel, *A Course of Lectures on Dramatic Art and Literature*, 2nd edn., trans. John Black (H. G. Bohn, London, 1846), i. 189.

[24] A. E. Haigh, *The Attic Theatre* (Clarendon Press, Oxford, 1889), 25.

[25] R. L. Green, *Two Satyr Plays: Euripides Cyclops and Sophocles' Ichneutai*, trans. with an introd. (Penguin, Harmondsworth, 1957), 11.

[26] M. Pohlenz, *Die griechische Tragödie*, vol. i, 2nd edn. (Vandenhoeck & Ruprecht, Göttingen, 1954), 134.

[27] C. T. Murphy, summary of 'Quae ratio inter fabulas satyricas et comoediam antiquam intercedat', diss. Harvard, *HSCP* 46 (1935), 206–9; F. Lassere, 'Le Drame satyrique', *RFIC* 101 (1973), 273–301.

an 'eroico', 'parodico', or 'amoroso' plot failed to perceive that the 'amorousness' of the genre is, in contradistinction to tragedy, apparently a male monopoly.[28] Indeed, the level of most critics' awareness of gender issues can be inferred from the fact that a prominent expert on satyr drama argued in print as late as 1980 that 'the general psychological principle is self-evident. Who of us has not received the advice that when going for an interview with a superior one should imagine him clad in his underwear?'[29]

Recently, however, critics have rightly been focusing on the religious and Dionysiac aspects of the genre. The poet Tony Harrison sees the physical conditions of the Athenian drama festivals, which united 'sufferer and celebrant in the same light', as the basis of the dialectical relationship between tragic and satyric drama.[30] Vase-paintings show that entourages of satyrs had been associated with the worship of Dionysos since well before the establishment of drama festivals. Pat Easterling therefore argues that the identity of the satyr chorus indicates that they enact something which has much more to do with Dionysos and his cult than either of the other genres.[31] F. Lissarrague's recent formulation defines the Dionysiac function of the satyrs as playing the same serious social issues as tragedy 'in a different key':[32]

we may say that satyrs reproduce the 'normal' values of Greek males by transforming them, according to a set of rules that are never random . . . Tragedy poses fundamental questions about the relation between mortals and gods, or it reflects on such serious issues as sacrifice, war, marriage, or law. Satyric drama, by contrast, plays with culture by first distancing it and then reconstructing it through its antitypes, the satyrs.

This anthropological interpretation is currently canonical, and invites further questions as to the way satyric drama plays with the 'serious issues' on which tragedy reflects. The economic and social implications of the encounter between man, monstrous giant, and satyr in *Cyclops* have been analysed by David Konstan. He argues that the contrast ultimately serves to present 'the human community . . . as the positive reali-

---

[28] *I drammi satireschi della Grecia antica* (Fratelli Bocca, Milan, 1940), 221–61.

[29] D. F. Sutton, *The Greek Satyr Play* (Hain, Meisenheim am Glan, 1980), 4.

[30] Tony Harrison, *The Trackers of Oxyrhynchus*, 2nd edn. (Faber & Faber, London, 1991), p. xiv.

[31] Easterling, 'A Show for Dionysos': the satyr play is a *culmination*, representing 'the performers ultimately getting nearest to their "true" cultic role of Dionysus' worshippers'.

[32] F. Lissarrague, 'Why Satyrs are Good to Represent', in J. J. Winkler and F. I. Zeitlin (eds.), *Nothing to Do with Dionysos?* (Princeton University Press, Princeton, 1990), 228–36, at 235–6.

zation of social relations', in contrast with both the monadic Cyclops and the unindividuated satyric collective.[33] It would be interesting to ask whether the motifs of slavery and release, and the communistic utopianism of the satyrs' group ideology, function as fantasy-correctives to the class-ridden city-state of Athens, founded on slave labour. But the question in hand is the relation between the satyrs' exclusively masculine viewpoint and the quite different perspective of tragedy, for satyr drama has been analysed by the male-dominated history of classical scholarship in a characteristically male-determined way—that is, by overlooking its gender dynamics altogether.

There is evidence that contemporary Athenians in the fifth century BCE viewed satyr drama's focus as distinctively masculine and sexualized. Aristophanes' *Thesmophoriazusae* (411) testifies to the early currency of a theory concerning dramatic representation, according to which a writer's own habits and perceived gender orientation influenced the characters he created. A 'womanish' man is thus more likely to create convincing parts for women characters than a 'masculine' one. Even adopting the dress and behaviour of women will help in writing tragedies about them. The interlocutors are the notoriously effeminate tragedian Agathon and a conspicuously 'butch' relative by marriage of the more famous tragedian Euripides (148–58):[34]

AGATHON. I change my clothing according as I change my mentality. A man who is a poet must adopt habits that match the plays he's committed to composing. For example, if one is writing plays about women, one's body must participate in their habits.

IN-LAW. So when you write a *Phaedra*, you mount astride?

AGATHON. If you're writing about men, your body has what it takes already, but when it's a question of something we don't possess, then it must be captured by imitation (*mimesis*).

IN-LAW. Ask me over then, when you're writing a satyr-play,[35] so I can collaborate with you, long and hard, from the rear.

The in-law's second joke illuminates the psychosexual orientation of satyr drama. To write a satyr play Agathon will need to be buggered. The transvestite Agathon's gender is ambivalent, for he is as effeminate as the Greek comic imagination could conceive a man to be. He is a man-

---

[33] 'The Anthropology of Euripides *Kyklops*', in Winkler and Zeitlin, *Nothing to Do with Dionysos?*, 207–27, at 227.

[34] Translation taken from A. Sommerstein (ed.), *Aristophanes' Thesmophoriazusae* (Aris & Phillips, Warminster, 1994), 33–5.

[35] The Greek text literally says 'when you are doing (or "making") satyrs' (*hotan saturous toinun poieis*): see above, n. 2.

woman who, the joke suggests, will collaborate in a satyr drama with the lustily masculine in-law while being anally penetrated by him. The success of the joke depends on the audience's assumption that the viewpoint of dramatic satyrs was collective, pointedly masculine, focused on the body, characterized by a hyperbolic sexual appetitiveness, and permitted both heterosexual and homosexual expression.

Do the remains of satyr drama substantiate the view of Euripides' in-law? Certainly Agathon's cross-dressing points to what seems to have been a regular satyric motif, for there is evidence for transvestite satyrs on vases.[36] There were also transvestite roles in satyr plays such as Ion's *Omphale*, where both Herakles and the satyrs, enslaved to the powerful Queen Omphale, seem to have donned women's attire.[37] Certainly the satyrs, unlike male characters in extant tragedy, are not exclusively heterosexual. Indeed, in Sophocles' *Lovers of Achilles*, in which *eros* was a topic of discussion generally (fr. 149. 8–9), Phoenix upbraided the satyrs for having turned from homoerotic to heterosexual ways, specifically for desiring women rather than boys (*ta paidika*, fr. 153). The homosexual tendencies of the satyrs are likewise implied in Achaeus' *Linos* (fr. 26), and documented on vases.[38] But the satyrs also despise effeminate males, for they taunt Dionysos himself with looking like a woman in Aeschylus' *Theoroi* (fr. 78a, 68). In Sophocles' *Trackers* Silenus boasts of the martial achievements of his youth, when he hung up trophies in nymphs' caves as evidence of his *manly* valour (*andreia*, fr. 314. 154).

One of the typical interests of the genre was invention, and even this motif was associated with (male) sexual arousal. Stage satyrs were privileged to be present at the introduction of fire to the terrestrial domain in Aeschylus' *Prometheus Firekindler*. In a fragment they envisage their domestic sex games now occurring in comfortable warmth (fr. 204b. 2–5): '[Throw down] your bright cloaks by the unwearying light of the fire. Often shall one of the naiads, when she has heard me tell this tale, pursue me by the blaze within the hearth.' The life-transforming arrival of fire allows the satyrs to fantasize that for once it will be they who are the

---

[36] See Brommer, *Das Satyrspiel*, nos. 118 and 118a.

[37] The female vocative plurals in Ion's *Omphale* ('maidens' and 'Lydian harp-women', frr. 20, 22), almost certainly apostrophize the satyrs temporarily dressed, like Heracles in service to Omphale, as women. In Euripides' *Skiron* the satyrs may either have dressed as women, or pursued female companions of Theseus (*The Oxyrhynchus Papyri*, 27 (1962), 57). Actors could put on additional (female) clothing over their satyric costumes (for a parallel see the goatskins in *Cyclops* 80); Seidensticker, 'Das Satyrspiel', 233; W. Steffen, 'The Satyr-Dramas of Euripides', *Eos*, 59 (1971), 203–26, at 207–8.

[38] Lissarrague, 'The Sexual Life of Satyrs', 64–5.

objects of erotic pursuit. The satyrs also tasted the first ever wine in Sophocles' *Dionysiskos* (of which one of the few fragments, Soph. fr. 173, is a masculine singular participle meaning 'drunk'), and the wine seems to have made them horny.[39]

In another Sophoclean play the satyrs actually participated in the invention of womankind. In a fragment of his *Pandora* one individual (Hephaestus?) is instructed by another to 'begin to manipulate the clay in your two hands' (fr. 482). This leaves little doubt that Pandora, the first woman, was actually constructed in the Athenian theatre, as she had been in Hesiod's accounts (*Theog.* 578–89, *Op.* 60–82). Other evidence links the satyrs with Hephaestus in the role of his workmen,[40] and the play had an alternative title, *Hammerers* (*Sphyrokopoi*), which indicates that the satyrs were involved. They either helped to craft Pandora, or hammered on the ground to release her from it, an interpretation perhaps supported by a vase-painting almost certainly inspired by this play, on which Pandora appears to rise from the earth (see Fig. 1.2).[41]

If the satyrs enjoy witnessing the creation of Woman, they also desire to win women as prizes in athletics. In a satyric dialogue probably composed by Sophocles, someone called Oineus or Schoineus converses with the chorus. [Sch]oineus has apparently announced that his daughter will be given to the victor in an athletics competition. When he asks the satyrs who they are, they deliver a manifesto of satyrdom (fr. 1130. 6–18):

We have come as bridegrooms, but are the children of nymphs, servants of Bacchus, and neighbours of the gods. Every proper art is embodied in us. On the one hand we can fight with spears, in wrestling matches, on horseback, in footraces, boxing, biting, and testicle-twisting; on the other hand musical song is implanted in us, and omniscient prophecy with no fakery, discriminating understanding of medicine, calculation of the heavens, dancing, and talking about the underworld. Is my attendance at this cult centre to prove fruitless? If you bestow your daughter upon me, you can take whichever of my skills you desire.[42]

This play therefore seems to have combined two of the satyrs' favourite physical activities: the pursuit of women (the princess's opinion is of

---

[39] For further references to drink enhancing sexual appetite in satyrs see above, n. 9.

[40] See A. C. Pearson (ed.), *The Fragments of Sophocles* (Cambridge University Press, Cambridge, 1917), i. 110, ii. 9, 136.

[41] An Attic red-figured volute-crater in Ferrara (T.579), dating from around 450 BCE. For a discussion and illustrations of the rest of the painting see A. D. Trendall and T. B. L. Webster, *Illustrations of Greek Drama* (Phaidon Press, London, 1971), 33 and pl. II. 7.

[42] My translation.

FIG. 1.2   Scene from a satyr play, perhaps Sophocles' *Pandora*.

course unlikely to have been taken into account), and athletics. The biting and testicle-twisting imply the most violent of the ancient combative athletic events, the *pankration*. This permitted almost any form of assault besides gouging out the opponent's eyes.

The surviving fragments of the satyr plays suggest that the sexual pursuit of females was not confined to the satyrs. Euripides' *Syleus* seems to have concluded with Herakles chasing Syleus' daughter (Xenodoke or Xenodike), through Syleus' vineyard.[43] Aeschylus' *Amymone* was the satyr play concluding his *Danaids* tetralogy, whose central topic had been the repudiation of marriage by Danaus' fifty daughters. The satyr play is likely to have enacted a marriage-related story preserved in Apollodorus (*Bibl.* 2. 1. 4), in which the Danaid Amymone was looking for water after a drought struck Argos. A satyr was about to rape her, but was disturbed by the arrival of Poseidon, who then had sex with her himself and revealed a spring to her. One of the only three fragments (fr. 13) has a male saying to a female that it is fated that she marry (or 'mate with'— *gameisthai*) him.[44]

From Sophocles' *Trackers* there survive about 180 lines of an altercation between the satyrs and the nymph Cyllene, who certainly fears their violence and shouting (fr. 314. 251–5). She is nursing the baby Hermes,

[43] *The Oxyrhynchus Papyri*, 27 (1962), 57–8.
[44] See D. F. Sutton, 'Aeschylus' *Amymone*', *GRBS* 15 (1974), 193–202.

who was borne by Atlas' daughter to Zeus (fr. 314. 267–76), but the satyrs are convinced that her cave conceals Apollo's cattle. They make no explicitly sexual threats against her, which may suggest that theatrical satyrs treated nymphs with more respect than human women. In Aeschylus' *Theoroi* (fr. 78a. 14–17) the satyrs seem to have a strong maternal attachment, and the satyrs' mothers are always nymphs. But the scene in Sophocles' *Trackers*, equally, may have concluded with an assault, perhaps a sexual assault, since the dialogue is turning into angry stichomythia just as the papyrus becomes unintelligible (fr. 314. 390–404).

The best example of heterosexual harassment in satyr drama is in Aeschylus' *Net-Fishers*, which dramatized the story of the baby Perseus. His mother Danaë was impregnated by Zeus (disguised as a shower of gold), locked up in a chest with the baby by her wicked father, and pushed out to sea. Eventually the chest arrived at the island of Seriphos and was hauled up in a fishing-net. The surviving scene involves an encounter between mother, baby, Silenus,[45] and the satyrs, in which Silenus plans to marry Danaë despite a (human) rival called Dictys. The text contains gaps, but it is clear that Danaë responds in horror to Silenus, calling on her ancestral gods to prevent her from being 'violated' (*lumanthesomai*) by the bestial satyrs (*knodalois*, fr. 47a. 765–85). Her register of speech is distinctly tragic, in comparison with the more colloquial and obscene vocabulary of the satyrs, which suggests that differentials in elevation of diction may have sometimes functioned in satyr drama to distinguish feminine from masculine speech.[46] Danaë contemplates suicide by hanging, a conventional method by which women kill themselves in tragedy.[47] Her fears are justified: even her child is at risk of sexual assault. For Silenus replies that her baby is smiling at his 'bald head'. Since the Greeks drew aural connections between their words for 'bald' and for 'phallus' (see above), this is almost certainly a euphemism

[45] Lloyd-Jones's case that Danaë's interlocutor in fr. 47a (765–72, 786–820) must be Silenus is overwhelmingly convincing (see *Aeschylus*, tr. H. W. Smyth, vol. ii, with an appendix by H. Lloyd-Jones (Harvard University Press, Cambridge, Mass., 1957), 33–5).

[46] It has been proposed that male heroes and satyrs used two different stylistic levels. W. Schmid argued that heroes had the same elevated diction as in tragedy, while the satyrs spoke in a lower register ('Der Hinzutritt des Satyrspiels', in W. Schmid and O. Stählin (eds.), *Geschichte der griechischen Literatur*, vol. i.2 (Beck, Munich, 1934), 83 n. 7). But Odysseus in *Cyclops* speaks just like Silenus.

[47] There is no justification for E. Lobel's view (*The Oxyrhynchus Papyri*, 18 (1941), 12) that Danaë's phrase 'Shall I then knot myself a noose' is influenced by slang: see Sophocles' *OT* 1374, Eur. *Hel.* 299. Her other allegedly untragic phrase, 'You have heard all I have to say', has a direct parallel at Aesch. *Ag.* 582.

for the tip of Silenus' phallus. He adds that 'the little one' is clearly a
'penis-lover' (*posthophiles*). An innocent critic once touchingly took this
scene as evidence that Aeschylus 'loved and knew infants intimately'.[48]
But Lissarrague much more plausibly draws attention to the equivalence
between a baby satyr and a phallus carried by two satyrs on the two sides
of an amphora in Boston.[49] In the male and highly sexualized world of
the satyr, bald heads and babies thus both become virtually indistinguishable from phalluses.

The papyrus' quality now improves. The satyrs envisage that Danaë
will marry Silenus rather than the rival Dictys, and believe her to be in
need of 'a good seeing to' (fr. 47a. 799–832):[50]

SILENUS. If I don't rejoice [at the sight] of you. Damnation take Dictys, who [is
trying to cheat] me of this prize [behind my back]. Come here, my dearie!
Don't be frightened! Why are you whimpering? Over here to my sons, so that
you can come to my protecting arms, dear boy—I'm so kind—and you can
find pleasure in the martens and the fawns and the young porcupines, and can
make a third in bed with your mother and with me your father. And daddy
shall give the little one his fun. And you shall lead a healthy life, so that one day,
when you've grown strong, you yourself—for your father's losing his grip on
fawn-killing footwork—you yourself shall catch beasts without a spear, and
give them to your mother for dinner, after the fashion of her husband's family,
amongst whom you will be earning your keep.
CHORUS. Come now, dear fellows, let us go and hurry on the marriage, for the
time is ripe for it and without words speaks for it. Why, I see that already the
bride is eager to enjoy our love to the full. No wonder: she spent a long time
wasting away all lonely in the ship beneath the foam. Well, now that she has
before her eyes our youthful vigour, she rejoices and exults; such is the bride-
groom that by the bright gleam of Aphrodite's torches . . .

Here the papyrus breaks off, but even this brief sequence is of unique
importance as the sole example of the satyrs of satyr drama in direct
colloquy with an object of their sexual desire. Danaë is indistinguishable
in this scene from a tragic heroine, but the pathos of her fear of rape is
undercut by the humorous presentation of the libidinousness of the
satyrs. The ageing Silenus' intentions towards Danaë may be more
domestic than erotic, and he seems to be more interested (in this scene,
anyway) in Perseus, the baby 'penis-lover', than in his mother. But the

[48] T. P. Howe, 'The Style of Aeschylus as Satyr-Playwright', *G&R* 6 (1959), 150–65, at 163.
[49] Lissarrague, 'The Sexual Life of Satyrs', 58.
[50] Translation by Lloyd-Jones, in *Aeschylus*, trans. Smyth, 537–41. Square brackets
enclose conjectural supplements.

satyrs themselves have only one thing in mind, and that is the delightful prospect of collective sexual intercourse with the woman before them. In the event Danaë was almost certainly spared the actual ordeal of multiple rape, and instead married Silenus' rival. But the intentionally comic fantasy of the satyrs speaks volumes about the psychosexual dynamics underpinning their group identity, and, by extension, that of their Athenian audience.[51]

Satyr drama, therefore, was characterized by an unapologetic obsession with male sexuality, visually represented in the satyric body, and a masculine, *homosocial* consciousness manifested in and articulated by its chorus of satyrs. The next stage in the argument requires establishing a distinction between this gender alignment and that of tragedy. First, some symbolism. On the rare occasions when the ancients represented the relationship between the two genres in visual or allegorical form, satyr play was certainly conceived as masculine in contrast with 'feminine' tragedy. On a vase from the last third of the fifth century a sexually excited satyr creeps up on a sleeping maenad significantly name-labelled 'Tragedy',[52] thus formulating the genre relationship of satyric to tragic drama as one of covert sexual assault (see Fig. 1.3). Another image is that of the matronly Tragedy in Horace's *Ars Poetica* (231–3): 'Tragedy does not deserve to blurt out trivial lines, but she will modestly consort a little with the forward satyrs, like a respectable lady dancing because she must on a feast day.'[53] Here tragedy is seen as coerced by satyr drama into revelry rather than into sexual activity.

Female characters and choruses are extremely prominent in Athenian tragedy. There are, admittedly, no plays without any men, which may have been unthinkable. But only one extant tragedy, Sophocles' *Philoctetes*, contains no women. Female tragic choruses in the surviving plays outnumber male by no fewer than twenty-one to ten. Some plays

---

[51] I have quoted *Net-Fishers* at length partly because antiquity held Aeschylus to have been by far the best writer of satyr dramas: Paus. 2. 13. 6; Menedemus quoted at Diog. Laert. 2. 133.

[52] See Fig. 1.3. Both Tragedy and Comedy are maenads chased by satyrs on a vase dated to about 430 BCE in New York (MM 24. 97. 25). It is just possible that the female figure holding a mask to the left of Ariadne on the 'Pronomos Vase' is a personification of satyr play (see E. Csapo and W. J. Slater, *The Context of Ancient Drama* (University of Michigan Press, Ann Arbor, 1995), 69 and pl. 8), but she is not represented in any relationship to tragedy.

[53] 'effutire leves indigna Tragoedia versus | ut festis matrona moveri iussa diebus, | intererit Satyris paulum pudibunda protervis.' Allegorical conceptions of tragedy as an imposing female are of course customary: see e.g. Plutarch's picture of Tragedy as an ornamented rich woman, with famous tragic actors serving her like beauticians and stool-bearers (*de glor. Athen.* 349).

FIG. 1.3   A satyr creeps up on a sleeping maenad named 'Tragodia'.

are named for their memorable female choruses (Aeschylus' *Supplices*, Euripides' *Bacchae*). Numerous tragedies were named for a female role (*Antigone*), or had a female protagonist,[54] a phenomenon replicated amongst the titles and remains of the lost plays.[55] Many plays named for a female chorus also had an important individual female role.[56] Even in many plays named for a male protagonist or chorus, the character on stage for the longest, or with the largest or most memorable part, may nevertheless be a woman (the queen in *Persians*, Clytemnestra in *Agamemnon*, Phaedra in *Hippolytus*). The ancients already sensed the important contribution of female characters to tragedy: in the satirist Lucian we find the somewhat exaggerated estimate that in these plays 'there are more females than males' (*de Salt.* 28, see also Ach. Tat. 1. 8). The assertiveness and articulacy of tragic women caused offence

---

[54]   The two *Electras, Medea, Hecuba, Andromache, Helen,* the *Iphigenias*.
[55]   e.g. Choerilus' *Alope*, Phrynichus' *Alcestis*, Aeschylus' and Sophocles' *Niobe*, Sophocles' *Phaedra*, Euripides' *Melanippe* plays, *Hypsipyle, Auge,* and *Andromeda*.
[56]   *Libation-Bearers, Eumenides, Trachiniae, Trojan Women, Supplices, Phoenissae*.

throughout antiquity: Aristotle recommends that women should not be depicted as clever or brave (*Poet.* 1454ᵃ23–4), Plutarch complains that tragedy represented women as adept rhetoricians (*de Aud. poet.* 28a), and the Christian Origen criticized Euripidean women for inappropriately expressing philosophical opinions (*Contra Celsum* 7. 36. 34–6).

Many reasons have been proposed for women's prominence in tragedy. Some are based on women's role in religion, their performance of funeral lamentation, and the phenomena of maenadism and transvestism in Dionysiac cult. Some draw on anthropological symbolism's findings that patriarchal cultures use the figures and bodies of women to imagine abstractions and think about their social order. Others point to the construction of women as more susceptible to invasive passions such as *eros* and daemonic possession.[57] Froma Zeitlin has importantly argued that theatrical representations of women, socially constructed as more emotionally expressive than men, offered a medium through which the Athenian male could legitimately explore a full range of emotions (including those denied socially to the 'ideal' self-restrained man), by watching his fellow-citizens 'playing the other' in the theatre.[58]

We know from an invaluable fifth-century source that the Athenian audience was once reduced to tears *en masse* by a tragedy, Phrynichus' *Sack of Miletus* (which almost certainly included female lamentation).[59] Reports attest to the emotive effect of tragic scenes on spectators, most of which relate to actors' performances in poignant female roles. The actor Polus used the urn containing the ashes of his own son to 'break the heart' of his audience when he played Sophocles' Electra lamenting Orestes (Aul. Gell. *NA* 6. 5). It was the sorrows of Hecuba and Andromache in Euripides' *Trojan Women* which forced even a cruel tyrant to leave the theatre in tears (Plut. *Vit. Pel.* 29. 4–6). When Athens had lost the Peloponnesian War in 404 BCE, the story goes that the allied

---

[57] For overviews and bibliography see H. Foley, 'The Conception of Women in Athenian Drama', in H. P. Foley (ed.), *Reflections of Women in Antiquity* (Gordon & Breach Science Publishers, London, 1981), 127–67; Edith Hall, 'The Sociology of Athenian Tragedy', in *Cambridge Companion to Greek Tragedy*, 93–126.

[58] F. I. Zeitlin, *Playing the Other: Gender and Society in Classical Greek Literature* (University of Chicago Press, Chicago, 1996), 341–74.

[59] Herod. 6. 21. 1. Phrynichus' women must have been striking, for a (probably untrue) tradition developed holding him responsible for the introduction of female characters into tragedy (*Suda* Φ 762). On the paradox whereby tragedy depicted forms of lamentation actively discouraged at Athens, see Helene Foley, 'The Politics of Tragic Lamentation', in A. Sommerstein et al. (eds.), *Tragedy, Comedy and the Polis* (Levante editori, Bari, 1993), 101–43.

generals opposing Athens were prevented from destroying the city by a man who performed the duet between Euripides' distraught Electra and her chorus of sympathetic women. His evocation of Electra's misery reminded the generals of the city's plight, and persuaded them to be merciful towards the conquered Athenians (Plut. *Vit. Lys.* 15. 2–3).

In Aristophanes' comedies the femininity of tragedy is consciously associated with Euripides and Agathon. In *Frogs* Aeschylus formulates the contrast between himself and Euripides primarily in terms of gender, and in particular of the active sexuality of Euripides' women. Aeschylus says that his heroes made every 'citizen man' (*andra politen*) warlike, and that he never created 'whores' (*pornas*) such as Phaedra or Stheneboea, nor ever portrayed a woman driven by erotic passion (*erosan ... gunaika*, 1041–4). Aeschylus claims that the poet has a special duty to conceal what is immoral, rather than dramatize it. For, while little children are taught by whomsoever addresses them, 'young men' (*toisi d' hebosi*) are taught by poets (1054–5). This juxtaposition of the objection to the sexually driven woman (*erosa gune*) in tragedy with the responsibility of poets to the moral education of youths adumbrates Socrates' objections to tragic mimesis in Plato's *Republic*.

The 'femininity' of tragedy is deeply implicated in its banishment by Socrates from the ideal polity. A function of poetry should be to make men brave (*andreioi*—literally, 'manly'): all lamentations and expressions of pity by men of note should therefore be excised from 'Homer and the other poets' (3. 387d1–2). Since the good man in reality grieves as little as possible when he loses 'a son or brother *or anything like that*', in literature, likewise, the laments attributed to notable men should be removed, and given to women (but not to serious women), and to cowardly men (3. 387e9–388a3). This applies to poetry in general, and the examples supplied suggest that the author is thinking as much of the gloomier parts of epic as of tragedy.

But Socrates subsequently focuses on drama, which he regards as particularly psychologically dangerous since it consists entirely of direct speech. First he establishes that the future guardians of his envisaged republic must not imitate anyone except brave, self-controlled, righteous, and free men, lest they become that which they imitate (3. 395c2–d3). The first type of person whom they must never imitate is, 'given that they are men, a woman' (*gunaika mimeisthai andras ontas*). Socrates then specifies types of activity typical of tragic women which he deems absolutely unsuitable for imitation: reviling a husband, boastfully competing with the gods, being overtaken by misfortune, mourning or lamentation, illness, lust (*erosan*), or childbirth (3. 395d5–e3).

Socrates next proscribes the imitation of slaves, bad men, cowards, the foul-mouthed, and madmen (3. 395e5–396a4). Yet the impersonation of women, which apparently damages spectators as well as actors,[60] takes overwhelming priority in his list of banned dramatis personae. And gender speedily resurfaces when Socrates later focuses more specifically on the audience. He is discussing the emotional impact made by performances of Homer and tragedy (10. 605c10–d5):

Take the best of us listening to Homer or any other of the tragic poets, when he is imitating a hero in grief and spinning out a long melancholy lamentation or imitating men singing and disfiguring themselves in grief: you know that he gives us pleasure, and we give ourselves up to following him; we sympathize and are seriously impressed, and praise as a good poet whoever most affects us in this way?[61]

On the other hand, says Socrates, we pride ourselves on the opposite reaction—on enduring the pain in silence—when enduring a real bereavement, 'because the latter is the reaction of a man, and the former is the reaction of a woman' (*hos touto men andros on, ekeino de gunaikos*, 10. 605d7–e1). The archaic poet Archilochus had long before defined grief as a womanish (*gunaikeion*) emotion to be avoided (fr. 13. 9–10 *IEG*), but in Plato it has become a reprehensibly 'womanish' thing even vicariously to undergo the experience of a grieving hero.

Plato's objections to tragedy reveal that even the classical Athenians were already aware that the theatre paradoxically licensed and even encouraged men to undergo emotional reactions, especially grief and lamentation, which in 'reality' would be disparaged as 'feminine'.[62] As Zeitlin states, 'theater uses the feminine for the purposes of imagining a fuller model for the masculine self, and "playing the other" opens that self to those often banned emotions of pity and fear'.[63]

Fifth-century Athenian tragedy seems actually to have preferred female choruses and is rich in important female roles. Comedy, likewise, offers many examples of both choruses and characters assuming female

---

[60] Penelope Murray (ed.), *Plato on Poetry* (Cambridge University Press, Cambridge, 1996), 176.

[61] Trans. A. D. Lindsay, *Plato: The Republic* (J. M. Dent & Sons, London, 1976), 309.

[62] In the *Laws* Plato speculates that the people in a hypothetical community who would regard tragedy as the most pleasurable genre would be 'the more educated' of the women, very young men, and the common herd (2. 658c10–d4).

[63] Zeitlin, *Playing the Other*, 363.

identities.[64] But defining features of satyr drama were its chorus of satyrs, with their over-developed bodily sexual characteristics, and probably the individual character of Father Silenus.[65] These features suggest that this dramatic genre included an obligatory and highly sexed masculine voice and viewpoint. A survey of the remains of the genre has not cast doubt on this inference; on the contrary, rape fantasies and the harassment of females have been found to be staples of the genre. Whatever conclusions are to be drawn from this startlingly gendered perspective must take into account satyr drama's function as the culmination of a quadruple tragic production at the City Dionysia, which recent scholarship has demonstrated functioned socio-politically as a celebration of collective *male* Athenian citizenship.[66]

Unfortunately it is impossible to discuss the configuring of gender in satyr drama further without speculation. The *Odyssey* was a regular source for satyric plots, yet we know neither whether Penelope appeared in Aeschylus' *Ostologoi*, nor how Circe was presented in his *Circe*. Other witches than Circe featured, yet we know nothing of the extent of Medea's involvement in Sophocles' *Daedalos* (or *Talos*). There may have been a satyric *Iambe* by Sophocles, representing a mythical female comedian, the personification of scurrilous iambic lampoon.[67] Supernatural or superhuman females appeared in Aeschylus' *Sphinx* and *Proteus* (Eidothea),[68] Achaeus' *Moirai*, and Aristias' *Keres*. The evidence for female divinities is present but frustratingly slight:[69] Sophocles wrote a *Krisis* which *may* imply the presence of Hera, Athena, and/or Aphrodite; there was *probably* a satyr play in which Athena competed with Marsyas on the aulos; Hera was *apparently* humiliated in Achaeus' *Hephaistos*; the

---

[64] Aristophanes' *Clouds, Lysistrata, Thesmophoriazusae*, and *Ecclesiazusae*; the phenomenon is replicated among the fragments of Old Comedy.

[65] Collinge, 'Some Reflections', 29.

[66] e.g. J. J. Winkler, 'The Ephebes' Song', in *Nothing to do with Dionysos?*, 20–62; Simon Goldhill, 'The Great Dionysia and Civic Ideology', ibid. 97–129; Zeitlin, *Playing the Other*; Edith Hall, *Aeschylus' Persians*, 13 and 19, 'The Sociology of Athenian tragedy', 93–126, and *Inventing the Barbarian* (Oxford University Press, Oxford, 1989), 201–10.

[67] According to the *Homeric Hymn to Demeter* (202–4), Iambe told jokes to console Demeter for the loss of Persephone: see Helene Foley (ed.), *The Homeric Hymn to Demeter* (Princeton University Press, Princeton, 1994), 45–6.

[68] R. G. Ussher, 'The Other Aeschylus: A Study of the Fragments of Aeschylean Satyr Plays', *Phoenix* 31 (1977), 287–99, at 290.

[69] R. J. Walker, in his edition *The Ichneutae of Sophocles* (Burns & Oates Ltd., London, 1919), 575, argues, while speculatively reconstructing Aeschylus' *Proteus*, that Apollo was 'more fitted' than Athena 'to be brought, without offence, into the satyric atmosphere'. Goddesses, presumably, might be shocked by the satyrs' riotous masculinity. I cite this only to show the extent to which scholars have allowed their own prejudices about gender roles to colour their work on satyr drama.

popular vase-painting motif in which the satyrs sexually assault Iris *may* suggest a plot for Achaeus' *Iris*.[70]

Yet despite the loss of so many texts, an attempt to decode the gender dynamics of satyr drama is crucial to our understanding of the total emotional experience undergone by the fifth-century spectator of tragedy. The protagonist of satyr drama is really its satyric chorus,[71] and the chorus consists of males quite incapable of regulating their own sexual appetites. In Freudian terms, the satyrs are all male id and no superego.[72] Eros is central also to tragedy, in which the plots are frequently motivated by inappropriate or excessive erotic impulses which endanger the entire household. Sometimes they affect the entire community, as Clytemnestra's relationship with Aegisthus destabilizes the Argos of the *Oresteia*. The sexually motivated character in tragedy is particularly dangerous if she is a woman. Although Aristophanes regarded the *erosa gune* as a particularly Euripidean phenomenon, she is anticipated by Aeschylus' Clytemnestra and Sophocles' Deianeira. But in satyr drama, rather than afflicting disturbed individuals of either sex, *eros* is a permanent attribute of the (male) choral collective.

At least one post-hippie critic has read the satyrs' sexuality as a proto-Rousseauan idealization of the innocent desires of Man in Nature before the restrictive social regulation of sexual relations in marriage: 'the satyr exists harmoniously with himself, with Nature, with Dionysus. He is the supreme embodiment of health. Although he is less than human, he embodies a kind of wisdom: he represents what Man can and should be.'[73] Besides the gender-blindness of this reading, which subsumes the entire human race under the sign of 'Man', its assumption that the satyrs represented an enviable model of freedom from psychosexual repression is wholly anachronistic. A diametrically opposite view diagnoses the satyrs as a sign of the Athenian male's negation of his own sexuality:

---

[70] For further discussion of all these plays, including bibliography and highly speculative reconstructions, see Sutton, *The Greek Satyr Play*.

[71] Seidensticker, 'Das Satyrspiel', 213.

[72] Psychoanalysts would be interested to learn that ancient men dreamt about satyrs. In the *Interpretation of Dreams* of Artemidorus, dreaming about any attendants of Dionysos, including the satyrs, is diagnosed as 'signifying great disturbance, dangers, and scandals'. Dreaming of actually dancing in honour of Dionysos 'is inauspicious for all but slaves. For most men, it foretells folly and harm because of the *ecstasis* of the mental processes and the frenzy' (2. 37, trans. Robert J. White, *The Interpretation of Dreams: Oneirocritica* (Noyes Press, Park Ridge, NJ, 1975), 118). If we can believe the pseudo-Callisthenic *Alexander Romance*, Alexander the Great 'saw in his sleep a satyr, one of the attendants of Dionysos, offering him a cheese made from milk' (35).

[73] Sutton, *The Greek Satyr Play*, 179.

Greek satyrdom is an expression of a basically misogynous outlook. In the vase-painting of the mid-fifth century—and undoubtedly on the stage—Greek satyrs are characterised as profoundly anti-female. By inventing the satyr to personify his fear, or disapproval, of natural sexuality—and by banishing him to the category 'animal'—the Greek is representing nature as incompatible with culture. He does not wish to be reminded that he is a sexual animal.[74]

While correctly appreciating the underlying misogyny of satyr drama, this reading surely overstates the ancient ambivalence towards male sexuality. Nearer to the mark is Konstan's interpretation of *Cyclops*,[75] in which both the satyrs' primitive communitarianism, and Polyphemus' anarchically monadic self-sufficiency, function as antitypes to the human community. Satyr drama thus sanctions humanity's internal relations (including its sexual mores and institution of marriage). To push this view to its limit, one function of the satyrs' pre-polis wantonness is to legitimize the regulation of wantonness in the polis.

Yet the most satisfactory definition of satyrdom available is undoubtedly that of Lissarrague. He argues that the satyrs reproduce the values of ancient Greek males by distancing them from their cultural norms, and systematically transform them according to a precise set of rules.[76] The only problem with this illuminating diagnosis lies in its *emotional neutrality*: it would be impossible for any female reader, let alone a conscious feminist, to contemplate the remains of satyr drama without a degree of emotional alienation. Lissarrague's 'rules that are never random' included the rule that male sexual aggression was a phenomenon to be riotously celebrated. This 'rule' poses an even greater problem to the *constructionist* feminist, who believes that the majority of gender role distinctions, including those defining sexual behaviour, are products of culture rather than of nature. For to her the genre must ultimately be seen to legitimize male sexual appetitiveness by *construing* it as embedded in nature, and to authorize it by theatrically tracing it in a special and hilarious form of charter myth to prehistory. Satyr drama offered an aetiological justification for Athenian male phallocentrism. 'We were all satyrs together once, and wasn't it fun?', the plays seem to me to shout noisily to the men of Athens.

Satyr drama sends the male spectator out of the theatre not only

---

[74] Herbert Hoffmann, 'Sexual and Asexual Pursuit: A Structuralist Approach to Greek Vase-Painting', *Royal Anthropological Institute of Great Britain and Ireland Occasional Paper* 34 (London, 1977), 3–4.
[75] Konstan, 'The Anthropology', 227.
[76] Lissarrague, 'Why Satyrs are Good to Represent', 235–6.

laughing rather than crying, but reassured of his place in the *male* collective. Tragedy has served its purpose by offering the assembled citizens of Athens an opportunity to indulge emotions socially constructed as feminine. But playing satyr drama's childlike, carnal, homosocial 'other' brings the spectator back into the psychological gender orientation appropriate to the City Dionysia, by substituting a joyous collective male consciousness physically centred on the phallus. A much cited definition suggests that in satyr drama tragedy subverts itself, 'and thereby effects insurance against the surfeit of the painful passions which it has unleashed'.[77] I would like to modify this definition so as to emphasize the gendered basis of the genre dichotomization: satyr drama offers the insurance of a reaffirmed sense of unindividuated masculinity, based in libidinal awareness, in order to protect against the painful 'feminine' emotions which tragedy has unleashed.

It might be objected that the satyrs do not apparently fulfil their sexual desires in satyr drama.[78] They are suspended in a state of eternal sexual excitement. While tragedy traces the consequences of dangerous sexualities through to their bitter end, satyr drama seems to have controlled the satyrs by foreclosing on its own invitation to sexual licence. But whatever the ideological implications of the apparently infinite deferral of theatrical satyrs' sexual gratification, the last and loudest voices heard whooping at the tragic competitions were male, uncouth, and lecherous. Satyr drama sent the Athenian male away from the tragic productions only after edifying him with at least an hour's worth of ithyphallic males behaving badly.

[77] 'und erwirkt sich dadurch Indemnität für das Übermaß der leidvollen Affekte, die sie entfesselt hat': Schmid, 'Der Hinzutritt', 82.
[78] Seidensticker, 'Das Satyrspiel', 244–5. M. Werre-de Haas (ed.), *Aeschylus' Dictyulci* (Brill, Leiden, 1961), 73.

2

'The Mother of the Argument': *Eros* and the Body in Sappho and Plato's *Phaedrus*

HELENE P. FOLEY

What else could one call the art of love of the Lesbian woman [Sappho] other than the Socratic art of love? For they seem to me to have practiced love after their own fashion, she the love of women, he of men. For they said they loved many, and were captivated by all things beautiful. What Alcibiades and Charmides and Phaedrus were to him, Gyrinna and Atthis and Anactoria were to her; what the rival craftsmen Prodicus and Gorgias and Thrasymachus and Protagoras were to Socrates, Gorgo and Andromeda were to Sappho. Sometimes she censures them, at other times she cross-examines them, and she uses irony just like Socrates.[1]

THIS arresting passage appears in an essay composed by the second-century CE sophist and Platonist Maximus of Tyre (18. 9), in which Maximus is attempting to justify the seeming contradiction between the ideal philosophical life and Socrates' frequently professed role as a technician of *eros* or erotic desire ('the dissimilitude of his practice in amatory affairs to his theory', 18. 5).[2] Why, Maximus asks, does this otherwise austere figure ('this lover of wisdom, who was superior to poverty, the enemy of pleasure and the friend of truth'), who so frequently asserts his ignorance, insist nevertheless that he is an authority on and practitioner of the art of *eros* (a *therapon tou erotos . . . ten technen deinos*, 18. 4)? Why does he make a point of calling attention, both in Plato and elsewhere, to

Due to limits of space and the immense bibliography on the issues addressed in this chapter, I shall cite only works that directly influenced or enriched my argument. I would like to thank M. M. McCabe, Maria Wyke, Christian Wolff, and Richard Seaford for their comments on an earlier draft of this chapter.

[1] Trans. D. A. Campbell, *Greek Lyric I* (Harvard University Press, Cambridge, Mass., 1982), 20. All citations and translations of archaic poets are from the Campbell edition unless otherwise noted.

[2] Trans. T. Taylor, *The Dissertation of Maximus Tyrius* (C. Whittingham, London, 1804); see the edition of M. B. Trapp, *Maximus Tyrius, Dissertationes* (Teubner, Stuttgart, 1994), 130.

the shocking, even maddening effects produced in him by the beautiful bodies of young men such as the irresistible Charmides (18. 4)? Why does Socrates enumerate as his preceptors in philosophical love three (unlikely) women, Aspasia the Milesian, Diotima the prophetess, and, in his *Phaedrus*, 'the fair Sappho' (18. 4, 18. 7)? Although puzzled that the expert lover Socrates banished the poets of old from his ideal republic (18. 5), Maximus nevertheless justifies Socrates' obsession with the love of boys by demonstrating the antiquity of his erotic practice among Greek archaic poets, especially Sappho and Anacreon. 'Whether a prophetess [Diotima] or a Lesbian [Sappho] was the mother of the argument (*he tou logou meter*), erotic discourses (*erotikoi logoi*) were not peculiar to Socrates, nor was he their inventor' (18. 7).

Maximus may be neither a subtle nor accurate reader of Plato or Sappho by our own contemporary standards. Yet he undoubtedly had a direct access to Sappho's *œuvre* that we ourselves do not. So did the participants in the Greek *symposia* ('drinking parties') frequented by Plato and Socrates, and, although we cannot be sure how familiar Plato was with the full corpus of her poetry, he pointedly cites Sappho in *Phaedrus*.[3] As an ancient reader, Maximus creates an imaginary dialogue between the works of Sappho and Plato that can, in my view, contribute to the larger contemporary debate on the dynamics of *eros* in both authors. In much recent (especially feminist) literature, Plato is, despite Socrates' notorious preoccupation with erotics, categorized as anti-body, and Sappho the reverse. In my view, Socrates' interest in erotics appears paradoxical only to those for whom erotics seems to be exclusively about bodies. I adopt the position that erotic desire plays a broader role in both Plato and Sappho and that the body and the language of the body function rather in both authors as a catalyst to more important poetic or philosophical issues and pursuits. Like Maximus, I believe that Sappho does serve in some critical respects as the 'mother' of Socrates' second argument about *eros* in *Phaedrus*.[4] Above all, a shared concern

---

[3] Athenians clearly had access to Sappho's poetry, depicted her in vase-paintings, mocked her in comedies, and sang her songs at *symposia* (see Campbell, *Greek Lyric I* test. 10 for Solon's admiration for one of Sappho's poems at a *symposium*), but we cannot be sure whether even educated Athenians had all of her poetry available to them or would have been familiar with it if they did.

[4] At *Phaedrus* 257b1–2 Lysias is called 'the father of [Socrates' first] *logos*'; at *Symposium* 177d3–5 Phaedrus is called 'the father of the *logos*', although he does not directly provoke the evening's series of speeches on *eros* (see further J. D. Moore, 'The Relation between Plato's *Symposium* and *Phaedrus*', in J. M. E. Moravçsik (ed.), *Patterns in Plato's Thought* (D. Reidel, Dordrecht, 1973), 65–6, 68). See also *Theatetus* 165c for the expression 'father of the *muthos*'. Maximus is clearly adapting these Platonic references to the roles of Sappho and

with erotic discourse, memory, and a less hierarchical and more reciprocal mode of homoerotic relations makes this possible. The exact relation
between Socrates' initial reference to Sappho in *Phaedrus* and his ensuing
two speeches about *eros* is difficult and controversial; nevertheless
archaic love poetry and Sappho in particular hover beneath the text's
surface and provide a cultural precedent for Socrates' argument in his
second speech.

In the passage in Plato's *Phaedrus* to which Maximus refers at 18. 7,
Socrates has just heard Phaedrus recite the orator Lysias' speech arguing
that it is better for a boy to gratify a non-lover ('one not in love') than a
lover ('one in love'), because the latter is likely to be fickle, jealous, and
irrational in his attentions. Socrates responds unenthusiastically to
Lysias' speech. If he agreed that Lysias had the last word on the subject,
'the men and women of antiquity and wisdom who have spoken and
written on the subject would refute me (*exelengchsousi*)'. He says that he
cannot tell Phaedrus offhand which ancients he has in mind, but he is
sure he has heard something better, 'from the fair Sappho maybe, or the
wise Anacreon, or perhaps some prose writers' (235c). Socrates' breast is
full[5] and he feels the urge to say something different from Lysias and no
worse; but due to his ignorance and a lapse of memory, he knows only
that 'he has been filled up through his ears like a vessel from someone
else's streams' (235c). Phaedrus finally coerces Socrates to compete with
Lysias and to make a speech about the dangers of the irrational lover.
After delivering this first speech with his head covered in shame, Socrates
goes on to refute his own speech with a palinode or recantation arguing
that it is, in the ideal case, to the boy's advantage to attach himself to a
lover rather than a non-lover. Socrates makes the archaic poet
Stesichorus the inspiration for and even the imagined author of this
second speech, and its object is by implication the beautiful Phaedrus
himself (243e).[6]

Diotima; he apparently means that Sappho is the inspiration for Socrates' speech (the
stream that has been poured into Socrates' ear comes in his view from this source), rather
than, as with Diotima, the maker of the speech or the originator of the discourse.

[5] Ronna Burger, *Plato's Phaedrus: A Defense of a Philosophical Art of Writing* (University of
Alabama Press, Birmingham, 1980), 32 sees this fullness as Socrates' 'awareness of that part
of the whole of *eros* suppressed by the speech of Lysias'.

[6] Phaedrus, whose name means 'Shining', was in fact not a boy at the time at which the
dialogue is set, but in his late thirties, about twenty years younger than Socrates; nor could
he have been in Athens, since he was exiled during 415–404 BCE for his supposed role in the
mutilation of the herms. For discussion, see further M. C. Nussbaum, *The Fragility of
Goodness: Luck and Ethics in Greek Tragedy and Philosophy* (Cambridge University Press,
Cambridge, 1986), 212.

Many scholars have thought Socrates' reference to Sappho and
Anacreon before his first speech represents irony typical of a man whose
disrespect for the authority of poets is elsewhere notorious.[7] If so, the
passage remains puzzling, because Sappho and Anacreon were consistently paired in antiquity as the originators and quintessential practitioners of the tradition of erotic poetry. How could poets who devoted their
whole lives to celebrating and practising the arts of *eros* be the inspiration
for a speech that urges the beloved to distrust and avoid the irrational
lover and love itself? The most recent commentator on the dialogue, C. J.
Rowe, dismisses as dramatically implausible the view of Léon Robin that
Socrates here anticipates his second rather than his first speech.[8] Rowe
argues that, in Socrates' first speech, Plato must be evoking Sappho and
Anacreon and unnamed others as the practitioners of non-philosophical
love, an irrational love of the body that entails little more than the pursuit
of pleasure. Hence paradoxically 'love poets give us better arguments in
favor of the non-lover than Lysias could ever muster'.[9]

From this perspective, Socrates' first speech parodies the worst excesses of archaic love poetry: the lover's shameless attempt to dominate
a resisting, indifferent, or even disgusted beloved,[10] or the lover's jealousy
and lack of concern for the beloved's economic welfare and for his
responsibilities to friends and family. Once the physical passion of
Socrates' irrational lover has cooled, his indifference to his former promises and his ingratitude force the beloved to pursue the lover. W. W.
Fortenbaugh interprets this as a parody of Sappho fragment 1, in which
Sappho asks Aphrodite to turn an indifferent woman into an active
pursuer of erotic gratification.[11] If so, the aggressive and irrational lover

---

[7] On Socrates' supposedly ironic treatment of inspiration from external sources, see P.
DuBois, *Sappho is Burning* (University of Chicago Press, Chicago, 1995), 85; Charles L.
Griswold, Jr., *Self-Knowledge in Plato's Phaedrus* (Yale University Press, New Haven, 1986),
53 (internal sources are more authoritative for Plato); and the sophisticated discussion of
alien discourses in Plato by Andrea Wilson Nightingale, *Genres in Dialogue: Plato and the
Construct of Philosophy* (Cambridge University Press, Cambridge, 1995), esp. 135–8 and
145–6.

[8] L. Robin, *Platon, Œuvres complètes*, iv.3: *Phèdre*, 2nd edn. (Les Belles Lettres, Paris,
1956), pp. xli–xlii, followed by G. J. de Vries, *A Commentary on the Phaedrus of Plato* (A. M.
Hakkert, Amsterdam, 1969), ad loc. See also Nightingale, *Genres in Dialogue*, 158 and
Burger, *Plato's Phaedrus*, 46, who argues that Socrates implies at 242c that he began the first
speech with the second already in mind: 'For all along, while speaking the first speech, I was
disturbed.'

[9] C. J. Rowe, *Plato's Phaedrus* (Aris & Phillips, Warminster, 1986), 151.

[10] G. R. F. Ferrari, *Listening to the Cicadas: A Study of Plato's Phaedrus* (Cambridge
University Press, Cambridge, 1987; repr. 1990), 107.

[11] 'Plato's *Phaedrus* 235c3', *Classical Philology*, 61 (1966), 108–9. See below for further
discussion.

of Socrates' first speech inaccurately reflects both a poetic tradition of pursuit and conquest in which the beloved can prove equally overwhelming to and even psychologically dominate the male lover,[12] and entirely misrepresents the Sapphic tradition, in which pursuit, conquest, and dominance apparently play at most a minimal role. Some Sapphic fragments could be argued, although not very convincingly, to represent such excesses. For example, Sappho's fragment 31 has been (controversially) interpreted as a poem about sexual jealousy. In Sappho fragment 16, Helen is said to have abandoned husband and family for love;[13] however, later in *Phaedrus*, the philosophical lovers also find that their relationship is more important to them than friends and family (255b5–7). The Sapphic fragments hardly urge an irresponsible pursuit of pleasure, inflict social isolation on the beloved, or express lack of concern for her welfare.

Moreover, as G. R. F. Ferrari has argued, Socrates' non-lover (who is in fact in love with the boy to whom he speaks, but pretends otherwise) is obsessively puritanical and, contrary to Greek tradition, sees no advantages whatsoever accruing to the boy from *eros*. Socrates' style reflects his content by deliberately refusing poetic inspiration full rein in this first speech, but allowing it in the second, where he integrates *eros* into the pursuit of virtue and philosophy.[14] Socrates first asserts, under the inspiration of Sappho and Anacreon, that he could give a speech different from and no worse than Lysias'. Phaedrus responds by insisting that Socrates offer a rhetorical response superior to that of Lysias; Socrates at once demurs, twice claiming that he cannot offer something different and more elaborate than that of Lysias (235e and 236b). Not only does he suggest from the start that he is ashamed to make the speech that Phaedrus demands, but he defines this speech as a product of deception, since the non-lover is only pretending to be so. How, then, can the first speech that Socrates delivers represent the different speech that he originally felt inspired to make? Ferrari suggests persuasively that Phaedrus, by trivializing Socrates' initial response, forces him to abandon his original inspiration;[15] indeed, at 244a Socrates even

[12] Ferrari, *Listening to the Cicadas*, 107.
[13] See also Alcaeus, fr. 283, Campbell, *Greek Lyric I*.
[14] Ferrari, *Listening to the Cicadas*, 96 and 110. The first speech is coloured by dithyrambic language and Socrates bursts into a final cynical verse to demonstrate that he is supposedly in the grip of an 'uncontrollable' divine inspiration.
[15] Ferrari, *Listening to the Cicadas*, 107; see the similar argument of Robin, *Phèdre*, p. xlii. Griswold, *Self-Knowledge*, 52 thinks that Socrates offers only a more comprehensive and better arranged speech, not, as in the second speech, a truer or nobler one.

attributes his first speech to Phaedrus, rather than, as earlier, to the Ligurian Muses (237a).[16]

Although a strictly ironic interpretation of Socrates' reference to his inspiration by archaic love poetry cannot be ruled out (and the ambiguity may be deliberate), a closer look at Socrates' second speech, which is explicitly attributed to yet another archaic poet, Stesichorus, son of Euphemus ('reverent in speech') from Himera ('Desireland'), and is represented as fully inspired by the Muses, confirms that the influence of archaic poetry plays a role in the second speech, but serves the different purpose of defending the ideal lover's relation to his beloved.[17] Socrates speaks of his initial critical response to Lysias' speech as poured into his ears from an external source; here he may in part be mocking not only traditional representations of poetic inspiration but Phaedrus' eagerness to absorb the words of others rather than think for himself. Yet despite Socrates' questioning of poetic inspiration in *Ion* and elsewhere, divine inspiration and madness continue to play an apparently serious role in *Phaedrus*, and the pouring and exchange of liquids becomes a critical image for the exchange of desire, knowledge, and dialogue between the philosophical lovers (255a).[18] Given Socrates' patent ambivalence on the subject of *eros* in this dialogue, I think it impossible to establish how much of the poetic trappings that Socrates attaches to his recantation represent a genuine and conscious appropriation and transformation of a tradition of erotic poetry of which Sappho is a major (and from the Greek perspective, historically the first) representative.[19] Yet I would conclude that if Socrates' first speech absurdly distorts some aspects of

[16] Other sources for the speech are some divine being (238d), local nymphs (241e), and Lysias (257b). Socrates later links his possession by gods here with forgetfulness (263d).

[17] Other sources for the second speech are Phaedrus (242b), Socrates' *daimonion* (divine internal voice, 242c), Ibycus (242d), and Socrates himself (243d, with Phaedrus at 265a) and his prophetic soul (242c). Socrates aligns himself with the two lyric poets Stesichorus and Ibycus, in being moved by fear of offending the gods. M. C. Nussbaum, ' "This Story Isn't True": Poetry, Goodness, and Understanding in Plato's *Phaedrus*', in J. Moravçsik and P. Temko (eds.), *Plato on Beauty, Wisdom, and the Arts* (Rowman & Littlefield, Totowa, NJ, 1982), 81 and *Fragility of Goodness*, 202–3 sees *Phaedrus* as a genuine recantation of Plato's own views in his middle dialogues. In her opinion, the first speech nevertheless offers a view that we must take with some degree of seriousness, in that it represents in an exaggerated form Plato's own earlier hostility to pleasure.

[18] The passage here evokes as well the love of Zeus for Ganymede, his cup-bearer and wine-pourer. Beauty emits an effluence called *himeros* (derived from *mere+epionta+reonta*, 'particles coming in a flood', 251c6–7). The effluence flows from the beloved into the eyes of the lover; the excess flow is then reflected back through the eyes of the beloved and fills and awakens his soul (see further Moore, 'Relation', 58).

[19] See D. A. Campbell, *Greek Lyric II* (Harvard University Press, Cambridge, Mass., 1988), test. 2 on Anacreon.

the traditional mad lover of erotic poetry to serve its anti-erotic argument, the second speech permits archaic erotic poetry to serve its truthful argument. Furthermore, it is above all Sappho's representation of *eros*
and erotic relations, rather than that of Anacreon or others, that proves
to be most suggestive for Plato in a number of dimensions.

Even if Plato evokes Sappho ironically, he goes out of his way to create
a setting for his dialogue that displaces Socrates from his normal urban
environment into one traditionally linked in myth and poetry to erotic,
and especially to female erotic, experience.[20] While the *locus amoenus*—
in particular, a natural spot distinguished by grass, trees, flowers, or
water—can occasionally be linked with young unmarried males (as in
archaic poetry that describes the pursuit of the beloved as a hunt in a wild
environment or in Euripides' *Hippolytus*), it more generally serves as the
setting in which virginal young women become the object of erotic
pursuit by men;[21] or, in the case of Sappho's poetry, it can represent the
environment, also defined by flowers, fruit, trees, and water, in which
erotic relations among women are conducted.[22] *Phaedrus* explicitly
evokes the myth of the abduction of the Attic maiden Oreithuia, daughter of Erectheus, by the wind god Boreas. To be sure, the actual site of the
maiden's abduction is said to be several stades off or perhaps elsewhere
(Socrates is not willing to pursue the question of the myth's historicity
with any certainty),[23] and Phaedrus' *locus amoenus* takes on a distinctly
philosophical cast by being overshadowed by a plane tree (the name
platanos may suggest Plato's name) and the *agnus castus* (a willow-like
plant associated with chastity).[24] Nevertheless, the playful link with the

[20] At first, Socrates insists that landscape and trees have nothing to teach him, but only
people in the city (230d4–5); later he seems to give a serious role to the wild deities of the
place (262d, 263d, 279b), and thus to become more responsive to the poetic implications of
the setting.
[21] On the *locus amoenus* in literature, see especially André Motte, *Prairies et jardins de la
Grèce antique* (Palais des Académies, Académie Royale de Belgique, Brussels, 1973) and, on
the visual representation of scenes of sexual pursuit, Christiane Sourvinou-Inwood, '*Reading' Greek Culture: Texts, Images, Rituals and Myths* (Clarendon Press, Oxford, 1991), 25–
144. The setting in *Phaedrus* also includes statues of and votive offerings to nymphs and the
river god Achelous, which may also evoke erotic pursuit as well as inspiration.
[22] Frr. 2 and 96 offer particularly good examples of the enchanted natural environments
created in Sappho's poetry. Her poems were said in Demetrius' *On Style* 132 to consist of
'gardens of nymphs, wedding hymns, and love affairs' (Campbell, *Greek Lyric I*, test. 45).
[23] See Ferrari, *Listening to the Cicadas*, 10. For Socrates, the historical truth of myth is less
important than the truth about oneself and who one might become. On Socrates' attitude
to myth here, see also Griswold, *Self-Knowledge*, 37–8, 140–1, Burger, *Plato's Phaedrus*, 15,
and David A. White, *Rhetoric and Reality in Plato's Phaedrus* (SUNY Press, Albany, NY,
1993), 19–22.
[24] Due to its supposed anti-aphrodisiac properties, women sat on beds of *agnus castus* in
their celebration of the religious festival for Demeter, the Thesmophoria.

Oreithuia myth lingers, as Socrates is more or less abducted by Phaedrus into these environs, seduced into a speech against his will (see 236d), and finally inspired with erotic madness.[25] He even swears in this passage by Hera, a goddess of marriage normally invoked by women (230b2). The dialogue repeatedly calls attention to the effect of the setting on Phaedrus and Socrates,[26] and Socrates invokes Pan and the nymphs as part of the wild inspiration for his second speech (262d, 263d, 279b).

Stesichorus' palinode, the inspiration for Socrates' second speech, claimed that Helen did not go to Troy; instead the Greeks fought for her image throughout the famous war; in essence Stesichorus denies a poetic tradition that blames female *eros*, irrationality, and lack of self-control for actions deliberately undertaken for other reasons by men. Socrates' recantation might thus include his distortion of archaic erotic poetry in his first speech. A noble man, say Socrates, would think the first speech the product of those brought up among vulgar sailors ignorant of love among free men (243c), whereas the second speech is a hymn to Eros (257a–b); Sappho and Anacreon were above all known as composers of hymns, and Plato was reputed in later antiquity to have been an admirer of Sappho (Aelian, *Historical Miscellanies* 12. 19, *Palatine Anthology* 9. 506; see also Plutarch, *Erotikos* 18).

In any case, when in his second speech Socrates describes the symptoms of an awakening *eros*, the strange shudder, sweats, and fevers that seize the lover at the sight of the beloved (251a), his audience may well have noticed the initial similarity of these symptoms to those of the lover in archaic poetry, above all, those felt by the poet herself in Sappho's famous fragment 31:[27]

For when I look at you for a moment, then it is no longer possible for me to speak; my tongue has snapped, at once a subtle fire has stolen beneath my flesh, I see nothing with my eyes, sweat pours from me, a trembling seizes me all over, I am greener than grass, and it seems to me that I am little short of dying.[28]

To be sure, this image is evoked only to be displaced, as Sappho's bodily fevers evolve into confusingly androgynous images (moistened lips com-

---

[25] The appropriation of mystery terminology in Socrates' second speech might also evoke among other things the similar story of the abduction of Persephone by Hades on which the Eleusinian Mysteries were based.

[26] Ferrari, *Listening to the Cicadas*, 10–12.

[27] These sweats and shudders are also linked with the experience felt by initiates in mystery cults. *Phaedrus*, like Sappho, also stresses the mixed pleasures and pains of love.

[28] Trans. Campbell, *Greek Lyric I*.

bined with a hot and swelling stump).[29] A stream of beauty from the boy enters the fevered lover's eyes, opens the sealed lips of his soul's feathers, and warms, moistens, and makes its quills swell. The subsequent itching, tickling, throbbing, and inflammation in the lover's soul is compared to the pain caused by teething in an infant's gums. Once lover and beloved share these erotic symptoms, the two go on to exchange metaphorical streams of liquid (251de, 253ab, 255b–d). Although the philosophical lovers' relationship will ideally remain unconsummated, the desires of the body remain a vital (if subordinate) part of their developing pursuit of philosophy. They will caress and touch even if they refrain from the act of love, and their mutual desire will form a basis for their future, lifelong devotion and friendship (255b–256e; less than ideal couples will occasionally give way to desire).[30]

In archaic love poetry, the lover is typically maddened by the forces of *eros* from without; streams of beauty from the beloved similarly flow into and arouse to madness the soul of Plato's philosophical lover.[31] As with the lovers of *Phaedrus* (252a2–30), Sappho and her erotic partners envision the beloved as a deity to be worshipped (96. 4–5).[32] It has been argued that Plato borrows from the archaic poets, then transforms the motif of desire giving wings to the lover, as well as the lover's internal division between passion and reason ('I am in love and not in love, I'm crazy and not crazy', Anacreon 428; see also Sappho fragment 51, 'I do not know what I should do; my thoughts go in two directions').[33] In short, I

---

[29] Ferrari, *Listening to the Cicadas*, 154; see also Page DuBois, 'Phallocentrism and its Subversion in Plato's *Phaedrus*', *Arethusa*, 18 (1985), 97–8.

[30] This is well emphasized by Nussbaum, *Fragility of Goodness*, 217, 220, 222, following G. Vlastos, 'The Individual as an Object of Love in Plato', in *Platonic Studies*, 2nd edn. (Princeton University Press, Princeton, 1994), esp. 38–42. Unlike the lovers of male erotic poetry, however, Plato's lover does not wish to possess his beloved, but to help him fashion himself after his particular god.

[31] Sappho is unusual in stressing the internal as well as external impulses that produce this erotic madness. See Lyn Hatherly Wilson, *Sappho's Sweetbitter Songs: Configurations of Female and Male in Ancient Greek Lyric* (Routledge, London, 1986), 62, who notes that Sappho is sensitive to visual stimuli and experiences fevers, winds, and fires but in the extant fragments she is not a victim of *eros*'s other weapons, such as nets, arrows, hammers, boxing gloves, bits, or bridles. On Eros' weapons, see Anne Carson, *Eros the Bittersweet: An Essay* (Princeton University Press, Princeton, 1986), 148. Griswold, *Self-Knowledge*, 75 is typical in arguing that in Plato 'divine erotic madness is not so much sent from the gods external to the individual as sparked from a source within him, as is suggested by its association with *anamnesis*'. But Nightingale, *Genres in Dialogue*, 159–60 makes a forceful case against this view.

[32] See also Campbell, *Greek Lyric II*, test. 7 on Anacreon.

[33] Anacreon fr. 428, Campbell, *Greek Lyric II*. For references on wings, see Carson, *Eros the Bittersweet*, 155–7, 172.

am in agreement with Andrea Wilson Nightingale that in the palinode Socrates 'yields to the discourse of lyric love poetry in fundamental ways'. She does not suggest that 'Plato defers to the genre of love poetry on every point; far from it. Nonetheless, the extent to which he respects and preserves the "voice" of this genre is quite remarkable. Indeed, it is precisely by leaving the genre of love poetry—with its discourse of madness, invasion, and the destruction of boundaries—more or less intact that Plato is able to create one of the most extraordinary paradoxes in his entire corpus: the notion that reason and madness, at a certain level, converge.'[34]

Socrates' speech thus apparently appropriates and then fundamentally transforms for philosophy a tradition that had its roots in representations of erotic experience in myth and in the archaic poetic tradition.[35] Plato offers here no substantial recantation of his earlier views on poetry. In *Phaedrus*, poets remain in the sixth rank of lives to be pursued by the soul, whereas the life of 'the lover of wisdom or beauty, or devoted to the Muses and to love' (248e) is to be preferred above all others.[36] Poets, or at least contemporary poets, can no longer compete in the pursuit of knowledge and truth with philosophy, which has superseded poetry in the pursuit of truth;[37] instead, philosophy becomes inspired, manic, and muse-loving, as it appeals to emotion by incorporating into its discourse metaphor, poetic devices like personification, and colourful, rhythmic language.[38] The irrational element in the soul is rehabilitated as

---

[34] Nightingale, *Genres in Dialogue*, 159 and 161. See also, Griswold, *Self-Knowledge*, 72–3 and 77, who stresses that 'Although the language of ordinary opinion, poetry and religion is not that of argument and analysis, it is nevertheless appropriate to articulate the ascent of language' and 'the fantasies of love'.

[35] See further Ferrari, *Listening to the Cicadas*, esp. 111. Later at *Phaedrus* 159d, Erato, the muse who presides over lyric poetry, cannot compete with Calliope and Ourania, who preside over philosophy, which nevertheless retains a poetic element (*mousike*) of its own. The passage once again gives a place to erotic lyric, even if it is secondary to philosophy.

[36] At *Republic* 598c, Plato argues that for a poet to be an acceptable contributor to the ideal state, he must create with understanding (*eidota poiein*). Nussbaum, 'This Story', 90 shows that this requirement creates the fundamental problem for rehabilitating poetry. She argues that Plato in *Phaedrus* instead reinterprets the *Republic*'s distinction between philosophy and poetry. Ferrari, *Listening to the Cicadas*, 117 rejects the effort of some commentators to argue that it is only uninspired and second-rate poets that belong in the sixth rank; in his view, if Plato had wished to make this distinction, he would have made it explicit in the text. See also Griswold, *Self-Knowledge*, 102–3 and White, *Rhetoric and Reality*, 70 and 114–15. In *Republic* 10, Socrates finds hymns to gods and praises of famous men acceptable poetic themes. In *Phaedrus*, inspired poets glorify past achievements and teach them to future generations (245a).

[37] Ferrari, *Listening to the Cicadas*, 117–19.

[38] See Nussbaum, 'This Story', 98 and *Fragility of Goodness*, 226–7.

a source of motivational energy for the philosophical pursuit.[39] Neverthe-less, when Socrates appropriates the Muses and archaic poetry for phi-losophy, he implies that he retains a greater respect for what ancient, as opposed to modern, tradition had to offer: the ancients, who lived in a pre-philosophic age, are twice cited as authorities on matters of divinely inspired madness (244b–d; see also 274c and 275b–c), even if they may be sources of true opinion rather than philosophic knowledge.[40]

Yet neither the male poetic tradition, nor the broader tradition in both poetry and prose that defines the protocols of erotic experience between male lover and beloved, prepares us for Socrates' argument in favour of a full and permanent reciprocity between lover and beloved.[41] Both of the philosophic lovers in *Phaedrus* actively reach out to the other with desire (*anteran*, although the boy's desires are initially weaker), both are recep-tive to the other's influence, and each ultimately takes active responsibil-ity for the development of their relationship.[42] By contrast, the standard pederastic lover plays the active role to a younger partner who does not respond erotically to his advances; pederastic poetry tends to stress se-duction, the exhilaration of conquest, and the transitory nature of the relationship. Even though erotic reciprocity traditionally defined the heterosexual relationship, heterosexuality is permanently marked, like the male pederastic relation, by inequality and a pattern of dominance and submission, and is thus unavailable as a model for Plato's argument in *Phaedrus*.

To be sure, in the classical period the male erotic tradition, while it formally insisted on the passivity and sexual indifference of the beloved, urged him to resist bestowing favours on all but the most honourable and virtuous lovers, and protected him from the exploitative advances of older men, was in practice undoubtedly complex (see generally Pausanias' speech in Plato's *Symposium*).[43] In Xenophon's *Symposium*

---

[39] See Nussbaum, 'This Story', 98. She suggests that in the description of the food of the soul's horses (*trophe doxaste*, 'the food of opinion', 245b) there may be a reference to poetry.

[40] Ferrari, *Listening to the Cicadas*, 114–15.

[41] See D. Halperin, 'Plato and Erotic Reciprocity', *Classical Antiquity*, 5 (1986.1), 60–80 on erotic reciprocity in Plato and its absence in the broader male tradition of pederasty.

[42] See esp. *Phaedrus* 252de and 255ab and Nussbaum, *Fragility of Goodness*, 216 and 219 and Ferrari, *Listening to the Cicadas*, 175–6. As Halperin, 'Erotic Reciprocity', 66–7 points out, although women are often said to love in return (*anteran*, Xenophon, *Symposium* 8. 3), the word is not used for men except in *Phaedrus* (255e).

[43] See further Halperin, 'Erotic Reciprocity', 65 n. 13. The problem was to avoid putting the boy, as a future citizen and active lover, into a passive sexual role. The *eromenos* not only avoided pursuing the *erastes*, but intercrural intercourse was the preferred mode because the boy could avoid penetration and faced the lover.

(4. 10–28), for example, the beautiful Critobulus, who is said to have begun pursuing his age-mate Cleinias (both are just beginning to grow beards), is also the apparent object of attentions from Socrates. It strains credulity to believe that the sexual ideology governing relations between *erastes* (lover) and *eromenos* (beloved), which apparently prevented a man from being both lover and beloved to the same man, maintained that someone who had already played the role of lover could pretend that he was entirely indifferent to desire in the role of beloved. In the archaic period it is not even clear that the same rigid protocols obtained. Here vase-paintings display the occasional aroused beloved.[44] Moreover, the poet Theognis' fickle beloved can receive satisfaction from sexual inter-course and yet go on to pursue other lovers repeatedly for himself. His beloved is compared both to a well-fed horse who once again desires a good rider (2. 1249–52) and pleasant pastures, and to a horse satisfied with barley who nevertheless once again takes on another man (2. 1267–70).[45] In both *Symposium* and *Phaedrus* there are hints of a breakdown in the traditional pattern: in *Symposium*, the younger man Aristodemus is said to be an *erastes* of Socrates, Socrates plays the *eromenos* to the younger Alcibiades (217d and, more generally, 222b), and Pausanias and Agathon are long-term adult lovers; in *Phaedrus* Socrates and Phaedrus frequently switch roles.[46]

Hence, despite Plato's marked lack of interest in examining the rela-tions between female lovers mentioned in Aristophanes' speech in *Sym-posium* (191e),[47] the only cultural precedent for the kind of pointedly less hierarchical and more egalitarian erotic reciprocity shared by Socrates' lovers in *Phaedrus* is apparently, as David Halperin and others have suggested in passing, to be found in female homoerotic relations.[48]

---

[44] On the vase-paintings, see further K. J. Dover, *Greek Homosexuality* (Harvard Univer-sity Press, Cambridge, Mass., 1978), 91–103 and Halperin, 'Erotic Reciprocity', 64 n. 11.

[45] Although in the first example the text is uncertain, both passages almost certainly contain veiled sexual references.

[46] On *Symposium*, see Halperin, 'Erotic Reciprocity', 68–71; on *Phaedrus*, see Griswold, *Self-Knowledge*, 29. Plato's strategy permits both lovers to be active, thus avoiding the charge that pederasty endangers the beloved by putting him in a passive role (Halperin, 'Erotic Reciprocity', 67).

[47] At *Laws* 636c Plato calls both sexual relations among males and among females contrary to nature.

[48] D. Halperin, *One Hundred Years of Homosexuality* (Routledge, New York, 1990), 129, 136. As E. F. Keller, 'Love and Sex in Plato's Epistemology', in her *Reflections on Gender and Science* (Yale University Press, New Haven, 1985), 32 puts it: 'In the end, Plato's definition of a new form of pederastic love remained constrained by cultural models available to him and the restrictions these imposed on acceptable forms of desire in men. Given these restrictions, the only imaginable model that might have offered an instance of reciprocal

Recent criticism on Sappho has generally taken for granted a greater reciprocity and mutuality in female than in male homoerotic relations in Greece, although the fragmentary nature of the evidence does not make this entirely certain.[49] Visual evidence may depict relations among female partners as less hierarchical than comparable representations of men.[50] In the *Partheneia* or Maiden Songs of the Spartan poet Alcman, young unmarried women express desire for women who are apparently their peers or only slightly older.[51] In Sappho, we cannot identify the age or status of most of the women in her poems with any certainty; the roles of lover and beloved in Sappho may not even be culturally differentiated as they are among men. In Sappho fragment 1 the goddess Aphrodite promises to turn a woman resistant to Sappho's advances into a pursuer of love. The text is ambiguous as to whether the new object of the woman's love will be Sappho or another woman, although the former seems more likely.[52] If the object of her pursuit is to be Sappho, then the female homoerotic relation is reversible in a manner contrary to that represented among males. Sappho's extant fragments offer only this one example of sexual pursuit, and here she does not celebrate victory in the game of love in the predatory fashion common to male erotic poets.

consummated sexuality, not automatically evoking aggression and inviting domination, would have come from female homosexual experience or from a female perspective on heterosexual experience.' M. Skinner, 'Woman and Language in Archaic Greece, or, Why is Sappho a Woman?', in N. Rabinowitz and A. Richlin (eds.), *Feminist Theory and the Classics* (Routledge, New York, 1993), 137 notes, however, that Halperin does not mention Sappho; nor does Keller. I agree with Skinner's point (pp. 137–8) that Sappho's female discourse gives Plato a chance to 'play the other', although she does not address the complex way in which *Phaedrus* relates to Sappho. On Plato's appropriation of the feminine in *Phaedrus*, see also DuBois, 'Phallocentrism', esp. 95–101.

[49] For reciprocity in Sappho, see the pioneering article of E. S. Stigers, 'Sappho's Private World', in H. P. Foley (ed.), *Reflections of Women in Antiquity* (Gordon & Breach, New York, 1981), 45–6 and Skinner, 'Women and Language', 125–44. Keller, 'Love and Sex', 29 argues that the Platonic relation, due to the lover's maturity, inevitably retains hierarchy, but is free of domination.

[50] For visual evidence depicting possibly less hierarchical relations among female lovers than male in archaic Greece, see M. Williamson, *Sappho's Immortal Daughters* (Harvard University Press, Cambridge, Mass., 1995), 124.

[51] Alcman, frr. 1 and 3 in Campbell, *Greek Lyric II*.

[52] In this poem Sappho apparently asks not for erotic justice (although there is a possible hint of this in the woman's turn to pursuit even if she is unwilling), but for success in love. Compare Anacreon's wish, described by Himerius in Anacreon fr. 445, Campbell, *Greek Lyric II*. See further A. Giacomelli, 'The Justice of Aphrodite in Sappho frag. 1', *Transactions and Proceedings of the American Philological Association*, 110 (1980), 135–42, Ellen Greene, 'Apostrophe and Women's Erotics in the Poetry of Sappho', *Transactions and Proceedings of the American Philological Association*, 124 (1994), 51–3, and Williamson, *Sappho's Immortal Daughters*, 163–4.

While the male poet aims at domination of the passive beloved, Sappho in poem 1 is ultimately granted either a restored mutuality (we cannot imagine that the ardent Sappho would resist the pursuing woman or adopt a passive role for long) or the desired woman will suffer comparably from the pangs of love. Although we can never be certain of the exact erotic relation among women who engage in dialogue in Sappho's poems, these dialogues, as we shall see below, seem to reflect an implicit equality and shared emotions (see fragment 94. 4) rather than assuming or establishing hierarchy; the duration of the relations is uncertain, but Sappho's poems repeatedly make a point of establishing their permanence in memory and song. The poems thus eroticize not a transient phase of life, but its whole course;[53] the process of love and a range of shared experiences take precedence over a specific goal.[54]

Margaret Williamson makes a good case for what she calls an elision of subject positions and a circulation of desire among the women in Sappho's poems.[55] In fragment 22, to give but one example, Sappho, as singer of the poem, elides herself with the subject position of the woman whom she commands to sing about her desire for a third woman:

I bid you, Abanthis, take [your lyre?] and sing of Gongyla, while desire once again flies around you, the lovely one—for her dress excited you when you saw it and I rejoice.

Relations among female lovers were unlikely to reflect with any consistency the hierarchies of a political life from which they were formally excluded, although they could have been pedagogical or initiatory. Since women married as early as 12 or 13, they were logically understood (as in Alcman) as potentially desiring subjects from puberty on. Hence I think it is safe to say, with Williamson, that 'in Sappho the range of voices, positions, and self–other relationship in the expression of desire is far

[53] See the valuable discussion of Thomas M. Falkner, *The Poetics of Old Age in Greek Epic, Lyric, and Tragedy* (University of Oklahoma Press, Norman, 1995), 92–107. The process extends even into old age; see Sappho's fr. 24. 3–4, where the speaker tells the beloved how she will remember the beautiful things they did in their youth.

[54] J. J. Winkler, 'Gardens of Nymphs: Public and Private in Sappho's Lyrics', in Foley (ed.), *Reflections of Women in Antiquity*, 69 stresses 'the ebb and flow of conflicting emotions, of sorrow succeeded by joy, of apprehensiveness followed by relief, of loss turning into victory'.

[55] Williamson, *Sappho's Immortal Daughters*, 129–30 and M. Williamson, 'Sappho and the Other Woman', in Sara Mills (ed.), *Language and Gender* (Longman, New York, 1995), 76–94; for a summary of her views, see esp. 93 n. 13. See also J. J. Winkler, *The Constraints of Desire: The Anthropology of Sex and Gender in Ancient Greece* (Routledge, New York, 1989), 167, on Sappho's ability to integrate in one poem 'several personal perspectives, whose multiple relations to each other set up a field of voices and evaluations'.

wider and far more subtly modulated' than in the male erotic tradition.[56] The claims for greater reciprocity in female than in male homoerotic relations made by other critics are also plausible if finally unprovable.

An unusual model of homoerotic relations is not the only aspect of the erotic scenario shared, although in very different ways, by Plato in *Phaedrus* and Sappho, however. As Maximus points out, each practised the art of love in a circle peopled by colleagues and rival practitioners of philosophy or poetry and by younger males or by (possibly younger) females who were the objects of their attention, erotic and otherwise.[57] These circles clearly differ fundamentally, and Sappho's is virtually impossible to recreate.[58] Yet more than Alcaeus or Anacreon or any other archaic poet, Sappho's *œuvre* gave to Maximus the impression of a carefully delineated world in which the poet repeatedly encounters the same or similar characters, takes internally consistent stances toward *eros* and beauty, and deploys rhetorical techniques used by Plato (irony, cross-examination, or censure). Maximus' remarks at 18. 9 are particularly interesting because the fragments that have come down to us offer few glimpses of this last aspect of Sappho's poetry. Certainly, several fragments express criticism or censure.[59] Irony is harder to find, although Sappho treats herself ironically in fragment 1. The one example that Maximus gives us, where he compares Socrates' ironic greeting to the rhapsode Ion (whom he is about to expose as ignorant) to Sappho's greeting to the daughter of Polyanax ('Mr Lord Over Many'), must remain opaque.[60]

---

[56] Williamson, 'Sappho and the Other Woman', 81.

[57] For the most recent discussion of the age of the members of Sappho's circle, see A. Lardinois, 'Subject and Circumstance in Sappho's Poetry', *Transactions and Proceedings of the American Philological Association*, 124 (1994), 57–84. I agree with him that, despite the lack of definite evidence, most of the women represented as objects of desire in Sappho's poetry are likely to have been young.

[58] For recent discussion, see H. N. Parker, 'Sappho Schoolmistress', *Transactions and Proceedings of the American Philological Association*, 123 (1993), 309–52, Lardinois, 'Subject and Circumstance', C. Bennett, 'Concerning "Sappho Schoolmistress"', *Transactions and Proceedings of the American Philological Association*, 124 (1994), 345–8, and Williamson, *Sappho's Immortal Daughters*. See further below.

[59] The following fragments, in Campbell, *Greek Lyric I*, apparently include blame or censure: 3, 5, 55, 57, 68, 71, 90, 91, 93, 209. Maximus compares Socrates' mockery of a sophist's garment and his manner of reclining with Sappho's mockery of a woman's [her rival Andromeda's] rustic dress (Maximus 18. 9 and Campbell 57; the phrase is also quoted by Athenaeus). Other Sappho fragments reflect rivalry between Sappho and other women (26, 37, 131, 144, 171, 202).

[60] Maximus says, 'for Socrates says, "Good day (*chairein*) to you, Ion", and Sappho says: "I wish the daughter of the house of Polyanax a very good day"' (fr. 155, trans. Campbell, *Greek Lyric I*). The father's name and the pointed and possibly sarcastic alliteration of *p*'s in

Yet both Socrates and Sappho do pointedly conduct relations erotic and otherwise with interlocutors through dialogue. Can this be part of what Maximus means by cross-examination (*elengchei*)? Again, dialogue is a feature of Sapphic poetry, which, while not exclusive to this poet, certainly differentiates her (at least on the basis of the fragments that have come down to us) from her peers.[61] Maximus may, in 18. 9, have in mind only cross-examination by Socrates or Sappho that exposes the ignorance of their interlocutors. (Notice that Socrates at *Phaedrus* 235b threatens Lysias' speech with cross-examination by the men and women of antiquity; this turns out to include Sappho and Anacreon, but the mention of women (see also *Meno* 81a) is initially striking in a Greek context.) Yet, as Maximus suggests in his phrase 'erotic discourses' (18. 7), both Plato and Sappho use a dialogic and argumentative mode for a broader range of serious purposes. Platonic dialogues often lead Socrates' interlocutors to another level of understanding (see *Phaedrus* 261a), whether the issue under discussion is, for example, *eros*, beauty, or virtue. As we shall see below, Sappho's fragmentary poems like 94 or 96 gently lead her interlocutors to a new perspective on the pain of erotic loss that aims both to re-envision and to assuage it. Platonic *elengchus* ('cross-examination') and dialectic rely on active participation by living persons engaged in dialogue and the potential for a certain degree of independence among participants in the dialogue (at least the ability to agree and disagree). Among Sapphic fragments that contain a dialogue, fragment 94 includes her reported conversation with a woman departing her circle which contrasts the woman's initially different perspective on that departure with Sappho's own.[62] In others, such as fragment 16, Sappho challenges other points of view on beauty and aims to persuade the hearer of her view. At the highest level, such as among the ideal philosophical lovers in *Phaedrus*, philosophical dialogue depends on the potential equality of the interlocutors. In *Phaedrus*, dialogues among putative equals involve mutual struggle and exploration and can create reciprocity in love and permanent friendship (255b). The elision of subject positions in Sappho identified by

the Greek may suggest social pretension on the woman's part. The family of Polyanax may elsewhere be attacked in a fragment attributed either to Sappho or Alcaeus (Campbell, *Sappho*, fr. 99).

[61] Archilochus' Cologne fragment (P. Colon. 7511), for example, includes dialogue as part of a narrative (as does epic), but the fragments of Sappho's fellow lyric poets contain little dialogue.

[62] Sappho's extant fragments might be better characterized, however, as discourses about *eros*, rather than as dialogues among lovers.

Williamson can implicitly put the partners in Sapphic dialogue on an equal footing.

In fragments 94 and 96 Sappho creates for separated or soon-to-be separated women a permanent and beautiful memory of the past. As B. Gentili puts it, in Sappho 'memory is not simply, as in Homer, a means of evoking emotion and sensations: it reactualizes shared experiences in a paradigmatic fashion and offers assurance that the life lived together exists as an absolute *reality* beyond space and time'.[63] At the early stages of their encounter, Socrates' philosophical lover in *Phaedrus* merely retains a Sapphic-style pleasurable memory of the desired boy when he is absent (251d6–7).[64] When they are together, both Socrates' lover and the beautiful boy are ultimately awakened by desire to a transcendent memory of eternal beauty and of the god with whom their souls once journeyed. The status of the philosophic lovers' memories obviously differs considerably from that in Sappho, as does Platonic dialectic from Sapphic dialogue, but the process of conducting matters relating to *eros* through dialogue and memory by Sappho and Plato is in some way comparable.[65] Maximus' seemingly facile attempt to make Sappho Plato's predecessor in 'erotic discourses' may be less absurd than might appear at first glance.

Sappho's poetry, as Maximus notes, names numerous female objects of desire, of her own and of others, and Socrates normally refuses to imagine attaching himself to any particular young man. Thus, despite the named individuals and the concrete relationships depicted in both Sappho's poems and Plato's dialogues, *eros* should always be understood in each *œuvre* as desire, an emotion fundamentally more impersonal than love. Although Sappho's world sometimes and probably often excluded lifelong attachments among female lovers, she insists on memorializing in song and thus making permanent each relationship, so that it can be shared both by the inevitably separated lovers and by the poet's larger audience. Similarly, Socrates generally plays the lover or beloved to many, even if *Phaedrus* raises the possibility of a lifelong attachment between philosophical lovers. In *Symposium*, Diotima interprets the

---

[63] *Poetry and its Public in Ancient Greece: From Homer to the Fifth-Century*, trans. A. T. Cole (Johns Hopkins University Press, Baltimore, 1988), 84.

[64] See further Ferrari, *Listening to the Cicadas*, 152 and 158.

[65] DuBois, *Sappho is Burning*, 81 argues that Plato denies corporeal desire and 'sublimates it into another memory, that sight of ideas that keeps men hunting for truth and beauty'; Sappho converts desire to memory rather than to metaphysical aspiration (p. 98). This interpretation of Plato applies better to *Symposium* and to Plato's other dialogues than to *Phaedrus*.

move from desiring one to desiring all beautiful bodies as a higher stage in the pursuit of beauty and philosophy (221d); Sapphic poetry makes a comparable generalizing move.

Despite Sappho's unapologetic celebration of desire, Sapphic poems often deal with the failure to attain or to make permanent the erotic relationship. While Sappho's lovers never regret their immersion in the world of concrete experience, her poetry nevertheless dwells not on presence but on absence or on transcending loss. Permanence and pleasure are ultimately lodged in the world of poetry and the imagination, not in the consummation of desire or in the possession of the beloved. It is song, simile, festal and religious performance, and the signs of shared experience that will link the lovers across time and space. As T. McEvilley puts it, Sappho usually 'seems to resolve the difficulties of life—from which the poems generally begin—by affirming that art and imagination are creators of stronger, healing realities'.[66] In fragment 16, Anactoria, the object of Sappho's desire, is celebrated in her absence and used to demonstrate a general point about the nature of *eros* and beauty. Sappho and Plato, especially in *Symposium*, seem to share the insight that *eros* pursues what it does not and cannot possess, but seeks rather to perpetuate itself as a motive for creation and/or the pursuit of knowledge.[67] In *Symposium*, the response to the beloved's beauty leads to procreation and the birth of discourses in beauty (206c-e); in Sappho, the relation between lover and beloved leads to the creation of therapeutic memories and their perpetuation in song. Page DuBois's claim that, in contrast to Plato, 'Sappho speaks of desire without imagining its transcendence except in the act of writing' gives insufficient emphasis to this critical exception.[68] Our fragments clearly demonstrate Sappho's ambitions for and explicit claims to poetic immortality,[69] and the substitution of song for presence is by no means as innocent as it might appear. In fragment 96, for example, the speaker consoles Atthis by stating that her beloved in faraway Sardis thinks about and remembers her with desire, honoured her as a goddess and delighted in her song, and is consumed because of Atthis' fate. Desire plays its role in this description, but the stress is on song, memory, and Atthis' godlike attributes, on the songs of Atthis and

---

[66] 'Sappho, Fragment Ninety-Four', *Phoenix*, 25 (1971), 8.

[67] See further Halperin, 'Erotic Reciprocity', 67 and 'Platonic *Eros* and What Men Call Love', *Ancient Philosophy*, 5 (1985), 169; erotic desire is not like other appetites in this respect (Halperin, 'Platonic *Eros*', 168).

[68] *Sappho is Burning*, 80.

[69] See Campbell, *Greek Lyric I*, frr. 55, 147, 150, 193.

by implication on the song of Sappho itself. I stress this point not so much to create a strained analogy between Sappho's and Plato's very different modes of recognizing the power of *eros* and its role as an inspiration for creating something more than corporeal, but to counter a tendency in the recent criticism that pits Sappho as the paradigmatic celebrant of the body against Plato's philosophic aim to transcend it.

Despite Diotima's, Aspasia's, and, I would add, Sappho's appearance in Plato's texts, DuBois and others have aimed to demonstrate that women—and with them the body and the material world—are in the end consistently excluded from the scene of Platonic philosophy.[70] In *Sappho is Burning*, DuBois begins her chapter on Plato and Sappho by asking what would it mean

To measure Sappho's absence from the text of Plato, her exclusion from the scene of philosophy? Is Sappho's exclusion necessary? Are her body and its desires intolerable, its speech too lyrical, too hysterical, too caught up in the battle of love, scenes of marriage, physical longing for the beloved to participate in the sober work of philosophy, even for an erotic philosophy like Plato's?[71]

In DuBois's view what Sappho most wants is to reconstitute the beloved in her absence, to dwell in the material sphere of the body and in the concrete details of everyday life.[72] The philosophical desire to transcend pleasure and the body in a Platonic fashion for the more exciting life of the soul is seemingly absent from all archaic poetry, not just Sappho's. Yet for neither Plato nor Sappho is erotics limited to the body and the corporeal realm. For Plato, *eros* is a catalyst to knowledge for both body and soul. When in fragment 22 Sappho urges Abanthis to sing under the provocation of her erotic response to Gongyla's dress, desire also serves as a catalyst for the creative process. Jane Snyder argues, in her discussion of this fragment, that the Sapphic lover often seeks not possession but 'a heightened experience of what is beautiful, a fluttering excitement aroused by motion and by visual stimulus' that generates song.[73] In *Symposium* Diotima urges the budding philosopher to transcend a devotion to particular bodies as well as the seductive trappings of desire such

---

[70] DuBois, *Sappho is Burning*, 93. See also Halperin, *One Hundred Years*, 113–52, esp. 142, 145, and 150 on the role of Diotima and the feminine in *Symposium*, DuBois, *Sappho is Burning*, 92, and P. DuBois, *Sowing the Body: Psychoanalysis and Ancient Representations of Women* (University of Chicago Press, Chicago, 1988), 169–83.

[71] DuBois, *Sappho is Burning*, 79, 85.

[72] Ibid. 81, 87.

[73] J. Snyder, 'The Configuration of Desire in Sappho', *Helios*, 21.1 (1994), 7, and 3–8. The erotic reach for the unpossessible does appear in a Sapphic wedding fragment (105a).

as chains of gold or dress (211d) in the pursuit of beauty itself. Yet Socrates' recantation within *Phaedrus*, which is both intensely lyrical and inspired by poetic madness, makes it clear that both the body and the concrete experiences of daily life play a critical role in generating the philosophical lovers' pursuit of philosophy.[74]

Furthermore, just as *Phaedrus* brings Plato to some degree into Sappho's camp, by retaining a more extensive catalytic role for the body and its desires in the philosophic relationship than in other dialogues, Sappho's poetry—as Maximus hints—can be suggestively proto-philosophical.[75] In the case of fragment 16, for example, Sappho aims to persuade the hearer of her view that 'the most beautiful thing on earth is what(ever) one loves':

> Some say that the most beautiful thing
> upon the black earth is an army of horsemen;
> others, of infantry, still others, of ships;
> but I say it is what[ever] one loves.

> It is completely easy to make this
> intelligible to everyone; for the woman
> who far surpassed all mortals in beauty,
> Helen, left her most brave husband

> And sailed off to Troy, nor did she
> remember at all her dear child
> or her dear parents; but [the Cyprian]
> led her away . . .

> [All of which] has now reminded me
> of Anaktoria, who is not here . . .

> Her lovely walk and the bright sparkle of her face
> I would rather look upon than
> all the Lydian chariots
> and full-armed infantry.[76]

In Page DuBois's view, 'at least as important as Anaktoria, and praise of Anaktoria, is the poet's attempt to universalize her insight, to speak in logical terms of the ways in which men's love of the display of battle,

---

[74] On the inextricable links between sexual and intellectual desire in *Phaedrus*, see Anne Lebeck, 'The Central Myth of Plato's *Phaedrus*', *Greek, Roman and Byzantine Studies*, 13 (1972), 267–90, esp. 273.

[75] The bibliography even on the philosophical aspects of this controversial fragment is too enormous to cite here; those cited give extensive references to earlier discussions.

[76] Trans. J. Snyder, *The Woman and the Lyre: Women Writers in Classical Greece and Rome* (Southern Illinois University Press, Carbondale, 1989), modified.

Helen's love, her own love for Anaktoria, belong within some more englobing strategy'.[77] 'Sappho is progressing toward analytical language, toward the notion of definition, of logical classes, of subordination and hypotactic structure.'[78] She 'moves toward abstraction' inductively and 'arrives at a version of a definition of the beautiful through the accumulation of detail, through example and personal testimony'.[79] DuBois agrees with Bruno Snell that Sappho is not simply asserting her personal taste about beauty here, but she does not follow him in arguing that Sappho is in a Platonic fashion 'evidently concerned to grasp a piece of genuine reality: to find Being instead of Appearance'.[80] In DuBois's view, Sappho is not saying that Anactoria *is* the most beautiful thing; instead, Sappho's poetic insight may be conditioned by the recent invention of money, which allowed 'things, even men, to be measured by a common standard'.[81]

For Hermann Fraenkel, Garry Wills, William Race, and others, by contrast, Sappho is in fragment 16 a precursor of the sophists.[82] For Fraenkel,

the implications of Sappho's astonishing thesis [in fragment 16] are very far ranging; it contains the potentiality of overthrowing any absolute value. For all values which are to be obtained are subsumed under the conception of the beautiful, so that 'the beautiful' becomes the yardstick for practical activity. According to Sappho, Helen, herself the most beautiful and most desired of women, found life with Paris more beautiful than the life she had previously led; and she thought and behaved as she did because she was seized by love. We do not desire what is in itself beautiful, but we find what we desire beautiful. This anticipates half of the dictum of the sophist Protagoras, according to which man is the measure of all things. Not infrequently, in this age, poetry precedes philosophy and prepares the way for it.[83]

[77] DuBois, *Sappho is Burning*, 105. See more generally, P. DuBois, 'Sappho and Helen', in John Peradotto and J. P. Sullivan (eds.), *Women in the Ancient World: The Arethusa Papers* (SUNY Press, Albany, NY, 1984), 95–106 and *Sappho is Burning*, 83, 85, 105–7, 110, 114.

[78] 'Sappho and Helen', 97–8.

[79] DuBois, *Sappho is Burning*, 107.

[80] B. Snell, *The Discovery of the Mind: The Greek Origins of European Thought*, trans. T. G. Rosenmeyer (Harper & Row, New York, 1960), 50.

[81] 'Sappho and Helen', 99. See also Sappho's evaluation of Kleis in fr. 132 Campbell.

[82] H. Fraenkel, *Early Greek Poetry and Philosophy*, trans. M. Hadas and J. Willis (Harcourt, Brace, Jovanovich, Oxford, 1962); G. Wills, 'The Sapphic *Umwertung aller Werte*', *American Journal of Philology*, 88 (1967), 434–42; W. H. Race, 'Sappho, fr. 16 L-P and Alkaios, fr. 42 L-P: Romantic and Classical Strains in Lesbian Lyric', *Classical Journal*, 85 (1989–90), 16–33.

[83] Fraenkel, *Early Greek Poetry*, 187. Wills, 'Sapphic *Umwertung*', agrees with Fraenkel, arguing that Sappho's principle 'precludes differentiation on any scale of objective merit'

Similarly, for Race, Sappho shows a sophistic confidence (line 5, 'it is completely easy to make this intelligible to everyone'), and uses a mythical exemplum to justify private passion and to reject the value of family, marriage, and public interests (war) in a sophistic and amoral fashion.[84] Anne Burnett takes the opposite view by arguing that Sappho avoids making a lover's (in contrast to the military man's) preference merely subjective, because the lover alone is uniquely inspired and authorized by Aphrodite.[85]

The claim that Sappho prefigures sophistry and cultural relativism in my view oversimplifies and distorts her poem. In *Phaedrus*, each lover of beauty responds at first most strongly to beauty in a particular form, whether to beauty in a beloved, or at a later stage to the beauty represented in leadership or philosophy ('each selects his love from the ranks of the beautiful according to his disposition' (252d5–e5)); yet, like Sappho, Plato is not arguing overall for a subjective view of beauty. In fragment 16, Sappho makes what seems to be the revolutionary gesture of defining all human response to and valuation of beauty and nobility in terms of *eros*.[86] The priamel form that begins fragment 16 ends by denying hierarchy among those objects valued as most desirable and noble and challenges standard cultural boundaries between public and private worlds.[87] Sappho's claim that 'whatever one desires' is most beautiful allows her to put men's response to armed forces (generally expressed in epic or poetry celebrating public achievements in

(p. 437). Yet in his view, 'Sappho goes beyond Protagoras in her vision of a beautiful and destructive anarchy . . . If logic destroys all objective values for Plato and Sappho, as for Nietzsche, this is only that she may create a newly evaluated world by sheer personal assertion and creativity' (p. 441).

[84] Race, 'Sappho and Alkaios', esp. 18–20, and 23.

[85] *Three Archaic Poets: Archilochus, Alcaeus, Sappho* (Harvard University Press, Cambridge, Mass., 1983), esp. 280, 287–8. Glenn Most, 'Sappho fr. 16.6–7L-P', *Classical Quarterly*, 31.1 (1981), 13, similarly argues that Sappho here anticipates Aristotle, *Rhetoric* 2. 23, in appealing to an authority that can settle the case because of non-rational factors (faith, respect, sanctity, or prestige, e.g. of the gods). The beautiful Helen's authority to judge is confirmed by the logic of 'like to like' (p. 15); in *Symposium*, Plato also concludes his investigation of the relation of *eros* to the beautiful by praising the spiritual beauty of Socrates (p. 16). Burnett, *Three Archaic Poets*, 281–2, sees Sappho as playing ironically with masculine logic and discourse in a 'too philosophic priamel' (p. 284). Sappho's praise of Anactoria is 'frankly disproportionate' (p. 280). The poem declares the 'aesthetic supremacy of erotic values over accepted moral ones', but not 'the pursuit of fairest flesh', since Sappho's own beloved cannot be possessed (pp. 289–90).

[86] As Gorgias points out in his *Encomium on Helen* (16), military formations (like *eros*) can cause an irrational response (panic) in viewers.

[87] Overlapping details blur the boundaries between examples here. I do not mean to argue that Sappho is strictly contrasting male and female worlds.

war)[88] or to the famous cause of war (Helen) on a par with an individual's desire for a beloved man or woman in the private (and conventionally less valued) sphere. The mythic example of Helen (and the presentation of Sappho's own argument) evokes for Sappho not the actual sight of her beloved but the elusive and unpossessible memory of the absent Anactoria, whom she would prefer to see over all other beautiful objects. This final example, by making Anactoria an object of memory and imagination, unites the entire set of beautiful things mentioned as objects worthy of poetic celebration and immortalization in epic poetry and erotic lyric rather than as random objects of sensual and aesthetic response in a lived present. If all Sappho's examples represent categories of poetic celebration, we can understand why they seem so categorically distant from each other and represent an apparently narrow range of beautiful objects,[89] as well as why Sappho is undermining the standard priamel form, which aimed to persuade the hearer of the poet's own specific conception of what is best.[90] Instead, Sappho's priamel, by substituting an embracing generalization ('the most beautiful thing ... is whatever one loves') for the expected concrete example, does *not* reject what went before, and comes to her own preference only by way of a second priamel.[91] To argue, as Fraenkel does, that for Sappho all human evaluation of beauty is merely subjective ('beauty is in the eye of the beholder') would undermine her implicit claim that these particular objects of desire are united by being the most worthy objects of poetic celebration, and that love poetry, with its celebration of beloved individuals, is not an inferior poetic genre. In this last claim, Sappho was followed by countless other love poets in antiquity.

In fragment 16, as in Plato, the lover responds not just to the beloved, but to beauty in the beloved. Indeed, the very insistence that *eros* defines beauty in so many seemingly dissimilar realms and motivates its pursuit puts Sappho in a comparable position to Plato's, when he motivates the pursuit of philosophy by *eros*, and makes beauty the unifying force that

---

[88] Helen obviously plays a critical role in epic, but 7th-century poetry apparently introduced sparring over the finest form of military activity and equipment. For examples, see Burnett, *Three Archaic Poets*, 282 and n. 11.

[89] Wills, ('Sapphic *Umwertung*', 435 and Race, 'Sappho and Alkaios', 18, who complains that Sappho narrows her examples abruptly from military activities to lovers and beloveds. Burnett, *Three Archaic Poets*, 283 gives examples of similar archaic priamels which end with a cap celebrating pleasure or success in love. Sappho's avoids this pursuit of possession.

[90] Wills, 'Sapphic *Umwertung*', 436.

[91] Here I agree with Wills, 'Sapphic *Umwertung*', 435 and 437, who insists that Sappho would not have used a neuter pronoun ('whatever') in line 4 if she had meant to exalt *eros* over admiration of military spectacle (p. 438).

explains the attraction of all the virtues.[92] As Burnett puts it, Sappho taught her hearers 'that their present experiences of love, enhanced by song and volatilised by memory, would let them recognize beauty later on, in all of its various forms'.[93] Sapphic generalization does not deliberately anticipate the Platonic abstraction of the incorporeal from the corporeal, but it takes a step in that direction by moving the listener beyond beauty in the visual world to beauty in the world of the imagination and to potential poetic permanence. Finally, the sharply diverging interpretations that this fragment has met among recent scholars suggest that Sappho's ancient readers—and Plato among them—could have found in it the seeds of a variety of arguments that claim it for philosophy.

Let us return to the question of the apparent hostility between Plato's and Sappho's view of *eros* and the body posed by DuBois. In her analysis of fragment 94, Ellen Greene argues that the use of pronouns and apostrophe (a move from third, to second, to first person plural) progressively erases the distinction between self and other to create 'a nearness so pronounced, that it makes all discrimination of identity, and thus all forms of property, impossible', as the 'environment dissolves into a totality of sensation'.[94]

> 'Honestly, I wish I were dead.'
> Weeping many tears she left me behind
> and said this also.
> 'Oh what terrible things we have suffered
> Sappho. I leave you against my will, I swear.'
>
> And I made this reply to her.
> 'Go and remember,
> for you know how we cherished you.
>
> If not, I want to remind you . . .
> of the beautiful things we shared.
> At my side you decked yourself

[92] See the argument concerning beauty in Plato's *Hippias Major*. I do not think that Sappho here tests hypotheses philosophically by cross-examination, engages in the dialectical process of division and collection outlined at *Phaedrus* 2665d ff., or aims to show that beauty itself unifies diverse examples of beauty. (On dialectic in *Phaedrus*, see further Herman L. Sinaiko, *Love, Knowledge, and Discourse: Dialogue and Dialectic in Phaedrus, Republic, Parmenides* (University of Chicago Press, Chicago, 1965; repr. 1979).)

[93] *Three Archaic Poets*, 224–5.

[94] Greene, 'Apostrophe and Women's Erotics', 44–5 and 49; DuBois, *Sappho is Burning*, 138–44 offers a similar analysis of pronouns in 94.

with many wreaths of violets
and roses and crocuses.

And many plaited garlands
made of flowers . . .
round your tender neck,

And . . . with much royal
and flowery perfume . . .
you anointed . . .

And on soft beds
. . . delicate . . .
you satisfied . . . desire

And there was no . . .
no shrine . . .
from which we were absent,

. . . no grove . . . nor choral dance.'[95]

By contrast, Anne Burnett's interpretation makes Sappho's poem far more abstract. She asserts that Sappho's

'Remember me!' has expanded, in the lines that follow, to become 'Remember beauty and pleasure!'—and the larger remembrance is offered as a talisman that can be taken anywhere . . . The girl is to remember not her lover but herself, and of herself, not her own person, not even vivid moments of her own history, but a schema of experience. She is to think of a series of three habitually repeated gestures, and these will lead her to an equally prismatic memory of satisfied desire.[96]

In so far as the gaps in the papyrus permit us to tell, the poem mentions putting on wreaths, garlands, and perfume and satisfying desire on beds, not hair, flesh, and love-making with a named partner at a concrete moment in time. Indeed, in the extant fragments, Sappho discreetly mentions only those aspects of a woman that can represent her desirability on public and festal occasions: face, eyes, walk, voice, details of clothing, wreaths and garlands. These are the aspects (voice and movement excluded) of feminine beauty that also appear on the famous and closely contemporary statues of maidens or *korai*, whose bodies are draped to show feminine curves, but are never nude. Indeed, it is Plato, whose world is characterized by nude male statues and athletic nudity, who

[95] My translation.
[96] A. P. Burnett, 'Desire and Memory', *Classical Philology*, 74 (1979), 18 and 23. For a different view, see Wilson, *Sappho's Sweetbitter Songs*, 130.

occasionally refers to the breathtaking details of bodily beauty that must be resisted by the would-be philosopher.[97]

By (apparently) mentioning the woman's satisfaction of desire, Sappho 94 is unusually explicit among her fragments, but remarkably discreet in comparison to a poem like Archilochus' Cologne fragment (P. Colon. 7511), which dwells on a woman's breasts and hair and moves to an explicit sexual climax. Both the Greek and the gaps in Sappho's text make it uncertain whether the woman satisfies her own desire, that of other women, or is definitely engaged in sexual activity at all.[98] Sappho's role (if any) in her sexual activity is also uncertain. As Burnett remarks of Sappho 94, 'nothing can change the fact that sex both is and is not here'.[99] In Burnett's view the final lines of the poem do not offer, as DuBois suggests, a regrettable destruction of intimacy; instead, the real goal of the poem is the burst of festal activity at the close of the fragment.[100] The woman will be replaced in Sappho's circle, but 'her own experience is indestructible'.[101] At the same time both her past sensual experiences and her shared memory of festal and religious events become, I would argue, something that she can take with her, perhaps even to another festal activity, marriage, where she will also don garlands and perfume.[102]

'The essential quality' of this poem and of all the longer Sapphic pieces, Burnett argues, 'is not raw emotion but perfected meditation'.[103] When Sappho records raw emotion and bodily symptoms, as in frag-

---

[97] See e.g. *Charmides* 155d, where Socrates is inflamed by his glance within Charmides' cloak at the gymnasium.

[98] For a subtle discussion of the problems of interpreting these lines, see Williamson, *Sappho's Immortal Daughters*, 146. Archaic male poets were apparently similarly discreet about erotic relations among men; hence one would not expect Sappho to be explicit about such details. Archilochus' explicit description occurs in a poem which blames rather than praises women.

[99] Burnett, 'Desire and Memory', 25. On the question of Sappho's 'lesbianism', see for the ancient evidence, A. Lardinois, 'Lesbian Sappho and Sappho of Lesbos', in J. N. Bremmer (ed.), *From Sappho to de Sade: Moments in the History of Sexuality* (Routledge, London, 1989; 2nd ed. 1991), 15–35. For further discussion, see Williamson, *Sappho's Immortal Daughters*, 90–132. Sappho apparently avoids describing directly the embraces of women that may have occurred offstage in the real environment that produced these poems; there may, however, be veiled references to erotic zones such as the clitoris in Sappho's poems; see Winkler, *Constraints of Desire*, 162–87.

[100] Burnett, 'Desire and Memory', 25; DuBois, *Sappho is Burning*, 144. McEvilley, 'Sappho Ninety-Four', 11 argues instead that since no other participants are mentioned at these festal activities, the poem creates a 'ghost city', where Sappho and her friend 'may wander, as through a "forest of symbols" that suggest the condition of their hearts'.

[101] Burnett, 'Desire and Memory', 25.

[102] For the way that the language of this passage may hint at a wedding rite, see McEvilley, 'Sappho Ninety-Four', 10–11.

[103] Burnett, 'Desire and Memory', 27.

ment 31 (see above), she is, as critics have shown, in the process of objectifying (her gaze depersonalizes her own body) and regaining some control over them.[104] The incomplete poem's last line apparently hints at a resolve to endure her failure to communicate with the desired woman: 'But all must be endured since even a poor man . . .'. The same is true of poem 94. As Burnett puts it, 'love is not a discrete experience' for Sappho. Sappho's celebrations of sensuous detail are part of a process of transforming the body's pleasures into an almost paradigmatic experience that also points beyond the body to a broader and more complex role for erotic desire in human life.

I stress this point because the influence of Luce Irigaray has lured Sappho's recent feminist critics such as Ellen Greene, Marilyn Skinner, and Lyn Hatherly Wilson into representing Sappho as a highly embodied and essentially different female voice. For Irigaray, 'speaking as woman . . . takes place on a timeless, almost wordless plane beyond patriarchal "compartments" and "schemas", where only the body's truths are valid'. Female lovers 'meld into one composite being through simultaneous *jouissance*, and this exchange of inexhaustible orgasmic pleasure constitutes a sharing of consciousness'. Writing 'poses the danger of reinscription as object within a prefabricated patriarchal account'.[105] Skinner, whose account of Irigaray I quote here, wants to argue that Sappho's song escapes inscription in patriarchy because it grew out of and served a female oral tradition. Its continued appeal to a male audience thus does not fundamentally change her poetry's representation of a truly female desire and a genuine 'feminine subjectivity'.[106]

Yet, regardless of orality or literacy, Sappho lived in and must inevitably have been shaped by both the cultural tradition which demanded her separation from beloved women and the male poetic tradition to which she explicitly refers (see especially fragments 1 and

[104] For a good discussion, see T. McEvilley, 'Sapphic Imagery and Fragment 96', *Hermes*, 101 (1973), 368–71. Vivid lists are one technique for creating this effect. If we translate, with some scholars, the word *tolmaton* in the final line as 'ventured' rather than 'endured', the ending has different implications.

[105] L. Irigaray, *This Sex Which is Not One*, trans. C. Porter with C. Burke (1977; Cornell University Press, Ithaca, NY, 1985), 212–16, interpreted by Skinner, 'Women and Language', 136. Skinner (p. 131) speaks of Sappho's 'open, fluid, polysemous—and hence conspicuously non-phallic'—strategies that 'are employed to convey the passionate sexual longing felt by a woman'. See also Greene's use of Irigaray in 'Apostrophe and Women's Erotics', 45, and Wilson's extensive discussions, including Hélène Cixous's attempt to 'write the female body', Julia Kristeva, and others as well as Irigaray, in *Sappho's Sweetbitter Songs*, esp. 11–18, and 191–201.

[106] Skinner, 'Women and Language', 134. See her n. 10 on the influence of Sappho on the visual and rhetorical tradition.

16).[107] Wilson, recognizing but in the end unable to escape from this same problem, opts for a model of Sappho's poetry in which a male-dominated world encloses a smaller, internally discrete women's sphere. Both social sectors are presumably bounded by phallocentric codes, language, and symbols, but the more private female and bilingual world can nevertheless 'construct a symbolic world that is formulated on more female, collective lines' and give voice to a uniquely female consciousness and desire that to some degree bypasses 'the laws and patterns of logocentric thought'.[108] There are indeed many ways in which Sappho's erotic poetry apparently differs from that of her male peers. But whether it is possible to define an essentially different, ahistorical female voice, somehow independent of the dominant discourses around it, yet in many ways resembling what is conventionally characterized as 'feminine', remains problematic. Is the feminine difference not constructed by and in relation to the male 'norm'? Furthermore, writers in antiquity such as Plutarch use Sappho and Anacreon to demonstrate that the art of poetry is the same whether practised by a male or a female (*Virtues of Women* 243b; see also Longinus, *On the Sublime* 10. 3 on Sappho, fragment 31).

Greene's observation about the shift in the use of pronouns in fragment 94 is well taken. Yet despite the intense intimacy among women that Sappho's poetry records, the experiences are frequently presented as displaced into past or future and generalizable. The poems repeatedly evoke the same symbols (garlands, beautiful clothes, flowers), similar erotic spaces, and similar events (songs, dances, festivals, or picnics in groves). Individual women are important in Sappho's poetry. Nevertheless, in so far as we can tell from the fragments, Sappho does not consistently name either the narrator or the loved women in her poems; nor is it clear whether her first persons are singular or plural (to be sung by a chorus). In fragment 31 the desired woman is unnamed, the man sitting beside her is potentially generic.[109] In addition, as Glenn Most has argued, the repeated use of the neuter pronoun in Sappho's love poems may have allowed later interpreters to confuse the gender of the beloved, and to make Sappho's female beloveds into men; it also makes her poetry 'not less personal . . . but less bound to specific and unrepeatable occa-

---

[107] See Winkler, *Constraints of Desire*, 162–87.

[108] pp. 12–13 and 15; see also pp. 199–201. Wilson builds here on the work of Winkler, 'Gardens of Nymphs', 63–89. Space does not permit me to do justice to Wilson's arguments here.

[109] *Contra* DuBois, *Sappho is Burning*, 134.

sions'.[110] For example, in fragment 31, the use of the neuter pronoun *to* ('that') in line 5 has an uncertain referent:

He seems as fortunate as the gods to me, the man who [or whatever man, *ottis*] sits opposite you and listens nearby to your sweet voice and lovely laughter. Truly *that* sets my heart trembling in my breast.[111]

Similarly, Sappho's emphasis in her poems on the repeated dimensions of erotic encounters among women (see the use of the word *deute* or 'again' in Sappho one or fragment 22) also renders individual encounters more paradigmatic/repeatable.

In *Phaedrus*, 'Plato is fully alive to the sense of particularity that informs any passionate erotic attachment'.[112] His lovers respond to each other and share daily life in both intimate and public environments. Yet his philosophical lovers also paradigmatically serve the larger argument, and Plato stresses the description of what takes place within the souls of the individual lovers even more than the relation between them.[113] Sappho is not making a philosophical argument, and hence her effort to generalize and make erotic experience repeatable is harder to explain. If her poems were performed publicly and Sappho, like Socrates, represented herself (as Maximus argues from his impression of her whole *œuvre*) as a lover of many beautiful girls and of many beautiful things, the paradigmatic quality of these seemingly intense, specific, and intimate poems is precisely what invited their female audience to participate in a unified experience, may have allowed the poet to reuse them on different occasions, and incidentally made them accessible and attractive to men as well. As Burnett argues, 'memory preserves, and the conceit of a ritual confers a permanence, for a rite holds within itself all of its past and all of its future performances'.[114] Sappho's poems are often set at and

---

[110] G. W. Most, 'Classics and Comparative Literature', a paper presented at a panel at the American Philological Association, 1994 and forthcoming in revised form (unavailable to me) as 'Reflecting Sappho', in Ellen Greene (ed.), *Re-reading Sappho II* (University of California Press, Berkeley and Los Angeles, 1997), 11–35. He also argues that contemporary male poets are far less non-specific than Sappho.

[111] Trans. Campbell, *Greek Lyric I*. Wilson, *Sappho's Sweetbitter Songs*, 55 makes a similar point about the reference of 'the lovely one' at the beginning of the fourth stanza of fr. 22 (line 13), which might refer to any of the women previously mentioned or to love itself.

[112] Halperin, 'Platonic *Eros*', 183 and 185. 'There is no repression in the correct approach to erotics because there is no motive to restrain or deny the desire to give birth to virtue; there is no sublimation because the authentic object of desire never changes during the upward journey towards the Form' (p. 186). See further Nussbaum, *Fragility of Goodness*, 202, 220.

[113] Ferrari, *Listening to the Cicadas*, 161–72, Griswold, *Self-Knowledge*, 126, 128, and 129, and White, *Rhetoric and Reality*, 146–7.   [114] *Three Archaic Poets*, 30.

make reference to ritual; the paradigmatic quality of her poetry and its emphasis on memory assimilate it to these aspects of ritual and endow its seemingly quotidian events with a striking poetic permanence.

Thus Sappho and Plato both construct a dynamics of homoerotic desire that apparently involves less pointed hierarchy and more implied reciprocity and equality than that represented in contemporary male poets or elsewhere. I have suggested that Sappho offers a possible precedent for Plato's views in *Phaedrus*. More important, however, for both Plato and Sappho erotics involves far more than the body. The erotic discourses of Plato and Sappho can lead their interlocutors beyond the specific to the paradigmatic, and beyond bodily pleasure and possession in Sappho to memory, song, and religious festivity and in Plato to a pursuit of philosophical knowledge and truth where memory (*anamnesis*) and beauty play a catalytic role. I have also tried to interpret *eros* and the body in Sappho on different terms from feminist scholars like Skinner, Greene, Wilson, or DuBois—terms that incidentally make her poetry more accessible to appropriation by Plato in *Phaedrus*, as well as by other male writers of antiquity.

Maximus argues that Sappho practised the Socratic art of love after her own fashion among women, while Socrates did so after his among men. Greek culture logically produced different erotic relations among women from those among men, since these relations must have served different cultural functions.[115] It has been argued that the standard hierarchical and non-reciprocal relation between male lover and beloved was rooted in Greek belief in an initiatory scenario.[116] In return for the favours of the beloved, the lover ideally offered him an often long-term *philia* ('friendship'), guidance, and gifts. He initiated the beloved into the world of war, politics, and love. Once mature, the beloved offered the same as lover to a younger man. The system initiated the beloved into his adult role as citizen of the polis.[117] And in Athens at least, each adult male ideally went on from this phase of his life to mature devotion to family and polis. As Foucault and others have stressed, the emphasis on self-control and behaviour worthy of a citizen in this carefully prescribed scenario is best explained by its links to the reproduction of power and a governing class.[118] While philosophy remains for other reasons attached

---

[115] See further Williamson, *Sappho's Immortal Daughters*, 130.

[116] See Dover, *Greek Homosexuality*, esp. ch. 4.

[117] See Demosthenes, *Erotic Essay*, for a representative view.

[118] See M. Foucault, *The Use of Pleasure*, trans. R. Hurley (Vintage, Random House, New York, 1985), Winkler, *Constraints of Desire*, and Halperin, *One Hundred Years*.

to the transcendence of pleasure and self-restraint, the kind of lifelong, reciprocal, more egalitarian, and far less hierarchical relation formed between two specific individuals for the mutual pursuit of philosophy in *Phaedrus* implicitly marks a radical withdrawal from the social and political world that produced the standard homoerotic relation.[119] Again, this makes it more logical for Plato to borrow from the Sapphic scenario, which, although it may have integrated women in some way into a social world, could not have aimed at reproducing participants in political power.

We have no idea how Sappho's world actually worked, or to what degree it imitated as well as differentiated itself from masculine circles. The battle still rages as to whether Sappho's circle was formed and united by engagement in religious cult, choral performance, pedagogy, or private festal occasions; we cannot be certain, although it seems likely, that women left Sappho's circle for marriage rather than some other reason.[120] Yet it seems no accident that just as Sappho's poetry recreates for the memory idealized erotic spaces to be shared in perpetuity by lovers who cannot live out their relationship in reality, Plato sets *Phaedrus* outside the city in a place where love is now, as in poetry, a powerful divinity rather than, as in *Symposium*, the daemonic offspring of Poverty and Resource; where the Muses find a place at the side of philosophy; and where an archaic poet becomes the imaginary author of a Socratic speech. Plato's formulation of a new erotic relationship in *Phaedrus* has no obvious place in the city and its reproduction (political or biological).[121] This may be one of the reasons why the model of homoerotic philosophical love in *Phaedrus* did not prove popular with Plato's philosophical followers and successors;[122] nor does it appear elsewhere in Plato. In *Symposium* Diotima outlines a new model of philosophical procreation of discourses that hints at a greater reciprocity

---

[119] See Griswold, *Self-Knowledge*, 34 and 136 and Burger, *Plato's Phaedrus*, 60 and 62 on philosophical withdrawal from the public world and its values. Nussbaum, *Fragility of Goodness*, esp. 229 argues that Plato's relation with Dion of Syracuse stands behind the lovers of *Phaedrus*. If so, this relation with Dion proved to be untenable in reality.

[120] For recent discussion with further bibliography, see Parker, 'Sappho Schoolmistress', Lardinois, 'Subject and Circumstance', Bennett, 'Concerning "Sappho Schoolmistress"', and Williamson, *Sappho's Immortal Daughters*. I think that the fragments suggest a picture too complex to be fully comprehended by any one of these theories, although the representation of Sappho as 'schoolmistress' seems least convincing.

[121] If Dion of Syracuse is Plato's inspiration here (see n. 119 above), he is envisioning a relation lived in a civic environment outside Athens. Note the stress in both Plato and Sappho on moving beyond the world and into environments presided over by deities.

[122] Halperin, 'Erotic Reciprocity', 70.

among interlocutors but does not explicitly reject the hierarchical model of homoerotic relations shaped by the goals of the city that is assumed by the earlier participants in the dialogue. This reticence suits Socrates' pursuit of philosophy in the civic world of often errant citizens and potential leaders. By contrast, the pastoral dream of *Phaedrus* can only find a precedent in the erotic memories created by Sappho.

3

Talking Recipes in the Gynaecological
Texts of the *Hippocratic Corpus*

ANN ELLIS HANSON

T H E Hippocratic writers of the fifth and early fourth centuries BCE were
quick to pounce upon what they considered unsophisticated aetiologies
for disease and upon remedies they claimed bore no logical relationship
to the sickness being treated. The scorn these authors heaped upon those
who professed irrational causes and cures is well known. The writer of
Sacred Disease criticized witch-doctors, faith-healers, quacks, and charla-
tans, whose aetiology for epilepsy and sudden seizures invoked attacks
from the gods and whose therapies consisted of purifications, incanta-
tions, prohibition of baths and specific foods, lying on goatskins and
eating the flesh of goats.[1] The writer of *Diseases of Young Girls* censured
women who followed commands from Artemis' priests to dedicate
costly garments to the goddess in the effort to cure madness in the
premenarchic young girl.[2]

In common with most Hippocratics, these two writers imagined that
the interior of the human body consisted of humours, or bodily fluids,
sometimes four in number, and interior organs which served as recep-
tacles for the humours. Although there was wide variation among the
treatises of the *Corpus* in matters of detail, most Hippocratics would
none the less agree that the receptacle for phlegm was the head from

[1] Hippocrates, *Morb. sacr.* 1. 1–46, 60–6 Grensemann. Works from the Hippocratic and
Galenic corpora are cited in the text by English titles, in the notes by Latin abbreviations,
as reported in Gerhard Fichtner, *Corpus Hippocraticum: Verzeichnis der hippokratischen
und pseudohippokratischen Schriften* and *Corpus Galenicum: Verzeichnis der galenischen
und pseudogalenischen Schriften* (Institut für Geschichte der Medizin, Tübingen, 1990). Full
bibliography for the editions of the Greek texts upon which I depend, and which are
identified in the notes by page and surname of the editor, are given in Fichtner. (Where
pertinent, I also include volume and line numbers.) Exceptions are those in the Loeb
Classical Library, cited with page reference, as LCL v, vi, and viii Potter and LCL vii Smith
(Harvard University Press, Cambridge, Mass., 1988–95).

[2] Hippocrates, *Virg.*, viii. 468–70 Littré.

which phlegmy fluids flowed in abundance and that the uterus was the receptacle for women's excess blood to be evacuated monthly. Most also believed that human health depended upon a balance among the bodily humours and upon a humour's ability to flow freely from the receptacle organ through the interior passageways on and out, mixed with urine, faeces, menses, and sweat. Maintaining equality among the humours required not only an aesthetic balancing of the intake and evacuation of food and drink, but also vigilance to combat unhealthy influences from the locality and the changing seasons.[3] Hippocratics' aetiology for disease was grounded in morbid accumulation of one bodily humour and in blockage of the inner passageways which trapped the humour within. This disease process lies at the core of the two writers' explanations for sudden seizures and premenarchic madness. Sitting still for too long and having one's feet go to sleep because excess blood had accumulated in the feet seemed to both writers an appropriate analogy for the numbness that extinguished the senses in those afflicted by the seizures and madness, and both based their therapies on promoting evacuation of the noxious fluid from the vital areas at the centre of the patient's body.

It was important to Hippocratics to absorb all human diseases within their medical craft, including the difficult sicknesses of seizures and madness, and to this end these medical writers not only assigned mechanical causes that were in harmony with the anatomy and physiology they endorsed, but they also employed therapies they claimed countered and reversed the diseased conditions according to the same mechanical principles.[4] If imbalance, accumulation, and blockage were causes of diseases, restoration of balance and free-flowing evacuations were cures. The overly dry was moistened and the overly wet dried; the overly hot was cooled and the overly cold warmed; the overly rough was smoothed and the overly smooth roughened; the overly hard was softened and the overly soft strengthened. Writers of the Hippocratic *Epidemics* assured their readers that medicaments possessing these capacities could be discovered.[5] The precept that opposites cure opposites (*alia aliis*) was a deliberate intellectual stance, at odds with the like-to-like principles of cure (*similia similibus*) that prevailed in the older systems of sympathetic magic and religious ritual.[6]

---

[3] For a layman's summary of basic medical principles current at the beginning of the 4th century BCE, see Xenophon, *Cyropaedia* 1. 6. 15–17.

[4] Ann Ellis Hanson, 'Conception, Gestation, and the Origin of Female Nature in the *Corpus Hippocraticum*', *Helios*, 19 (1992), 31–71, esp. 33–4.

[5] Hippocrates, *Epid.* 2. 2. 12 and 6. 2. 1, LCL vii. 34 and 224 Smith.

[6] The notion that 'opposites cure opposites' is frequently expressed in the *Corpus*: Hippocrates, *Nat. hom.* 9. 1–2, 188 Jouanna; *Flat.* 1. 5, 104 Jouanna; *Morb.* 2. 16, LCL v. 220–

No group of related treatises within the *Hippocratic Corpus* was more amply equipped with recipes and therapies than the gynaecological treatises, and the medicaments and therapeutic procedures were both embedded in and affixed as addenda to treatises on women's diseases. The recipes, along with the gynaecologies themselves, have been dismissed, for example, as mere repositories of women's irrational beliefs and practices from folk medicine.[7] Feminist scholars rightly objected, because a treatise such as *Diseases of Young Girls* and other portions of the gynaecologies were clearly participating in the same intellectual ferment of the fifth century BCE as were the Hippocratic treatises of general medicine. Helen King has underscored, however, how mired in unwarranted assumptions were attempts to attribute the source of gynaecological medicaments either exclusively to male doctors (as medical enforcers of the patriarchal oppression of women) or to a woman's oral tradition passed down from mother to daughter.[8] While King went on to view Hippocratic gynaecology and its medicaments as a dialogic system in which both doctors and female patients pursued strategies of self-interest and to suggest how women patients of the fifth and fourth centuries BCE had space in which to manipulate the Hippocratic system, this chapter focuses upon Hippocratics and the recipes they subsumed into their gynaecological collections. I begin by historicizing the medicaments, setting forth evidence that Hippocratic collections were multi-layered and assembled from a variety of sources over some two centuries. Within this temporal space doctors, Hippocratics and their predecessors, manipulated the medicaments into the form in which they now appear in the *Corpus Hippocraticum*. As Hippocratics recontextualized old recipes into new surroundings, they sometimes retained them in their original form, but at other times they reshaped the therapies to suit changing circumstances of time and place. Hippocratic methods of manipulation seem to resemble those employed by their latter-day descendants, the compilers of recipe books during Hellenistic, Roman, and Byzantine

---

2 Potter; *Loc. hom.* 12 and 34, LCL viii. 42–4 and 74–6 Potter. Helen King, 'Sacrificial Blood: The Role of the amnion in Hippocratic Gynecology', *Helios*, 13 (1987), 117–26, and Heinrich von Staden, 'The Spiderwoman and the Chaste Tree: The Semantics of Matter', *Configuration*, 1 (1993), 23–56.

[7] e.g. James Longrigg, *Greek Rational Medicine: Philosophy and Medicine from Alcmaeon to the Alexandrians* (Routledge, London, 1993), 3–4, nor were the recipe collections included in editions of portions of *Mul.* 1 and 2 by Nicolas Countouris and Hermann Grensemann.

[8] Helen King, 'Self-Help, Self-Knowledge: In Search of the Patient in Hippocratic Gynecology', in Richard Hawley and Barbara Levick (eds.), *Women in Antiquity: New Assessments* (Routledge, London, 1995), 135–48, with a survey of earlier bibliography on the recipes.

times. I then turn to mediating between the multi-layered collections and individual recipes, identifying changes which distance some medicaments away from less sophisticated patterns of thought and move them into closer alignment with mechanical explanations for causes and cures of diseases. Such shifts not only alter the messages recipes are speaking, but also represent changes in the medical construction of gender on female bodies, since women patients became ill and recovered according to Hippocratic paradigms.

Collecting, recording, and rearranging therapeutics was a job undertaken throughout antiquity by medical writers, the majority of them certainly men.[9] Modern appeals to the efficacy of medicinal ingredients do not serve as a necessary guarantee that the therapies resulted from successful empirical testing by generations of ordinary women.[10] The evidence, in fact, never carries us back to the moment when a particular Hippocratic recipe first came into being, nor does it clarify the process through which the recipe won a place within Hippocratic collections. None the less, once written down, a recipe acquired a history and has yet a story to tell.

The impact of writing on medicine and the interplay of oral and written sources in the *Corpus* has, to date, received only brief attention. The medical profession did make early and vigorous use of writing for their prose texts, and Hippocratics relied on written collections of therapies.[11] The writer of *Affections*, a treatise of general medicine,

---

[9] There are exceptions, but they are few: Galen, for example, attributed one recipe to a midwife (*de comp. med. per gen.* 5. 13, xiii. 840. 2–10 Kühn) and cited from a work on cosmetics attributed to Cleopatra, for which see Cajus Fabricius, *Galens Exzerpte aus älteren Pharmakologen* (Walter de Gruyter, Berlin, 1972), 201–2.

[10] The arguments on behalf of efficacy have been played out largely on recipes for contraceptives, of which the *Corpus* offers only a few explicit examples: the *atokeion*, repeated with minor variations in two collections (*Mul.* 1. 76, viii. 170 Littré=*Nat. mul.* 98, 121 Trapp); the statement that venesection causes miscarriage in the pregnant (e.g. *Aph.* 5. 31). For arguments on behalf of efficacy, see John M. Riddle, *Contraception and Abortion from the Ancient World to the Renaissance* (Harvard University Press, Cambridge, Mass., 1992); arguments for efficacy are accepted by e.g. Nancy Demand, *Birth, Death, and Motherhood in Classical Greece* (The Johns Hopkins University Press, London, 1994), p. xvi. Contraceptive and abortive information was more likely to have been of interest to, and tested by, specialized sub-populations, such as professional prostitutes: see e.g. Ann Ellis Hanson, 'Phaenarete: Mother and *Maia*', in Renate Wittern and Pierre Pellegrin (eds.), *Hippokratische Medizin und antike Philosophie* (=*Medizin der Antike* i) (Olms-Wiedemann, Hildesheim, 1996), 159–81, esp. 164–6; Robert Sallares, *The Ecology of the Ancient Greek World* (Duckworth, London, 1991), 154–60; and for the Roman world, Bruce W. Frier, 'Natural Fertility and Family Limitation in Roman Marriage', *Classical Philology*, 89 (1994), 318–33.

[11] For discussions of orality and writing in the *Corpus*, see e.g. Iain M. Lonie, 'Literacy and the Development of Hippocratic Medicine', in François Lasserre and Philippe Mudry

assures us that the recipe collection upon which he was drawing circulated in written form: 'If pain in the back or side is likewise present for this patient, give what has been written in the *Remedies* (*Pharmakitis*) for pleuritic pain.'[12] The eight references to the *Remedies* collection suggest that it included analgesics, anti-febriles, and appropriate food-stuffs and potions. The gynaecological treatises *Diseases of Women* 1 and 2 also advised medicaments drawn from a collection called *Women's Remedies* (*Gynaikeia*), although the form in which the collection circulated is not made clear: when treating uterine lesions, 'in the evening give her a thick potion and whatever is suitable to drink from the *Women's Remedies*'; when medicating a red flux, 'make up her bed with the foot-end higher and administer as a drink an acceptable prescription from the *Women's Remedies*'.[13] The fact that the same gynaecological therapies were absorbed into several collections re-inforces the notion that written sources were also available to writers of gynaecology.[14]

If Hippocratics were moving toward the practices of Hellenistic and Roman doctors in regard to the collecting of recipes, they were drawing therapies and recipes from a variety of sources, rearranging and revising what they collected to suit their own purposes. A Greek-speaking physi-cian living in Egypt during the fourth century CE commissioned a scribe to draw up a recipe book for him. After the scribe finished, the physician doubled the number of recipes in his notebook by copying additional

(eds.), *Formes de pensée dans la collection hippocratique: Actes du IVe colloque international hippocratique* (Librairie Droz, Geneva, 1983), 145–61; Knut Usener, ' "Schreiben" im *Corpus Hippocraticum*', in Wolfgang Kullmann and Michael Reichel (eds.), *Der Übergang von der Mündlichkeit zur Literatur bei den Griechen* (Gunter Narr Verlag, Tübingen, 1990), 291–9; Jutta Kollesch, 'Zur Mündlichkeit hippokratischer Schriften', in Juan Antonio López Férez (ed.), *Tratados hipocráticos* (*Estudios acerca de su contenido, forma, e influencia*): *Actas del VIIe colloque international hippocratique, Madrid, 24–29 de septiembre de 1990* (Universidad Nacional de Educación a Distancia, Madrid, 1992), 335–42; Ann Ellis Hanson, 'Fragmenta-tion and the Greek Medical Writers', in Glenn W. Most (ed.), *Aporemata*, i (Vandenhoeck & Ruprecht, Göttingen, 1997), 289–314, esp. 304–14.

[12] *Remedies=Pharmakitis* in Hippocrates, *Aff.* 9, LCL v. 16 Potter; also *Aff.* (15), 18, 23, 28, and 40, LCL v. 28, 32, 42, 50, and 64 Potter; but *Pharmaka* in *Aff.* 18 and 29, LCL v. 30 and 50 Potter.

[13] Hippocrates, *Mul.* 1. 64 and 2. 113, viii. 132. 22–24 and 244. 4–5 Littré.

[14] For the argument that earlier written materials stand behind the gynaecologies in our present *Corpus*, Hermann Grensemann, *Knidische Medizin, i: Die Testimonien zur ältesten knidischen Lehre und Analysen knidischer Schriften im Corpus Hippocraticum* (Walter de Gruyter, Berlin, 1975), 72–9 and 215–17, with earlier bibliography; for the view that all layers of the Hippocratic gynaecology identified by Grensemann have access to the earlier mate-rial, Antoine Thivel, *Cnide et Cos? Essai sur les doctrines médicales dans la Collection hippocratique* (Belles Lettres, Paris, 1981), 94–5.

ones into its copious margins.[15] Galen, who lived and practised at Rome in the latter half of the second century CE, published several of the recipe collections he said he had put together for his own use. At one point he noted that the recipe for baldness he had just copied into the first book of his compound therapies had been found by his friend Claudianus in a leather notebook formerly belonging to a physician who had died.[16] Later in the same work Galen devoted eight chapters to medications for the scalp and hair, and this section included recipes drawn from the now-lost works of previous medical writers—Heras, Crito, Cleopatra, Archigenes, Asclepiades of Prusa, Soranus, Apollonius. Some of these latter had themselves taken recipes from even earlier medical writers, such as Heracleides of Tarentum, practising in the early decades of the first century BCE.[17] Advertising the fact that one was relying upon written sources, whether private notebooks of practitioners or authored collections in public circulation, made clear to fellow practitioners and patients alike that the recipes were serious and authoritative.

Referring to a therapy or recipe by the name of the doctor with whom it was associated, either as originator or popularizer, became a frequent practice only in Hellenistic and Roman times.[18] The naming of names, however, gives us the means to show that the collections drew from earlier material; when doctors, such as Galen, produced their new collections, they juxtaposed recipes which were modern and up to date with others that were already a century or more old. As later medical writers excerpted, the names of the earliest physicians were particularly likely to disappear, sometimes lost through negligence, or deliberately replaced by the name of the writer who recontextualized and modernized the recipe.[19] Naming a recipe after a physician occurs but once in the gynaecological collections of the *Corpus*, when a medicament for uterine suffocation was named a *philistion* after the medical writer Philistion, living

---

[15] Louise C. Youtie, *P.Michigan* XVII 758: *The Michigan Medical Codex* (Scholars Press, Atlanta, 1996). For other examples of recipes of Greek doctors, preserved on papyrus in the dry sands of Egypt, see Isabella Andorlini Marcone, 'L'apporto dei papiri alla conscenza della scienza medica antica', in Wolfgang Haase (ed.), *Aufstieg und Niedergang der römischen Welt*, 37.1 (Walter de Gruyter, Berlin, 1993), 458–562.

[16] *De comp. med. sec. loc.* 1. 1, xii. 422–6 Kühn.

[17] Cajus Fabricius, *Galens Exzerpte*, 126–7, 143–4, 200.

[18] Examples ibid. 180–205, and Andorlini Marcone, 'L'apporto dei papiri', 462–3. Cf. also Fabulla, a woman for whom a prescription was compounded, in Galen, *de comp. med. sec. loc.* 9. 2 and 10. 2, xiii. 250. 9 and 341. 9 Kühn.

[19] Examples in Marie-Hélène Marganne, 'Une étape dans la transmission d'une prescription médicale: P. Berl. Möller 13', in Rosario Pintaudi (ed.), *Miscellanea papyrologica* (Gonelli, Florence, 1980), 179–83, and Youtie, *The Michigan Medical Codex*, fos. A 6–13 and E 5; for examples from Galen, Cajus Fabricius, *Galens Exzerpte*, 80 and n. 26a.

in Sicily about the middle of the fourth century BCE.[20] Although earlier scholars understood the appearance of Philistion's name as a chronological marker that supplied a date in the mid-fourth century for composition of the gynaecological treatises, Hermann Grensemann convincingly argued that some portions were receiving written form in the first decades of the fifth century BCE.[21] One plank in Grensemann's argument was the fact that a few recipes employed Aeginetan measurements for their ingredients, although the weights and measures of Aegina were not only losing their dominance in the eastern Mediterranean after the defeat of Persia, but the island itself was forced to adopt the Attic standard after being subsumed into the Athenian Empire some years before mid-century. Hence, as a chronological marker, the *philistion* was more likely to be one of the later medicaments incorporated into the collection, marking the end of the process of composition, rather than its inception.

A recipe in the Hippocratic gynaecological collections for a restorative gruel was already in use a century or two earlier, the time at which this recipe received written form outside the *Corpus*. Gruels of various consistencies, made from barley, water, and other ingredients, were a staple in the diet of the infirm throughout antiquity and are omnipresent in therapeutic and dietetic treatises. Only in a few instances, however, do Hippocratic and other medical writers add the herb pennyroyal to the barley and water mixture; in the *Corpus*, the barley and pennyroyal gruel appears only among gynaecological medicaments. After recommending the administration of an acceptable drink from the *Women's Remedies* for a woman suffering from the red flow noted above, recipes for potions follow, including one in which pennyroyal was sprinkled over barley groats and mixed (with water).[22] The potion of barley groats and

---

[20] *Mul.* 2. 201, viii. 386. 9–10 Littré, and *Nat. mul.* 32, 94. 15 Trapp. The Galenic lexicon considered *philistion* a plant (xix. 151. 9 Kühn), but *Nat. mul.* 32 treated it as a medicinal compound.

[21] e.g. [Johannes] Gossens, *Pauly-Wissowas Realencyclopädie der classischen Altertumswissenschaft*, viii.2 (Druckenmüller, Stuttgart, 1913), cols. 1801–52, s.v. 'Hippokrates'; for the earlier date, Hermann Grensemann, *Knidische Medizin*, i. 49–52, 195–202, and *Knidische Medizin*, ii (Steiner, Stuttgart, 1982), 72–3; cf. Antoine Thivel, *Cnide et Cos?*, 90–106, on the treatise *Superf.* from the latest stratum, which also had access to recipes with Aeginetan measurements. Important also is Heinrich von Staden, 'Women and Dirt', *Helios*, 19 (1992), 7–30, esp. 12–13 and n. 42, where he stresses the fact that the chronological implications of Grensemann's arguments have greater consequence for the gynaecological treatises than does his attachment of the gynaecological treatises to the so-called 'School of Cnidus'.

[22] *Mul.* 2. 113, viii. 244. 9 Littré, and cf. also *Mul.* 3. 242, viii. 456 Littré, where pennyroyal gruel medicates the woman who miscarries unwillingly.

pennyroyal was recontextualized by the late compendiast Oribasius, court physician to the mid-fourth-century CE Roman emperor Julian. Oribasius said the gruel was a restorative remedy for those afflicted by acute sea sickness and he claimed he excerpted it from Dieuches, a physician of the late fourth or early third centuries BCE.[23] The nourishing properties of the pennyroyal gruel were also known to laymen through a story told about the pre-Socratic philosopher Heracleitus. Plutarch used the episode in his essay *On Garrulity*, and the fourth-century CE rhetor and philosopher Themistius presented a fuller version in his oration *On Virtue*, now surviving only in a Syriac adaptation. The citizens of Ephesus were accustomed to abundant supplies of food until they were besieged by the Persians; as food ran low and hunger sorely pressed them, they came together to confront the issue. When no one dared to advise his fellow-citizens to restrict their eating habits, Heracleitus took barley groats, mixed them with water, added pennyroyal, and consumed the gruel as a silent lesson in moderation and the eating of simple foods. When the enemy heard that the citizens of Ephesus had learned to regiment their diet in accordance with Heracleitus' advice, they lifted the siege, 'defeated', as they said, 'by the barley gruel of Heracleitus'.[24]

As a restorative gruel, the potion's earliest appearance in written form occurs in the *Homeric Hymn to Demeter*. The goddess, who arrived at the house of Celeus and Metaneira worn out and grieving, her head veiled, was offered red wine. This she refused as inappropriate, asking instead for 'barley and water, mixed with gentle pennyroyal'; she then drank this, breaking her fast 'for the sake of the rite' (vv. 208–11).[25] In the *Hymn* Demeter's drinking of the restorative and nourishing gruel explained the origin of the potion her worshippers would drink for centuries to come in remembrance of their goddess's tribulation and recovery. The *Hymn* is usually dated in the latter decades of the seventh century BCE,[26] and from the perspective of the Hippocratic gynaecologies, it

[23] Dieuches fr. 19 Bertier (Oribasius, *Synopsis* 5. 33. 1–7); the recipe is repeated in Paulus Aegineta, *Epitomae* I 56.

[24] D–K 22 A 3b; for the full text of Themistius with discussion, see J. Gildemeister and F. Bücheler, 'Themistios περὶ ἀρετῆς *Rheinisches Museum für Philologie*, 27 (1872), 438–62.

[25] For the 'Eleusinian potion' (*kykeon*), see Helene P. Foley, *The Homeric Hymn to Demeter* (Princeton University Press, Princeton, 1994), 46–8, 68–70, with earlier bibliography.

[26] No later than *c*.600 BCE, Wilhelm Schmid and Otto Stählin, *Geschichte der griechischen Literatur*, vol. i. 1 (Beck, Munich, 1929), 242; between 650 and 550 BCE, Foley, *Homeric Hymn to Demeter*, 29.

shows their recipe in use more than a century or two before a medical writer subsumed it into his collection. In addition, however well known the pennyroyal gruel became as the Eleusinian *kykeon* to celebrants of the rites of Demeter, Greek medical writers in the course of more than a thousand years, from the Hippocratics and Dieuches to Oribasius and Paulus Aegineta, passed over in silence the religious resonances of the potion. The medicinal drink was restorative and easy to digest; it calmed and strengthened; for these reasons women drank it, including the grieving Demeter, and so did travellers by sea.

Repetition of a medicament or therapy both within the *Corpus* and in other sources not only testifies to the fact that the collections took shape over time, but also exemplifies the ways in which Hippocratic recipes modulated and changed in the course of subsequent recontextualizations. A sophisticated improvement in technique seems apparent, for example, in the substitution of a chair for administering uterine fumigations and fomentations, as opposed to having the woman insert one end of a reed into a pot and the other end into her vagina, as she squatted over a hole in the ground. The chair was to have a corded seat through which extended the tube delivering fumes from the pot on the fire directly into the woman's uterus as she sat upon the chair.[27] That the medical writers considered the chair safer and more comfortable for the woman seems underscored by the concerns they expressed: she who fumigated while squatting over the hole must worry that the fire not get too hot and that she fumigate in good weather, when there was no wind, lest she be chilled. She who fumigated while sitting on the chair was merely cautioned to sit down when the fumigation was cool and to get up when it had again cooled. A footstool before the chair added further to her comfort.

A collection of gynaecological recipes from Ptolemaic Egypt, dated to the third or second century BCE, not only testifies to a subsequent recontextualization of Hippocratic medicaments, but exemplifies the consequences of setting recipes into a different time and place. The mutilated sheet of papyrus contains on its front side fragmentary remains of three columns of gynaecological medicaments, among which is a contraceptive (*atokeion*) whose ingredients included oak galls and

---

[27] *Mul.* 2. 133, 19. 9–21. 12 Countouris (hole in the ground); *Mul.* 3. 230, viii. 438–40 Littré (chair); *Mul.* 1. 75, viii. 162. 9–11 Littré (chair and footstool). For doctors' involvement in the construction of gynaecological equipment, see Ann Ellis Hanson, 'A Division of Labor: Roles for Men in Greek and Roman Births', *Thamyris*, 1 (1994), 157–202, esp. 159–70.

pomegranate seeds.[28] Two prescriptions in the central column claim to medicate uterine suffocation (*hysterike pnix*):[29]

For suffocation from the uterus: prescribe dried otters' kidneys, three fingers' worth; take this in fragrant wine. It also helps pains in the testicles (*didymoi*) and is a clyster for the uterus.

Another: if coughing occurs together with the suffocation, 2 (obols)[30] of realgar (*sandarake*), an equal amount of unfired sulphur, five or 4 almonds; cleanse and mix well; [administer] in fragrant wine. (*P.Ryl.* 3.7 531, col. 2, ll. 12–20)

A series of potions to medicate uterine suffocation are also gathered together in the Hippocratic *Diseases of Women* 2, the first and fourth of which closely resemble the two recipes juxtaposed in the papyrus:

For suffocation from the uterus: have her drink castoreum and fleabane (*konyza*) in wine, separately and together . . .

If the uterus causes suffocation together with coughing, as much as an obol of realgar (*sandarake*), and an equal amount of unfired sulphur; mix in cleansed bitter almonds, three or four, and administer in fragrant wine.[31]

Both pairs of recipes appear in a gynaecological context, although the recipes on the front of the papyrus are recontextualized into a broader environment, by no means exclusive to uterine suffocation. The relocation of the first recipe into an Egyptian milieu apparently brought the substitution of dried otters' kidneys for castoreum, the potent substance from beaver testicles that was a staple in Mediterranean medicine. Both Herodotus and Aristophanes Grammaticus noted that otters lived in the waters of the Nile, and these creatures were perhaps more conspicuous and more plentiful in an Egyptian setting than beavers.[32] Significant in

---

[28] *P.Ryl.* 3. 531=Mertens-Pack[3] 2418=107 Andorlini Marcone, 'L'apporto dei papiri', 518; for the non-gynaecological recipes on the back, Marie-Hélène Marganne, *Inventaire analytique des papyrus grecs de médecine* (Droz, Geneva, 1981), 283–6. For oak galls and pomegranate in later contraceptives, Riddle, *Contraception and Abortion*, 25–6, 33, 51–3, 94–7, etc.; for uterine suffocation, Helen King, 'Once upon a Text: Hysteria from Hippocrates', in Sander L. Gilman, Helen King, Roy Porter, G. S. Rousseau, and Elaine Showalter (eds.), *Hysteria beyond Freud* (University of California Press, Berkeley and Los Angeles, 1993), 3–90.

[29] The word 'hysteria' was not used by Greek and Roman writers, and the term apparently entered the English language only late in the 18th century: for references, see Mark S. Micale, *Approaching Hysteria: Disease and its Interpretations* (Princeton University Press, Princeton, 1995), 113–14, 120–9.

[30] Read in line 16 on the photograph, pl. 8 in *P.Ryl.* 3; the ed. prin. (*P.Ryl.* 3, p. 167, n. to line 16) worries about the symbol after *sandarake*, but does not see it as expressing quantity.

[31] Hippocrates, *Mul.* 2. 200, viii. 382. 12–13 and 15–18 Littré; for similar therapies, *Mul.* 2. 125 and 201, viii. 268. 15–17 and 384. 4–7 Littré.

[32] For otters in the Nile, Herodotus 2. 72 and Aristophanes Gram., *Historiae animalium epitome* 1. 11. 1. According to the ed. prin. of the papyrus otter's kidneys were not used for

the same recipe is the use of *didymoi,* literally 'twins', yet the Alexandrian anatomist Herophilus, systematically dissecting human bodies under the patronage of Ptolemy Philadelphus in the mid-third century BCE, was infusing the term *didymoi* with anatomic specificity, employing it not only for testicles in the male, but also for ovaries in the female.[33] When the papyrus version of the first medicament notes that it was also useful for pains in the testicles, the employment of modern and up-to-date anatomical language from Alexandria marks the observation as an addition, added in the course of recontextualization. A Hippocratic would most likely have written *orchies.*

When the same medicament is recorded more than once within the collections of Hippocratic gynaecologies, differences among the recipe's versions reveal the kind of reshaping Hippocratics themselves undertook. A therapy for the woman vomiting blood after childbirth, when the vein on her liver has been severed, was repeated three times in two long versions and a short one. No version explains which aspect of birthing caused the vein to rupture, but it seems likely that the underside of her liver was lacerated by the kicks and blows from her rumbustious infant, as it endeavoured to disentangle itself from the confining membranes of the womb and accomplish its birthing.[34] The short version of the therapy is chronologically latest: it derives either from one of the two long versions, or from their source, and cannot account for the similarities between the two long versions. One long version of the therapy, embedded in the narrative discussing postpartum diseases in *Diseases of Women* 1, reads:

If a woman vomits blood after she has delivered her child, a hair (*thrix*)[35] on her liver has been lacerated; pain wanders to her interior organs, and her heart is convulsed. It is necessary to wash her with much hot water and insert those fomentations which are particularly receptive. Have her drink milk of an ass for

medical purposes by other Greek writers, although medieval writers did substitute otter's testicles for castoreum; so also Marganne, *Inventaire,* 284 and n. 2.

[33] Heinrich von Staden, *Herophilus: The Art of Medicine in Early Alexandria* (Cambridge University Press, Cambridge, 1989), 231.

[34] For Hippocratics' ignorance of uterine contractions, see Ann Ellis Hanson, 'Continuity and Change: Three Case Studies in Hippocratic Gynecological Therapy and Theory', in Sarah Pomeroy (ed.), *Women's History and Ancient History* (University of North Carolina Press, Chapel Hill, 1991), 73–110, esp. 87–95; for possible awareness in the latest stratum of the Hippocratic gynaecology, see Ann Ellis Hanson, 'A Hair on her Liver has been Lacerated: Hippocratic Physiology for the Digestive Tract and the Birth Canal', in Daniela Manetti and Amneris Roselli, (eds.), *Atti del IXe International Colloque Hippocratique, Pisa, 25–9 Sept. 1996,* (forthcoming).

[35] Hippocrates, *Mul.* 1. 43, viii. 100. 20–102. 4 Littré (*thrix* in MS Theta); other versions (with *syrinx*) at *Nat. mul.* 52, 111. 5–11 Trapp, and *Mul.* 1. 78, viii. 196. 5–8 Littré.

seven days, or five. Afterward, have her drink milk of a black cow, while she abstains from solid food, if possible for forty days; toward evening have her drink ground sesame. This sickness is dangerous.

The other two versions speak not of a hair on her liver, but a tube (*syrinx*), and the Galenic lexicon assures us that 'hair' was the word employed by those who sacrifice to designate the narrow vein, straight and black, on the concave underside of the liver in the right lobe.[36] By choosing to speak of the tube on the liver, these two versions deliberately distanced their terminology away from that used in religious hepatoscopy.[37]

The short version, appearing among the prescriptions adjoined to the end of *Diseases of Women* 1, likewise dispensed with the adjective 'black' as qualifier for the cow whose milk the woman was to drink. This change effectively severed the connection between the cow's colour of skin and the milk the physician prescribed, and while the black cow remained in the two longer versions, this is the only cow in the *Corpus* whose skin colour is noted before its milk is recommended as a medicament.[38] At one point in time the milk needed to medicate the black vein on the liver had to be from a black cow in order to be effective; but at a later point concern about the colour of the cow's skin had ceased to be a medical priority, and the connection between the black vein and the black cow was eliminated.

As the preceding examples suggest, Hippocratic recipe collections, in common with those of later antiquity, preserve therapies long in use. Sometimes medical writers reshaped older therapies to reflect current medical theory and practice, and at other times they passed on in silence what earlier copies of the recipe presented, content merely with setting the recipe into new contexts. Except for the author of *Sacred Disease* cited at the outset, Hippocratics neither discuss amulets nor inform us about the use their patients made of medicinal charms. Even so, an amulet has made its way into a series of nine *okytokia*, therapies that promote quick delivery for the woman labouring in diffi-

---

[36] Galen, *Ling. s. dict. exolet. expl.*, s.v. θρίξ, xix. 104. 13–15 Kühn.

[37] *Syrinx* occurs in the *Corpus* in two meanings, 'duct or channel within the body', often the bronchial tube or other tubes in the lungs, and 'fistular sore'. For the first meaning, pertinent here, see especially *Int. aff.* 1, LCL vi. 70 Potter, and *Morb.* 4. 56. 1–8, 119–22 Joly, the latter together with the commentary by Iain M. Lonie, *The Hippocratic Treatises 'On Generation', 'On the Nature of the Child', 'Diseases IV'* (Walter de Gruyter, Berlin, 1981), 361–3.

[38] Cf. Robert Joly, *Le Niveau de la science hippocratique: Contribution à la pyschologie de l'histoire des sciences* (Belles Lettres, Paris, 1966), 37–8.

cult childbirth (*dystokia*).[39] The majority of the recipes prescribe herbal compounds, although one recommends phlebotomy (or bloodletting) at the ankle, provided the woman is young, at the peak of her strength, and full-blooded. The *okytokion* which precedes the apparently up-to-date venesection therapy, a procedure whose popularity increased in Hellenistic and Roman periods, reads: 'smear fruit of a wild cucumber already white on wax, wind up on red-coloured fleece and fasten around the parturient's loins.' This prescription identifies itself as a magic amulet through its material (red fleece); its means of application (attachment to the exterior of the woman's person); its action (the redness of the fleece appeals to and summons the blood that exits the parturient during and after birthing). Dioscorides, a writer of pharmacology in the first century CE and a physician with experience in the Roman army, was himself often sceptical about the efficacy of amulets in his influential book on medicinal drugs. None the less, he noted that everyone supposes amulets from red jasper to be prophylactic and to promote quick delivery when worn on the thigh[40]—thereby testifying to the existence in the Roman period of an amulet made of red jasper which replicated in a more permanent medium the Hippocratics' perishable amulet of red fleece.

There is no way to know when and under what circumstances the amulet entered the list of Hippocratic *okytokia*, but unless it was the last item added to the list, some Hippocratic contributors missed the fact that this medicament was appealing to the magico-religious principle that like cures like. After all, it was contextualized among other serious medicinal therapies, such as herbal compounds and venesection. Soranus of Ephesus, living and practising medicine in Rome in the first years of the second century CE, also failed to notice that this was an amulet. When criticizing as ineffectual the *okytokia* prescribed by the followers of Hippocrates, Soranus remembered this medicament as 'the fruit of the wild cucumber, infused into a cerate made from dates and fastened on the loins'.[41] In recalling the amulet more in the form of a medicament, forgetting about the red fleece and its action, Soranus not only failed to reproduce the Hippocratic language with precision, which

---

[39] Hippocrates, *Mul.* 1. 77, viii. 172. 2–4 Littré; cf. Ann Ellis Hanson, 'Uterine Amulets and Greek Uterine Medicine', *Medicina nei secoli*, 7 (1995), 281–99, and Dietlinde Goltz, *Studien zur altorientalischen und griechischen Heilkunde Therapie, Arzneibereitung, Rezeptstruktur* (Steiner, Wiesbaden, 1971), 242. For venesection in Hippocratic gynaecologies, see Hanson, 'A Division of Labor', 186–7 and n. 81.

[40] Dioscorides, *de materia medica* 5. 142, iii. 100. 16–17 Wellmann.

[41] Soranus, *Gynaikeia* 4. 13. 2, 144. 2–7 Ilberg.

was frequently his habit, but his memory of what he once read in the *Corpus* aligned the prescription more closely to the other *okytokia* among which it was embedded.[42]

Elsewhere in his *Gynaecology* Soranus declared amulets ineffective, whether women appealed to them as contraceptives, or as staunchers of uterine haemorrhage, although he permitted the latter to retain their amulets, because the hope they provided made the women more cheerful.[43] Soranus' failure to classify the Hippocratic medicament as a charm, less sophisticated intellectually and medically than the herbal remedies or the phlebotomy, suggests that the intellectual stance Hippocratics claimed for themselves influenced Soranus not to expect amulets in the *Corpus*, and he passed over the message the therapy was speaking.

Soranus did think he heard an unsophisticated message in another group of therapies prominent in the gynaecologies of the *Corpus* and he was articulate in expressing his objections to the odour therapies doctors employed to treat women suffering from uterine suffocation:

But the majority of the ancients and nearly all followers of other sects employ ill-smelling odors (such as burnt hair, . . . and all substances that are thought to exhibit oppressive smell), as though the uterus flees from evil odours. As a result, they have also fumigated with sweet-smelling substances from below, and have approved of suppositories made with spikenard and storax, so that the uterus, fleeing the former, but pursuing the latter, might transfer from the upper to the lower parts of the body.[44]

At first glance Soranus' evaluation seems accurate, since medical writers, not only those who compiled the gynaecologies of the *Hippocratic Corpus* half a millennium before, but also Soranus' contemporaries and those who followed him for a millennium to come, prescribed for the noses and vaginas of their female patients fetid and sweet fumigations and pessaries in order to influence uterine movements in the manner Soranus described.

The notion that Soranus alone of the medical community heard an inconcinnate message in the odour therapies—the message that the uterus was a sentient and auto-directed creature, roaming at will about the female body and wreaking havoc wherever it went—merits closer inspection. Soranus' words recall Timaeus' description of the womb in

[42] Danielle Gourevitch, 'Les Lectures hippocratiques de Soranos d'Ephèse dans son traité *Des maladies des femmes*', in López Férez (ed.), *Tratados hipocráticos*, 597–607.

[43] Soranus, *Gynaikeia* 1. 63. 3 and 3. 42. 3, 47. 16–20 and 121. 26–31 Ilberg.

[44] Soranus, *Gynaikeia* 3. 29. 1, 112. 4–14 Ilberg.

the Platonic dialogue bearing his name. Galen quoted an extensive portion from the same part of the *Timaeus*, yet Galen's emphasis was on the improbable female anatomy the passage implied, and he stressed the fact that Hellenistic dissections proved uterine travel most unlikely, because ligaments rooted the organ in its place.[45] Soranus' attention, however, was focused not on anatomical matters, but on treatment, and his quarrel was with the foul-smelling medicaments. Soranus' agenda was to discredit malodorous fumigations and pessaries and to drive them from the gynaecological pharmacopoeia, in the same spirit as he elsewhere attacked therapies and ingredients employed by his predecessors, because the old remedies were harsh and as likely to damage the patients as to heal them.[46] Pungent fumigations caused congestion and must be rejected except in extreme cases.[47] At the same time, Soranus recontextualized therapies employing pleasant odours among the medicaments he approved, prescribing, for example, sweet things to smell for the patient afflicted by external uterine prolapse.[48] In reshaping the odoriferous therapies, Soranus was at pains to make the actions of pleasant odours accord with the sophisticated anatomy of Herophilus, who described not only the multiple layers of muscle tissue that composed the uterus and other organs, but also the ligaments that fastened the organ in the lower body cavity.[49] Soranus also expressed the therapeutic actions of pleasant odours in terms of the medical concepts employed by the Methodist sect to which he adhered.[50] That is, to Soranus the pleasant odours at the nose made the uterus and its ligaments constrict, due to the odours' cooling properties, and this constriction overcame the organ's overly relaxed condition that had caused the outward prolapse in the first place.

[45] Plato, *Timaeus* 91b–c; Galen, *de loc. aff.* 6, viii. 425–6 Kühn. For a brief summary of earlier discussion of the Plato passage, as well as a novel interpretation, Mark J. Adair, 'Plato's View of the Wandering Uterus', *Classical Journal*, 91 (1996), 154–63.

[46] e.g. Soranus, *Gynaikeia* 3. 29. 5 and 4. 36. 11, 113. 1–6 and 149. 25–7 Ilberg; at *Gynaikeia* 1. 8. 1–2, 7. 14–19 Ilberg, Soranus briefly noted the anatomical improbability of uterine movement. Cf. also Ann Ellis Hanson and Monica H. Green, 'Soranus of Ephesus: *Methodicorum princeps*', in Wolfgang Haase (ed.), *Aufstieg und Niedergang der römischen Welt*, 37.2 (Walter de Gruyter, Berlin, 1994), 968–1075, esp. 988.

[47] Cf. Caelius Aurelianus, *Tardarum passionum* 2. 75 and 113, 590. 3–6 and 612. 6–14 Bendz; for Caelius Aurelianus as translator and adapter of Soranus, see e.g. Hanson and Green, 'Soranus of Ephesus', 973–80.

[48] Soranus, *Gynaikeia* 4. 38. 3, 151. 11–12 Ilberg.

[49] e.g. von Staden, *Herophilus*, 167–9.

[50] Danielle Gourevitch, 'La Pratique méthodique: Définition de la maladie, indication et traitement', in Phillipe Mudry and J. Pigeaud (eds.), *Les Écoles médicales à Rome: Actes du 2ème colloque international sur les textes médicaux latins antiques, Lausanne, septembre 1986* (Droz, Geneva, 1991), 253–68.

Soranus' outburst failed to note that already in Hippocratic hands odoriferous fumigations, fomentations, and pessaries had modulated to the point of medicating according to mechanical principles: wet to moisten, dry to desiccate, hot to warm, cool to extinguish heat.[51] However correct Soranus may be about the implications inherent in aromatic medicaments for the uterus, Hippocratic gynaecologies did not suggest that the uterus responded to odours as did an animal.[52] Rather, Hippocratic accounts tracked the movements of a desiccated and overheated uterus toward moist organs, such as the liver or the lungs, in accordance with their mechanical aetiologies for uterine displacements:

Uterine suffocation happens especially to those women who do not have intercourse, and to older women rather than young ones, since their wombs are lighter. The main reason for its occurrence is the following: when a woman is empty and distressed more than usual, her womb, now heated by hard work, turns because it is empty and light-weight. There is, in fact, empty space for it to turn in, since her belly is empty. The turning womb heads toward the liver and lies there; it moves toward the abdomen. The womb is rushing along and going upward toward the moisture, because it has been unduly dried out by hard work, and the liver is full of moisture. When the womb heads toward the liver, it produces sudden suffocation, as the womb occupies the breathing space around the belly.[53]

The therapies Hippocratics employed to counteract uterine displacements responded to their mechanical aetiologies: cool and moist douches to medicate the uterus when it was too hot and too dry, or warm and softening agents for external prolapse that made it too cold and too hard. Or they prescribed binders that mechanically held the uterus down in its place, or pessaries that propped it up; succussion on a ladder, with the woman tied to it upside down, shook the womb back to its proper position.[54] The aromatic fomentations and fumigations seem comfortably recontextualized into medicaments that are within the Hippocratic effort to link through logical argument the mechanical explanations for how sicknesses arose with the therapies that cured them. Soranus' charge that employing aromatic fumigations and pessaries required those who prescribed them to espouse the view that the uterus was a sentient

---

[51] Cf. Hippocrates, *Acut.* 21. 1–3, 44. 25–45. 15 Joly; Galen's commentary on the chapter offers helpful expansions, *in Hipp. Acut. comment.* 2, xv. 519–26 Kühn.

[52] Stressed by Helen King, 'From παϱθένος to γυνή: The Dynamics of Category' (Ph.D. diss., University College, London, 1985), 113–16, and 'Once upon a Text', 25–8, 42.

[53] Hippocrates, *Mul.* 1. 7. 1–4, 100. 18–28 Grensemann; cf. also *Mul.* 1. 32. 1–8, 122. 19–124. 14 Grensemann; *Mul.* 2. 133 and 137–8, 15–43 Countouris.

[54] Hanson, 'Continuity and Change', 81–7.

creature ignored doctors' habits of reshaping and recontextualizing recipes they considered useful, in order to make the recipes better accord with the theories they espoused—a practice in which Soranus himself participated. The notion that the womb was an animal and responded to odours may well have had currency in the Greek-speaking world at other points in time and other intellectual climates. Both pre-Hippocratic medicine and medical magic have been suggested as possible loci for such views.[55] The inconcinnity in aromatic therapies that so exercised Soranus did not, however, speak this message to the majority of ancient physicians, because their medical predecessors had sufficiently reshaped odoriferous therapies into medicaments that operated according to sophisticated, mechanical principles.

Heinrich von Staden has pointed out that excrement occurs as an ingredient only in gynaecological remedies, and that Hippocratics instructed only their female patients to medicate themselves with dried animal dungs and bird droppings.[56] About half of the excrement recipes appear in similar form in more than a single treatise, and the textual quality of the variants suggests that the medical writers were drawing from written sources.[57] Cow dung occurs most frequently, usually as an ingredient in uterine fumigations; on one occasion the Hippocratic writer cautioned that something should be set on the dung so that it did not smell—otherwise it was better not to fumigate at all.[58] Fumigations with cow dung returned the uterus to a salubrious position,[59] healed a uterine flow,[60] treated unnatural accumulation of fluid in the womb due to miscarriage, abortion, or retained menses,[61]

[55] Giulia Sissa, *Greek Virginity* (Harvard University Press, Cambridge, Mass., 1990), 41–52, where she associates odoriferous therapies with the Pythia's prophetic inspiration on the tripod; King, 'Once upon a Text', 43–4, where she notes that the 3rd–4th-century CE papyrus *PGM* VII 260–72 preserves the concept of an animate and sentient womb.

[56] von Staden, 'Women and Dirt', 7–30, but see also *Herophilus*, 19 and n. 65.

[57] Cf. below, in nn. 58–61, 64, 66, and the specific example from Hippocrates, *Mul.* 1. 89, cited in n. 62.

[58] Hippocrates, *Mul.* 2. 195, viii. 378. 18–19 Littré; the version at *Nat. mul.* 34, 100. 4–13 Trapp, mentions a number of fragrant ingredients, but does not note that these temper the bad smells of dung. For cow dung in fumigations elsewhere in the *Corpus*, see section 8 in the 'gynaecological chapter' in Hippocrates, *Loc. hom.* 47, 78. 24–7 Joly.

[59] Hippocrates, *Mul.* 2. 203, viii. 390. 11–12 and 390. 16–392. 4 Littré (=*Nat. mul.* 34, 100. 21–2 and 101. 4–16 Trapp).

[60] Hippocrates, *Mul.* 2. 195, viii. 376. 23–378. 3 Littré (=*Nat. mul.* 103, 123. 1–3 Trapp); *Mul.* 2. 195, viii. 378. 17–19 Littré (=*Nat. mul.* 34, 100. 4–13 Trapp), and cf. *Mul.* 1. 206, viii. 398. 13–17 and 400. 19–402. 1 Littré.

[61] Hippocrates, *Mul.* 1. 59, viii. 118. 8–9 Littré (=*Nat. mul.* 2, 70. 22–71. 3 Trapp).

medicated sterility,[62] cleansed indurations from the uterus.[63] Goat turds in fumigations rectified uterine displacement[64] and provoked menses.[65] By contrast, mule dung was principally a stauncher of blood, used in treatments for uterine flows, whether administered in a drink, a vaginal pessary, or as a fumigation;[66] on one occasion a fumigation of mule dung opened and straightened a closed and deviated uterine mouth.[67] Other excrements occur less frequently in gynaecological recipes: mouse turds in a vaginal suppository expelled a dead foetus;[68] bird droppings in a uterine infusion medicated wind or breath in the womb and excessive uterine pain;[69] hawk droppings in a drink aided in opening a closed uterine mouth, as did a lotion containing droppings of the fox-goose in rose oil applied topically.[70] A plaster of pigeon droppings treated baldness.[71]

Von Staden observed that use of excrement therapy was a cross-cultural phenomenon in the ancient world, employed by the healers of Egypt and Mesopotamia, as well as appearing in Chinese, Talmudic, and Indian medicine. He also noted that dungs represented an element of continuity within Greek medicine, since later writers of Hellenistic, Roman, and Byzantine times continued to record similar applications and accepted excrement therapies without criticism for men, as well as for women. What was distinctive about the dungs in Hippocratic medicaments, in contrast to the other traditions, was their gender-specific application—for women only. Von Staden underscored how Greek ritual, magic, and religion resonated with beliefs about the susceptibility of women to impurity and pollution, and that Greek authors, both early and late, rehearsed the theme that women were filthy creatures.[72] None the less, it does not necessarily follow that Hippocratics themselves were

---

[62] Hippocrates, *Mul.* 1. 85, viii. 210. 7–10 Littré; cf. similar fumigations at *Mul.* 1. 86 and 1. 89, viii. 210. 19–21 and 212. 13–16 Littré, but in the latter replacing cow urine (*ourou boeiou*) with bitter vetch (*orobiou*).

[63] Hippocrates, *Mul.* 2. 206, viii. 398. 13–19 Littré.

[64] Hippocrates, *Mul.* 2. 203, viii. 390. 5–6 and 10–11 Littré (=*Nat. mul.* 34, 100. 17–18 and 20–1 Trapp).

[65] Hippocrates, *Nat. mul.* 32, 89. 8–11 Trapp.

[66] Hippocrates, *Mul.* 2. 192, viii. 374. 7–9 Littré (=*Nat. mul.* 90, 118. 22–3 Trapp); and *Nat. mul.* 82, 117. 14–15 Trapp; at *Mul.* 3. 245, viii. 458. 21–2 Littré, mule turds medicate a pregnant woman who bleeds.

[67] Hippocrates, *Superf.* 32. 1, 90. 18–25 Lienau; a male mule must provide the turds.

[68] Hippocrates, *Mul.* 1. 78, viii. 186. 11–12 Littré.

[69] Hippocrates, *Mul.* 2. 177, viii. 360. 9–11 Littré.

[70] Hippocrates, *Mul.* 1. 89, viii. 214. 8–13 Littré.

[71] Hippocrates, *Mul.* 2. 190, viii. 370. 3–4 Littré.

[72] Full bibliography on all topics in von Staden, 'Women and Dirt', 5–18.

responsible for introducing magico-ritual purifiers, including excrement, into therapies for the womb, since they too, in common with their medical successors in the millennium following, may have found such ingredients embedded in their sources of medicaments for women and they too may have accepted and quietly passed on the excrement therapies, even as they also accepted and transmitted the *okytokion* of red fleece. Nor does it necessarily follow that, when prescribing such medicaments for female patients, Hippocratics were consciously responding to the dynamics of magic and religion in order to combat female filth of the womb with animal and avian filth.

A number of alternative scenarios can, I believe, be constructed to explain the gender-specific presence of *Dreckapotheke* in the Hippocratic gynaecologies, and the one I outline here appeals to dynamics operative in some of the medicaments already surveyed—the hair on the liver and the milk from the black cow, the amulet of red fleece, the odour therapies and the sentient and auto-directed uterus, the gruel of barley groats and pennyroyal. In other contexts these items too resonated with potent, magico-religious meaning, yet in the gynaecologies of the *Corpus* their contextualization in the midst of medicaments that conformed to the mechanical paradigms of curing through opposites tempered the force of their messages. Probing later writers' views on the medicinal properties of dungs suggests the directions in which excrement therapies were moving already in Hippocratic hands, modulating away from the paradigms that invoked their powerful purifying properties toward paradigms that valued excrements for their curative properties, such as heating and drying, moistening and softening, strengthening and smoothing. This process of modulation eventually made dungs suitable medicaments for Greek men, as well as for Greek womenfolk, as the acceptance of dung in medicaments by Dioscorides and Galen makes clear.

Conspicuous is the continued prominence of excrement, especially mouse dung, in topical lotions and creams to medicate baldness.[73] The long-lived confidence that some excrements stimulated growth of hair in the bald recalls the use of excrement as fertilizer for farmers' fields.[74] Hippocratic gynaecology borrowed the vocabulary of ploughing the

---

[73] e.g. Galen, *de comp. med. sec. loc.* 10. 1, xii. 402–4, 407–9, 416–19 Kühn.

[74] Bird droppings in the agricultural compendium *Geoponica*: from the goose, 12. 11, 356.3 Beckh; from the pigeon, 14. 1. 1, 405. 8–12 Beckh. The notion that ancients may have viewed medicinal dungs as fertilizer was suggested by William H. S. Jones, 'Ancient Roman Folk Medicine', *Journal of the History of Medicine and Allied Sciences*, 12 (1957), 462.

fields to describe the process by which childbirth broke down the young girl's lean, hard, and compact body into the spongy flesh that character-ized the mature woman, and Hippocratics found Mother Earth good to think with when composing gynaecological theory.[75] Their concern to enhance the ability of female patients to take up the liquid of intercourse, a mixture of seed from the man and seed from the woman, and carry it as a foetus to birth perhaps influenced them to revalorize some dungs as enhancers of female fertility and fertilizers for the womb.

Although von Staden's observation that Hippocratics placed no gender-based restrictions on the employment of urine is correct, their exclusive use of urine in medicaments for the uterus and the anus may have been influenced not only by the anatomical similarity of these two bodily conduits and their anatomical proximity in the female body, but also by the roles each conduit played in evacuation. Urine appears in four gynaecological therapies as the liquid of choice for vapour baths, in-tended either to cleanse the uterus and enhance its fertility, or to soften and straighten the uterine mouth. The urine employed in general medi-cine was the important liquid either for a douche to be injected after excising or cauterizing fistulas and haemorrhoids, or for an unguent to be applied after the excision.[76] The cleansing properties of urine were emphasized in Galen's discussion: he used urine externally many times on slaves and country folk, as well as for those who travelled without a doctor, and he applauded the farmer who doused his wounds with his own urine, as long as the lacerations were not on his head or face. Especially in the case of head wounds that were difficult to heal, properly prepared child's urine was by no means disgusting.[77]

Dioscorides' report on the many uses of goat droppings shows that while this excrement continued in gynaecological remedies, it was also employed to treat conditions common to men and women. In potions, goat turds cured jaundice, provoked menses, aborted an embryo; when dried and mixed with vinegar, they provided a topical lotion to staunch female flux and other blood flows; when burnt and mixed with vinegar or oxymel, they medicated baldness; smeared on with lard, they helped gout; boiled in vinegar or wine, they provided a lotion for lesions and the tonsils.[78]

---

[75] Hanson, 'Conception, Gestation', 37–41.

[76] For the uterus: Hippocrates, *Mul.* 1. 75, viii. 162. 8–11 Littré (*kyeteria*); *Mul.* 2. 134, viii. 302. 18–304. 1 and viii. 304. 14–17 Littré; *Mul.* 1. 85, viii. 210. 7–13 Littré; *Mul.* 1. 46, viii. 322. 3–8. For the anus: *Haem.* 3 and 5. 2, 148. 1–6 and 149. 13–16 Joly; *Fist.* 141. 10–13 Joly.

[77] Galen, *de simpl. medicament. temp.* 10, xii. 286–7 Kühn.

[78] Dioscorides, *de materia medica* 2. 80–1, 1. 161–5 Wellmann.

Von Staden used a passage from the tenth book of Galen's discussion of the qualities and powers of simple drugs to demonstrate that Greeks regarded excrement as dirty and disgusting, and, in religious contexts, able to pollute sacred space. Excrement is dirty, but Galen's disgust was primarily levelled at the ingestion of all products derived from the human body—sweat, urine, menstrual blood, and faeces—and he railed against Xenocrates, 'not a medical writer of ancient times, but in the generation of our grandfathers', for continuing to prescribe drinks made from these substances.[79] Galen was, however, by no means finished with such substances, and he went on to report about the products from animals which were useful for humans. Although he claimed he had tested these personally, his account often veers into stories other doctors and pupils had told him. Galen continued to reiterate his revulsion toward the use of human faeces in medicaments because of their disgusting smell, but he praised the turds of cows, goats, land crocodiles, and especially those of dogs and wolves fed exclusively on bones, because these turds were white, had no bad odour, and were among the best inducers of sweat. The cleansing and drying properties of such excrements medicated wounds and dissipated swelling and induration from bites and stings.

A major thrust in Galen's discussion of the medicinal uses of excrement was that the best doctor needed to know every remedy and should choose the better one according to the circumstances: he knew of a doctor who prescribed potions of goat turds with wine to medicate jaundice and with frankincense for female flows, although he never prescribed such drinks for sophisticated and important city dwellers. He might do so, however, for travellers and hunters, if nothing better was available, or for farm labourers with hearty bodies. He thought most dungs too potent for the soft skin of women and children, but the refined ladies of Rome found that dung of the small land crocodile made their complexions radiant and smooth.[80] Galen employed pigeon excrement

---

[79] *de simpl. medicament. temp.* 10, xii. 245–309 Kühn, esp. 297–308; von Staden, 'Women and Dirt', 9, quotes xii. 249. 1–9 Kühn.

[80] Women's employment of crocodile dung as a cosmetic at Rome seems to have attracted considerable attention from laymen as well. The poet Horace noted that the complexion of an old hag was painted with crocodile dung ('colorque | stercore fucatus crocodili', *Epode* 12. 10–11), and Acron, explicator of Horace's text, provided in his commentary to the line much the same information as Galen: 'this is for maintaining the skin, or for creating a luminous effect, as women were reported (to do)', 'Hoc enim ad conservandam cutem uel candorem faciendum mulieres uti dicebantur' (496. 15–16 Hauthal). The elder Pliny reported that the land crocodile fed upon very sweet-scented flowers and its intestines produce *crocodilea* which, among other things, cleared the complexion, removed freckles, pimples, and all spots (*NH* 28. 28. 108–9).

in plasters for chronic ailments of city folk because it too had no bad odour and exhibited potent drying properties. He used goat turds very frequently in topical applications because they warmed and dried without at the same time chilling or moistening; a plaster of goat turds helped one patient immensely, when he was afflicted with a hardened swelling on his knee that resisted other treatments. However applied, Galen attributed to certain approved dungs the ability to heat, dry, cleanse, smooth, and soften the surfaces with which they came into contact. It is my contention that Hippocratics were already moving excrement therapies into these dynamic patterns.

Galen knew much about the interior of the female body from the writings of Herophilus and he personally dissected and vivisected female animals. Hippocratics practised neither systematic dissection of animals nor of humans and they knew nothing of what Herophilus would subsequently achieve a century and a half later. They were, as a result, far less successful than Herophilus in demystifying the womb: he saw the uterus lying in the body cavity, fastened in its place by ligaments, and he observed that it was made from layers of muscular tissue, the same stuff as in other bodily parts.[81] Hippocratic concerns in the gynaecologies lay elsewhere than in accurate descriptions of uterine anatomy. Important to them was that the uterus be pliant, straight, cleansed, and open at the proper time, rather than closed due to induration or bending, clogged with blood and other fluids at inopportune moments. Such concerns respond well to the warming, softening, cleansing properties Galen attributed to the approved dungs.[82] Hippocratics intended to aid their female patients in making their wombs able to receive and take up the seed in pregnancy, for in the *Corpus* barrenness was a woman's disease.[83] To enhance the likelihood of pregnancy Hippocratics urged their female patients to warm and dry, soften and smooth their wombs, recontextualizing dungs in the direction of uterine cosmetics that enhanced the pliability, corrected the humidity, and promoted luminous cleanliness in the uterus. However resonant Hippocratic medical vocabulary is with the language and concepts of religion and magic, the trajectory along which excrement therapies were moving was toward closer integration with the mechanical principles that motivated

---

[81] Herophilus, T193 (=Soranus, *Gynaikeia* 3. 3. 4, 95. 17–21 Ilberg, with commentary by von Staden, *Herophilus*), 296–9.

[82] Cf. Hippocrates, *Epid.* 6. 5. 1, 104 Manetti-Roselli, a passage that grouped menses and lochial flows together with urine and faeces, as did Galen.

[83] Hanson, 'Conception, Gestation', 46.

Hippocratics' aetiologies for other diseases and into greater harmony with the medicine Hippocratics currently practised. In isolation, such therapies and medicaments bespeak fascinating images that looked to other times and other modes of thinking, yet when embedded in Hippocratic contexts the recipes were being taught to mute unsophisticated messages and to participate instead in curing through logical constructs, such as the principle that opposites cure opposites.

Eliminating the black cow from a therapy, recasting fragrant and malodorous fumigations as warming and drying agents, and revalorizing excrement therapies in the direction of fertilizers and cosmetics for the uterus, rather than purifiers of filth, are changes that signal shifts in doctors' views about the female body and in the principles by which they felt obliged to medicate diseases of the womb. Hippocratics gave medical voice to gender constructs current at the end of the fifth century BCE, expressing gender difference through an anatomy that emphasized woman's soft and spongy flesh, the anatomical opposite of firm, male flesh, and in a physiology dominated by a superabundance of blood, ever threatening to accumulate in excess and remain trapped inside the woman's body with deadly consequences that never threatened the male.[84] None the less, Hippocratics tried to cure diseases of women in accordance with the same mechanical principles they applied to the afflicted bodies of men, for the mechanical paradigms enhanced their ability to intervene in sicknesses, telling them what to do, when to do it, and how to convey to the patient their authority in matters of health and disease. As medical aetiologies for disease shifted away from viewing sicknesses as punishments sent by gods to malfunctions in a mechanical process, remedies shifted as well. Reticent as Hippocratics were about the specific properties of the ingredients in their therapies, other than that this medicament cured sterility, or that therapy straightened a bent uterine mouth, the changes they effected in matters of detail document their efforts, and at times those of their predecessors, to draw older therapies within more modern paradigms.

One Hippocratic writer chastised his fellow professionals who were unaware that women had diseases all their own and could not be healed in the same way as men.[85] He knew doctors who made such mistakes, and women's lives were lost in the process—menstrual blood could be

---

[84] Discussed extensively by Lesley Dean-Jones, 'The Politics of Pleasure: Female Sexual Appetite in the Hippocratic Corpus', *Helios*, 19 (1992), 72–91, and *Women's Bodies in Classical Greek Science* (Clarendon Press, Oxford, 1994), 38–44, 110–19, 247–53.

[85] Hippocrates, *Mul.* 1. 62, 112. 23–114. 7 Grensemann.

trapped anywhere within the female body, and ignorance of this fact led unenlightened doctors into errors fatal to the women involved. He knew many professionals who lanced a red swelling in the groin of women suffering from amenorrhoea, unaware that this was displaced menstrual blood; as a result, these doctors created a second path of exit for menses and brought the women to their deaths. Another Hippocratic knew of a medical colleague who did not realize that the body of a young girl at menarche would not benefit from a nosebleed, as an alternative means to expel displaced menstrual blood, in the same way as would the body of a mature woman. The young girl died, but the doctor did not understand.[86] The punctilious Hippocratic needed at the outset to question his female patients in the same way he questioned his male patients. The process of drawing responses from the woman might be difficult, since the questions were about her reproductive functions: did her menses come, did she have intercourse with her husband, had she conceived a child and carried it to birthing? Although Hippocratics isolated gynaecological therapies and medicaments in treatises on diseases of women, or in discrete sections of treatises of general medicine, and although they employed some medicaments on a gender-specific basis, their remedies cured female bodies according to the same mechanical principles that explained in logical fashion how therapies and medicaments cured all patients. Women's bodies got sick with female diseases and recovered from these not because mysterious and inexplicable forces were at work, but in accordance with the rules Hippocratics enunciated. Such a stance was, to be sure, in the self-interest of professional physicians, for it enabled them to absorb women's diseases within their medical craft. At the same time, their confidence that women experienced disease and recovery according to Hippocratic principles underscores how successful these professional physicians had been in tempering the unsophisticated messages inherent in many of their medicaments and therapies.

---

[86] e.g. *Mul.* 1. 2. 26–30, 94. 25–96. 3 Grensemann (lancing the red swelling); *Epid.* vii. 123, LCL vii. 414 Smith (the young girl whose nose bled, but who died anyway). For discussion of the latter, see Helen King, 'The Daughter of Leonides: Reading the Hippocratic Corpus', in Averil Cameron (ed.), *History as Text: The Writing of Ancient History* (University of North Carolina Press, Chapel Hill, 1989), 13–32.

4

Controlling Daughters' Bodies in Sirach

JON L. BERQUIST

ANCIENT Israel's literature ranges over many interests, from the distant matters of international politics to the most intimate realities of common existence. The texts concern themselves with world-changing history and with everyday happenings, such as the activity of one's body and the interrelationships of family life. Such a combination of interests certainly appears in the Book of Sirach, a text depicting life in Jewish communities during the early Hellenistic period, probably during 200–175 BCE.[1] The book is similar in form and tone to Israel's earlier wisdom literature, especially Proverbs.[2]

The Book of Sirach, however, depicts life in Jewish communities during the early Hellenistic period. In fact, the date of the book's writing can be closely approximated. Sirach 50: 1–24 contains praise of the Jerusalem Temple's recently deceased high priest, Simon son of Onias (or

---

[1] This book is known by several names, including the Wisdom of Ben Sira and Ecclesiasticus. The most extensive recent commentary is Patrick W. Skehan and Alexander A. DiLella, *The Wisdom of Ben Sira*, Anchor Bible 39 (Doubleday, New York, 1987); see also Jack T. Sanders, *Ben Sira and Demotic Wisdom*, SBL Monograph Series 28 (Scholars Press, Chico, Calif., 1983); R. A. F. MacKenzie, *Sirach*, Old Testament Message 19 (Michael Glazier, Wilmington, Del., 1983); and Alexander A. DiLella, 'Wisdom of Ben-Sira', in David Noel Freedman (ed.), *The Anchor Bible Dictionary*, vi: *Si–Z* (Doubleday, New York, 1992), 931–45. For an extended discussion of women in Sirach, see Warren C. Trenchard, *Ben Sira's View of Women: A Literary Analysis*, Brown Judaic Studies 38 (Scholars Press, Chico, Calif., 1982). The best presentation (despite its brevity) of the question of women in Sirach can be found in Claudia V. Camp, 'Understanding a Patriarchy: Women in Second Century Jerusalem through the Eyes of Ben Sira', in Amy-Jill Levine (ed.), *'Women Like This': New Perspectives on Jewish Women in the Greco-Roman World*, Early Judaism and its Literature 1 (Scholars Press, Atlanta, 1991), 1–39, esp. 34–7 on the daughter.

[2] Though some trends within scholarship have suggested the presence of other canonical wisdom texts, most scholars consider there to be five wisdom books: Proverbs, Job, Ecclesiastes/Qoheleth, the Wisdom of Solomon, and Sirach. For an overview of Israelite wisdom literature, see the treatments by James L. Crenshaw, *Old Testament Wisdom* (John Knox, Atlanta, 1981) and Roland E. Murphy, *The Tree of Life: An Exploration of Biblical Wisdom Literature*, Anchor Bible Reference Library (Doubleday, New York, 1990; repr. Eerdmans, Grand Rapids, Mich., 1996).

Yohanan). Simon was high priest from about 219 to 196 BCE.[3] The book does not show any awareness of the Maccabean uprising that attained (partial) sovereignty and a rededication of the Jerusalem Temple in 164 BCE. Thus, the Book of Sirach can be dated with certainty between 196 and 164 BCE, and most likely reflects a time between 195 and 175 BCE, when memories of Simon were clear but Antiochus IV Epiphanes had not yet begun his reign in the area of Palestine, which led to the Maccabean revolt.[4]

In many ways, Sirach is a disheartening and misogynistic book that denigrates women repeatedly and viciously, even though most scholarly treatments of the book avoid these realities and concentrate elsewhere. When scholarship has noted this hostility, its response has varied from embrace to embarrassed acknowledgement to rejection of its dangerous values. The majority of scholarship on the portrayal of women in Sirach has focused on the adult women, most of whom figure in the text as wives of dominant men. However, Sirach offers a unique entrance to the study of daughters in ancient religious tradition. Of ancient Israel's five key wisdom texts, only Sirach mentions daughters.[5]

Why does Sirach introduce this concern with young women, when earlier wisdom literature ignored them? The interpretation of the passages concerning daughters requires a foray into Sirach's particular rhetoric about them, a rhetoric infused with violence directed against the bodies of these young women.[6] The body metaphors draw the reader into the text through their multivalence and lure the reader into the text's ideology. Of course, the very production of discourse about bodies and

---

[3] Josephus, *Antiquities*, 12. 4. 10.

[4] See John G. Snaith, 'Ecclesiasticus: A Tract for the Times', in John Day, Robert P. Gordon, and H. G. M. Williamson (eds.), *Wisdom in Ancient Israel: Essays in Honour of J. A. Emerton* (Cambridge University Press, Cambridge, 1995), 170–81, esp. 170–2.

[5] Furthermore, Sirach's attention to daughters is only in the context of the father–daughter relationship. In so far as this is only one aspect of a young woman's life (and is actually a denotation of her in terms of her father rather than as herself), this limited perspective continues to occlude the visibility of young women as themselves and in their varied contexts. Of particular interest may be the absence of any trace of the mother–daughter relationship. See Janet Liebman Jacobs, *Victimized Daughters: Incest and the Development of the Female Self* (Routledge, New York, 1994), esp. ch. 2, entitled 'Incest and the Destruction of the Mother–Daughter Bond'.

[6] The sociology of the body and of body rhetoric are subjects receiving great attention in scholarship, including Arthur W. Frank, 'Bringing Bodies Back in: A Decade Review', *Theory, Culture & Society*, 7 (1990), 131–62; Mike Featherstone, Mike Hepworth, and Bryan S. Turner (eds.), *The Body: Social Process and Cultural Theory*, Theory, Culture & Society (SAGE, London, 1991); Sue Scott and David Morgan (eds.), *Body Matters: Essays on the Sociology of the Body* (Falmer, London, 1993); and Chris Shilling, *The Body and Social Theory*, Theory, Culture & Society (SAGE, London, 1993).

about sexuality controls bodies and their sexuality. In this sense, the writing about sexual bodies is a marginal activity, producing a margin *around* sex in the form of a text *about* sex; this *about*-activity is a limiting function.[7] Sirach's body rhetoric constructs a network of social relations, both inside and outside the family.[8] The network of social relations produced by this discourse is inherently hierarchical, and so the relationship of parents to children (as a relationship produced *by* sex but not necessarily *about* sex) receives especially strong expression.

Although Israelite wisdom literature concerns itself little with families and child-rearing, the general demeanour of its remarks on the topic is well known.[9] Israel's wisdom values social order, and in this vein Proverbs urges discipline for a child (Proverbs 3: 12) and connects parental prestige to the child's success (Proverbs 10: 1). In response, the child honours the parents and maintains the parents' name and inherited property after they are deceased (Proverbs 13: 22). This upper-class ethical system perpetuates social stratification through learned values and economic institutions. The Book of Sirach falls within this tradition, emphasizing the honour and respect due to one's elders and superiors (Sirach 3), but it belabours the inherent risks.[10] Children represent a potential loss to the parent, both in terms of wealth and of honour. Thus, Sirach warns, 'Do not desire a multitude of worthless children, and do not rejoice in ungodly offspring. If they multiply, do not rejoice in them, unless the fear of the Lord is in them' (Sirach 16: 1–2; scripture citations are from the New Revised Standard Version). Children are not good or bad *per se*, but they have potential in both directions, from the parental viewpoint (cf. Sirach 22: 3–6). This requires a disciplinary vigilance far

---

[7] See David M. Gunn and Danna Nolan Fewell, *Narrative in the Hebrew Bible*, Oxford Bible Series (Oxford University Press, Oxford, 1993), 155–8, 189–94.

[8] For a stunning development of this issue that begins with Foucault's realizations of sex-discourse as a regulatory practice, see Judith Butler, *Bodies that Matter: On the Discursive Limits of 'Sex'* (Routledge, New York, 1993).

[9] Of the few instances of the term 'daughter' in the five books of wisdom, several of them are metaphorical, such as the leech's daughters in Proverbs 30: 15 and the daughters of song in Qoheleth 12: 4. For an insightful feminist investigation of the father–son motif that established patriarchy at the beginning of the Book of Proverbs, see Carol A. Newsom, 'Woman and the Discourse of Patriarchal Wisdom: A Study of Proverbs 1–9', in Peggy L. Day (ed.), *Gender and Difference in Ancient Israel* (Fortress Press, Minneapolis, 1989), 142–60.

[10] For a compelling discussion of Sirach in the light of a father's personal and financial investment in his daughter's sexual purity, see Léonie J. Archer, *Her Price is beyond Rubies: The Jewish Woman in Graeco-Roman Palestine*, Journal for the Study of the Old Testament Supplement 60 (JSOT Press, Sheffield, 1990), 25–9.

beyond the 'spare the rod, spoil the child' notion of Proverbs 13: 24. In a section entitled 'Concerning Children', Sirach writes:

He who loves his son will whip him often, so that he may rejoice at the way he turns out . . . Bow down his neck in his youth, and beat his sides while he is young, or else he will become stubborn and disobey you, and you will have sorrow of soul from him. Discipline your son and make his yoke heavy, so that you may not be offended by his shamelessness. (Sirach 30: 1, 12–13)[11]

The tone of Sirach's words about raising sons prepares us well for the harshness of his warnings about daughters, but Sirach's concerns about daughters, even though expressed in a mere two passages, include not only issues of economics and honour—he also targets the daughters' sexuality. The first of these passages is Sirach 26: 10–12:

> Keep strict watch over a headstrong daughter,
>   or else, when she finds liberty, she will make use of it.
> Be on guard against her impudent eye,
>   and do not be surprised if she sins against you.
> As a thirsty traveller opens his mouth
>   and drinks from any water near him,
> so she will sit in front of every tent peg
>   and open her quiver to the arrow.

This passage makes use of two types of body rhetoric regarding daughters.[12] First, it characterizes general emotional states in terms of body parts (a *head*strong daughter with an impudent *eye*). Then the metaphors change direction; instead of using concrete body terms to describe emotions, the text develops terms from the physical world to connote body parts. The use of blunt terms for female sexual organs in Greek literature typically depicts women as excessively sexual creatures.[13] The second passage is Sirach 42: 9–13, which appears in the midst of a collection of household advice shortly before Sirach's lengthy Hymn in Praise of the Ancestors:

---

[11] See John J. Pilch, ' "Beat His Ribs While He Is Young" (Sir 30: 12): A Window on the Mediterranean World', *Biblical Theology Bulletin*, 23 (1993), 101–13.

[12] Some commentators have translated the word for daughter as 'wife', turning the passage into a rejection of an unfaithful spouse. However, such a translation of *thugater* ('daughter') seems highly unlikely; neither textual evidence nor clear indications of context argue in its favour.

[13] Holt N. Parker, 'Love's Body Anatomized: The Ancient Erotic Handbooks and the Rhetoric of Sexuality', in Amy Richlin (ed.), *Pornography and Representation in Greece and Rome* (Oxford University Press, New York, 1992), 90–107.

A daughter is a secret anxiety to her father,
 and worry over her robs him of sleep;
when she is young, for fear she may not marry,
 or if married, for fear she may be disliked;
while a virgin, for fear she may be seduced
  and become pregnant in her father's house;
 or having a husband, for fear she may go astray,
 or, though married, for fear she may be barren.
Keep strict watch over a headstrong daughter,
 or she may make you a laughing-stock to your enemies,
 a byword in the city and the assembly of the people,
 and put you to shame in public gatherings.
See that there is no lattice in her room,
 no spot that overlooks the approaches to the house.
Do not let her parade her beauty before any man,
 or spend her time among married women;
for from garments comes the moth,
 and from a woman comes woman's wickedness.

These two passages share many of the same basic attitudes as Proverbs: social order requires that parents limit a child's experiences and that the child brings honour to the parents, at least by protecting inheritance rights through a clean line of descent.

This last issue—inheritance rights and connected property concerns—dominates much of the scholarship on Sirach's discourse on women, as well as biblical sexuality in general. According to the property argument, men control the bodies of their wives and children as part of their ownership of all the property of the household.[14] Certainly, Sirach was part of a patriarchal system in which men controlled many aspects of women's lives and bodies.[15] Bryan S. Turner argues that the premodern regulation of the female body's sexuality was based upon 'household authority and the distribution of property'.[16] Fathers carried a financial burden in their daughters that could be satisfied only through their sale at marriage, but sexual activity would sharply devalue the human commodity. Furthermore, a promiscuous daughter would violate social norms and would render the father dishonoured before his friends and colleagues, ruining his life. For these reasons,

[14] Bryan S. Turner, *The Body and Society: Explorations in Social Theory*, Theory, Culture and Society (Basil Blackwell, Oxford, 1984), 118.

[15] Skehan and DiLella, *Wisdom of Ben Sira*, 90.

[16] Turner, *The Body and Society*, 3.

the wise father maximized wealth and honour by limiting the daughter's sexuality.

Certainly, this explanation is not without truth. Such shame/honour issues were important in the ancient world, and there were clearly a host of political and economic advantages from marrying off one's daughter well. In this interpretation, Sirach's concern with a daughter's virginity is not just a preoccupation; it represents a financial investment.[17]

Turner's explanation of woman's body as property assumes a sociological constant: a custom of marriage that remains unchanged throughout the Mediterranean world for a millennium. Such an explanation would also require the existence of a pre-modern view of sexuality that reduced *all* issues of sexual ethics and body rhetoric to economic concerns.[18] Though such a uniform social value is not impossible, it is difficult to defend in light of the fact that none of the other wisdom writings reflects the same concerns. Though the absence of such references does not negate the possibility of socio-economic explanation, it encourages the investigator to look further for explanations that deal with both the presence and the absence of such images. The questions asked of the text, therefore, move to issues of the psychology of paternity.

What did the author mean by these particular texts in the Book of Sirach? What life experiences embedded themselves within this text? These sorts of questions, of course, would violate the authorial fallacy, but perhaps other sorts of questions would be appropriate. Do these texts embody some sort of psychodynamic that exists regardless of authorial experience? Such an exploration could benefit from a psychoanalytical framework, especially one that struggled to identify common human experiences. Freudian psychoanalysis (as well as most heirs and rebuttals) emphasizes the textual nature of the psychoanalytic object. Thus, the narrative of childhood abuse (whether 'accurate' or not) may be more important to the psychoanalytic process than the experience itself (whether or not it actually existed). Mental reality dominates historical reality, thus paralleling a rhetorical analysis. As another example, con-

---

[17] Note, however, Gerda Lerner's argument that the exchange of women pre-dates private property (*The Creation of Patriarchy* (Oxford University Press, Oxford, 1986), 50, with reference to Claude Meillassoux, 'From Reproduction to Production: A Marxist Approach to Economic Anthropology', *Economy and Society*, 1 (1972), 93–105).

[18] As Turner, *The Body and Society*, 118–20, would imply. But note that Turner only considers the mother–son dyad, as an instance of the father's control of wife and of son. Turner's avoidance of the father–daughter dyad betrays the limits of the economic approach.

sider Freud's treatment of parapraxes, where what the text *says*, not what the analysand *meant*, is the object for analysis.

Whereas Sirach's son-talk focuses exclusively on issues of dominance and honour, his talk about daughters demonstrates an erotophobia: a fear of the daughter's body and of the father's inability to control sexuality.[19] Certainly this erotophobia is tied to the paternal ambivalence regarding a daughter; that is, the economic reality requires the daughter as father's property to remain inviolate until she is given away to a husband. By social norms, the father's possession is asexual; the husband's possession is the opposite. The male parent's task is to prepare a pristine virgin as an object of male desire without admitting any desire himself. A father owns each member of his household, including rights to the sexuality of any women inside, with the singular exception of the daughter.[20] If there is a limit to the father's control, it is only in that he does not have permanent control of her sexuality; that right belongs to her husband, the as-yet absent male.[21]

But this assertion about fatherhood reads our own morality into the silence of a text such as Leviticus 18, which forbids sexual intercourse between a man and his mother, sister, aunt, cousin, sister-in-law, niece, daughter-in-law, granddaughter, and other female descendants. The daughter's role is silent, fraught with unspoken possibilities. She increases her sexual desirability in order to increase her father's wealth; the law grants control of her body to her father, and the law requires her virginity, but the law does not forbid her father's advances. Thus, the need to keep the daughter within the family (to 'protect' her) sexualizes the family dynamics.

The cultural problematics of this pattern conflict with the notion of exogamy. The patriarchal exogamous family requires the exchangeability of the daughter, the only woman within the household who is 'available' for the transaction.[22] As Lynda E. Boose writes,

[19] For an analysis of the construction of female sexual uncontrollability (and its relation to notions of female irrationality) in the ancient and modern worlds, see Carol Groneman, 'Nymphomania: The Historical Construction of Female Sexuality', *Signs: Journal of Women in Culture and Society*, 19 (1994), 337–67.

[20] See Michel Foucault, *The History of Sexuality*, 3 vols., trans. Robert Hurley (Vintage, New York, 1978–86), ii. 147, iii. 35. For information about the official acceptability of incest in Egypt contemporary with ancient Israel's canonical literature, see Russell Middleton, 'Brother–Sister and Father–Daughter Marriage in Ancient Egypt', *American Sociological Review*, 27 (1962), 603–11.

[21] Lynda E. Boose, 'The Father's House and the Daughter in It: The Structure of Western Culture's Daughter–Father Relationships', in Lynda E. Boose and Betty S. Flowers (eds.), *Daughters and Fathers* (Johns Hopkins University Press, Baltimore, 1989), 19–74.

[22] Lerner, *Creation of Patriarchy*, 24–5.

Thus, if the prohibition of incest is essentially a mechanism to control internal family sexuality so that outward exchanges can take place, then the incest taboo would seem to have a special applicability to one particular pair. And if it is true, as anthropology asserts, that the origins of culture are synonymous with the evolution of kinship, then culture has essentially been built upon the relationship it has seemed least eager to discuss—that between father and daughter.[23]

This is precisely the social position missing from the Hebrew Bible's incest discourse.

The father's economic need to make his daughter desirable yet to refrain from his own desire entwines itself with a madonna/whore complex. The more pure the daughter, the more suspect her motives. Thus Sirach assumes that this pure creature, kept within the bonds of fatherly control and confined to the protection of the house, is in actuality a craven sexual animal. This assumption transfers the desire from the father to the daughter, and objectifies her in the process.[24] Within the sexualized family dynamics, the daughter becomes her mother's sexual rival for the father's attention. The father's fantasy creates the Electra complex, if only in his own mind.

This explains much of Sirach's rhetoric. In Sirach 26, the father describes a daughter who purposefully seeks out sexual experiences at any occasion she finds. She opens herself and invites sexual liaisons indiscriminately. In her father's eyes, she is wilfully sexual, actively seductive. The passage never admits any interest on the father's part, but harshly condemns the daughter's sexuality.

The rhetoric of the daughter in Sirach 26 is in the midst of a chapter dealing mostly with the husband–wife relationship. If the wife is good, the husband is happy, despite whatever else happens (Sirach 26: 1–4). However, a jealous wife brings heartache and sorrow, especially when she announces her jealousy (Sirach 26: 6). Only three verses of denunciation, culminating in the possibility of the wife's infidelity, separate that statement of the wife's jealousy from the need to control the

---

[23] Boose, 'Father's House and the Daughter in It', 19–20.

[24] In Freud's writings also, the emphasis upon the daughter's repressed desire supersedes the role of the father's seduction. For a discussion of female desire v. male seduction in Hellenic culture, see Eva C. Keuls, *The Reign of the Phallus: Sexual Politics in Ancient Athens* (1985; repr. University of California Press, Berkeley and Los Angeles, 1993), 116. Boose argues that the advantages of kin-group linkages that result from the exchange of the daughter are a psychic defence against the loss of the daughter: 'For losing one's daughter through a transaction that the father controls circumvents her ability ever to choose another man over him, thus allowing him to retain vestiges of his primary claim' ('Father's House and the Daughter in It', 31).

daughter in verse 10. Could the daughter be the rival that brings about jealousy?

After the discourse condemning the daughter's sexuality, Sirach turns to talk of the wife's sexuality—it is delightful, especially when she is silent (Sirach 26: 13–14); she is charming and beautiful, if she is in a disciplined home (vv. 15–16); she is beautiful, shapely, stately (vv. 17–18). Sirach then advises men to stay with the wife of their youth, rather than dispersing themselves among strangers; the offspring should be confident of their descent (vv. 19–21). As a whole, the passage discusses the danger of a jealous wife, emphasizes the need to control a daughter's wanton sexuality, and then praises the beauty of the wife in an admonishment to the men to stay faithful.

From a psychoanalytic viewpoint, this passage frames the male fantasy of the seductive daughter within the context of socially mandated monogamy. Paternal desire for the daughter receives denial, supported by male rhetoric and fear of the shame produced by a publicly vengeful wife. Sirach expresses well the sexualization of the household required by the production of the chaste yet desirable daughter.

The psychodynamic explanation matches much of Sirach's rhetoric, but it is unclear whether the match indicates a corollary or a causation. Again, such an explanation explains the presence of the sexualized daughter rhetoric in Sirach with a hypothesis that these concerns are common, almost universal; the absence of such rhetoric in Proverbs and other wisdom literature argues against the ready acceptance of that hypothesis. Thus, the Freudian psychoanalytic exploration of common human experiences runs into difficulties as it attempts to explain the specifics of Sirach's rhetoric, which stems from a culture quite distant from the modern era.

Whereas psychological interpretations of rhetoric tend to emphasize the commonalities within human experience, sociology is more sensitive to change, and may thus be a tool more suited to differential explanations. Proverbs does not discuss daughters, and Sirach shares much of the same world-view, but adds rhetoric about the body to decry the daughter's sexuality. What changed between the time of Proverbs and the second-century date of Sirach's first writing?

The answer that many biblical scholars would find obvious is Hellenization. Some biblical interpreters seem to view Hellenism as a thoroughgoing cultural revolution that offers a single, tidy explanation for every perceived difference between earlier and Hellenistic cultures. This is the judgement of Rudolf Smend, who commented in 1906 that

Sirach is motivated by a hatred of all things Greek and evidences a complete rejection and avoidance of any Greek thought within the book.[25] For most of this century, however, scholarship has moderated this opinion, understanding that the Book of Sirach represents a partial assimilationist stance to Hellenistic culture[26] while maintaining some distinctions.[27] Although scholars differ in their understanding of Sirach's balance of assimilation v. distinctiveness, virtually all scholarly options recognize the need to combine these views. Thus, a comment such as the following by Edmond Jacob is much more representative of current scholarship than is Smend's opinion:

During Ben Sira's lifetime Hellenism in Palestine was no longer a foreign reality which had to be stemmed. Since at least the third century B.C., the Greek language, and with it a large part of the Greek spirit, had found its way into the country. One could no more ignore it than the air which he breathed daily.[28]

Despite the dangers of the overly general category of 'Greek thought', the fact remains that Jerusalem experienced a major cultural shift in the years and centuries after Alexander's defeat of the Persian Empire in 333 BCE. Of course, such changes in roles and values proceed at uneven paces, varying with numerous factors such as social sector and geography. Nevertheless, Hellenistic culture's understanding of the adult–youth relation and the father–daughter relationship in particular differed from patterns in earlier Israelite or Jewish cultures.[29]

Historically, Israelite and Jewish families had included multiple

[25] Rudolf Smend, *Die Weisheit des Jesus Sirach erklärt* (Reimer, Berlin, 1906), p. xxiv and *passim*.

[26] John G. Gammie, 'The Sage in Sirach', in John G. Gammie and Leo G. Perdue (eds.), *The Sage in Israel and the Ancient Near East* (Eisenbrauns, Winona Lake, Ind., 1990), 355–72, esp. 360–4; and Leo G. Perdue, *Wisdom and Creation: The Theology of Wisdom Literature* (Abingdon, Nashville, 1994), 243–90, esp. 246.

[27] Alexander A. DiLella, 'The Meaning of Wisdom in Ben Sira', in Leo G. Perdue, Bernard Brandon Scott, and William Johnston Wiseman (eds.), *In Search of Wisdom: Essays in Memory of John G. Gammie* (Westminster John Knox Press, Louisville, Ky., 1993), 133–48, esp. 136.

[28] Edmond Jacob, 'Wisdom and Religion in Sirach', in John G. Gammie, Walter A. Brueggemann, W. Lee Humphreys, and James M. Ward (eds.), *Israelite Wisdom: Theological and Literary Essays in Honor of Samuel Terrien* (Scholars Press, Missoula, Mont., 1978), 248.

[29] For analyses of Greek notions of a daughter's sexuality, see Mark Golden, *Children and Childhood in Classical Athens* (Johns Hopkins University Press, Baltimore, 1990), 94–6; and Jeffrey Henderson, 'Greek Attitudes toward Sex', in Michael Grant and Rachel Kitzinger (eds.), *Civilization of the Ancient Mediterranean: Greece and Rome*, 3 vols. (Scribner's, New York, 1988), ii. 1251. For a description of the problems inherent in reconstructing women's lives from the extant Greek sources, see Marilyn A. Katz, 'Ideology and the "Status of Women" in Ancient Greece', in Richard Hawley and Barbara Levick (eds.), *Women in Antiquity: New Assessments* (Routledge, London, 1995), 21–43.

generations in one household, regardless of the household's economic level.[30] In pre-Hellenistic Israel, there was no recognition of any rights of children, nor any discussion of the concepts of legal majority and minority. Children were completely under the power of their parents, especially their father, until they became adults.[31] For women, the status of adulthood was clearly achieved at marriage, wherein they transferred from one man's house to another. Children were only identified with respect to their father. Girls and boys alike were put to work collecting fuel or performing other simple foraging tasks at about ages 5 or 6, under the supervision of their mothers (or other women within the family).[32] Israelite women had children as part of their economic contribution to family survival.[33]

Fathers owned their daughters.[34] They could even sell daughters into marriage or slavery (Exodus 21; 2 Kings 4: 1–7; Nehemiah 5: 1–5).[35] Fathers certainly controlled the daughter's sexuality and could give away sexual access to the daughter, at least in some circumstances (Genesis 19: 8; Judges 19: 24). Israelite law treats damage to a daughter as compensatable through financial arrangements with the girl's father (Exodus 22: 16–17; Numbers 30: 3–16). Virginity was not an absolute cultural value in ancient Israel. A daughter's virginity was a good that the father owned and which he could sell or give to others at his own initiation. The law protected the father's investment from those outside the family, but there was nothing against the father employing his daughter's sexuality in whatever way he found most to his benefit. Incest remained one of those possible uses of her sexuality.

Marriage was never a matter of individual choice; it was an economic

---

[30] Carol L. Meyers, 'Everyday Life: Women in the Period of the Hebrew Bible', in Carol A. Newsom and Sharon H. Ringe (eds.), *The Women's Bible Commentary* (SPCK, London; Westminster John Knox Press, Louisville, Ky., 1992), 244–51, esp. 246. See also C. J. H. Wright, 'Family', in Freedman (ed.), *Anchor Bible Dictionary*, vol. ii: *D–G* (Doubleday, New York, 1992), 761–9, esp. 766–7. For an overview of the status of sociological and archaeological research on the family in ancient Israel, see Karel van der Toorn, *Family Religion in Babylonia, Syria and Israel: Continuity and Change in the Forms of Religious Life*, Studies in the History and Culture of the Ancient Near East 7 (E. J. Brill, Leiden, 1996), 190–205.

[31] Archer, *Her Price is beyond Rubies*, 63.

[32] Carol Meyers, 'The Family in Early Israel', in Leo G. Perdue, Joseph Blenkinsopp, John J. Collins, and Carol Meyers, *Families in Ancient Israel*, Family, Religion, and Culture (Westminster John Knox Press, Louisville, Ky., 1997), 28.

[33] Ibid. 30.

[34] G. I. Emmerson, 'Women in Ancient Israel', in R. E. Clements (ed.), *The World of Ancient Israel: Sociological, Anthropological and Political Perspectives* (Cambridge University Press, Cambridge, 1989), 371–94, esp. 380–2; and Joseph Blenkinsopp, 'The Family in First Temple Israel', in Perdue et al., *Families in Ancient Israel*, 66–76.

[35] Wright, 'Family', ii. 767.

connection between households.[36] According to Joseph Blenkinsopp, the purposes of marriage were 'to make alliances, renew the household's labor pool, and in general promote its economic interests. The laws governing forbidden degrees of consanguinity in Leviticus 18: 1–18 [the incest prohibitions] are motivated by these concerns and by the need to preserve order within the household, not by eugenics.'[37] Jewish women usually married at age 12.[38] Men, however, were encouraged to wait until age 20 in order to gain some education.[39]

The changes in Jewish culture brought by Hellenistic influences were not instantaneous.[40] Martin Hengel argues that the process of Hellenization only began in Palestine and many parts of the Greek-dominated world in the middle of the third century, about seventy-five years or more after Alexander's conquest. According to Hengel, political and social issues, such as family structure, experienced the first impacts, whereas philosophical, literary, and religious aspects became of con-sequence only in subsequent centuries.[41] Hellenization was not an imperialization, in the sense that there was no central bureaucracy for-cing the adoption of new cultural ways. Instead, Hellenism spread when local non-Greeks, such as Jews in Jerusalem, perceived social advantage from mimicking Greek ways. Because the Greeks were prosperous and enjoyed high prestige, they gained the attention of local persons by constructing a new social hierarchy, at the top of which were Greeks.[42] Jews who wished to advance themselves in Jerusalem society, as well as in the larger context of the Hellenistic world beyond Palestine, could ascend

---

[36] Thus, anthropologists can speak in terms of the economics of honour and shame, or the finances of sexuality. For an application of this thought to Sirach, see Camp, 'Under-standing a Patriarchy', 2–4.

[37] Blenkinsopp, 'Family in First Temple Israel', 59.

[38] Archer, *Her Price is beyond Rubies*, 95; Blenkinsopp, 'Family in First Temple Israel', 77.

[39] Archer, *Her Price is beyond Rubies*, 96.

[40] For an example of continuing cultural conflicts and the long-term ambiguities of cultural contact, see Judith Romney Wegner, 'Philo's Portrayal of Women—Hebraic or Hellenic?', in Levine (ed.), *'Women Like This'*, 41–66.

[41] Martin Hengel, 'The Interpenetration of Judaism and Hellenism in the Pre-Maccabean Period', in W. D. Davies and Louis Finkelstein (eds.), *The Cambridge History of Judaism*, ii: *The Hellenistic Age* (Cambridge University Press, Cambridge, 1989), 167–228, esp. 178–9. See also Elias J. Bickerman, *From Ezra to the Last of the Maccabees: Foundations of Postbiblical Judaism* (Schocken, New York, 1947), 54–71; Arnoldo Momigliano, *Alien Wisdom: The Limits of Hellenization* (Cambridge University Press, Cambridge, 1975), 88–96; and Jonathan Goldstein, 'Jewish Acceptance and Rejection of Hellenism', in E. P. Sanders, A. I. Baumgarten, and Alan Mendelson (eds.), *Jewish and Christian Self-Definition*, ii: *Aspects of Judaism in the Graeco-Roman Period* (Fortress, Philadelphia, 1981), 64–87.

[42] Shimon Applebaum, *Judaea in Hellenistic and Roman Times: Historical and Archaeo-logical Essays*, Studies in Judaism in Late Antiquity 40 (E. J. Brill, Leiden, 1989), 30–46.

the social ladder through copying Greek lifestyles.[43] This meant becoming Hellenized, beginning with local institutions such as family life:

The primarily economic trend of Hellenistic civilization and its limitation to the upper classes and the cities resulted in a relaxation of *life-style* which during the course of the third century probably found an entry even into Palestine and certain circles in Jerusalem. The eloquent warnings of the latest part of Proverbs in particular, against adultery with the 'strange woman', the picture of enjoyment of life and the delight of feasting on the one hand and the warning against a luxurious way of life on the other suggest that the 'Graeculi' were not just a phenomenon in the Rome of the late republic, but were also to be found in Palestine.[44]

In Israel, women were ignored. In Greece, they were villainized and the source of impurity, a notion that appears only late in Israel's legal codes.[45] Pre-Hellenistic Israelite literature tended to exclude the daughter from narrative as part of the social devaluation of women;[46] Hellenistic Judaism, in contrast, excluded women from society by keeping them in their father's house.

The Hellenistic world treated youth in a different way, for both boys and girls. Boys would stay by themselves, rather than living within their father's house, beginning at about age 12 and continuing at least until age 18.[47] Women under the age of 12 were kept within the home in the early Hellenistic period, to limit the possibility of their contamination of the public world of men.[48]

Hellenistic Judaism in general believed in the woman's uncontrollable allurement. This resulted in a renewed emphasis on premarital chastity.[49] But another move was at play here. Whereas previously Israelite law had

---

[43] Hengel, 'Interpenetration', 179–81.

[44] Martin Hengel, *Judaism and Hellenism: Studies in their Encounter in Palestine during the Early Hellenistic Period*, i: *Text* (Fortress, Philadelphia, 1974), 54.

[45] For the Greek rejection of women, see Anne Carson, 'Putting Her in Her Place: Woman, Dirt, and Desire', in David M. Halperin, John J. Winkler, and Froma I. Zeitlin (eds.), *Before Sexuality: The Construction of Erotic Experience in the Ancient Greek World* (Princeton University Press, Princeton, 1990), 134–69.

[46] Ilona N. Rashkow, *The Phallacy of Genesis: A Feminist-Psychoanalytic Approach*, Literary Currents in Biblical Interpretation (Westminster John Knox Press, Louisville, Ky., 1993), 65–84.

[47] Barry S. Strauss, *Fathers and Sons in Athens: Ideology and Society in the Era of the Peloponnesian War* (Princeton University Press, Princeton, 1993); Clause Mossé, 'Women in the Spartan Revolutions of the Third Century B.C.', in Sarah B. Pomeroy (ed.), *Women's History and Ancient History* (University of North Carolina Press, Chapel Hill, 1991), 138–53, esp. 141–2. See also Xenophon, *Lac. pol.* 1. 6.

[48] Archer, *Her Price is beyond Rubies*, 105.

[49] Ibid. 106.

justified a young woman's separation from society outside the family on the basis of the woman's need for protection, the later Hellenistic literature rationalized such isolation on the basis of the male society's need for safety from the woman's rampant and polluting sexuality. As Léonie Archer summarizes, 'by the Graeco-Roman period, therefore, the purity of women had without doubt been placed centre stage, with virginity being viewed in terms of a morality overtly far removed from the philosophy of earlier years'.[50] Again, according to Archer:

The new social ordering and moral consciousness of the Second Commonwealth rendered the preservation of the girl's virginity a matter of utmost importance, but the period's increased urbanization, with its possibilities for increased sexual laxity, presented great problems as to how exactly the required degree of purity was to be attained. The rapidly developing view of women as domestic beings with no part to play in the public life of the state . . . provided the purists with the solution to their problem: women would simply be kept in seclusion within the home ordering their household affairs.[51]

Philo writes of Jewish houses with special chambers reserved for the virgin daughters, so that no one else in the household could enter their quarters. Likewise, these quarters were shielded from the street by the public quarters and those set aside for men and married women; no visitor could reach a young woman without going through the rest of the densely occupied house.[52] This was a clear change from Jewish society in ancient Israel, where women, both married and unmarried, were present in public at a variety of occasions (Genesis 18, 24; Judges 21: 19–20). Greek morality considered an ideal marriage to begin with a woman of age 14 and a man of age 30, since the culture required a woman's bridal virginity but believed that young women were lustful.[53] Sirach shares this expectation that young women would seek out sexual involvement.

---

[50] Archer, *Her Price is beyond Rubies.* 111.

[51] Ibid. 113.

[52] Ibid. 117. See Philo, *Leg. all.* 3. 40, 3. 98; *Spec. leg.* 3. 169; *in Flaccum* § 89; cf. also 2 Macc. 3: 19; 3 Macc. 1: 18; 4 Macc. 18: 7–8; *Assumption of Moses* 11: 12.

[53] Paul Veyne (ed.), *A History of Private Life*, i: *From Pagan Rome to Byzantium* (Belknap, Cambridge, Mass., 1987), 20–5; and Foucault, *History of Sexuality*, ii. 154, 216. A more nuanced historical view can be found in Beryl Rawson, 'Adult–Child Relationships in Roman Society', in Beryl Rawson (ed.), *Marriage, Divorce and Children in Ancient Rome* (Clarendon, Oxford, 1991), 7–30, esp. 27. For an overview leading into rabbinic customs, see also David Biale, *From Intercourse to Discourse: Control of Sexuality in Rabbinic Literature*, Center for Hermeneutical Studies (Graduate Theological Union, Berkeley, Calif., 1990). A more thorough discussion of the Greek sources (especially Aristotle) can be found in Sarah B. Pomeroy, *Goddesses, Whores, Wives, and Slaves: Women in Classical Antiquity* (Schocken Books, New York, 1975).

These trends of Hellenization continued. A few centuries later, young Greek and Roman men were allowed to have a time of sexual freedom, but such behaviour was still not allowed for young women, of whom virginity was expected.[54] The economic motivation seems to be missing and replaced with a moral or habitual explanation for the maintenance of the same custom of requisite (or at least preferred) virginity. Yet this preference for female virginity at marriage was not some abstract valuation of the concept of virginity. According to Peter Brown, 'the girl's loss of her virginity was, simply, a bad omen for her future conduct. A girl who had already enjoyed furtive love affairs might do the same when she was married.'[55] Such errant behaviour was a reversal of sexual roles for women, since Greek culture expected women to be recipients of sexual advances, never the initiators.[56] For Hellenistic Jewish communities as well, the meaning of virginity was moving away from purely economic senses to have a more symbolic connotation, representing purity of heart.[57]

In short, Sirach's Hellenistic Jewish world was facing a series of cultural shifts and instabilities, in the midst of which it became increasingly difficult to maintain basic social patterns and the associated honour system.[58] Certainly, Sirach fears women with sexual initiative, since they

[54] Veyne, *History of Private Life*, 23–5; Foucault, *History of Sexuality*, iii. 129. For an analysis of how the Hellenistic concept of virginity extended its hyperbolic valuation of the virgin into the Roman and Christian eras, see Giulia Sissa, 'Maidenhood without Maidenhead: The Female Body in Ancient Greece', in Halperin et al. (eds.), *Before Sexuality*, 339–64. But see Thomas Wiedemann, *Adults and Children in the Roman Empire* (Yale University Press, New Haven, 1989), who discounts Veyne's notions of childhood sexuality as 'controversial' and repeatedly denies juvenile sexuality in the ancient world, just as many do today. However, the influences of this notion of adolescent sexuality as (almost) unrestrainable are clear in e.g. Victorian culture, as demonstrated by this quote from one of that period's commentaries on sexuality: 'It is well known that rigid continence is seldom observed about the age of puberty' (Michael Ryan, *The Philosophy of Marriage in its Social, Moral, and Physical Relations*, 3rd edn. (H. Balliere, London, 1839), 64).

[55] Peter Brown, *The Body and Society: Men, Women and Sexual Renunciation in Early Christianity*, Lectures on the History of Religions 13 (Columbia University Press, New York, 1988), 29.

[56] Female sexual passivity encodes itself in linguistics as well as in literature; female sexuality is expressed in passive verbs. See Bella Zweig, 'The Mute Nude Female Characters in Aristophanes' Plays', in Richlin (ed.), *Pornography and Representation in Greece and Rome*, 78; Nicole Loraux, *The Experience of Tiresias: The Feminine and the Greek Man* (Princeton University Press, Princeton, 1995), 230; and Foucault, *History of Sexuality*, ii. 46. See also Aristotle, *History of Animals*, 9. 5. 637^a; 7. 1. 581^b; *Politics* 3. 1274^{b}38–1275^{a}23.

[57] Tal Ilan, *Jewish Women in Greco-Roman Palestine: An Inquiry into Image and Status*, Texte und Studien zum antiken Judentum 44 (J. C. B. Mohr [Paul Siebeck], Tübingen, 1995; Hendrickson, Peabody, Mass., 1997), 98.

[58] See the conclusions of Burton Mack, *Wisdom and the Hebrew Epic* (University of Chicago Press, Chicago, 1985).

deny cultural expectations. This is clear from his much earlier comments in chapter 9:

> Do not be jealous of the wife of your bosom,
>   or you will teach her an evil lesson to your own hurt.
> Do not give yourself to a woman
>   and let her trample down your strength.
> Do not go near a loose woman,
>   or you will fall into her snares.
> Do not dally with a singing girl,
>   or you will be caught by her tricks. (Sirach 9: 1–4)

Sirach disdains the woman who takes initiative, whether by learning 'an evil lesson' about the possibilities for sexual infidelity, or in the woman who tramples a man's strength. Other women have 'snares' and 'tricks' by which they take charge in sexual relations.

But earlier Israelite and Judean culture was no different in its expectations of women's passivity and fear of female assertiveness. In fact, Sirach's general pronouncements against the sexually assertive woman are little different from those found in Proverbs 7, where the 'loud' woman takes an active role and leads a man astray:

> With much seductive speech she persuades him;
>   with her smooth talk she compels him.
> Right away he follows her,
>   and goes like an ox to the slaughter,
> or bounds like a stag toward the trap
>   until an arrow pierces its entrails.
> He is like a bird rushing into a snare,
>   not knowing that it will cost him his life. (Proverbs 7: 21–3)

Proverbs and Sirach share related notions of the danger of the sexually assertive woman. The social differences behind the rhetorical differences in Proverbs and Sirach, especially the metaphors for the daughter's body, must reside elsewhere. Hellenism's cultural shift involved not only sexual roles, but also the changing expectations placed upon persons in different age categories.[59]

Ancient Israel's understanding of sexual development seems to reflect

---

[59] For an analysis of cultural variation in age role expectations, see A. Bame Nsamenang, *Human Development in Cultural Context: A Third World Perspective*, Cross-cultural Research and Methodology 16 (SAGE, Newbury Park, Calif., 1992).

two stages: childhood and adulthood.[60] All children are clearly the father's property.[61] At the time that a child became physically able to procreate, the person became an adult, with full expectations for marriage, children, family life, and adult contributions to society as a whole. On the other hand, Hellenistic society perceived the matter differently, often referring to a three-stage system of childhood, adolescence, and adulthood.[62] The beginnings of procreative ability did not signal a transition into adulthood. In the Hellenistic world, young men were expected to seek out sexual encounters, and the literature tells many tales of high degrees of youthful sexual expression. Whereas adulthood should be a time of restraint and responsibility, a man's youth was a period of freedom and frolic, in which an adolescent man participated in a wide variety of experiences (sexual and otherwise) with a group of his peers.[63] Adolescence created a society of young men apart from the world of adult males and the male children kept in that world with them. Hellenism thus introduced to the Jewish context a new sexual morality, in which there was a new category of men (adolescents) who had expectations for high sexual activity.[64] This cultural dissonance created a range of tensions and social shifts.

Cultural contact is never a simple, linear phenomenon. In this case, it precipitated a Jewish resistance to several features of Greek and Roman society, while at the same time Jewish culture embraced other aspects of Hellenistic culture. Cross-cultural interaction is clearly visible in changes in the range of sexual norms and expressions. One of the Jewish reactions to Hellenized views of sexuality involved abstinence, asceticism, and isolation. At Qumran, sexual abstinence among the men was believed to make them like God's angels in a holy army.[65] Greeks understood the presence of women to cause divisions between men, based in lust and

---

[60] Léonie J. Archer, 'Notions of Community and the Exclusion of the Female in Jewish History and Historiography', in Léonie J. Archer, Susan Fischler, and Maria Wyke (eds.), *Women in Ancient Societies: 'An Illusion of the Night'* (1994; repr. Routledge, New York, 1995), 56–7.

[61] So even as late as the Mishnah; see Judith R. Wegner, *Chattel or Person: The Status of Women in the Mishnah* (Oxford University Press, Oxford, 1988), 20–39.

[62] Sue Blundell, *Women in Ancient Greece* (Harvard University Press, Cambridge, Mass., 1995), 99–100.

[63] Foucault, *History of Sexuality*, i. 46; ii. 46, 59. See also Emiel Eyben, *Restless Youth in Ancient Rome*, trans. Patrick Daly (Routledge, London, 1993), 6–9, 14–16, 107–27, 231–8.

[64] For a later Jewish recognition of female adolescence, see *Nid.* 5. 7, *Ketub.* 4. 5, and Archer, *Her Price is beyond Rubies*, 43–4.

[65] *Community Rule*, 4.

jealousy.[66] Accepting such beliefs yet rejecting some of the Hellenistic norms of sexual activity, some parts of Jewish society avoided male–female contact in favour of practices of isolation.[67]

In the text's body rhetoric, Sirach partakes of isolationist tendencies. Sirach recognizes the Hellenizing influences of the new adolescence and reacts to it in two ways. For young men, Sirach warns them against the temptations of sexual encounters. These passages are rather neutral in their imagery, and they take seriously the role of the young male as subject. This allows Sirach to fit new expectations into his former values; in effect, he treats adolescent males as adult males, assuming that both adolescent and adult males have a number of sexual drives that are real, but that those drives should be the focus of the male's self-control.

The case of the daughter, however, remains much more problematic. She represents the ambiguities of the changes in gender and age expectations, and Sirach refuses to collapse the categories of age for her as he does for the male adolescent. This problem of ambiguity plays itself out in multiple social contexts of the daughter's adolescence. As Boose writes,

> Her adolescence seems, in fact, to crystallize the paradox of her place within the family. On the one hand, since she is its one female who is a full blood member, the loss of family blood that marks the threshold of her maturity symbolically asserts the subtraction she signifies and physically defines her as the breach in the wall of family enclosure . . . At the same time, however, since menstruation marks the daughter's entrance into the margins of desire, her presence likewise threatens to invite incestuous desire and hence pollution within the family boundaries.[68]

However, Sirach's reaction to daughters is different in several ways. First, Sirach's body metaphors convert the daughter's body into a rhetorical object.[69] She is not the subject of her own sexuality; she possesses

---

[66] Brown, *The Body and Society*, 39.

[67] This is typical of the use of power to limit sexuality as it limits other possibilities in the rest of life. See Foucault, *History of Sexuality*, i. 83.

[68] Boose, 'Father's House and the Daughter in It', 35. Likewise, the Victorian re-emphasis on adolescence accompanied the rise in rape, incest, and other sexual contact between adults and adolescents or children. See James R. Kincaid, *Child-Loving: The Erotic Child and Victorian Culture* (Routledge, New York, 1992).

[69] In the process of this convers(at)ion, Sirach's attention directs itself to young female bodies as constructed by discourse, and specifically by a phallocratic discourse that continually produces rigid power for the father. Cf. Zillah R. Eisenstein, *The Female Body and the Law* (University of California Press, Berkeley and Los Angeles, 1988), 81. Camp, 'Understanding a Patriarchy', 11 n. 23, recognizes that the term for 'peg' is used also in Sirach 27: 2, and remarks that Sirach 'habitually mixes sexual and economic language'. This clearly adds to the objectification.

no possibility for self-control, and thus her body—especially her organs of sexuality—become mere objects. She is dehumanized, seen only as an object and yet perversely as the subject of intense sexual desire. The father's desires are transferred to the daughter, robbing her of any recognition of her own emotions and objectifying her.[70] Sirach never refers to the daughter as a being capable of choice; she works by physiological instinct.[71] Her body does not even receive anatomical names; the problem is her open quiver.

Sirach denies female agency in favour of strictly instinctual motivations, as if the daughter had no mind with which to choose, but instead was merely a slave of her body.[72] But her body is also denied the chance to be a body in Sirach's rhetoric; it is merely an inanimate object. The dichotomy of activity and passivity becomes highly problematic; though he condemns the daughter's active interest in sex, he also condemns her passive acceptance of lovers.[73] Thus, he encourages fathers to take the 'appropriate' steps; they should lock up their daughters where nothing can happen. This allows fathers to take the active role in regulating their daughters' sexuality, and forces the daughters into the proper passive role, satisfying the morality of Hellenistic Judaism.

In response to the new social construct of adolescence, Sirach treats the adolescent male as an adult, but considers the adolescent female as a child, still under the father's protection. This strategy allows a tacit rejection of the new culture (by denying that there really are three separate age categories) at the same time as it embraces the new cultural ideology (by accepting notions of adolescent sexual drives

---

[70] Jacobs, *Victimized Daughters*, 49.

[71] For descriptions of comparable Greek female lust, see Blundell, *Women in Ancient Greece*, 100–5.

[72] The denial of agency and subsequent objectification of the daughter in Sirach is clearly a reaction to fear. This paternal fear is paralleled by the belief inherent in Greek tragedies: once the father loses possession of the daughter, his own death is close at hand. See Nancy Sorkin Rabinowitz, 'Tragedy and the Politics of Containment', in Richlin (ed.), *Pornography and Representation in Greece and Rome*, 36–52; and Veyne, *History of Private Life*, 25–9.

[73] The dichotomy between activity and passivity is even more problematic than it may seem at first instance. Not only is the daughter's role involved, but the men's roles are as well. Do the men actively pursue the daughter (but if so, then the daughter is to blame only for her passivity in accepting such affronts), or are the men passive in their response to young female beauty (but then the men are passive in their own sexuality; i.e. they passively accept the 'active' role in a sexual liaison)? Notice how Sirach's discourse moves against the recognition of male sexuality as either active or passive through the absence of male sexual rhetoric. The men's bodies remain outside the discourse, even the very discourse designed to encapsulate female bodies. See the discussion of men's missing bodies in Leonard Duroche, 'Male Perception as Social Construct', in Jeff Hearn and David Morgan (eds.), *Men, Masculinities & Social Theory* (Unwin Hyman, London, 1990), 170–8.

that are not 'ready' for marriage). Sirach both rejects and consumes Hellenism.[74]

The rhetoric of the daughters' bodies, then, is a rhetoric of control, and specifically of control by isolation.[75] This fits well with much of Sirach's thoughts about life and morality. Along with the dominant wisdom tradition as reflected in Proverbs, Sirach favours self-control and restraint. The actions prescribed with regard to the daughter are at one level only another case of this general principle—even though there is certainly more going on here. Sirach favours a strong patriarchal control of the father over all members of the household, especially over the financial concerns that still come into play concerning a marriageable daughter's virginity. Furthermore, he strongly favours self-control, especially for a man's sexuality; a wise man resists the attractions and temptations of seductive women wherever they are. Even when the woman is his wife, the virtuous and honourable man must show restraint.[76] Thus, a man controls family, wealth, and self.

Sirach's rhetorical and social construction of male and female bodies is hardly surprising. In fact, it parallels common techniques of social organization.[77] As young men become public figures, learning to exert increasing control over self, body, and the surrounding physical and social environment, society forces women inside. Women experience 'the channeling of their *very bodies* into the reserved containment and the ideal immobility towards which they must strive'.[78] By such restriction, women learn to relinquish both bodily autonomy and social power. Colette Guillaumin argues that this symbolizes and creates the accessibility of women's bodies to the men around them. Isolation and enclosure

---

[74] Note that M. Hengel, *Judaism and Hellenism* (Fortress Press, Philadelphia, 1974), i. 138–53, understands Sirach as arguing against Greek liberalism while demonstrating strong Hellenistic influences.

[75] Kathy Newman, 'Re-membering an Interrupted Conversation: The Mother/Virgin Split', *Trivia*, 2 (1983), 45–63. Part of the process of control lies in isolating the daughter (virgin) from other women. For female isolation in ancient Greece, see Katz, 'Ideology and the "Status of Women"', 29; and Carson, 'Putting Her in Her Place', 135–69. For an extended feminist consideration of the isolation of woman from woman in literature, see Helena Michie, *Sororophobia: Differences among Women in Literature and Culture* (Oxford University Press, New York, 1992).

[76] Camp argues this effectively in relation to Sirach 9: 1a ('Understanding a Patriarchy', 20–2).

[77] See Lynn Hunt (ed.), *Eroticism and the Body Politic*, Parallax: Re-visions of Culture and Society (Johns Hopkins University Press, Baltimore, 1991).

[78] Colette Guillaumin, 'The Constructed Body', in Catherine B. Burroughs and Jeffrey David Ehrenreich (ed.), *Reading the Social Body* (University of Iowa Press, Iowa City, 1993), 48.

constructs women's bodies as, in her words, 'bodies-for-others', bodies defined by their required availability.

Sirach therefore restricts the daughter's body in order to maintain its availability for men. In another sense, Sirach confines the daughter to maintain his own social mobility within a culture where female purity signified male status by demonstrating the male's control of his own household. But this operates in the realm of norms—that is, statements about preferred behaviour. Sirach stays closer to traditional *norms* than to *values*, since he moves toward acceptance of certain Hellenistic notions. He recognizes and accepts the belief in adolescent sexuality. Within Hellenistic culture, the young virgin adolescent is the ideal of female beauty driven toward sexual passion. Sirach accepts the cultural logic of new values while maintaining more traditional norms, for he assumes the daughter's highly charged sexuality while attempting to limit it by keeping it within the household. As Ingrid Walsøe-Engel argues is the case in modern German drama, Sirach and other men in Hellenistic Jewish society trap the 'scandalous ambiguities of their daughters' fatal sexuality' between the 'competing imperatives of posses-sive retention and the avoidance of incest'.[79] He believes that his nubile daughter will have sex with any male she sees, and so the only solution is to keep her at home—precisely where she sees no adult male but the father, whose actions are governed, one presumes, by self-control of the father and of the household.

Sirach's solution to rampant adolescent female sexuality is to bring that sexuality into the home, the cultural place of safety and control.[80] As long as the daughter remains within the household, the father is able to exercise control, at least in the understanding of Hellenistic Jewish cul-ture.[81] The command to stay in the house finds a parallel in Sirach 42: 12, which disallows conversation between the virgin daughter and sexually active married women.[82] This presents an immediate problem. Sirach's

[79] Ingrid Walsøe-Engel, *Fathers and Daughters: Patterns of Seduction in Tragedies by Gryphius, Lessing, Hebbel and Kroetz* (Camden House, Columbia, SC, 1993), 1.

[80] Of course, this is precisely *not* Sirach's solution, but instead Sirach's statement about a solution. When Sirach claims to trap the daughter inside the house, he succeeds at trapping the daughter inside a text about/around her.

[81] The reality of domestic violence contradicts this emphasis on the home as the place of male control. Cf. Jalna Hanmer and Sheila Saunders, 'Blowing the Cover of the Protective Male: A Community Study of Violence to Women', in Eva Gamarnikow, David H. J. Morgan, June Purvis, and Daphne Taylorson (eds.), *The Public and the Private* (Heinemann, London, 1983), 28–46.

[82] While scholars usually emphasize Sirach's supposed assumption that contact with other women makes women more sexually active, the household limitation prevented

typical father admits that his daughter is a sexual being, and thus one with a sexuality that needs control. What of her relationships with the males within the household? If her sexuality is nearly beyond control, then it seems likely that she will create sexual tensions and opportunities within the domestic context as well. This raises the possibility of incest, especially in the father–daughter dyad.[83]

Incest relationships place sexual abuse/violence within family connections. Social understandings of incest frequently assume that there is a *relationship* involved; that is, both father *and* daughter contribute to the maintenance of the situation.[84] In the terms of Sirach 26: 10–12 and 42: 9–13, the father's desire for the incestuous relationship leads then to Sirach's claim that the daughter was 'asking for it' (her quiver is always open to any arrow; she spreads herself before every tent peg; her thirst is never sated). Her own lust and wanton behaviour caused any sexual tensions within the household. Interpreters often echo this ambiguous relationship, as does Tal Ilan:

Thus in *Ben Sira*'s eyes a daughter is a constant aggravation to her father, especially as a source of sexual temptation. Accordingly he cannot treat her with affection but locks her up behind bars. *Ben Sira*'s continual fears point to a rather impersonal, loveless relationship between father and daughter.[85]

When Ilan writes of the daughter as 'a source of sexual temptation', is she implying that the father is tempted? If so, then the imprisonment and the 'loveless relationship' is either a forced removal or a forced incest, but which one Ilan intends is not clear.

Freud replaced his original notion that incest was frequent and was causative of adult trauma with his belief in subconscious desires. Daughters enact their sexual development by rejecting the mother and desiring the father and the phallus. Freud's opinion was that actual instances of incest were rare, but were frequent in female fantasy. Incest only occurred in those cases where the seductive daughter was

---

women from easily identifying with other women, leading further to the mother/virgin dichotomy of male-identified female sexuality. See Newman, 'Re-membering an Interrupted Conversation'.

[83] For a discussion of incest in modern legal discourse, see Vikki Bell, 'Health, Harm or Happy Families? Knowledges of Incest in Twentieth Century Parliamentary Debates', in Sue Scott, Gareth Williams, Stephen Platt, and Hilary Thomas (eds.), *Private Risks and Public Dangers* (Avebury, Aldershot, 1992), 57–73.

[84] Not surprisingly, such assumptions parallel social tendencies to blame the victim. See Emily Driver, 'Introduction', in Emily Driver and Audrey Droisen (eds.), *Child Sexual Abuse: Feminist Perspectives* (Macmillan, London, 1989), 18–19.

[85] Ilan, *Jewish Women in Greco-Roman Palestine*, 49.

successful.[86] But this places all agency within the daughter, negating any sense of agency from the adult male, the society's most powerful figure. Furthermore it does little to explain the concentration on incestuous relationships within the Hebrew Bible narratives.[87]

Some feminist psychoanalysts root such seductive behaviour, when it occurs, in the daughter's recognition that the male world offers advantages, especially those advantages tied to access to the outside world.[88] Within this perspective, there is a connection between the father's power and his covert attractiveness to his daughter. To refer to the father's attractiveness is to continue Sirach's fantasy of female desire for the male, a fantasy that obscures the possible woman–woman connections within the family and within the larger world.[89] The more the father limits access to the outside world, the more pathological the family. Though domination is not causally connected to incest, they express related forms of family pathology. Some feminist psychoanalysts identify incest as an extreme form of female socialization. This point is of special interest, since Sirach's subject is socialization. The power expressed in controlling the family is the same socio-political and family-institutional power that produces incest.[90] As a result of and in parallel with this incestual control, Sirach turns the family's attention inward, further defining the boundaries between inside and outside, between Jewish cultural purity and Hellenistic enculturation.[91] Incest, whether potential or actualized, manifests and symbolizes the father's sexual and social control of the daughter.

---

[86] Cathy Waldby et al., 'Theoretical Perspectives on Father–Daughter Incest', in Driver and Droisen (eds.), *Child Sexual Abuse*, 88–93. Luce Irigaray reads Freud as a father afraid of seducing his daughter (*Speculum of the Other Woman*, trans. Gillian C. Gill (Cornell University Press, Ithaca, NY, 1985), 41); see also Jane Gallop, *The Daughter's Seduction: Feminism and Psychoanalysis* (Cornell University Press, Ithaca, NY, 1982), 70–9.

[87] Rashkow, *Phallacy of Genesis*, 68–9, points to the following incestuous (or questionable) relationships in Genesis: Adam–Eve, Cain–Cain's wife, Noah's wife–Ham, Abram–Sarai, Lot–Lot's daughters, Isaac–Rebekah, Jacob–Leah–Rachel, Reuben–Bilhah, and Judah–Tamar.

[88] See Judith Herman, *Father–Daughter Incest* (Harvard University Press, Cambridge, Mass., 1981); and Jessica Benjamin, *The Bonds of Love: Psychoanalysis, Feminism, and the Problem of Domination* (Pantheon, New York, 1988).

[89] In this fantasy, the assertion of paternal attractiveness displaces the original maternal attraction. This other dyad, ignored by Sirach, is recognized by many lesbian critics. See Elaine Marks, 'Lesbian Intertextuality', in Susan J. Wolfe and Julie Penelope (eds.), *Sexual Practice, Textual Theory: Lesbian Cultural Theory* (Blackwell, Cambridge, 1993), 271–90, esp. 273.

[90] Waldby, 'Theoretical Perspectives on Father–Daughter Incest', 99–102.

[91] Irving Kaufman, 'Father–Daughter Incest', in Stanley H. Cath, Alan R. Gurwitt, and John Munder Ross (eds.), *Father and Child: Developmental and Clinical Perspectives* (Little, Brown, Boston, 1982), 491–507, esp. 493–4.

Sirach, however, seems closer to the Lacanian model of family relations, which places the phallus as the standard of value, possessed by the father and desired by the daughter, but displaced into law:[92] 'The daughter submits to the father's rule, which prohibits the father's desire, the father's penis, out of the desire to seduce the father by doing his bidding and thus pleasing him.'[93] Even obedience is related to seduction. Sirach would certainly agree with the primacy of the law, embodied in male power and sexuality, and the need for all members of the house, especially the wayward daughter, to come under that phallic authority.[94]

There is a reciprocal relationship between socially/textually constructed notions of sexual desire and socially/textually constructed forms of political authority.[95] In Foucault's words, 'the phenomenon of the social body is the effect not of a consensus but of the materiality of power operating on the very bodies of individuals'.[96] Sirach constructs a family with a strong tension between controlling father and wilful adolescent daughter. Isolation is the only means to prevent the violation entailed by intercourse, yet isolation forms incestuousness. In both, the dominance of the father's law is crucial. The father's power operates on the materiality of the daughter's body, with effects in the social body.

Sirach's concerns with contact between different cultures form the basis of much of his writing. He adopts the form of the Book of Proverbs,

[92] See, for example, Jacques Lacan, 'The Signification of the Phallus', in *Écrits: A Selection* (Norton, New York, 1977), 281–91. Even more to the point would be Lacan's notion of incest as the prohibition of sex with mother or sister (but not daughter) in 'Function and Field of Speech and Language in Psychoanalysis', *Écrits*, 66; Lacan ties the incest prohibition directly to the symbolic rule of the father and thus to the larger issues of symbolic order and the presence of the Law, all connected to the discourse of prohibition and the signification of speech/language/law.

[93] Gallop, *Daughter's Seduction*, 70–1.

[94] In the light of Lacan's emphasis on language, it may be reasonable to assert a relationship between the daughter's silence (especially in relationship to other women) and her coming under the paternal phallus.

[95] Nancy Armstrong and Leonard Tennenhouse, 'The Literature of Conduct, the Conduct of Literature, and the Politics of Desire: An Introduction', in Nancy Armstrong and Leonard Tennenhouse (eds.), *The Ideology of Conduct: Essays on Literature and the History of Sexuality* (Methuen, New York, 1987), 2–3. Note that Sirach combines the male/female and public/private dichotomies and blurs the distinctions into a concentrated discourse of power. This blurring can be found in many other societies as well; see Linda Imray and Audrey Middleton, 'Public and Private: Marking the Boundaries', in Gamarnikow et al. (eds.), *The Public and the Private*, 12–27.

[96] Michel Foucault, 'Body/Power', in *Power/Knowledge: Selected Interviews and Other Writings, 1972–1977*, ed. Colin Gordon (Pantheon, New York, 1980), 55. Not without relevance are Foucault's comments about the control of children's masturbation in 18th-century Europe (pp. 56–7).

notable for its beginning with fears of foreigners and foreign thought, metaphorically described as fear of the female body. Male contact with women must be carefully controlled in Sirach, just as contact with Hellenistic culture must be controlled.[97] Almost all of Sirach's comments about children emphasize the control, even the violence, necessary to raise them up in the traditional Jewish way. The influences of cultural change take root in the actions of the young—a group that attains greater status as a distinct stage of sexual and social development in Greek thought and practice.

Finally, the Book of Sirach concludes with the well-known Hymn to the Ancestors, which praises tradition (Sirach 40–8). In that sense, Proverbs and Sirach form a continuity, to be read together; Sirach may well have been written with conscious reference to the much earlier Book of Proverbs. Proverbs' initial emphasis on the fear of the foreign woman finds its outcome in Sirach's presentation of the Jewish man. Proverbs fears the future when a man encounters a strange woman in the streets; Sirach finds everything of value inside his study, in the past, in ancient men. Despite the similarities of metaphor, Sirach's own position is clear in contrast to Proverbs. Whereas Proverbs maintains an optimism that indigenous culture can triumph over foreign influences, Sirach is an isolationist.

The treatment of the daughter in Sirach reflects the general cultural isolationist attitudes of the book. Sirach faces the seductiveness of something that the culture now values anew, but that his tradition proclaims as forbidden to touch. As Sirach isolates himself from the new Hellenized culture, he isolates the daughter inside the house, and he declares her pristine, despite debaucherous intentions and a lack of self-control in refusing the evil. Of whom does Sirach speak? At the same time that he feels the pull of the new, Hellenistic culture, he hides himself away, locked in the traditions of the past, when all were children, when all were innocent, and no inappropriate thoughts had yet entered pristine minds.

Does Sirach touch the daughter's forbidden body? One never knows. But he does embrace the assumptions of Hellenism, including the perception of adolescent sexuality as a non-adult phenomenon. He partakes of the assumptions and refuses the content, just as he keeps the daughter inside the house, claiming that her sexuality belongs to him. Incest,

---

[97] The metaphorical value of the unattached woman as a signifier of rebellion against cultural constraints (here as a rejection of traditional Jewish culture) is a common theme in many feminist literatures. See Marks, 'Lesbian Intertextuality', 276–8.

whether emotional or physical, results. Interpreters must remember that this is a rhetorically incestuous *text* as well. Sirach's grandson translates the book into Greek so that it can become accessible to a wider audience, since in the intervening years Greek has increasingly become the lingua franca even in Jewish communities of the Diaspora. Although the book was written as a praise of Jewishness against Hellenistic influences, within two generations the text touches the forbidden—and becomes Greek. The prologue commends the book to those who love learning and those who desire the law—now available in a language that the translator admits is not a little different from the words of the fathers.

The control of bodies parallels a desire to control the body politic. Sirach attempts to distance the Greek influences on Jewish culture, including such problematic values as the tripartite construction of sexuality. But Sirach's entry into this discourse points to the (partial) assimilation of Greek cultural values. The text embodies a politics of control and isolation as it entextualizes the control of women's isolated bodies— yet the attraction of intercourse with forbidden temptations is present, engendered in the rhetoric of the body.

5

Austerity, Excess, Success, and Failure in Hellenistic and Early Imperial Italy

EMMA DENCH

MY aim in this chapter is to analyse ancient definitions of ethnic identity and military power by exploring the history of uses of images of austerity and decadence in Hellenistic and Roman Italy. In the moralizing rhetoric of ancient Greece and Rome, decadence, along with traits associated with it, such as lust and lack of self-control, is commonly conceptualized as feminine. Austerity and self-control are most usually identified as desirably masculine virtues defined in opposition to these feminine vices. The identification of moral superiority as masculine explains and justifies the holding of power by males in ancient Graeco-Roman societies, and is supposed to guarantee social, political, and military success. Assertion of the unusual susceptibility of women to luxury, lust, and self-indulgence may in certain contexts indicate their incapability of holding power. In other contexts, however, it indicates the threat that they may pose to the society's success, and their need to be controlled in order to eliminate or minimize this threat. In ancient thought, the feminine sphere is frequently elided with other conceptual categories, such as foreigners, slaves, and animals, which, if uncontrolled, may pose a similar threat to society. These masculine virtues and feminine vices are frequently conceptualized as being written on the body of the individual, in the form of clothing, gesture, sexual behaviour, appetites, and physical activity.[1]

---

[1] J. Davidson, *Courtesans and Fishcakes: The Consuming Passions of Classical Athens* (Harpercollins, London, 1997), esp. 138–82; M. Foucault, *The Use of Pleasure: The History of Sexuality* vol. ii (Eng. trans.; Penguin, London, 1995); T. Barton, *Power and Knowledge: Astrology, Physiognomics, and Medicine under the Roman Empire* (University of Michigan Press, Ann Arbor, 1994), esp. 115–19; C. Edwards, *The Politics of Immorality in Ancient Rome* (Cambridge University Press, Cambridge, 1993), esp. 63–97; M. Gleason, *Making Men: Sophists and Self-Presentation in Ancient Rome* (Princeton University Press, Princeton, 1995). For an excellent general introduction to sociological approaches to the body, see S. Scott and D. Morgan (eds.), 'Bodies in a Social Landscape', in *Body Matters* (Falmer Press, London, 1993), 1–21.

However, in the ancient Graeco-Roman world, even within a single social group and a short chronological period, the application of these constructed categories is neither static nor simple. This is particularly true in times of profound social and political change, such as at the end of the Roman Republic, when tensions between the traditional ideal of an essentially aristocratic system of power shared among the elite, and the newer model of monarchy, are most clearly visible. First, it is important to note that accusations of feminine vices such as decadence are most usually made by and against male members of the Roman elite. The ancient rhetoric of Otherness is sophisticated in its ability to detect attributes of Otherness in the male citizen: the qualities of the female, the foreigner, and even the animal.[2] The rhetoric of female vices is open to an intense degree of manipulation. In the case of the competition for power between Mark Antony and Octavian, the future emperor Augustus, at the end of the Republic, we are fortunate to have preserved both sides of the slanging match. Accusations of effeminacy were made by each side against the other: the rhetoric of feminine vices was both useful and highly adaptable. Thus, for example, Cicero's *Philippics* mount a full-scale attack on the uncontrolled appetites of Antony: his drunkenness, debauchery, and lust.[3] Taunts against Octavian recorded in Suetonius' *Life of Augustus* include generalized effeminacy, the prostitution of his body to Aulus Hirtius, and the depilation of his legs using hot nutshells.[4]

The case of the exchange of insults between Mark Antony and Octavian is particularly interesting. While both sides certainly appealed to the rhetoric of feminine vices in order to discredit the legitimacy of the claims of the other to be a suitable holder of power, other wars of words and images were taking place at the same time but in different contexts. In these different contexts, Mark Antony and Octavian set themselves up as representatives of different models of power. Octavian appropriated for himself the model of power over others legitimized and justified by self-control and austerity, while Mark Antony took for himself the model of flamboyant consumption associated with the Hellenistic ideal of kingship pursued by his consort Cleopatra.[5] Such 'feminine' traits of

---

[2] S. Ortner and H. Whitehead, *Sexual Meanings: The Cultural Construction of Gender and Sexuality* (Cambridge University Press, Cambridge, 1981), 9; Edwards, *Politics*, 24–5; Barton, *Power and Knowledge*, 115.

[3] e.g. 2. 3. 6; 2. 18. 44; 2. 18. 55; 2. 34. 85; 2. 41. 104.

[4] 68.

[5] P. Zanker, *The Power of Images in the Age of Augustus* (Eng. trans.; University of Michigan Press, Ann Arbor, 1988), 33–53; M. Wyke, 'Augustan Cleopatras: Female Power

conspicuous consumption and self-indulgence could be reappropriated as an advertisement of absolute power which was demonstrated by the ability to satisfy one's appetites.

The models appropriated by each side were, of course, portrayed unfavourably by the other. Despite the positive value that was frequently assigned to manly austerity and self-control, one's position in the social and political hierarchy of the competitive world of the Roman elite was constantly open to debate, and the rules of the game were of course never clearly established. Manly austerity was all very well, but the Roman elite in various contexts also wished to pride itself on cultured sophistication (*urbanitas*). One man's austerity could be viewed by another in one context as highly desirable, but in another as the boorishness of a country bumpkin.[6] Mark Antony's model of flamboyant consumption has its roots also in this alternative aspect of the aristocratic male ideal. Rhetoric in this competitive climate is notoriously slippery.

Turning from the portrayal and self-perception of Roman individuals, Roman literature also contains idealized portrayals of Rome, Romanness, and Romans collectively. As holders of an imperial power, Romans collectively, the quality of Romanness they embody, and the city itself are frequently made to embody qualities of manly austerity and self-control. In these cases, the qualities are defined in opposition to the feminine vices of foreign peoples who have been subjected to Roman rule, or who ought to be subjected to Roman rule in the future. Once again, however, these qualities are slippery. For example, in the famous statement of Augustus' boast to have found the city of Rome built of brick, but to have left it built of marble, the language used (*ornatam*), suggests feminine adornment and display.[7] As the capital of empire, Rome is perceived to need elements of flamboyant display. In other contexts, such elements may be interpreted unfavourably, as decadence to be contrasted with a worthy and manly past, or even with the simplicity and manliness of foreigners.

The cases of the ancient Italian societies which I shall discuss in this chapter are peculiarly complex. We are dealing with a number of Greek and non-Greek societies that were highly conscious of these alternative models of power and success rooted in the thought of Athens of the fifth

and Poetic Authority', in A. Powell (ed.), *Roman Poetry and Propaganda in the Age of Augustus* (Bristol Classical Press, Bristol, 1992), 98–140.

[6] E. Ramage, *Urbanitas: Ancient Sophistication and Refinement* (University of Oklahoma Press, Norman, 1973), 52–110; Edwards, *Politics*, 96.

[7] Suet. *Aug.* 28. 3.

century BCE. However, these ancient Italian societies appropriated and adapted these models to a variety of different ends. The military, social, and political environment of Italy between the fourth and first centuries BCE was highly competitive. This competitiveness is visible both between societies and between individuals within a particular society, and at times involved differing conceptions both of the individual successful male body and of the superior body politic as a whole.

1. *Classical Models*

On one level, the use of images of austerity and decadence in the culturally diverse environment of Hellenistic and Roman Italy represents an ethnocentric attempt on the part of Greeks and Romans to project and explain the relative positions of themselves and other peoples within the world by recourse to explanatory frameworks of competition, success, and failure appropriated from classical Athens of the fifth and fourth centuries BCE. However, such classical explanatory frameworks are prone to shift. One obvious example is the idea of *hybris*, which means overstepping the moral, religious, legal, and/or political boundaries set by an individual ancient society in such a way as to cause the humiliation or dishonour of others, incurring the anger and resentment of the victim, and subsequent disaster for the perpetrator.[8] *Hybris* is a trait attendant on successes which are not controlled by moderation, and in consequence those in possession of absolute power and of empires are particularly prone to it: the immoderation of *hybris* associates it closely with the feminine traits of decadent behaviour, or *tryphe*. In other words, success is itself a potentially very dangerous thing, and may carry within it the seeds of its own destruction.[9]

It is also very important to note that different societies appropriated and reinterpreted classical ideology in a number of different ways, according to the individual concerns of each society. In particular, concepts of ethnicity in Hellenistic Italy may not be perceived to carry with them a specifically 'Greek' label. One of the most commonly used figures of thought by means of which to express conflict and superiority in ancient Western cultures is that of the 'barbarian'. In origin, the barbar-

---

[8] I follow here the account given by N. Fisher in '*Hybris* and Dishonour: 1', *Greece and Rome*, 23.2 (1976), 177–93.

[9] In general, J. de Romilly, *The Rise and Fall of States According to Greek Authors* (University of Michigan Press, Ann Arbor, 1977). J. McGlew, *Tyranny and Political Culture in Ancient Greece* (Cornell University Press, Ithaca, NY, 1993), esp. 34.

ian is a Greek invention *par excellence* and the very figure against which fifth-century ideas of Greekness could be articulated. As I have already suggested, in ancient thought, the categories of female and barbarian are frequently elided into a composite Other against which masculine success and power may be articulated. Strikingly and ironically, in Hellenistic Italy, the figure of the 'barbarian' is used in a number of non-Greek contexts, in order to assert the superiority of one non-Greek people over another, or even over Greeks. Given the elision of the categories of female and barbarian, the assignment of gender categories is similarly open to ironic shifts of this kind.

Decadence (*tryphe*) is one persistent model that recurs in classical Greek literature as a means of organizing and explaining how the world is perceived to be, or ought to be: in particular, it is a way of thinking about appropriately masculine behaviour by defining it in opposition to inappropriate decadence. Within the thought of democratic, fifth-century Athens, *tryphe* is the antithesis of masculine self-control, one of the prime characteristics of the enemy whose very flamboyance is an early warning sign of the military disaster that is to follow. Decadence is played out in the form of opulent material possessions, dubious relationships between the sexes, and softness of behaviour manifested in the customs of that society as seen through an Athenian 'grid'.

In the first half of the fifth century, Persia functioned as the primary anti-Athens, and in Aeschylus' *Persians* (first performed in 472 BCE), Persian decadence in the form of a dominant queen, abundant gold, wealth, and despotism seems to anticipate the news of the defeat of the Persian king Xerxes at the hands of the Greek hoplite and naval forces: in the *Persians*, the political dimensions of ethnic self-definition are all-important.[10] Decadence is a particular characteristic of the eastern barbarian of the full-blown fifth-century manifestation, and Greek writers provide a variety of methods to explain this connection. According to one tendency, the world in fifth-century Greek thought is 'mapped' according to the framework of environmental determinism: this ancient theory, which may have its roots in attempts to explain susceptibility to various kinds of disease, supposes that human physique, character, and habits are dependent on the physical environment and climate within which peoples live. Thus, for example, in the late fifth-century

---

[10] E. Hall, *Inventing the Barbarian: Greek Self-Definition through Tragedy* (Clarendon Press, Oxford, 1989); id., 'Asia Unmanned: Images of Victory in Classical Athens', in J. Rich and G. Shipley (eds.), *War and Society in the Greek World* (Routledge, London, 1993), 108–24.

anonymous 'Hippocratic' work *Airs, Waters, Places*, the world is divided up into 'Europe' and 'Asia'. The bracing and changing climate of 'Europe' encourages manly bravery within her inhabitants, while the over-pleasant and stable climate of 'Asia' encourages a corresponding tameness, cowardice, and laziness.[11] 'Environmental determinism' is one of a number of explanatory frameworks suggested by Herodotus in his *Histories* (probably completed in the 430s BCE), a work concerned with tracing the recent Persian Wars from their supposed roots in myths of conflict between East and West, and which is deeply concerned with models of explanation, including the relationship between customs and environment.[12] The work ends enigmatically, after dealing with the Persian defeat, with a 'flashback' of a reported warning to the Persian king Cyrus, the great imperialist, not to exchange their hardy environment for a soft one.[13] The effect of such a change might well convert the success connected with struggle against a tough environment to the decadence and overblown luxury associated with a soft one.

The author of *Airs, Waters, Places*, like some of his contemporaries, however, expresses doubts about whether human characteristics are fixed 'by nature'—in this case at conception—or whether cultural forces can prevail.[14] For other ancient authors, luxury and the closely related trait of *hybris* appear to be more prone to shift. In Herodotus' narrative, for example, luxury seems to be highly contagious, particularly at the moment when a decadent people is conquered: the acquisition of new wealth and attendant lifestyle on the part of the conquerors can cause its own problems. It is surely not accidental that Herodotus attributes to the Persians, whose military defeat at Greek hands forms the climax of the work as a whole, the trait of being peculiarly susceptible to the luxuries (*eupatheiai*) of the peoples they encounter.[15] The Greek word itself is rooted in the notion of receptiveness, that is the antithesis of the success-

---

[11] Ch. 24. NB the Greek term for bravery is *andreia*, a noun which is cognate with *aner* (man as opposed to woman, rather than *anthropos*, human as opposed to god or animal). Similarly, in Latin, *virtus*, manly virtue which includes bravery, is cognate with *vir*, man as opposed to woman. For the latter, see Edwards, *Politics*, 20.

[12] For other forms of explanation, see J. Gould, *Herodotus* (Weidenfeld & Nicolson, London, 1989), ch. 4. For the so-called *nomos/physis* (nurture/nature) debate in later 5th-century Athens, see W. Guthrie, *The History of Greek Philosophy*, iii: *The Fifth-Century Enlightenment* (Cambridge University Press, Cambridge, 1969), 55–134.

[13] Herod. 9. 122. Herodotus implicitly draws contrasts between the reign of Cyrus, under whom empire was acquired, and that of Darius, and above all Xerxes, under whom empire was lost. The idealization of Cyrus will appear in full-blown form in Xenophon's *Cyropaedia*, which may be based on long-standing traditions, both Greek and Persian: see D. Gera, *Xenophon's Cyropaedia: Style, Genre, and Literary Technique* (Clarendon Press, Oxford, 1993), introd.

[14] Ch. 24.

[15] 1. 135.

ful and 'masculine' holding of power through self-control in ancient thought. We learn here that such feminine traits may be acquired through success itself.

The supposed risks of overreaching oneself, and becoming overblown, closely associated with conquest and imperialism, were ones of which classical Greek authors were at times acutely aware, and perhaps no one more so than Thucydides. Through Thucydides' narrative of the Peloponnesian War (which breaks off in the course of the events of 411 BCE) runs a preoccupation with tyranny. Traditionally in Athenian thought, tyranny functioned as a useful counterpoint to democracy, the tyrant representing on an individual scale all the dangers of power unmoderated and an accompanyingly overblown lifestyle. The tyrant is characterized by his cruelty, display and consumption of luxury goods, and by sexual lust. The immoderation and lack of self-control of the tyrant places him, in classical Athenian thought, within the female sphere. It is, however, possible to view the flamboyance of the tyrant in a more positive light as an alternative model of power through the involvement of the advertisement of superiority through conspicuous consumption, and the unreined indulgence of appetites.

The tyrant of Greece's past enjoys a close association in behaviour with the present 'oriental' despot, and the glorious defeat of the last of Athens' tyrants is as much a turning-point as is the defeat of the barbarian in her collective mythology of democracy. Within Thucydides' narrative, however, awkward questions are raised about the convenient oppositions of tyranny/despotism on the one hand, and democracy on the other.[16] For Thucydides, there are problems with the received view of the glorious end of tyranny at Athens: the incident is, in his view, little more than a lovers' tiff that misfired, since Harmodius and Aristogeiton set out to destroy not Hippias the actual tyrant, but his brother Hipparchus.[17] Thucydides goes considerably further: one important underlying idea within his narrative as a whole is that the Athenian Empire has itself become a tyranny, with all the implicit risks of *hybris* and subsequent political disaster.[18]

Even in fifth-century Athens, then, ascriptions of female luxury and decadence are subject to shifts. One further area of tension in fifth-

---

[16] McGlew, *Tyranny and Political Culture*, 124–56; cf. N. Loraux, *The Children of Athena: Athenian Ideas about Citizenship and the Division between the Sexes*, trans. C. Levine (Princeton University Press, Princeton, 1993), 155.

[17] Thucydides 6. 53–9.

[18] e.g. 3. 37 for Cleon's speech on Mytilene; cf. C. Macleod, 'Thucydides and Tragedy', in *Collected Papers* (Oxford University Press, Oxford, 1983), 140–58.

century Athenian thought on ethnicity and political success concerns conceptualizations of Sparta, whose chequered relationship with Athens had led in 431 BCE to the outbreak of the Peloponnesian War, which Athens eventually lost in 404, suffering in addition the imposition of a Spartan-backed oligarchic regime. One of the strands of traditional Athenian thought about the Spartans makes them the epitome of austerity and self-control. Sparta's reputation for having a highly disciplined and well-ordered society, resistant to tyranny, could make her the antithesis of 'Asiatic' luxury, or even of the Ionians, who supposedly came from the same stock as Athens.[19]

In other contexts, Sparta could become the authoritarian 'Other' against which to set Athens, the latter being supposedly representative of openness, freedom, and, above all, moderation through the avoidance of excess. Thucydides puts into the mouth of Pericles, in his famous 'funeral speech', a praise of Athens that implicitly attacks the ways of Sparta in such terms.[20] Sparta's self-consciously archaic and aristocratic outlook could look conservative in the extreme to late fifth- and fourth-century Athenians, while the difference between their socio-political environments led to an ideological tendency to push Sparta into the mental category of tyranny.[21] Athenian authors were also interested in ascribing meaning to the different economic and social position of women in Sparta: ancient ethnographical interest frequently focused on relations between the sexes as an important means of characterizing and interpreting Otherness.[22] Hence, the rights of Spartan women to inherit and own property could be construed as a sign of a decadent society, in contrast with the very restricted economic role of women in classical Athens.[23]

Nevertheless Sparta's military success, and her very different social and political organization, also meant that she had keen admirers in Athens, not least the Laconizing Critias, a prominent member of the Spartan-backed junta of 404 BCE, who praised the self-restraint of

---

[19] For this and what follows, see E. Rawson, *The Spartan Tradition in European Thought* (Clarendon Press, Oxford, 1969), chs. 1–7.

[20] 2. 37–41.

[21] e.g. Aristophanes' *Wasps*, *passim*.

[22] Cf. for Herodotus' interest in such matters, M. Rossellini and S. Said, 'Usages des femmes et autres nomoi chez les "sauvages" d'Hérodote', *Annali della Scuola Normale Superiore di Pisa*, series 3, 8.3 (1978), 94–105.

[23] Most famously, Aristotle, *Pol.* 1269ᵃ, with P. Cartledge, 'Spartan Wives: Liberation or Licence?', *CQ* 31 (1981), 84 ff.; cf. Plato, *Laws* 7. 806c. For Spartan female prominence more favourably construed under the early Roman Empire, see the much later collection of uplifting stories in Plutarch, *Mor.* 240c–242d.

the Spartans, exemplified by their *syssitia*, or simple 'common meals'.[24] The most famous classical treatise on Sparta is, of course, the *Constitution of the Lacedaemonians*, attributed to Xenophon, with its heavy emphasis on the order and physical training of Spartan men and women alike. The association between the physical training of male bodies and political success is found frequently in ancient thought. However, the interest of fourth-century Athenian philosophical writers in the ideal of the physical training of female bodies is striking. For example, Plato in the *Republic* imagines that both music and gymnastic training are appropriate for the wives of the guardians, those judged most fit to rule his ideal state. Such women will thus be fit to play their role in warfare and guardianship of the state. This training and these duties are adapted from those appropriate to the men of this class, to take into account the supposed greater weakness of the women.[25] This interest in the physical training of women seems to be related to a growing fascination with non-democratic political systems within which public and private spheres were much more blurred than they were in classical Athens. Divisions between the public, masculine sphere of power-holding, and the private, feminine sphere were far from clear-cut in such societies. We can see authors grappling with the problem of delineating roles for 'good' women, and for the 'good', healthy, non-democratic body politic as a whole.[26] What we find is the application of carefully adapted models of traditionally masculine self-control, physical exertion, and hard work to create such roles.

2. Hellenistic Italy

The various societies in the western Mediterranean were to reinterpret the ideology of the barbarian in a number of different ways. One striking aspect of classical and Hellenistic Greek self-definition is the multitude of experiences among the Greek cities which were represented through the rhetoric of superiority to the barbarian. Major differences occurred in

[24] Frr. 6–9 (Diels–Kranz).

[25] 5. 453–7; cf. *Laws* 7. 804d–e.

[26] Ischomachos' training of his wife, as portrayed in Xenophon's *Oeconomicus*, is an interesting example of the application of the ideal of female self-control, hard work, and physical exercise within an imagined classical Athenian context, where the wife is emphatically located within the house. The use of political metaphors applied to this internal context is striking: e.g. the wife is said to be the *nomophylax* of the household (9. 15). Cf. S. Pomeroy, *Xenophon* Oeconomicus: *A Social-Historical Commentary* (Clarendon Press, Oxford, 1994), 33–9.

the relationships between individual Greek cities and non-Greek peoples, especially in the case of the Greek colonies, whose survival was, broadly speaking, generally dependent in terms of economy and/or manpower on dealings with non-Greek peoples. Fifth-century Athenian use of the ideology of the barbarian as a figure by means of which hegemony could be claimed and the benefits of democracy asserted is one part of a much larger picture: within the Greek world much more broadly defined, opposition to the barbarian seems to have become something like a necessary condition for the proclamation of one's polis as part of the civilized world. In addition, and paradoxically, it will later emerge that claims of superiority to the barbarian were not restricted to communities which were of Greek foundation, or which could remotely have passed for Greek in the eyes of the Greeks themselves.

Despite the importance of the rhetoric of superiority over the barbarian among Greek and non-Greek peoples alike, the conceptualization of the relationship between selves and barbarians is not always a simple one. For southern Italy in the late fourth and third centuries BCE, the tastes of Macedon were a great inspiration. The eastern conquests of Alexander the Great reawakened interest in the orientalized styles of clothing and decoration associated with the Eastern barbarian. These tastes have left their mark on the material culture of southern Italy of this period, and vase-painting in particular is an important indication of the tastes of the Greek elites.

Depictions of Persians were particularly in vogue in southern Italy during the decades after Alexander's Eastern conquests, as can be seen in the famous case of the Darius painter's large volute-crater (Naples 3253) found at Canosa, which shows the conflict between Persia and Hellas as a three-tier concept, the divine sphere at the top, human rule in the middle, and vassals at the bottom. Reading the vase vertically, one can see the protection of Hellas by Athene, while Asia is lured to her doom by a Fury. The Persian king Darius himself sits in full 'oriental' costume directly underneath Zeus, while the vassals in the differentiated dress of particular parts of Persia grovel before the king. In so doing, they perform the gesture of flattening the body on the ground before superiors that so fascinated Greek audiences, and which was associated with the despotic regime of Persia, as opposed to the masculine and free conduct of Athens.[27] In the case of such sumptuously executed material objects,

[27] A. D. Trendall and A. Cambitoglou, *The Red-Figured Vases of Apulia*, ii: *Late Apulian* (Oxford University Press, Oxford, 1982), 495, and pl. 176.1; E. D. Francis, *Image and Idea in Fifth-Century Greece: Art and Literature after the Persian Wars*, ed. M. Vickers (Routledge,

one is struck forcibly by the aesthetic enjoyment that was presumably gained from depictions of such barbarian 'Otherness'. The rhetoric of superiority over barbarian sumptuousness engages its speakers and listeners in sumptuous depictions of it.[28]

More tantalizing is a later fourth-century series of helmets of largely southern Italian and Etruscan provenance. The sort of decorative work used on the helmets—particularly lines of hair, motifs of leaves (especially acanthus leaves), and masks—has long been associated with Tarentine craftsmen. The shape of the helmet is a Phrygian bonnet, an imitation in metal of the soft-pointed caps which are traditionally depicted as the headgear of Persians and peoples to the north-east of Greece. Finds both of actual metal helmets and of depictions of them suggest that they were particularly in vogue in Macedon, and it is apparently from Macedon that the fashion spread to southern Italy.[29] The appearance of some of the helmets of Tarentine production in non-Greek funerary contexts would suggest that some of these helmets were either worn or used ritually by non-Greek peoples. The significance of the helmets for the wearers or users themselves is hard to determine, whether in the case of the non-Greeks of southern Italy, or the Macedonians. Even if the Greekness of the Macedonians was open to speculation in some quarters at least, it seems to stretch belief to suggest that their wearing of the Phrygian bonnet-type helmet was an advertisement of their dubious ethnic identity and the effeminacy that was associated with it.

It is similarly important not to jump to conclusions about the southern Italian versions of the helmet. As I shall try to show in the course of this chapter, shifts of meaning are particularly characteristic of the Hellenistic world. Continuity of classical terminology does not necessarily imply a continuity of meaning. In the post-classical world, the wearing of the Phrygian helmet seems unlikely to have been supposed to signify the effeminacy of its warrior wearer or user, but might perhaps be an attempt to harness the terror inspired by barbarian cruelty, like the portrayal of Medusa on a shield. As always, in ancient definitions of gender and ethnicity, the context is all-important, and it may well have been possible to appropriate one feature of the barbarian and use it within the assertive

London, 1990), 36–9; H. Metzger, 'A propos des images apuliennes de la bataille d'Alexandre et du conseil de Darius', *REG* 80 (1967), 308–13.

[28] Cf. Edwards, *Politics*, 204 on the moralizing rhetoric of the Roman Empire.

[29] A. Adam, 'Remarques sur une série de bronze ou Tarente et les Barbares dans la deuxième moitié du IV s. av. J.-C.', *MEFRA* 94 (1982), 7–32.

self-image of the warrior. Alternatively, the wearing or use of Phrygian helmets might have been directed at social distinction within the group, an advertisement of the exotic and fashionable taste of the wearer that appealed to models of distinction other than those of self-control and austerity. As we have seen in the case of elite rhetoric at the end of the Roman Republic, appropriately masculine behaviour might involve a complex combination of display and restraint that was always open to challenge.

Elsewhere in Hellenistic Italy, the familiar iconography of superiority over the barbarian seems at first sight to be used in a more straightforward manner. A late fourth-century series of vases from Arpi, an Oscan-speaking community in the plainland to the east of the Samnite mountains of the Central Apennines, depicts familiar scenes of conflict with the barbarian, the latter being portrayed in the losing position. However, close analysis of the costumes worn by the respective parties reveals these to be no standard scenes of Greeks conquering Eastern barbarians. In the clearest examples, the barbarian role is played rather by figures dressed in costume familiar from other parts of Oscan-speaking Italy: the 'anatomical' cuirass that imitates the naked male chest; the helmet with its high, resplendent plumes. The corresponding conquering figure seems to be wearing characteristically Roman battledress: the button-top helmet and greaves. The conquering Greek has become a Roman, the conquered barbarian a Samnite. Looking at this case in isolation, it is hard to read the nuances of these paintings; to know, for example, if the Samnite barbarian carried associations of the softness, luxury, and decadence that were associated in Greek thought with the Eastern barbarian.[30]

In this context, however, Livy's narrative of the Samnite Wars is suggestive. While one of the layers of Livy's account is undoubtedly early Augustan, the detection of late fourth-century structures is plausible, and accords well with the series of vases from Arpi.[31] In Livy's account of the wars between the Romans and Samnites, there is great emphasis on the resplendence of the Samnites' battledress, which the Roman general is made to contrast with the plain, serviceable character of that worn by

[30] M. Mazzei, 'Nota su un gruppo di vasi policromi con scene di combattimento, da Arpi (FG)', *AION* 9 (1987), 167–88; cf. E. Curti, E. Dench, and J. R. Patterson, 'The Archaeology of Central and Southern Roman Italy: Recent Trends and Approaches', *JRS* 86 (1996), 170–89, at 184.
[31] A. Rouveret, 'Tite-Live, *Histoire romaine* ix, 40: La Description des armées samnites ou les pièges de la symétrie', in A. Adam and A. Rouveret (eds.), *Guerre et sociétés en Italie (V–IV s. avant J.-C.)* (École Normale Supérieure, Paris, 1986), 91–120.

the Roman army.[32] There are similar Roman literary traditions concerning the Sabines, conquered at the same time as the Samnites, and in later thought closely associated with them. Despite a strong later tradition of the Sabines as being of exemplary moral character and discipline, the antiquarian tradition preserved alternative constructions of their ethnic identity. Most notable is the Augustan Dionysius of Halicarnassus' claim that Fabius Pictor, the first Roman historian, had said that the Sabines during the Regal period wore rings and bracelets, a sign for the Romans of their effeminate lifestyle, comparable with that of the Etruscans.[33] In Graeco-Roman literature, the Etruscans are portrayed as being notoriously decadent.[34] I believe that this is largely an interpretation of the Etruscans' highly stratified society, and of the modes of elite self-advertisement within that society.

One explanation of the Livian account of Samnite arms might be that it is an exaggerated form of real difference. There is no surviving evidence of the use of gold or silver in Samnite armour, but vase- and tomb-painting would certainly suggest a taste for resplendent dress in the form of the ornate cuirasses and plumed helmets I mentioned above. What this dress meant in a Samnite context we do not really know, but the overtones are likely to have been very different from those in Livy's account. Tomb-paintings from Oscan-speaking Paestum suggest that such dress, along with the depiction of the individual on horseback, indicated the elite masculine ideal of the young warrior within this society. His success in warfare is not infrequently shown by the portrayal of enemy spoils carried home on his lance, sometimes graphically bloodied. The ideal of the young warrior seems to have been one role within a society that self-consciously ordained a number of roles for other individuals within the family, or groups within the body politic. Women are assigned a prominent ritual role, particularly in relation to the returning warrior: they are frequently shown offering him a libation. The indications are that this is a society that is concerned with clearly delineated gendered roles, as well as appropriate roles for young and old men respectively.[35] There is a mismatch here between Roman portrayal of effeminate barbarians, and an apparent portrayal of selves as

---

[32] 10. 39. 16, cf. 9. 40, where the Samnite arms are described in detail.

[33] *Ant. Rom.* 2. 38=Fabius Pictor fr. 8 (P.)=Cincius fr. 5 (P.).

[34] e.g. Athenaeus, *Table Talk* 12. 517d–518b for their sexual immodesty and drinking habits; 4. 153d for sumptuous Etruscan dinner-parties, complete with nude waitresses.

[35] E. Dench, *From Barbarians to New Men: Greek, Roman, and Modern Perceptions of Peoples from the Central Apennines* (Clarendon Press, Oxford, 1995), 64–6.

belonging to a restrained and well-ordered body politic on the part of the Oscan-speaking Paestans.

The ideology of superiority over the barbarian, however, represented only one of a number of frames for conceptualizing relations between peoples in the complex cultural world of southern Italy. There are also stories centred on late fourth-century BCE Tarentum of an 'invention of tradition' which constructs close links between Tarentum and her Oscan-speaking neighbours, the Samnites. Some of these traditions are explicitly linked with Aristoxenos of Tarentum, a philosopher who defined himself as Pythagorean, and who apparently wrote a hagiographical account of Archytas of Tarentum, who had lived a generation before Aristoxenos.[36] Traditions explicitly linked with Aristoxenos, and others which are similar in theme, seem to have operated both for internal purposes within Tarentum and among other Italian peoples, and for external purposes, as a way to characterize relationships between the Tarentines and non-Greek peoples of southern Italy. These themes, associated with a southern Italian brand of Pythagoreanism, often revolve around the strict regulation of individual, elite behaviour—these are aristocratic themes for aristocratic societies— and the successful running of the state, set up in opposition to behaviour that is to be avoided. Ideal behaviour involves the avoidance of *tryphe* (decadence) and tyranny, the preservation of self-sufficiency, and the promotion of austerity, accompanied by the denial of pleasure.[37] In other words, ideal behaviour involves all the hard attributes traditionally associated with successful, masculine power-holding in antiquity. While this masculine ideal is at times appropriated to project the success of Tarentum as a whole, on an individual level, the good general is idealized: it is the philosopher general Archytas, a symbol of the golden age of Tarentine independence, in whom such values are embodied. For Tarentum herself, this projection of collective self-control is meant to recall that of her mother-city, Sparta: this is a good example of the appropriation of earlier ideology to serve the specific needs of a later society.

[36] For a fuller account of Pythagoreanism in Tarentum, see Dench, *Barbarians*, 53–61, with references. I allude to the collection of essays in E. Hobsbawm and T. Ranger (eds.), *The Invention of Tradition* (Cambridge University Press, Cambridge, 1983).

[37] For inscriptions relating to the self-representation of south Italian Pythagoreans, with emphasis on the delineation of female virtue through chastity and unadorned clothing, see H. Thesleff (ed.), *The Pythagorean Texts of the Hellenistic Period* (Åbo Akademi, Åbo, 1965), 151–4; cf. V. Lamprodopoulou, 'Some Pythagorean Female Virtues', in R. Hawley and B. Levick (eds.), *Women in Antiquity: New Assessments* (Routledge, London, 1995), 122–34.

For late fourth-century Tarentum, however, these austere values embodied in the general Archytas are contextualized explicitly within a contemporary environment and opposed to the hedonistic atmosphere of Syracuse, ruled by tyrants and bound for disaster. This opposition is a reminder that southern Italy at this time is a world that is both highly competitive, and in turmoil, set in an age of shifting alliances not just involving the Greek cities themselves, but also the powerful non-Greek peoples of Italy.[38] In the case of late fourth-century Tarentum, one of the major problems it faced was the growing power of two competing non-Greek peoples, the Latin-speaking Romans and the Oscan-speaking Samnites, both apparently well versed in forming relationships with the Greek cities of southern Italy.

The Augustan geographer Strabo tells us about a Tarentine fiction relating to these years—that the Samnites themselves were descended from Spartans and even numbered among themselves 'Pitanates', a supposed force of Spartan crack troops whose historicity was doubted even in antiquity.[39] As ethnographical proof of this relationship, Strabo gives the example of the supposedly remarkable Spartanate custom of marrying off the 'best' Samnite man to the 'best' Samnite woman. This is another example of ancient ethnographical interest in the sexual relationships of their subjects. Given the importance in Graeco-Roman thought of gender roles as an indication of both ethnic identity and political, military, and social success, such information is of great significance. In this case, such a marriage custom is presumably meant to say something about the desirable regulation of sexual relations by the society as a whole, with concern for the maintenance of a strict social hierarchy. It is well worth noting the significance of the 'best' woman here, who is given a weight equal to that of the 'best' man. As in the case of the idealized versions of Spartan customs that this detail is clearly meant to recall, ancient thought is addressing the issue of a social structure and social and political ideals unlike those of classical, democratic Athens. The blurring of public and private spheres within this aristocratic society and the greater visibility of women outside a strictly secluded environment appear to require in this case a careful delineation of these female roles through the adaptation of traditionally masculine ideals of austerity and self-control.

It is probably also to the late fourth century that we should date the

---

[38] See, especially, N. Purcell, 'South Italy in the Fourth Century BC', in *Cambridge Ancient History*, vol. vi (Cambridge University Press, Cambridge, 2nd edn., 1994), 381–403.

[39] 5. 4. 12=p. 250 C; cf. Thuc. 1. 20 *contra* Herod. 9. 53.

attribution of Spartan practices and values to other peoples supposedly related to the Samnites, including the Sabines, Lucanians, and Oenotri: the latter, believed to be a prehistoric southern Italian people, were even thought to have held common meals in the Spartan tradition.[40] As we have already seen, such common meals were constructed in idealizing classical Athenian thought as an indication of the self-restraint and austerity of a society that collectively displayed features of a positive, masculine model of political and military power. It seems clear that the Tarentines were resorting to an ideological device not uncommon in Graeco-Roman antiquity, the invention of shared origins backed up by proofs of shared customs, which survive in the form of these ethnographical snippets about Samnitic peoples which concentrate on their supposed Spartan austerity and the strict regulation of relations between the sexes.

In addition, the origins of hagiographical traditions which centred on the Samnite 'wise man' Pontius Herennius, another philosopher leader in the southern Italian Pythagorean ideological tradition, should be related to this environment. He is the father of the general who defeated the Romans at the Caudine Forks, and is a figure closely associated with Archytas in ancient literary accounts.[41]

In brief, if this particular brand of austerity functioned internally within Tarentine ideology as an apparent advertisement of masculine power and success, the ascription of such values, alongside Spartan origins, to the Samnites may be explained partly in terms of a desire to put a favourable gloss upon the Tarentine use of Samnite manpower to supplement their fighting forces. While non-Greek mercenaries were in fact used widely in Hellenistic Italy,[42] as indeed in other parts of the Hellenistic world, in ideological terms their use is fraught with dangers, being associated with decadence and lack of independence, that is precisely the kinds of vices against which late fourth-century Tarentum set itself up. Use of Samnite military manpower by the Tarentines is thus constructed as a brotherhood of two austere groups, rather than as the importation of men to fight for a lush society incapable of fighting for itself.

Interestingly enough there are also signs of non-Greek peoples pro-

---

[40] Lucanians: Justin 23. 1. 3–7; Oenotri: Aristotle *Pol.* 7. 10. 1329[b]; Sabines: Dionysius of Halicarnassus, *Ant. Rom.* 2. 49. 2=Cato, *Orig.* 2. 21 (ed. M. Chassignet (Budé, Paris, 1986)).

[41] Cicero, *de senectute* 41.

[42] G. Tagliamonte, *I figli di Marte: Mobilità, mercenari e mercenariato italici in Magna Grecia e Sicilia* (Bretschneider, Rome, 1994).

moting images of austerity for their own ends. For example, it appears that the Samnites themselves during the course of the fourth century BCE might have been regulating expenditure over burials. At least there is an increasingly noticeable decline in the quantity and quality of goods placed within tombs during this period, a decline that cannot be explained simply by reference to a generalized economic decline.[43] In the famous painted chamber-tombs of Oscan-speaking Paestum, from around the mid-fourth century, there are indications of an iconographic emphasis on a particular variety of female virtue. Paestan women are not infrequently represented as working wool, or riding in the style of Roman *matronae* in a mule-cart. In the contemporary iconography of their near-neighbours, the Campanians, in contrast, women tend to be portrayed attending to their appearance—holding a mirror, for example—or relaxing with a flower or a bird in their hands.[44] Within these Campanian portraits, female self-interest and leisure seem to be held up as an ideal. The contrasting Paestan and Campanian representations of idealized female behaviour appear to act as a vehicle for their differentiation from their neighbours.

3. *Republican and Augustan Rome*

Traditions relating to Rome during the period of her wars with the Samnites suggest that the Romans too promoted their own austerity, and it is in the Roman context that the competitive aspect of this austerity is most clearly apparent. Traditions abound concerning contemporary Roman interest in Pythagoreanism, both individually and collectively. This interest should be understood within the broader context of southern Italian Pythagorean interest in idealized behaviour of individuals and societies. 'During the Samnite War', according to Pliny the Elder, the Romans set up statues to Pythagoras and the Athenian general Alcibiades in the assembly, as 'the best and wisest of the Greeks'.[45] Worthy sayings and doings of these men were preserved in later collections, suggesting the intensity of Roman promotion of images of their own austerity in the

[43] W. Johannowsky, 'Il Sannio', in *Italici in Magna Grecia: Lingue, insediamenti e strutture* (Edizioni Osanna, Venosa, 1990), 13–21.

[44] A. Rouveret and A. Pontrandolfo Greco, 'Pittura funeraria in Lucania e Campania: Puntualizzazioni cronologiche e proposte di lettura', in *Ricerche di pittura ellenistica: Lettura e interpretazione pittorica dal IV secolo a.C. all'ellenismo* (Quaderni dei Dialoghi di Archeologia, Rome, 1985), 91–100, 103.

[45] *NH* 34. 26. Pliny does not tell us which Samnite War is meant. On all this, see F. Zevi, 'Considerazioni sull'elogio di Scipione Barbato', *St. Misc.* 15 (1970), 65–73.

middle Republic. The fact that Plutarch collected Roman, as well as Spartan, pithy sayings (*apophthegmata*) is more than a coincidence. Most famous of all is Manius Curius Dentatus, conqueror of Sabines and Samnites, whose legendary austerity seems to have been reinvented in a number of generations.[46] In one uplifting version, he is surprised by the Samnites on his small and simple estate while eating turnips from a plain, earthenware plate. According to tradition, he refused the Samnites' bribe of gold, 'because he would rather be the conqueror of those who had the gold than have the gold himself'.[47] The connection between bodily austerity and gaining the military upper hand is made explicit, while there is an implied corollary: the connection between having flamboyant material possessions (particularly gold) and military failure. Another 'famous saying' associated with Manius Curius is also suggestive: he was meant to have made a terrible boast on the extent of his conquest of the Sabines, in terms of both men and land. It is tempting to read this Roman tradition as the hybristic boast of the conqueror who has over reached the boundaries of both individual and society, inviting the doom attendant on the acquisition of empire.[48]

The ideological climate of second-century Rome was rather different. Contemporary and near-contemporary sources suggest that, towards the middle of the century, a Roman sense of having achieved a world empire was being associated with the kinds of perils that are familiar from the earlier classical Greek context.[49] In particular, focus on the moral and social problems of the Roman elite, resulting from the acquisition of empire, is best illustrated by Polybius' vignette of the dissipated and self-indulgent behaviour of the peers of the young Scipio Aemilianus, summed up by a remark plausibly attributed to the Elder Cato in a public speech, namely that the world had really started going downhill when pretty boys and caviar reached higher prices than farm equipment.[50] One should note here the mental link between consumption of luxury food and conspicuous sexual consumption that we have observed also in the appetites traditionally ascribed to the tyrant in classical Athenian thought. There are indications that pretty boys were primarily problematic to some Romans in so far as they were regarded as a luxurious import, alongside such other goods as fancy foodstuffs and furniture.

[46] See esp. Plutarch, *Apophthegmata M. Curii*.
[47] Val. Max. 4. 3. 5; cf. Pliny, *NH* 19. 87; Plutarch, *Cato Maior* 2; Cicero, *de senectute* 55.
[48] Dio fr. 37. 1.
[49] For a more detailed discussion of ideological developments in 2nd- and 1st-century Rome, see Dench, *Barbarians*, 67–108.
[50] 31. 25.

Cato's perception of ideal, successful behaviour among the Roman elite entails the condemnation of luxury in the form of the fruits of conquest.[51]

It is against this background that we find the very beginnings of the location of images of continence outside the city of Rome, the construction of a moral alternative to the perceived contemporary decadence that has accompanied the acquisition of empire. At times this moral alternative is not set geographically with any precision, but rather delineated by means of suitable physical activity, activity of a strenuous and non-indulgent kind being the key. In the work of the Elder Cato, we have, however, the tentative beginnings of the long history of the location of moral excellence within the Sabine countryside. Defeated and subsequently enfranchised by Rome, the Sabines came to lose their barbarian, luxurious aspect in Roman eyes. Their remaining hint of distinctness and outsider quality no longer a threat, they were treated within Roman ideology as a sub-group of Rome within which moral excellence could conveniently be located.[52] Already in a fragment of a speech by Cato the Elder, the Sabine landscape had been converted into an unequivocally rough one, a suitable environment for *parsimonia*, *duritia*, and *industria* ('frugality, hardness, and hard work').[53]

The ideology of 'new men', in its Ciceronian and Sallustian manifestations, is in many ways a direct inheritance from second-century ideological traditions: the case of the Sabines had essentially provided a model for the self-perception and self-promotion of Roman senators who did not come from Roman 'noble' families, and of the new Roman upper classes formed from the mass enfranchisement of Italians after the Social War. *Novus homo* ('new man'), like the *nobilis* ('noble') with whom he is implicitly or explicitly contrasted, is a social not a legal term, and its meaning consequently changes according to context. In some contexts, a 'new man' is someone whose family has not yet produced a consul, while in others he is someone whose family has not yet produced a praetor. 'New man' ideology entails the advertisement of values defined against those ascribed to the 'noble'. In 'new man' ideology, the 'noble' is

---

[51] One needs to be careful about describing Cato's attitude as a concern primarily to distinguish Romans from Greeks: it is what the Romans do with the profits of empire that is given most emphasis in contemporary accounts. The best account of Cato's complex attitude to Greek culture is still to be found in A. Astin, *Cato the Censor* (Oxford University Press, Oxford, 1978), 157–81.

[52] Dench, *Barbarians*, 90–2.

[53] Festus, p. 350 L.=H. Malcovati (ed.), *Oratorum Romanorum Fragmenta* (4th edn., 1976), no. 8, 128.

ascribed all the decadent and self-indulgent traits with which we are now familiar from our analysis of ancient concepts of effeminacy.[54] Hence the 'noble' is supposed, in the speech attributed to Marius by Sallust, to indulge his physical appetites by hiring specialized chefs, and to get his knowledge of battles from books. In contrast Marius, the 'new man', stresses his taste for exacting physical exercise, alertness, and vigilance.[55] There were other sides to the argument, however, as worthy 'new man' ideology could be perceived by the *nobiles*, or even by fellow 'new men', as nothing less than rusticity, and the perceived failure to live up to the flamboyant standards of urbanity judged reprehensible. The writings of Cicero, himself a 'new man' happy to reinvent himself and his friends, protégés, and enemies according to the requirements of the individual context, suggest the complexity and competitiveness of self-definition among the Roman elite.[56]

The Samnites had suffered at the hands of Sulla as retribution for their support of Marius, and it is not until the Augustan age that both the first Samnite senator is attested, and the Samnites and neighbouring tribes who had also been at the forefront of war against Rome in 91–89 BCE appear in idealized contexts. Like the Sabines before them, it was only after their defeat and incorporation as a sub-group within the Roman citizenship that these peoples could be made to embody values that the Romans themselves were considered to have lost. The concept of the importance of the strength and quality of the military manpower of the ex-rebel tribes is of particular ideological importance in early imperial literature: the threat, both real and apparent, that this manpower had once posed to Rome was now lost, the Italians' military strength appearing both as safely incorporated within Rome, but also as an alternative to the perceived decadence of the contemporary urban population.[57]

The major theme of Horace's *Odes* 3. 6, written in the early Augustan period, is the connection between military success or failure and lifestyle. Contemporary Rome is portrayed as militarily weak overseas and ridden with civil faction at home; there is an explicit connection between moral

---

[54] For the term, P. Brunt, '*Nobilitas* and *novitas*', *JRS* 72 (1982), 1–17; more generally, T. P. Wiseman, *New Men in the Roman Senate 139 BC–AD 14* (Clarendon Press, Oxford, 1971).

[55] *Jugurtha* 85.

[56] For Ciceronian notions of the *urbanitas* of himself and his friends, see Ramage, *Urbanitas*, 52–64. Clodius' public assessment of Cicero was somewhat different, however: 'What would a man from Arpinum want with hot water?', he allegedly asked (Cicero, *ad Atticum* 1. 16); cf. also Edwards, *Politics*, 201 for a discussion of the exaggerated self-conscious frugality of Piso.

[57] Dench, *Barbarians*, 106–7.

misbehaviour (*culpa*) and near disaster on a collective scale. The prime example of misbehaviour is an adulterous woman, schooled in sexual excess, including 'Ionic movements', her husband turning a blind eye to her erotic adventures:

The maiden, ripe for plucking, delights to be taught Ionic movements and is trained in the arts of love even now, and imagines affairs unrestrained by decency, quivering with sensation from fingertips to toes. Soon, she seeks out younger lovers at her husband's drunken revels, nor is she choosy about the target for her illicit pleasures, doing it quickly with the lights out. She gets up brazenly in front of her husband, whoever it is who bids her, whether he be a pedlar, or the captain of a Spanish ship, a spendthrift purchaser of shame. (vv. 21–32; my translation)

This disgraceful scene is contrasted with a 'flashback' to the great days of Roman military success in the third and early second centuries BCE:

Not from such parents as these were born the youth who fouled the sea with Punic blood, and brought low Pyrrhus, and Antiochus the Great, and terrible Hannibal, but the masculine offspring of country soldiers were they, taught to turn the clods of earth with Sabellian hoes, and to carry home hewn logs to please their strict mother. (vv. 37–44)

There are striking connections here between military success, a rustic, non-urban Sabellian landscape, the masculine austerity of the soldiers, and the austere but influential role of the mother. Underpinning the contrast between these two vignettes is the moral ideal of self-restraint and avoidance of excess that is a central feature of classical Greek and Hellenistic thought about 'masculine' behaviour and the prerequisites for power or good rule.

Despite the continuity of themes here, it is nevertheless important to emphasize the socio-specific aspects of Horace's poem. One aspect of Horace's poem that is very 'Roman' is the Italian landscape within which the idealized scene is set, in contrast with the foreign—specifically Ionic—elements of the scene of decadence. It is in the late Republic and early Augustan age, two or three generations after the Social War which had led to the enrolment into the Roman citizenship of all the peoples of peninsular Italy, that there is a proliferation of uses of Italy and Italians within ideologically laden contexts. There is, above all, a good deal of emphasis on the austere moral lifestyle of the Italians. Once again, in Roman ideology regarding Italy, we can observe a close connection between morally upright lifestyles and the healthy body politic as exemplified in the military and political spheres. In general terms, this idealization of Italian morality is a way of thinking about a newly exten-sive Roman identity. Italy in Roman thought functions not least as a vast 'rustic' environment which can be used in certain contexts to provide an austere contrast to and commentary on the contemporary decadence of Rome.

In early Augustan ideology, this emphasis on Italian moral superiority, and the military and political success that was linked with it, was to gain impetus. Such an idealization of Italy is crucial in the portrayal of the Battle of Actium as a conflict between Octavian, who could be seen as a 'new man' and representative of Italian values,[58] and the effeminate Antony dominated by the exaggeratedly Eastern queen Cleopatra. Sig-nificantly, much seems to have been made at around this time of Antony's appropriation of Asiatic style, including his Asiatic rhetorical style, in contrast with the self-conscious restraint of the future Augustus' own style. The negative assessment of Asianism has deep roots in the negative classical Athenian assessment of Ionianism that I mentioned above. As we frequently observe in Graeco-Roman antiquity, the rhe-torical style makes the man, or, as in this case, less of a man. Ancient authors describe prose style in explicitly sexual terms: for Dionysius of Halicarnassus, the Attic style played the respectable woman to the Asiatic style's whore. Antony's appropriation of this flamboyant style of present-ing himself becomes in the rhetoric of his enemies an indication of his receptive, un-Italian nature.[59]

In Horace's poem, it is highly significant that the 'Sabellian' landscape of idealized behaviour in the middle Republic is an ethnic name that is an artificial amalgam of Sabines and Samnites, which first appeared in Roman literature of the late Republic. This new ethnic name effectively links up the now defeated and safely incorporated Samnites to the long enfranchised and ideologically useful Sabines.[60] This link between Sabines and Samnites was shortly afterwards to be written on the Augustan map of Italy composed of newly created regions. The Sabines and Samnites were now united in Regio IV, along with other Central Apennine peoples with whom they were associated in moral terms.[61]

---

[58] Suet. *Aug.* 2–4; cf. Cic. *Phil.* 3. 6. 15.

[59] D.H., *On Ancient Orators*, preface; cf. Suet. *Aug.* 86. 1–2; J. Griffin, 'Propertius and Antony', *JRS* 67 (1977), 17–26; Zanker, *Power of Images*, 57–64; cf. A. Wallace-Hadrill, 'Rome's Cultural Revolution', *JRS* 79 (1989), 157–64.

[60] Dench, *Barbarians*, 103–6.

[61] Pliny, *NH* 3. 106–9. The purpose of the regions remains obscure. See R. Thomsen, *The Italic Regions from Augustus to the Lombard Invasion* (Gyldendals Forlagstrykkeri,

Anxiety about female adultery was particularly acute in Horace's day, culminating in the extraordinary adultery law of 18 BCE, which bears the name of Augustus himself. This law sees the state acting as regulator of what was previously considered to be a private matter to be resolved primarily by the *paterfamilias* ('father of the household') within the individual household, and is the most striking attempt on the part of an ancient state in the Graeco-Roman world to regulate the sexual behaviour of its members.[62] The adultery law emphasizes control over women's bodies: this is a graphic illustration of the promotion of health of the body politic through control of female vices. Interestingly, the adultery law also represents one of the earliest examples of the projection of an image of Augustus as the *paterfamilias* of Rome collectively, an image that was in 2 BCE to be formalized in the honorific title of *pater patriae* ('father of the country').[63] The passing of the adultery law was advertised prominently in imperial ideology because of its supposed role in halting the turmoil of the end of the Republic which had been perceived in the characteristically overlapping spheres of morality, politics, religion, and warfare. This is a further reminder of the close connection in ancient Graeco-Roman thought between the regulation of the bodies of individuals and the health of the body politic.

The presence of the strict mother in the idealized scene of Horace's poem is a further indication of the importance in elite Roman thought of the need to adapt traditional gendered moral language to fit the increasing social prominence of individual upper-class women within the essentially aristocratic environment of later Republican and imperial Rome. Elements are appropriated from the traditionally masculine sphere of austerity and self-control in order to describe an ideal role for such women. This role is, however, circumscribed. While upper-class women are required to avoid excessive behaviour traditionally ascribed to the female sphere, it is important to preserve a sense of a conceptual boundary between the male and female spheres. While female bodies and appetites need to be controlled and regulated, this must be done in a

---

Copenhagen, 1946), esp. 103; C. Nicolet, *L'Inventaire du monde: Géographie et politique aux origines de l'empire romain* (Fayard, Paris, 1988), 221–3.

[62] D. Cohen, 'The Augustan Law on Adultery: The Social and Cultural Context', in D. Kertzer and R. Saller (eds.), *The Family in Italy from Antiquity to the Present* (Yale University Press, New Haven, 1991), 109 ff.; cf., more generally, G. Williams, 'Poetry in the Moral Climate of Augustan Rome', *JRS* 52 (1962); A. Wallace-Hadrill, 'Family and Inheritance in the Augustan Marriage-Laws', *PCPS* 27 (1981), 58 ff.; K. Galinsky, 'Augustus' Legislation on Morals and Marriage', *Philologus*, 125 (1981), 126 ff.; Edwards, *Politics*, 34–62.

[63] *RG* 35.

manner appropriate to the female. They should not, then, work out at the gym, just as they should not be seen wrangling in court or having intellectual pretensions.[64]

Control of female behaviour should be understood within the context of the particular Augustan emphasis on Roman identity as expressed by a hierarchical social order. Suitable roles were delineated for all sectors of society, and special attention was paid to the moral and social standing of the senatorial and equestrian elite, distinguishing them from other sectors. For example, there was apparently a ban for the first time on marriage between those of senatorial and those of freedman families,[65] while elaborate legislation on seating at the games emphasizes the divisions between various gender, age, and social groups.[66] The delineation of the class of respectable women was also apparently emphasized by encouraging the wearing of the modest *stola*. Here as elsewhere, this emphasis on the healthy and well-ordered body politic is meant to project an image of real, traditional, Romanness, and to maintain and justify Roman imperial greatness. Nevertheless, when viewed from a different perspective, in contrast with foreigners, the Romans looked rather more homogeneous: Augustus apparently promoted the wearing of togas, traditional Roman clothing for males, by quoting Virgil in the forum at wearers of dark cloaks.[67]

Italians and Augustan morality come together in a real-life association of 'Sabellians' with virtuous behaviour. It is surely no accident that one of the proposers of the Papian-Poppaean law, the second batch of Augustan marriage legislation, was M. Papius Mutilus. His name would recall for Romans that of the famous Samnite leader of the Social War, C. Papius Mutilus, probably his grandfather. Although Papius was, like his colleague in the consulship of 9 CE, notoriously a childless bachelor,[68] his Samnite origins must have seemed peculiarly appropriate in the context of legislation that was promoted as bound to ensure the successful

---

[64] I allude to Juvenal, *Sat.* 6; for the problems posed by Livia, see N. Purcell, 'Livia and the Womanhood of Rome', *PCPS* ns 32 (1986), 78–105; compare, for the new prominence of women in Greek cities in the Hellenistic and Roman periods, R. van Bremen, 'Women and Wealth', in A. Cameron and A. Kuhrt (eds.), *Images of Women in Antiquity* (Croom Helm, London, 1983; 1993), 223–42.

[65] Dio 54. 16. 2; 56. 7. 2. For Dio's muddles, see A. Watson, *The Law of Persons in the Later Roman Republic* (Oxford University Press, Oxford, 1967), 33–7.

[66] Suet. *Aug.* 44; E. Rawson, '*Discrimina ordinum*: The *lex Julia theatralis*', *PBSR* 55 (1987), 83–114.

[67] Suet. *Aug.* 40. 5; cf. Virgil, *Aen.* 1. 282; Zanker, *Power of Images*, 162–6.

[68] Dio 56. 9.

continuation of Rome not least through military success, via the medium of control over the sexual morality of individuals.[69]

However, as I suggested briefly earlier, Augustan Rome is not an unambiguous projection of masculine austerity and self-control. Besides the projection of the city of Rome herself as a fit world centre through a flamboyant physical appearance, ancient thought had also to grapple with the extraordinarily prominent position of Augustus himself, as well as that of his household—including his wife Livia, and his daughter and granddaughter—and that of his personal friends. For example, Suetonius, the Hadrianic biographer of the early emperors, related tales of Augustus' womanizing. Although these tales are partially rationalized as the political strategy of the wise emperor, such tales undoubtedly place Augustus within the very different sphere of the tyrant who, when viewed in a favourable light, exercises his power and dominance by indulging his appetites without constraint.[70]

This flamboyant aspect of Augustan Rome is also embodied in the person of Augustus' powerful friend Maecenas, patron of poets such as Horace, Virgil, and Propertius. Images of effeminate indulgence run through ancient assessments of Maecenas, including those apparently made by Augustus himself. His very prose style is described in revealing metaphors of hairstyle and perfume: 'curls dripping with myrrh'.[71] Interestingly, Maecenas himself apparently paraded his Etruscan royal origins, recalling the ancient association of Etruscans with archetypical luxury and indulgence of appetites.[72] Maecenas' pride in his Etruscan royal origins should probably be considered within the context of a more general Julio-Claudian antiquarian interest in Etruscology, and, more specifically, alongside contemporary interest in the idea of Etruscan input into the more civilized aspects of early Rome.[73]

The projection of images of imperial Rome in the early empire involved a complex combination of two different modes of advertising

[69] See, especially, Williams, 'Poetry in the Moral Climate of Augustan Rome', 28 ff.

[70] Suet. *Aug.* 69; cf. 71 for Livia as procuress of virgins for Augustus to deflower; cf. Edwards, *Politics*, 47–8; J. Dunkle, 'The Rhetorical Tyrant in Roman Historiography: Sallust, Livy and Tacitus', *CW* 65 (1971), 171–4.

[71] Suet. *Aug.* 86. 2; Wiseman, *New Men*, 14.

[72] e.g. Horace, *Odes* 1. 1. 1; 3. 29. 1; Propertius 3. 9. 1; *Elegiae ad Maecenatem* 1. 13; cf. Martial 12. 4. 2.

[73] D. Musti, 'Tendenze nella storiografia romana e greca su Roma arcaica: Studi su Livio e Dionigi da Alicarnasso', *Quaderni Urbinati*, 10 (1970), 5–158; M. Fox, *Roman Historical Myths* (Clarendon Press, Oxford, 1996), 127–32.

success and superiority—flamboyance and self-control. As we have seen, each of these has a long history of associations with spheres of both gender and ethnic identification. One of the most striking aspects of ideology concerning both Augustan Rome and Augustus himself is the image of Augustus and Augustan Rome as the culmination of history. At times, this is specifically Roman history, but elsewhere the notion of Augustus and Augustan Rome as a culmination of the local histories of Rome and Italian communities and peoples is emphasized.[74] Just as the combined flamboyance and austerity of Augustus himself could be seen to embody both models of superiority and success traditionally enacted by elite Roman males, so Augustan Rome itself embodied both the flamboyance and *urbanitas* ascribed to the Etruscans, and the moral rectitude ascribed to the Samnites. The well-explored emphasis on order and morality in Augustan ideology represents a variation on an ancient theme of the promotion of the idea of success and ethnic superiority sited on idealized bodies and genders.

[74] For specifically Roman history, see P. Zanker, *Forum Augustum: Das Bildprogramm* (Wasmuth, Tübingen, 1968); for Virgil and local histories, see A. Bernardi s.v. 'Italia', in *Enciclopedia Virgiliana* (Istituto della Enciclopedia Italiana, Rome, 1984). See also Velleius Paterculus' *Roman History*, written under Tiberius.

6

Poisonous Women and Unnatural History in Roman Culture

SARAH CURRIE

THIS is an essay about ancient Roman *veneficium* ('poisoning'), a practice which subverts any view of the ancient body as a stable locus.[1] Roman *venenum* ('poison') disrupts the relationship between bodies and subjects. It is that which inhabits the body, annihilates the boundaries of the self, and before which subjectivity itself collapses. *Venenum* spells loss of control over the body and identity.

The art of poisoning in ancient Roman society was associated with women. Yet poisoning's precise burden of gender has been under-analysed by modern commentators. Female poisoning at Rome and elsewhere has been characterized as a misogynistic stereotype or a strategy of power for women and an equalizer in the asymmetry of the sexes.[2] My aim is to go beyond the descriptive and ask the more difficult question of why women were associated with poison. Women too in Roman culture could be the victims of poison, sometimes administered by men. Yet *venenum* presents a peculiar threat to men, the ideal subjects, and to their investment in subjectivity.

Roman *veneficium*, the wielding of *venenum* either through its introduction into the body or in the form of a charm, was invasive. *Venenum* occupied and feminized bodies. Poisoning, unlike other forms of killing, spectacularized the familiar body and rendered it strange.

I would like to thank the Pembroke Center, Brown, for supporting my research and Maria Wyke for her comments.

[1] *Veneficium* connoted the employment of *venenum*, which incorporated witchcraft as well as poisoning; this double valency can be seen, for example, in the Cornelian homicide law of 81 BCE. The teacher of rhetoric Quintilian implies that the two operations can be easily distinguished in spite of their common name (*Inst. orat.* 7. 3. 7). I will be discussing *veneficium* chiefly in the sense of poisoning, yet such *veneficium* often bears traces of the magical.

[2] See Margaret Hallissy, *Venomous Woman: Fear of the Female in Literature* (Greenwood Press, Westport, Conn., 1990). She argues that between men and women, poison operates as 'an insidious equalizer', 12.

Venenum controlled or puppetized its victims, even compelling them to be spectators of their own death. In this sense, the art of poisoning in Roman culture exemplifies the psychoanalytical category of 'the uncanny'.[3] The uncanny is evoked by the estrangement of the familiar and its vocabulary incorporates fetishism, animism, and automatism. Poisoning in Roman culture arguably demonstrates key features of the uncanny; not only did it alienate the body, it also manifested a persistent residue of the magical.[4]

The uncanny is an aesthetic category and it finds some of its most potent expression in the visual domain. It is the appearance in Roman culture of poisoning as an uncanny, visual art which particularly concerns me. Poisoning was an artistic activity with the body as its medium. Yet it was a perverse and deadly art. If Roman poisoning is a manifestation of the uncanny, we can go beyond cataloguing venomous women and posit reasons for the association of women and poison and for poison's assumed feminizing power. The uncanny, as articulated by Freud, is an expression of the repressed fears of castration and death. Roman poisoning was predicated upon sexual difference and represents the intertwined horrors of death and castration; it is thus appropriate that women should be its agents. Yet at the same time poison is desirable and erotic. It uncovers a yearning for destruction, a desire for the inorganic, and a nostalgia for what was before.

I am taking as a case study poisoning as it appears in the natural history of Pliny the Elder. Pliny completed his *Historia naturalis* ('Natural History'), a catalogue of the phenomena of *natura* comprising thirty-one books, in 77 CE, though it was only published after the author's death in 79 CE.[5] In a highly idealizing moment, Pliny asserts that

[3] The concept of the uncanny, or the 'unheimlich', was proposed by Sigmund Freud in 'The Uncanny' (1919), standard edition, ed. James Strachey, vol. xvii (Hogarth Press, London, 1955), 253–82. For the uncanny in visual art I have found very helpful Hal Foster, *Compulsive Beauty* (MIT Press, Cambridge, Mass., 1995).

[4] The historian Tacitus provides us with startling examples of the poisoned as slaves whose bodies have become alien to them. For example, Germanicus, by his own testimony, is a creature of his poisoners (*Ann.* 2. 69), and Britannicus is reduced to a zombie-like state before his death, evoking a displaced, paralysing horror in Agrippina (*Ann.* 13. 16). This uncanniness is strengthened by poisoning's overlapping relationship with other magical dark *artes*; the latter story illustrates the relationship between *venenum* and *fascinatio* ('bewitchment').

[5] I have used the Loeb Classical Library edition of Pliny's *Natural History*, ed. H. Rackham and W. H. S. Jones, in 10 vols. (Heinemann, Cambridge, Mass., 1938–63), in conjunction with the text of C. Mayhoff (Teubner, Leipzig, 1899–1906). There are considerable difficulties in 'translating' Pliny's herbs. I have followed the Loeb's identifications; a comprehensive list is given at the back of volume vii. Other translations are mine.

his theme is nature, and that nature is synonymous with life (*pref.* 13). The neglect of death in Pliny's declared version of nature can be understood as a form of repression. Its chief return in the text is in the form of poisons. Books 21–7 of the *Natural History* deal with flora and they constitute the chief repository of Pliny's herbal, medicinal wisdom, both *remedia* ('cures') and *venena* ('poisons'). Pliny deals too with animal poisons, yet he is scornful of any remedial qualities in animal derivatives. It is in the herbal realm that we discover the disturbing inseparability of the poisonous and the therapeutic. The Roman medical discourse of the first century CE was very different from the Hippocratic which had concentrated on regimen, that is the discipline of the body through exercise and diet. Medicine for Pliny overwhelmingly dealt with the manipulation of drugs in an amalgam of native Italian folklore and Greek pharmacology; the body was no longer a field of play but a vessel for external substances. However, herbal poisons are a troubling and disruptive presence amidst Pliny's medical observations.[6] They subvert his intentions of creating a self-administered, native therapy. The poisons in Pliny's text, whether given to the self or others, by their nature invade and undermine bodily integrity.

Pliny subscribes to the association of women and the art of poisoning. Yet he is forced to resemble these poisonous women, dispensing deadly knowledge for the harmful manipulation of the body. Pliny appears unable to excise poisons and poisonous women from his text and is constantly readmitting both. Poisons function in the *Natural History* as a reminder of what has been suppressed in his account, that nature is also death.

Poisoning also appears in Pliny as a perverse aesthetic practice. Pliny's depiction of *natura* incorporates applications of the natural world as well as its manifestations; this is demonstrated by the inclusion of a much-excavated survey of the visual arts. Poisoning carries a particular burden as a deadly art, while bearing a disturbing resemblance to other arts, most conspicuously the plastic arts. *Venena* embodied, and bore away, the deadliness of nature. Yet, perhaps more intriguingly, they could also encapsulate and carry away the murderousness of art. Body arts which aimed at the improvement or representation of the body could be

[6] Mary Beagon, *Pliny on Roman Nature* (Clarendon Press, Oxford, 1992), sees a resolution to the presence of natural poisons in Pliny's benign nature in the antidote from the Temple of Aesculapius at Cos (20. 264), 240. Yet the antidote is for all animal (not herbal) poisons, except that of the asp. This modification significantly destroys its status as a 'universal' remedy.

idealized as life-giving and therapeutic. Yet in their shadows lurked a darker conception of such *artes* as deathly. These two faces of body art, the life-giving and the deathly, were schematically associated with men and women respectively. Poison, by distilling and isolating what was lethal, cured as well as killed.

Although the presence of poisons in the *Natural History* undermines Pliny's declared intentions, they are more than disruptive. The return to poisons and to the figure of the poisonous woman embodies an attempt, implicit rather than explicit, at inoculation against both castration and death. Poison is thus desirable as a way of seeking out, confronting, and preparing for death. Yet this is an inoculation which will never be complete and is doomed to continual repetition.[7] Pliny's poisons typify their status in Roman culture as inoculation and scapegoat.

In his discussion of flowers in the *Natural History*, Pliny begins by uncovering the worm in the bud. He cites the Elder Cato who claimed that the bloom and perfume of flowers lasted only one day. Nature thus provided a clear warning that the flower which is most pleasing to the eye fades soonest (21. 2).[8] The fleeting colours of flowers, according to Pliny, were none the less the envy of artists. Take as an example the rivalrous love-affair of Pausias and Glycera of Sicyon (21. 4). He was a painter and she was a garland-maker. He would copy her works in his paintings. So to spur him on, she would vary her designs. Thus there was a competition between art and nature, and among Pausias' extant paintings was *Stephaneplocos* ('The Garland-Maker'), a portrait of Glycera. Finally there is a footnote to the story in Pliny's chapters on art. A copy of Glycera's picture was purchased at Athens by the notoriously extravagant Lucius Lucullus (35. 125).[9]

We seem to have a story which is a barely appropriate illustration of Pliny's original point, that painters emulate in their works the colours of flowers. Indeed it is more effective as an exemplification of Cato's warning, for it is the artifical, not the natural garlands, which last. Pausias' picture is rendered as a *memento mori*. In the battle of art and nature, art has seemingly won, preserving the image of the garland-

[7] This impulse towards annihilation, as a means of preparing for it and warding it off, was described by Freud in his essay, linked to his examination of the uncanny, 'Beyond the Pleasure Principle' (1920), standard edition, ed. James Strachey, vol. xviii (Hogarth Press, London, 1955), 7–64.

[8] Cato, *de re rustica* 8. 2.

[9] Pliny in his later account gives the title of the picture as *Stephanoplocos*, or *Stephanopolis* ('The Garland-Seller'). In the latter case, Glycera's profession appears as a consequence of her poverty, and she is perhaps therefore less of an artist.

maker long after the flowers have faded. In Pliny's tale, art is associated with man and nature with woman. The work of art and male desire is also an erotic binding, superior to the work of nature which is depicted as the weaving of fragile flowers, symptomatic of death and dissolution. Yet Glycera's garlands come first; it is nature and death which are anterior to desire. Nature is deathly not so much because it stands for corporeal death but because it is that which stands before and threatens the self; it signifies where the self will return. Pliny makes the hedonistic Roman Lucullus buy Pausias' painting after the sybarite had been killed in his text with a love-philtre, a *venenum* (25. 25). Death again, it seems, is stronger than and prior to love.

The latent venom in Pliny can be seen in his citation of a warning by the Greek medical authorities Mnesitheus and Callimacus about the unseen dangers of flowers (21. 12). Worn in the form of garlands on the brow at banquets, they could be injurious to health, in particular that of the head. The pernicious effect comes from their strong smell which can steal up on the unsuspecting wearer frolicking at a drinking party. Take the case of Cleopatra and her customary wickedness. In the run-up to the Battle of Actium, Antony had become deeply suspicious of everyone and everything, including the attentions of the queen. All his food was tasted in advance. The story goes that on one occasion Cleopatra 'played' upon his paranoia by poisoning the tips of the flowers of a chaplet she then placed on his head. As the party warmed up, Cleopatra suggested that she and Antony 'drink their chaplets'. What could be more innocent? As Antony placed the pieces of his chaplet into his wine-cup, Cleopatra stopped him with her hand. She declared that it was she who was the source of Antony's anxiety, yet Antony lived by her will, not by her lack of opportunity or plan. To demonstrate this, she ordered a prisoner to be brought in and made to drink from Antony's cup. The man died on the spot.

What exactly is Cleopatra playing at? Her capacity to kill Antony is the evidence of her love. Yet Cleopatra's proof of her love is riddled with poison. And what is Pliny playing at? The story is introduced as if it illustrates the proposition that the odours of flowers can be dangerous especially if the victim is drunk. It does no such thing. The unnamed poison employed by Cleopatra is merely applied to flowers, not derived from them, and her method owes nothing to smell but is the favoured poisoner's trick of infusion in wine, albeit through the medium of the chaplet. Pliny's incorporation of the story was presumably informed by its interweaving of flowers and poison; the irresistible impression is that

Cleopatra herself was a poisoned flower whose heady aroma stole upon Antony sunk deep in his cups. Cleopatra was poison as well as poisoning. In this respect Cleopatra, who was supposed to have successfully poisoned her brother Ptolemy IV, is a model of the female poisoner.

Cleopatra 'plays' at poisoning Antony, saving him at the last moment. Cleopatra appears to be teaching Antony a lesson, but the moral, that he lives by her desire not by her lack of opportunity to kill him, is highly ambiguous. Beneath Cleopatra's simple lesson lies a stranger one and the death of the slave is a crucial detail. It transforms Cleopatra's game into theatre. Cleopatra stages for Antony the scene of a man dying of poison. She shows him what death, or loss of self, looks like, while mocking the redundancy of his precautions. Yet it is not Cleopatra whom Antony should fear but death itself. Cleopatra's theatre underlines the visual component of poisoning, the way that it spectacularized the body. But for readers of Pliny, Cleopatra's display of control over life and death is self-defeating. It is not Antony who will die through poison, but Cleopatra herself. The spectacle of death is for and before both of them.

Pliny's story about Cleopatra reflects his own troubled relationship to the poisons which appear in his 'medicine-chest' only to be disavowed. In his medical discussions, Pliny attempts to create an ideal of a non-alienated therapy, purely masculine and Italian, neither in the hands of old women nor Greek slaves. Pliny famously characterized the debilitating nature of slavery on Roman society in a remarkable image of bodily disintegration and alienation; 'We walk with the feet of others, we recognize with others' eyes, we acknowledge with others' memories, we live by others' endeavours' (29. 19). The yielding up of medical knowlege by Roman men to outsiders and inferiors was enervating and emasculating. Yet Pliny's ideal of a therapy for the Roman body, which remains within control of that body, is a fantasy. It is chiefly in his herbal medicines, in the imaginary landscape of the Italian garden as laid out by Pliny, that we can see its impossibility. For within the garden, *venena* and *remedia* are constantly overlapping. The fictitious nature of Pliny's Italian garden is also underscored by his heavy reliance upon Greek authors, most notably, in this context, Theophrastus.[10] Pliny attempts to expel both women and poisons from his garden, yet they both return to haunt it.

---

[10] Among Pliny's other sources were almost certainly the Greek herbals of Crateus, Dionysius, and Metrodorus. See Beagon, *Roman Nature*, 204, and for further details, John Scarborough, 'Pharmacy in Pliny's *Natural History*: Some Observations on Substances and Sources', in Roger French and Frank Greenaway (eds.), *Science in the Early Roman Empire: Pliny the Elder: His Sources and Influence* (Croom Helm, London, 1986), 59–85.

Pliny does not just contribute to the image of the venomous woman. He is forced to take up her position, to be like Cleopatra, to play with poison, to paint for his readers a picture of death. Pliny tries to negotiate this minefield by arguing that nature provides poisons as a means of suicide, a painless relief from existence, most notably to avoid starvation or wasting, an end especially unnatural to the beneficence of the earth; poisons were also an antidote to precipices and hanging, in other words capital punishment (2. 156). Poisoning of another, however, is absolutely an image of an 'unnatural' wasting. Again there is a chasm in Pliny between benign self-doctoring and destructive treatment by another. This is in contrast with the materialist Lucretius who posited a straight opposition between primitive man accidentally poisoning himself and civilized man consciously poisoning others (*de rerum natura* 5. 1608–9). For Lucretius, all knowing applications of poison were 'unnatural'. The challenge for Pliny is to play with poison in such a way as to neutralize its venom.

It is interesting to note further in this context that Pliny makes the plant *artemisia* ('wormwood') belong not to Artemis Ilithyia—the goddess of childbirth—as others do, but to Artemisia, the wife of Mausolus and creator of the famous Mausoleum (25. 73). The husband is commemorated in the funeral monument and his wife in the plant; the modes of commemoration are parallel. Pliny ascribes a deathly meaning to a plant conventionally associated with birth. It seems that flora are again placed on the side of death. The point of this association of the floral with death is nature's nostalgia, its persistent return to the inorganic. It is perhaps relevant that the posthumously published *Natural History* is also Pliny's own memorial. However, it is the provision of poisons which encapsulates most clearly nature's turning back to the inorganic.

There is a further intriguing tale in Pliny's *Natural History* which entwines women, flowers, and mortality. This deals with the emperor Augustus' shameless daughter Julia, ultimately banished for her adultery. She is banished by Pliny's text too and not given a name (21. 9). We are informed that flowers were of highly restricted use in Roman public life. Yet Julia, in the manner of Athenian revellers and during a nocturnal binge, placed a chaplet of flowers on the statue of Marsyas in the Roman forum, an action castigated in a letter of 'the god', that is Augustus himself. This is a rich and strange story and one which is told to evoke horror. In addition to the status of Julia's ritual as a nocturnal rite, an inversion of Roman religious norms and itself redolent of death, the mortal Marsyas was presumably a peculiarly indecent choice for such an honour. Marsyas had challenged the god Apollo to a musical contest and was flayed for his impudence. Apollo was a key figure in Augustus' personal mythology, seen for example on coinage or the sculptural programme from the Temple of Apollo on the Palatine.[11] Julia honours the mortal Marsyas with flowers in defiance of her ultimately deified father.

Poison was a distillate of the mortality to be found in nature. Latin *venenum* is usually contrasted with the Greek *pharmakon* ('drug'), whose benign or malign operations were determined by context. Yet it is a deception of *venenum* to offer itself to us as a more stable concept than the *pharmakon*. In legal contexts the term *venenum* demanded modification; for example, a text by the jurist Gaius asserted that *venenum* demanded qualification to be understood as harmful, and that it was interchangeable with *pharmakon*.[12] The term *venenum* was floating rather than just ambiguous. In one outrageous rhetorical context, for instance, water becomes *venenum*.[13] *Venenum* vacillated between a substance and an effect. It was liquid and solid, vegetable, animal, and occasionally mineral. It also demanded a context or differentiation in order to be activated. It was highly volatile. If opposed to other *venena* it could potentially neutralize them, leap to its own opposite, and become a *remedium*. If applied to the healthy body it often required a contrasting, therapeutic medium such as wine or honey to be most effective as *venenum*.

It is easier to treat *venenum* as a principle rather than a genus in Roman culture. Take one of Pliny's deadly poisons, *ophiusa* ('the serpents' drug'), from Elephantis in Ethiopia (24. 163). The herb is lead-coloured—a hint of the inorganic perhaps—and horrible to look at. If taken in a potion, it produces terrifying visions of snakes which force the victim to commit suicide. It is pure poison. Yet Pliny adds that it was used to execute those guilty of sacrilege. The poison is socially reintegrated, made into a remedy of a social ill. Pliny then adds that there

---

[11] See Paul Zanker, *The Power of Images in the Age of Augustus*, trans. Alan Shapiro (University of Michigan Press, Ann Arbor, 1988), 48–53, and 240.

[12] *Digest* 50. 16. 236 (in 'Meaning of Expressions'), Gaius, *XII Tables* 4, citing the Homeric description of *pharmaka*, 'many beneficial and many harmful'. It explains that any substance is *venenum* which changes the nature of that to which it is applied. There may be a simple, practical advantage in legislating for the Greek- and Latin-speaking parts of the Empire that *pharmakon* and *venenum* should be assimilated.

[13] This is the premiss of the rhetorical exercise *Minor Declamation* 350, attributed to Quintilian, in which a stepmother gives her ill stepson water, against the instructions of the doctor.

is a similar drug, *thalassaegle* or *potamaugis*, which drives men into a frenzy with visions (24. 164). There is no social use adduced for it; Pliny simply leaves a sting in the tail. According to Aulus Gellius, the second-century CE composer of an eclectic assortment of pieces of knowledge called *Attic Nights*, *venenum* was one of a number of Latin words which had once been benign or ambiguous but now had exclusively negative meanings (12. 9. 2). The other examples he cites are perhaps significant; *periculum*, which had meant 'experiment' before meaning 'danger', and *contagium* which connoted 'contact' before meaning 'contagion'. Gellius' semantic nostalgia seems to imply that *venenum* went to the heart of anxieties about the meaning of words, especially about the erosion and migration of meaning.

Venenum suffuses texts as it does bodies. *Venenum* could represent the pluralism and opacity of words. Language was poisoned because it was riddling and elusive. This relationship of *venenum* to meaning appears to underlie Pliny's portrayal of Mithridates, king of the Pontus and enemy of Rome (25. 5–8). Mithridates inoculates himself against assassination by poison by taking in anticipation all known poisons with their anti-dotes; he also makes a study of the Pontic ducks who live on poison. Pliny juxtaposes the immune king with praise for Mithridates' linguistic ability. He spoke twenty-two languages and no imperial subject of his was ever addressed through an interpreter. Mithridates attempted, in a similar manner as with poisons, to inoculate himself against the volatility of language. In his attempt to be completely immune to poison, Mithridates also strove to stabilize his relationship to language, to be before it and be free of its tyrannical mediation. Mithridates' studies then passed into Roman hands, and into Latin, through his nemesis, the Roman general Pompey, who defeated the king and gained possession of his written studies. In other words, a poison of the Roman empire was effectively transformed into a *remedium*, a source of useful knowledge for the imperial rulers.

In Cicero's *Brutus,* a dialogue on the decline of oratory, *venenum* appears as the specific ingredient or motor of the art of persuasion. Cicero's friend Atticus attacks the violence of rhetoric in the name of history. Through the art of rhetoric, the career of the rebellious Roman Coriolanus can be made to match that of the Greek general and hero of Salamis, Themistocles (42–3). In the Greek history of Thucydides, Themistocles died of natural causes, but in the Greek orators he died of drinking a draught of bull's blood, an appropriately tragic end, which could also be bestowed by oratory upon Coriolanus. The historian

Atticus sardonically enjoins Cicero to take the bowl—he will even provide the bull—to transform Coriolanus into a second Themistocles. The draught of poison to be taken by Coriolanus is that which will metamorphose history into rhetoric. It is a troubling image; living history is killed by the venom of rhetoric. Carlin Barton has characterized *venenum* as an equalizer, a positive agent in Roman culture's pharmacology as it moved between different poles of annihilation.[14] Yet Aulus Gellius' point, that *venenum* had lost its pluralism over time, suggests the term also contained within itself the possibility of a loss of mobility. In other words, *venenum* could embody an atrophy of meaning.

My concern is with poison as an uncanny art practised upon bodies and the metaphorical bodies of texts, which are inseparable in the *Natural History*. Poison was not merely a medium by which one individual controlled another; it was a force before which subjectivity itself collapsed. In a discussion of gems, Pliny described Demosthenes, the greatest orator of the Greeks, as wearing a ring containing poison (33. 25–6). Demosthenes thus carried with him the means of his own death; the master of spoken language was also the master of his own demise. Demosthenes' ring represents the ideal of man's strategic relationship to poison. Yet unfortunately *venenum* could be alienated and employed by others secretly against the body. This resembles the way seal-rings themselves, supposedly fixers of relations, could be manipulated in a fraudulent way (33. 26). Paranoia about poisoners overlay a deep-rooted fear about poison itself, specifically that poison preceded men. Demosthenes' death was before him, and he was its subject.

Poisoning was a body art which subordinated victim and perpetrator to *venenum* and which reduced the body to a host for its operations. Its contagiousness underlies the scope of legislation against poisoners, including those who merely possessed, prepared, and sold poison (*Digest* 48. 8. 3). This destabilizing and decentring power of poison can be discerned in the three commonly adduced etymological accounts of *venenum*.[15] One of them connected it with wine. The sixth-century CE etymologist Isidore of Seville, accounting for the name of wine, proposed that once upon a time *venenum* ('poison') was indistinguishable from *vinum* ('wine') (*Origines* 3. 2). To be precise, he says that wine was once called *vinenum*, but after the discovery of a *virus lethiferi succi* ('concoc-

[14] Carlin Barton, *The Sorrows of the Ancient Romans* (Princeton University Press, Princeton, 1993), 91.
[15] See Robert Maltby, *A Lexicon of Ancient Etymologies* (Francis Cairns Press, Leeds, 1991), 634.

tion of deathly juice'), it took the name *vinum*. This possibility of a primal admixture of wine and poison, a *virus* ('concoction') of *venenum* and *vinum*, or simply an undifferentiation of wine and poison implies a late attempt to distil this liquid into good and bad therapies; wine is usually a health-promoting remedy. *Venenum* often requires and seeks out its former companion wine to be effective. For Pliny, there is no more difficult or more abundant part of his work than wine, for it is not clear whether it generally does more good than harm. Even with the individual draught, it is not immediately clear whether it will be an *auxilium* ('a help') or a poison (23. 31). None the less, Pliny almost exclusively gives instances of wines as *remedia*. Pliny continues that wine was used long ago to promote sleep and banish worries. Wine generally appears in Roman culture as *venenum*'s companion and opposite. The body appears as just the background for the ebb and flow of *remedia* and *venena*.

The most frequently assumed etymological origin of *venenum* associated it with the goddess Venus. The goddess' cult was established in Italy in the third century BCE; it is argued that *venus*, meaning 'charm', was originally interchangeable with *venenum*. Hence *venenum* is assumed to have once been a love-philtre. Yet the idea of *venenum*'s fall from grace does not stand up to close scrutiny. The emperor Caligula was supposedly driven mad by a love-philtre and the sybarite Lucius Lucullus was killed by one.[16] Poison was erotic, and the erotic was poisonous. This is evident in Virgil's *Aeneid* when Cupid is exhorted by his mother Venus to infect Dido with fire and deceive her with poison (1. 688).[17] *Venenum* is Venus' drug; it represents a desirable dissolution. Another etymology, given to us in Servius' commentary on the same passage in the *Aeneid*, links *venenum* with *venae* ('veins'). *Venenum* was that which flowed through the veins, inhabiting and taking over its host. In this context, Pliny's description of *musta* ('musts') is intriguing (23. 29). Must is beneficial for the veins. Yet if taken too rapidly after a bath, it causes death.[18] According to the author of an earlier medical treatise in Latin, Celsus, it is much more difficult to treat poisons which have been taken

---

[16] Caligula: Suetonius, *Life of Caligula* 50. Lucullus: Plutarch, *Life of Lucullus* 43.

[17] Erotic poison is also, for example, a theme of Propertius, *Elegiae* 2. 1, especially vv. 51–6, though the terms *venenum/venena* are not used.

[18] Must is a complex *remedium/venenum*. It also gives headaches, is harmful to the stomach and throat, but is an antidote to aphrodisiacs, snake and reptile bites, and is good for the kidneys, liver, intestines, and bladder. Its oxymoronic status infiltrates its application. It is taken in oil and then vomited up; in other words, both consumed and not consumed.

internally, which conceal their presence and work their way from the inside outwards, than the poisons of bites and stings which work their way inwards from the outside (*de medicina* 5. 27. 11).

Poison implied bodily possession of poisoners and victims. A jurist on the Aquilian law on damages cites three separate means of introducing poison into the body, by mouth, by external application, and by *clyster* ('injection') (*Digest* 9. 2. 8. 1). Poison was fecund. For example, in his account of *boleti* ('fungi'), Pliny referred briefly to the famous murder of the emperor Claudius by Agrippina through the agency of a *boletus* (22. 92). This, in Pliny's description, was an act of poisoning that would only produce more *venenum*, namely Agrippina's son Nero. Poison begets poison. Pliny goes on to describe *boleti* as effectively poison-fixing, absorbing poison from decaying, unclean objects as well as from venomous snakes (22. 94–5). This description might also be applied to the genesis of Nero himself.

Poisoning entailed a loss of self, an undoing, the becoming of a mere host for the operations of *venenum*. Pliny's anger against the Greek medical writers' dissemination of destructive knowledge led him to a revealing juxtaposition. What possible excuse could they have for educating readers in poisons, abortives, and drugs which induced madness? (25. 25). Drugs which promoted abortion and insanity were modes of loosening comparable to poisoning. Pliny says he will leave alone abortives, love-philtres—because he remembers the famous general Lucius Lucullus—and magic spells, which he does not believe in. Abortion, and its inevitable alienation of reproduction, absolutely embodied fear of loss for Roman men. This sense of loss is fundamental. The true horror of poison was not death but castration.[19] The historian Sallust, in his account of the Catilinarian conspiracy, spelled it out; the contemporary vice of *avaritia* ('avarice'), like bad poisons, feminized both the body and the mind (11. 3). Roman culture returned repeatedly to the female poisoner in an attempt to expel such threats of death and castration.

Poisoning was a feminine and mimetic practice in Roman texts including the *Natural History*. Roman women as mimics, as deceivers, and as poisoners undoubtedly owed something to their social mobility. Women moved from household to household. There was hence a preoccupation with the secretly venomous *noverca* ('stepmother'), who bore a perverted resemblance to the nourishing *matrona*; the poisoning *noverca*

---

[19] At 26. 3, Pliny has an intriguing image of this loss when he talks of a strange facial plague striking down Roman nobles; women and slaves were immune.

was a specific development of the generally murderous Greek step-mother.[20] In the whole of Tacitus' *Annals*, there is only one *artifex* ('artist'), Lucusta. She was a notorious poisoner of the imperial court who skilfully practised her art until her execution under the emperor Galba (12. 66. 4). In Suetonius' account, Lucusta is permitted a terse defence of her aesthetic practice. After a flogging from the emperor Nero for a protracted dosing of his intended victim, his stepbrother Britannicus, Lucusta explains that she had adopted a slow, subtle poison-ing in order to conceal the crime, to protect Nero from the *invidia* ('hatred') its disclosure would provoke (*Life of Nero* 33. 2). Lucusta depends on the standard realist defence. Her art is a mimetic one, an art which conceals its art.[21] Lucusta is the paragon of the female poisoner as an uncanny artist.

Yet female poisoners could take a more simple-minded form, as ven-omous, serpentine monsters, instant bringers of death; according to Pliny, the snake-bite is the worst of all ills (25. 99). For Freud, it was the snaky-haired Medusa who was the epitome of the idea of female uncan-niness.[22] Snake venom was hot. The cold, calculating woman poisoner was a figure who opposed and even suppressed the hot, bestial poisoner, who deformed poisoning into an art. Medea, a notoriously hot poisoner and daughter of the Sun, is a muted presence in Pliny's *Natural History*. Indeed her most famous poisoning is, in the *Natural History*, not a poisoning at all. In Pliny's account, Medea killed Jason's new wife with *naphtha* ('naphtha') (2. 235). It was highly flammable and because of its mysterious affinity for flames caught fire quite naturally when the bride approached the altar to sacrifice. In contrast to the simulated atrophy of the cold poisoner, there is little artistry in the model of the hot poisoner, though sometimes cold poisoners had to be as quick as hot ones. Cleopatra at table with Antony uses a speedy poison and Lucusta is compelled by Nero to concoct a poison 'swift as steel' (Suetonius, *Life of Nero* 33. 2).

Cold, slow poisoning was repeatedly figured as a mimetic art. It mocked natural atrophy. The pharmacopoeia of the cold poisoner

---

[20] See Patricia A. Watson, *Ancient Stepmothers: Myth, Misogyny and Reality* (E. J. Brill, New York, 1995), 7–18.

[21] Lucusta thus resembles the mythical artist Pygmalion as depicted in Ovid's *Metamor-phoses*, discussed briefly below. Pygmalion is a hyper-realist who tricks himself, falling in love with his own statue of a girl, for 'so did the art conceal its art' (10. 253). Lucusta on the other hand is a deadly realist who tricks others.

[22] 'Medusa's Head' (1922/46), standard edition, ed. James Strachey, vol. xviii (Hogarth Press, London, 1955), 273–4. Medusa embodies a castrating threat in visual form.

reflected this mimicry. In the Greek conception of natural sympathies and antipathies portrayed by Pliny, mere resemblance could be sufficient for a herb to have an inoculative or therapeutic effect (20. 1). Yet mimicry was particularly intense with *venena*. Poisons produced resemblances of death. We have already commented on the hallucinogenics which produced such terror that suicide would inevitably result. Other herbs mirrored death. The seeds and leaves of hemlock possessed a *refrigetoria vis* ('freezing power'), chilling its victims at their extremities before killing them (25. 151). *Mandragora* ('mandrake') was an antidote to snake-bites. It also reproduced the death-like states of speechlessness, anaesthesia, and sleep (25. 150). This was all in addition to its power to kill. Dark poppies had anaesthetic properties, and the power to destroy sight and induce a death-like coma, which would ultimately end in death itself (20. 199). The bulb *scilla* ('squill'), drunk in a concoction of vinegar, was therapeutic for eye and stomach disorders, but too great a quantity produced briefly the appearance of death (20. 39). *Cuminum* ('cumin') when pounded and drunk with wine produces an artificial pallor (20. 57). Pliny reports that this was employed by the followers of the orator Porcius Latro in order, presumably, to enhance their rhetorical power with an affectation of emotion. The rebel Julius Vindex employed the same trick to fool legacy-hunters into believing he was dying.

Poisoning in the manner of mimesis was a deception. In yet another contradiction of his declared ethical stance, Pliny asserts that honey is good for concealing poison (21. 77). He also describes naturally occurring poisoned honeys; *maenomenon* from Pontus which drives men mad, and poisoned honey from Persis and Gaetulia. Such sweet traps were a warning to men to be less greedy and more careful (21. 78). *Trefolium* ('trefoil'), despite its recommendation by certain Greek authorities, was a particularly dangerous poison (21. 152–3). Its remedial effect came only from its capacity to neutralize the poisons of snakes and scorpions. Yet the leaves of poisonous trefoil could also be used, according to Pliny, in face ointment, to preserve the beauty of women's skin. Cosmetics, like poisons, were a mode of mimicry, a strategy by which women masqueraded as women. We find a significant confusion in Roman legal discourse between sellers of cosmetics and perfumes, *pigmentarii*, and sellers of poison. *Pigmentarii* were liable under the Cornelian homicide law if they dealt negligently in hemlock, salamander, monkshood, pinegrubs, poisonous beetles, mandragora, or Spanish fly.[23]

---

[23] *Digest* 48. 8. 3. 4 (Marcian, *Institutes* 14).

That poisoning was repeatedly figured as a mimetic art is intriguing given the ancient world's double-edged medicinal evaluation of mimesis, as both life-giving and death-dealing, as signalling absence and presence.[24] Through the medium of poison, we see a struggle to split mimesis into a female aesthetic of death-dealing and absence, and a male aesthetic of life-giving and presence; women's role as poisoners in Roman culture was informed by the perceived relationship of art and sexual difference. Pliny tells a story of the origins of *plastice* ('modelling'), which illustrates the relationship between these opposing aspects of mimesis and masculinity and femininity. Modelling was invented by Butades of Sicyon, a potter, at Corinth (35. 151–2). His daughter, anticipating that she would miss the young man she loved, who was leaving town, had the bright idea of sketching out his silhouette cast by the lamp upon the wall. Butades, noticing this, 'filled' in the drawing with clay which he then baked in his kiln, thus inventing modelling. The father filled in the empty picture and rendered an expression of absence into one of presence. While this is a charming story and the young woman's artistic expression poignant and eloquent, it associates women with an aesthetic of absence and emptiness and men with an aesthetic of presence and fullness. Yet Pliny adds a note of complexity. The portrait remained on display at Corinth until the city's violent destruction by the Roman Mummius in 146 BCE, when Greece was subjugated by the Roman empire. Butades' work too seems ultimately to signify loss.

We know that women participated in the visual arts in antiquity. Women painters receive a brief survey as curiosities in the *Natural History* (35. 147–8). They include, most notably, Iaia from Cyzicus. She appears to have negotiated anxieties around a female aesthetic practice by remaining unmarried. Her works included a self-portrait done with a mirror, a rendering of herself as an art-object and artist simultaneously. Moreover, Pliny also tells a negative tale about male desire for created women. Some of the oldest Italian paintings were to be found at Lanuvium and depicted Atalanta and Helen nude. When the emperor Caligula saw them he was filled with lust and would have taken them away with him if the plaster of the murals had not prevented it (35. 18). Caligula's desire is evidently foolish and potentially destructive.

None the less, male art and desire was generally idealized as purely

---

[24] For a fascinating account of the negative, Platonic assessment of mimesis with reference to Roman sculpture, see Yun Lee Too, 'Statues, Mirrors, Gods: Controlling Images in Apuleius', in Jas Elsner (ed.), *Art and Text in Roman Culture* (Cambridge University Press, Cambridge, 1996), 133–52.

creative, whereas female desire, and by extension female artistry, were condemned to death-dealing. It is not difficult to find evidence of the deadliness of female desire in Roman culture. Orators turned to Marcus Cato's assertion that every adulteress was the same as a poisoner, and that the two crimes of adultery and poisoning were inseparable. The rhetorical handbook known as *Rhetorica ad Herennium* provides a rationalizing defence of this position (4. 16. 23). A woman convicted of one crime was guilty of many transgressions. An unchaste woman was invariably a poisoner since, from fear of discovery, she would have no qualms about doing away with her husband, her parents, and others. A poisoning woman was also an adulteress. For she was bound to have poisoned through lust, and a corrupt soul was bound to inhabit a corrupt body. Did the same apply to men? Not at all. For each male crime was inspired by a distinct passion, whereas all female crimes were committed for one reason, lust.

The deadly, poisonous aspect of female desire found a parallel in the lethal aspect of mimesis. It was in particular the sculptor's art which female poisoners darkly parodied as they made warm bodies cold and lifeless. Sculpture indeed carried a particular mimetic burden. In his treatise on the sublime Longinus declares that what is valued in art, specifically statues, is accuracy, whereas in speech it is that which surpasses the human (*de sublimitate* 36). The intimate relationship of masculine desire and a masculine mimetic art, specifically sculptural, was given expression in Ovid's version of the legend of Pygmalion and his statue-turned-woman (*Metamorphoses* 10. 243–97). Through his desire, the artist transcends *imitatio* ('imitation') altogether. The cold statue becomes warm flesh through the intervention of Venus. The sculptor's aesthetic practice is a life-giving and an erotic one, a work of desire.[25]

Yet the story of Pygmalion is put by Ovid into the mouth of the widowed Orpheus in a string of tales of destructive and destroyed *amor*. In particular, the confirmed bachelorhood of the sculptor is induced by the spectacle of the Propoetides, sisters who rashly denied the divinity of Venus. The goddess dishes out an erotic punishment, making them prostitute themselves in public, while gradually turning them colder and harder until they become flints. The tale depicts Venus' power moving from the organic to the inorganic, in precisely the opposite direction from her gift to Pygmalion.

[25] For an examination of Ovid's Pygmalion, gender, and artistic creativity, see Alison Sharrock, 'Womanufacture', *Journal of Roman Studies*, 81 (1991), 36–49.

The cold, sculptural artistry of *veneficium* can be seen in the figure of Tacitus' Lucusta who assaults Britannicus through the appropriately chilly medium of iced water. He slips into a coma which passes as an epileptic fit, before eventually dying (*Ann.* 13. 15–17). In Suetonius' version, the future emperor Titus shares Britannicus' table and is also poisoned, but not fatally; interestingly, it is remarked that he later sets up two statues to Britannicus (*Titus* 2). Pliny too depicts a poisoned corpse as if it were a statue, though significantly he is defending the naturalness and non-violence of suicide through poison. After painless death through poison, the body remains whole, with the blood inside, and no birds or beasts will touch it but it is perfectly preserved (2. 63). Poison appears to petrify.[26] Poison's movement from the organic to the inorganic can also be detected in Pliny's account of the preservative *cedrus* ('prickly juniper'), used for treating book-rolls, which in turn gives diligent readers headaches (24. 17). Pliny remarks scornfully about the perverse operations of *cedrus*, that it keeps dead bodies uncorrupted but causes living ones to decay. *Cedrus* is an odd object of Pliny's wrath and has clearly been brought into play to construct a pleasing paradox. It sums up his anxieties about alien, deathly drugs, but in addition *cedrus* possesses a memorializing power.

One aspect of Roman poisoning which draws attention to its status as art is the marks left upon the body which operate as the signature of the poisoner. That a corpse was discoloured was a forensic proof that it had been poisoned.[27] Juvenal famously depicts a *matrona* instructing her ignorant neighbours in the art of poisoning and, afterwards, how to walk behind their *nigros maritos* ('black husbands') (*Sat.* 1. 72). In Tacitus' account of the death of Claudius, the emperor's corpse was kept in bandages. This was presumably to prevent detection of the poison, though this description of the unseen body concurs with Tacitus'

---

[26] There are no mineral poisons in the *Natural History*, only mineral therapies, but there is an interesting discussion of the *sarcophagus lapis* ('sarcophagus stone') (36. 131). Corpses surrounded by the stone are consumed within forty days and objects placed on the bodies are petrified. The stone, like herbal poisons, seems to manifest the contagion of the inorganic.

[27] *Rhet. ad Her.* 2. 8. 20; Quintilian, *Inst. orat.* 5. 11. 44. Although, as Quintilian at *Inst. orat.* 5. 11. 39 points out, this was not proof of the identity of the poisoner. Poisoning shared a vocabulary with dyeing. In particular clothes stained with *purpura* were 'poisoned'. This surely suggests dyeing to a point of no return; see, for example, Aulus Gellius, *NA* 10. 15. 27 and 20. 9. 3. In the case of an extract from Indian snakes, whose colour is not specified, it marks an aesthetic decay from the original four colours of Greek painting; Pliny disapproves of such exotic coloration (35. 50). He also attacks Greek quacks who ignorantly put poisonous *minium* ('red lead')—the tint used on the face by a celebrator of a Roman triumph—in their concoctions (29. 25).

hesitation about the source of the poison (*Ann.* 12. 67). More radically ambiguous was the tale of Germanicus' corpse, which may or may not have had the *signa* ('marks') of poisoning according to the sympathies of the viewer (2. 73). In Cassius Dio's version of the death of Britannicus, the corpse is covered with chalk to prevent the blackening being seen. However, when the body is laid out in the Campus Martius, by divine intervention torrential rain washes off the chalk (61. 7. 4). Cassius Dio cleverly negotiates the career difficulties which face Lucusta; as a successful poisoner she must be undetected, but as a famous one she must be discovered. Pliny virtually ignores this visual symptom of poisoning. This may be connected with Pliny's description of the natural source of poisons. The aesthetics of poisoning too are natural and without discoloration, the sign of art.

Pliny struggles to deal with safe and dangerous disclosures of medical knowledge. The fact that medicine has become an *ars*, a specialism, was itself a threat.[28] However it is Roman bodies in Greek hands which bother him. Those hands, according to Cato, belong to adulterers, legacy-hunters, and poisoners (29. 20–1). In Pliny's attack upon foreign, imported medicines, we are given an image of the Roman body politic being invaded and occupied by alien substances. He is alarmed by imported drugs with prices fixed by foreigners. Even Cato did not foresee this particular transformation of the Roman body into the profit of others (29. 24).

Poison suffuses Pliny's text. Many of his beneficial herbs are antidotes to poisons. Pliny repeatedly denounces *venena*, only to be compelled to reintroduce and dwell on them. He expresses a reluctance to elaborate upon a type of *trychnos* ('deadly nightshade'), then tells us that even in small doses it causes madness and hallucinations and, in larger doses, death. The irresponsible Greeks have made light of this (21. 178). He parades a reluctance to discuss a type of *trychnos*, *halicacabos*, called by some *morion* or *moly*, which in small quantities is a handy teeth-rinse, in larger, the cause of delirium. Nor will he talk of *buprestis* ('hare's ear'), which is poison to cattle. Why should poisons come up in relation to grasses? Simply because there are those who mistakenly think that *buprestis* is a potent aphrodisiac (22. 78). Only rarely does Pliny create a genuine mystery around poisons. For example, he mentions the presumably poisonous plant *cnecos* or *atractylis* ('safflower'), saying it would not be right to dwell on it, except that its external application grants immu-

---

[28] Discussed by Beagon, *Roman Nature*, 202–10.

nity from poisons, and complete anaesthesia from scorpions' stings (21. 184).

The inescapability of poison in Pliny's Italian pastoral is finally summed up by a female figure, Circe, the witch whose spells changed the shapes of her victims. Circe is undeniably a poisoner, a manipulator of potent herbs. She appears first in a discussion of the citrus-tree, when Pliny talks of Homer elevating Circe to the status of a goddess (13. 100). She is also an Italian. Circe had traditionally been located at Circeii, a promontory south of Latium. The Marsi from central Italy were supposedly descended from Circe's son Marsus, and they were purportedly immune to snake venom (7. 15). The Marsi were renowned for their magic, their snake-bite cures, and their grove to Angita, a goddess of healing.

In the *Natural History*, Circe appears as part of an intriguing discussion about the Italian garden. Pliny claims to have visited the garden of the long-lived Roman Antonius Castor, who is one source of his herbal wisdom. He contrasts the old man's healthy knowledge of nature with the ignorance of those who say women have power over eclipses through herbs. Pliny then cites Aeschylus' description of Italy as the site of powerful herbs, especially around Circeii where Circe lived, although Homer gave the prize for herbs to Egypt. Pliny alludes again to the Marsi, whom he makes, more than just immune to snakes, *domitores serpentium* ('snake-charmers') (25. 11). It seems that at the bottom of Pliny's native Italian garden lurks the poisonous witch Circe and her snake-handling descendants who are immune to poison. This would potentially make Pliny's Italian garden, and his native pharmacopoeia, poisoned at the root.

Pliny's Cleopatra at table with Antony was an artist of the uncanny, spectacularizing and manipulating the body and painting death in an unfamiliar light. Her behaviour was a parallel to the practice of the text of the *Natural History* which suppresses mortality but then reluctantly displays for us the workings of poisons and images of death. Cleopatra represents the inescapability and the desirability of poison even as she evokes its horror. Yet there are intriguing traces of an antidote to these dangerous feminine games with poison in the *Natural History* and it comes in the surprising figure of *Homerica Helena*. In an enigmatic moment Pliny comments that it was possible to tell from the painted images of Atalanta and Helen, by which Caligula was so enraptured, which was the virgin, that Atalanta was painted *ut virgo*. Pliny seems to be denying any secrecy to female sexuality. From one perspective this is just an attempt to fix Helen's whorishness, to deny in vain the slipperiness of women. Yet perhaps Helen in this picture seems what she is, definitely not a *virgo*, in a moment of transparency.

Helen appears chiefly in the *Natural History* in connection with another plant, her own, *helenium*, which sprang from Helen's tears and was very popular on the island of Helen (21. 59). It is a beauty aid for women, and said to make perfect the face and skin. It enhances sexual attractiveness (21. 159). Throughout his work, Pliny's cosmetic advice stresses the desirability of smoothness and perfection of skin; for example, he discusses how to eliminate blemishes and beautify the skin with cucumber (20. 9), rocket (20. 125), anise (20. 185), and tree-fungi (22. 98).[29]

The plant *helenium*, I would argue, symbolizes an appropriate, inward-turned aesthetic of self-adornment for women. It was used by women, not against foreign bodies, that is men's bodies, but upon themselves in order to make themselves smooth as statues. Cosmetics, and women's beauty generally, could be pure, deceptive *venena*. The positive evaluation of such female *cultus* ('cultivation') in Ovid's didactic poem on cosmetics depended precisely upon the exclusion of any magical means of self-enhancement, and the rejection of old women and their herbs and potions (*de medicamine facie* 35–42). Such magical practices were violent and aimed against the object of desire, rather than strategies of self-improvement. Elsewhere, Ovid constructs an elaborate analogy between the female application of cosmetics and artistic creativity (*Ars Amatoria* 3. 219–25). One of the images he employs is sculptural; the making-up of the female face, a repellent activity to be concealed from the potential lover, is like the classical Greek sculptor Myron's work upon a shapeless lump of marble.[30] Ovid's cosmetics have an oxymoronic quality as genuinely beautifying but also confirming women's underlying ugliness. Pliny's made-up women are living, breathing statues.

Pliny gives an ambiguous position in his text to the drug *nepenthes* ('opium poppy'), administered by Helen to the male heroes in Homer's *Odyssey* (*Od.* 4. 220–6). *Nepenthes* is given by Homer's Helen to the men as an antidote to their lamentations, but Telemachus still grieves (4. 290–1). Pliny's Helen in this context merely served before the meal a wine which banished cares; the properties of *nepenthes* are implicitly trans-

---

[29] At 30. 28–39, Pliny lists facial cures, again mainly for the removal of blemishes. They include lichen and rose-oil, mixed up in concoctions of animal derivatives.

[30] For the enduring idea of poisonous cosmetics, see Hallissy, *Venomous Woman*, 35–7.

ferred to the wine (23. 41). Furthermore *helenium* itself, when added to wine, displayed the qualities ideally attributed to *nepenthes*, giving joy and dispelling sadness; coming from Helen's tears it must have had an inoculative quality (21. 159). At 28. 117, Pliny, citing Democritus, says that *helenium* drunk from a chameleon's skin was a cure for melancholy; this seems a further example of an insidious, contagious redundancy among the herbs in the *Natural History*. *Helenium* also alleviates asthma, is a remedy for snake-bites when taken in wine, and kills mice (21. 159).

By giving the properties of *nepenthes* to both the wine served by Helen and her plant, *helenium*, Pliny avoids the troubling failure of *nepenthes* in Homer, as well as enhancing Helen's status as a doctor. We are told that Helen received her training in pharmacology from the queen in Egypt, a fact which Pliny gleans from Homer. This is raised as Pliny discusses Antonius Castor's Italian garden and mentions Homer giving the prize for herbs to Egypt (25. 12). In this context, Helen's pharmacopoeia now includes *nepenthes*, in spite of its odd omission when Pliny alluded to the Odyssean meal in Sparta. *Nepenthes*, which brought oblivion and forgetfulness of sorrow, becomes mysteriously in the *Natural History* a drug administered by Helen *omnibus mortalibus* ('to all mortals'). *Nepenthes* is Helen's gift to mankind in Pliny, not just Telemachus. The Egyptian origin of Helen's pharmacological knowledge may be an antidote to the troubling idea of Italy as drug-infested. In any case, Pliny's Helen was an obvious complement to his Cleopatra of Egypt. If Pliny's Cleopatra represented the risks of poison, of an alienated therapy which would fragment and invade the body, in the manner of natural sympathies it is a woman who holds out the cure. In contrast to the cold artistry of Cleopatra, Helen's therapy is warm and reassuring.

Poisoning in Pliny typifies its status in Roman culture as an uncanny visual art. The epitome of the cold, female poisoner in the *Natural History* is Cleopatra. She has a value, as a means of confronting annihilation. Yet the story of Cleopatra remains a dangerous confession of Pliny's own dubious practice as a medical writer who must delve into poisons as well as cures. Helen appears as an antidote. Struggling to suppress Homeric ambiguities, Helen's *ars* appears a self-possessed one and her drug aimed chiefly at self-administration. Helen holds out the fantasy of an appropriate and consolatory spectacularizing of only female bodies and an unambiguous therapy.

7

Discovering the Body in Roman Oratory

ERIK GUNDERSON

IN order to appreciate the stakes in the game of the deployment of the male body in public oratorical performance at Rome, we first have to take seriously the idea that the orator is a good man, a *vir bonus*. In the Roman tradition, Cato lays down the definition that the orator is a good man skilled at speaking, and the social morality of his definition persists throughout Latin literature.[1] The public speaker will be called upon to prosecute and to defend in the courthouse, to explain and to propose resolutions to the people, and to debate with peers in a legislative body. Yet when the orator is defined by way of his essence rather than his function, the space for an elaborate technology of presence opens up at the site of rhetorical performance: rhetoric in this case can never be 'mere rhetoric' as we say today. Moreover, the positing of a prior and virtuous presence to the orator has profound consequences for the orator's body:[2] this body must represent the virtue of the character

This is a condensed version of E. Gunderson, 'Contested Subjects: Rhetorical Theory and the Body' (dissertation, University of California, Berkeley, 1996), 55–88. I would like to thank T. Habinek, M. Griffith, M. Wyke, and an anonymous reader for their invaluable help at various stages in this project.

[1] The bibliography on the *vir bonus* is extensive. On the persistence of Cato's definition of the orator in Roman thought see G. Kennedy, *The Art of Rhetoric in the Roman World, 300 B.C.–A.D. 300* (Princeton University Press, Princeton, 1972), 56–7. A. Michel highlights the social usefulness of the good man in *Rhétorique et philosophie chez Cicéron; Essai sur les fondements philosophiques de l'art de persuader* (Presses Universitaires de France, Paris, 1960), 15–16. For the morality of oratory in general see pp. 19–38. A. Gwynn explains Quintilian's phrase by way of a general moral reaction against his age in *Roman Education from Cicero to Quintilian* (Oxford University Press, Oxford, 1926), 230–41. E. Laughton insists upon the Romanness of such a rhetorical morality in 'Cicero and the Greek Orators', *American Journal of Philology*, 82 (1961), 28.

[2] Useful sociological analyses of bodies and gestures can be found in J. Bremmer and H. Roodenburg (eds.), *A Cultural History of Gesture* (Cornell University Press, Ithaca, NY, 1992), P. Bourdieu, *The Logic of Practice* (Stanford University Press, Stanford, Calif., 1990), J.-C. Schmitt, 'Gestures: Introduction and General Bibliography', *History and Anthropology*, 1 (1984), 1–28, and L. Boltanski, 'Les Usages sociaux du corps', *Annales ESC* 26 (1971), 205–33. M. Mauss, 'Techniques of the Body', *Economy and Society*, 2 (1973), 70–87 remains

who bears it. Appearances must always correspond to some socially sanctioned vision of reality. The orator's body then is not so much a material substance, as a social one where its sex and station are vital concerns.

Who, or what, is a good man? Taken separately, the two sides of the term *bonus* (good) and *vir* (man) can be analysed by reference both to their lexical entries and to the broader social discourse of Rome. Such a distinction is perhaps tendentious to the extent that words can never be segregated from the society that uses them, but I would like to start from the dictionary and to proceed on from there to demonstrate the social scope of this phrase.

In Latin, a *vir* is an adult male. But the same word also signifies a man who is a husband or a soldier. Thus, in 'pregnant' uses, a man in Latin is a real man, a manly man. The term also designates a position of authority and responsibility: the adult is enfranchised while the child (or slave) is not;[3] the man rules his wife in the household; the soldier is the defender of the safety of the state. In short, the term evokes more than mere gender.[4]

On the other side of the phrase, *bonus* means 'good'. This goodness can be very open-ended and impute a broadly positive moral, aesthetic, or utilitarian quality to the term it modifies: a good person, a good painting, a good tool. More specifically, though, this goodness may indi-

---

a classic within this realm. G. Graf investigates Quintilian from this perspective in 'The Gestures of Roman Actors and Orators', in Bremmer and Roodenburg (eds.), *A Cultural History of Gesture*, 36–58. K. Tuite, 'The Production of Gesture', *Semiotica*, 93 (1993), 83–105 examines the semiotics of gestures. Within contemporary critical theory, one can look to works such as J. Butler, 'Foucault and the Paradox of Bodily Inscriptions', *Journal of Philosophy*, 86 (1989), 601–7, J. Butler, *Bodies that Matter: On the Discursive Limits of 'Sex'* (Routledge, New York, 1993), and S. Lash, 'Genealogy and the Body: Foucault, Deleuze, Nietzsche', *Theory, Culture, Society*, 2 (1984), 1–17. The problem of the performer's body and voice at Rome has been discussed at length in C. Edwards, *The Politics of Immorality in Ancient Rome* (Cambridge University Press, Cambridge, 1993), T. Barton, *Power and Knowledge: Astrology, Physiognomics, and Medicine under the Roman Empire* (University of Michigan Press, Ann Arbor, 1994), and M. Gleason, *Making Men: Sophists and Self-Presentation in Ancient Rome* (Princeton University Press, Princeton, 1995).

[3] In both Greek and Latin, the terms for child, παῖς and *puer*, can also mean slave. Hence the opposition between man and 'boy' revolves around the issue of either being in power and authority or being subject to someone else's power and authority.

[4] Wyke shows how the physical enactment of this gender plays in the social field. She concludes, 'In the practices of the Roman world, the surface of the male body is thus fully implicated in definitions of power and civic responsibility' in 'Woman in the Mirror: The Rhetoric of Adornment in the Roman World', in L. Archer, S. Fischler, and M. Wyke (eds.), *Women in Ancient Societies: 'An Illusion of the Night'* (Macmillan, Basingstoke, 1994), 135.

cate that a person is socially reliable or reputable: a good chap, a good citizen.[5] And, when used of men, it often indicates men of substance or social standing: a prominent citizen, a leading citizen.[6] Thus the masculine plural of the adjective standing alone, *boni* or 'good [men]', also implies the wealth that goes with station.[7] Good, then, is not so much a bland qualifier as it is a pointer to evaluation within a social context. In other words, a 'good man' is a man seen *tout court* in his full, dominant social capacity and one who has proven himself valuable within this society. He is an asset to the world, and in all likelihood has derived assets (*bona*) from the world. He is the man on top of society, and the man most invested in it. Similarly, as the orator becomes isomorphous with the political morality latent in the phrase 'good man', the public speaker, the prosecutor, the defender, and the senator becomes the man always already authorized so to express himself and the man to whom one must listen.

Not only the bodies of good men, but all bodies in general are subject to this action of primary acculturation. Contemporary critical thought on the body has taught us that the body cannot be seen as some raw material upon which some fully present and conscious agent acts, giving order to the chaos of his corporeal aspect. There is no fundamental facticity to the body, a body which stands independently of the law or a body which enters into a relationship with the symbolic order as an equal partner. The body here loses its status as a biological fact which is given meaning by the personality of its bearer: the body is another symbol in a world of symbols which the subject can never fully master.[8]

In seeking to secure a special social status for the orator's body as

---

[5] Compare J. Hellegouarc'h on the mercurial use of the term *boni* in *Le Vocabulaire latin des relations et des partis politiques sous la République* (Belles Lettres, Paris, 1963), 489–90. The appellation reflects partisanship, not a fixed content.

[6] For the political reading of *bonus* and the Latin words with which it is associated, see Hellegouarc'h, *Le Vocabulaire latin*, 184–95. P. Sinclair, 'The Sententia in "Rhetorica ad Herennium": A Study in the Sociology of Rhetoric', *American Journal of Philology*, 114 (1993), 561–80 covers the social status of the orator as leading citizen.

[7] The *Oxford Latin Dictionary* cites Plautus, *Captivi* 583: 'It's characteristic of the down-and-out to be spiteful and to envy good (i.e. affluent) men.'

[8] Judith Butler takes notions of body which have had a long and popular currency in Western thought, and reiterates Foucault's investigation of the mechanisms which stamp the body with intelligibility. See Butler, *Bodies that Matter*, 32–55. Employing notions found in Foucault's *Discipline and Punish* and *History of Sexuality* she produces a portrait of a body whose origin is not the soul but a constitutive power which resides outside any conscious subject. See especially p. 49 for 'the sex of materiality' as a point of inquiry logically anterior to 'the materiality of sex'. Assuming the latter without attending to the former dis-enables certain kinds of feminist inquiry.

exclusively a good and virile body, Roman rhetorical theorists such as Quintilian make new and special appeals to and readings of the truth of the body. The ancient theorists want to take the body of their student and secure for it a distinct and exclusive reading. The rhetorical theorist secures for the good man his goodness and his masculinity and protects the speaker from a potential collapse into illegitimate effeminacy. This same process, though, reveals the lines of power which trace the surface of the body, giving it its legible contours within Roman culture. While rhetorical theory may wish to derive the meaning of the ideal male body from the anterior principle of the good soul, when we read this ancient reading of the body, we can see instead a body which is shot through with the effects of the matrix of knowledge/power which allows for the transcription of meanings onto bodily surfaces. And this same knowledge/power which delineates the body also delineates a soul for the body, a bodily soul set off against other possible and possibly corrupt souls. Ancient theoretical speculation upon the body thus serves as part of a strategic production and reproduction of the Roman male subject as a whole, a subject read in both his physical and metaphysical aspects.[9] Indeed the very last words of the eleventh book of Quintilian's *Institutio oratoria* are meant to ward off the threats to the virile authority of the orator's ideal bodily performance. These crises emerge where the body is ill-regulated and incompletely understood by its bearer:

> But contemporary taste has adopted and demands a rather more excited delivery and in some circumstances this is suitable. Still, it must be kept in check lest while we seek the elegance of the actor, we lose the authority of the noble and serious man. (Quintilian 11. 3. 180–4)

I would like to take Quintilian's *Institutio oratoria* as my prime exemplar of the process of exposition and reflection to which the orator subjects himself. Quintilian published his massive work somewhere around the 90s CE. In his encyclopaedic survey of the departments of oratory he collects, sorts, and comments upon centuries of Greek and Roman thought on oratory. Quintilian's discussion of performance is the fullest extant, and for its author it represents a crowning gesture and culmination of a tradition of corporeal know-

---

[9] The orator is asked to recognize himself in these telling descriptions: he is met with a hailing such as Althusser describes as the inaugural moment of subjectivation, the moment of interpellation. The theory of the body thus becomes a hailing of both a body and a soul which inaugurates the twain within a sociality which was always waiting to catch them up. See L. Althusser, *Lenin and Philosophy*, trans. B. Brewster (Monthly Review Press, New York, 1971).

ledge.[10] Quintilian has outdone his predecessors, and in particular he far outstrips Cicero, his inspiration and his ideal. Quintilian's excellence leads at once to a consideration of the question of motives: what was failing in other rhetorical texts? Why was there a poverty of knowledge about the body? How was it that the body should need a longer and more detailed description? Quintilian promises little novelty, and certainly no innovations of 'substance', only those of detail.[11] Yet when it comes to performance, Quintilian's extension of knowledge of details represents the extension of the potentialities for the exercise of power on the Roman male body.[12]

In ancient theoretical depictions of the body, a discovery of the body takes place. This is a discovery in two senses. First, the body is disclosed: 'truths' are revealed about the body. Of course, these truths are vital fictions, products which themselves produce a social reality with real material consequences. This is the second sense in which discovery can be used: the revelation is an innovation. In this sense the rhetorical theorist is making up the body as he goes. The body revealed is revealed as specifically thus or so. The body which the theorist beholds is a body which has been constituted as legible, a body made for reading. The shapes which have been discovered are arbitrary to the extent that other knowledges of the body could be imagined, but they are specific and specifically efficacious to the extent that these readings of the body have real and worldly effects in Roman society.

Quintilian's discussion of performance yokes the body to the soul. Quintilian hopes to secure the validity of his enterprise by assuring his readers that the soul remains both the prison and the gaoler of the body. Quintilian routinely asserts that the 'inside' of the orator is reflected in the appearances he produces, that good oratory is a matter of true appearances. The inner man is readily revealed by the examination of external signs:

---

[10] An excellent discussion of later and mostly Greek material on performance can be found in Gleason, *Making Men*. E. Fantham examines Quintilian's relationship to earlier authors' discussions of performance in 'Quintilian on Performance: Traditional and Personal Elements in *Institutio* 11. 3', *Phoenix*, 36 (1982), 243–63.

[11] Quintilian apologizes for the extent of his analytics in 1. 7. 34–5: many great speakers have spent much labour on what would seem to be the least details of oratory.

[12] See M. Foucault, 'Prison Talk', in *Power/Knowledge: Selected Interviews and Other Writings, 1972–1977*, ed. C. Gordon (Pantheon Books, New York, 1980), 52: 'The exercise of power perpetually creates knowledge, and, conversely, knowledge constantly induces effects of power . . . Knowledge and power are integrated with one another, and there is no point in dreaming of a time when knowledge will cease to depend on power.'

Now it is time to speak of what a suitable delivery is. It is surely that which is accommodated to those things about which we speak. This accommodation the very movements of our souls furnish for the most part, and the voice rings as it is struck. (Quintilian 11. 3. 61)

A radical reading of this last piece of advice would obviate the need for Quintilian's own text, as one would need only to feel a thing in order to speak it. This is in fact the position of some of the nameless theoretical enemies who appear in Quintilian's text.[13] However, Quintilian heads off such a threat by asserting that some passions are genuine but need art to shape them.[14]

The structure of Quintilian's arguments here and elsewhere has an important consequence for his student: the contest between affectation and belief can never be decided in the case of Quintilian's version of oratory. Quintilian has pre-empted the reading of his orator for affectation with his *natura* (nature) and *cura* (labour) formulation: 'nothing is perfect where nature is not supplemented by labour' (11. 3. 11). Belief is now always also a matter of affectation rewritten as *cura*. That is, the orator can only really perform with sincerity after first learning, investigating, and knowing his own body. This discipline supplements the nature it discovers and complements it, but discipline also insinuates itself in the place of nature.[15] The ancient rhetorical handbook then becomes a necessary prop for male subjectivity and a tool without which the orator is lost to himself. The text ensures that there will be no body without the text, and, accordingly, that there will be no soul without the theorization of the soul.

The motions of the body and the modulations of the voice serve as their own sort of language, a *sermo corporis*, that is, 'a language of the body'.[16] Accordingly the body itself is opened up to the full critical vocabulary of the Roman rhetorical tradition. All concerns and regulations which may have been directed at the orator's verbal style can potentially be rethought with regard to the physical aspect of perfor-

---

[13] 11. 3. 11.

[14] On the other hand, fictions suffer from the lack of passions to inspire them. In the latter case, Quintilian's advice is to begin imagining for oneself thoughts which would inspire the passions one would feign and so to be moved by one's own fictions. Thus even in the case of fictions, if they are to be done well, they should have a kernel of truth to them.

[15] This is Derrida's 'dangerous supplement'. See J. Derrida, *Of Grammatology*, trans. G. Spivak (Johns Hopkins University Press, Baltimore, 1976).

[16] The Latin phrase appears in Quintilian 11. 3. 1 which is referring to Cicero, *de oratore* 3. 222. Bodily eloquence, *eloquentia corporis*, also mentioned in 11. 3. 1 is taken from Cicero, *Orator* 55.

mance as well. The fetishism of the language in which oratory participates thus becomes a fetishism of bodies. And as is the case with any fetish, this new body is invested with mystical potency. Yet the source of this power is ultimately disavowed and deferred.[17] The orator's status is dependent upon the mystification of his cultural capital as a 'gift' which naturally adheres to his person, to his inmost self. And the technical manual participates in the bestowing of this gift while ostensibly only discovering truths about performance, a *natura* which *cura* supplements. It is by the text's *cura* that the student's body becomes naturalized. At the same time this *cura* or discipline revolves back on the question of the gift as a whole, exposing the basic ficticity of the soul which animates the elite male performer.

The body of the Roman orator is always on the verge of failing; it needs a prop and training. The theoretician's gaze catches within its scopic field a body which is always in need of reworking within the terms of that same vision.[18] In this sense, Quintilian is a producer of knowledge/power, and he stands against the nameless others of 11. 3. 11 who think it enough to be born in order to be a good orator. Their version of hegemonic and virile bodily performances, for them, proceeds without question. But Quintilian always needs to supplement nature with effort. In so doing, he exposes the body to a different regime of truth, one of discipline and surveillance, even if discipline's goal is the salvation of the authentic good man. Yet as observation and self-knowledge collapse, Quintilian ensures that spectatorship is a socially significant act. Whether an audience or a theoretical text watches him, the orator must know that he is watched. And in the case of the watching of a text like Quintilian's, the orator is asked to take up a self-reflexive gaze: watch yourself first, foremost, and most carefully. In every instance watching is cruel, an activity always implicated not just in evaluation, but in hostile evaluation.

The student of Roman oratory cannot be master of his appearances, yet he is a creature who is given to the senses. In contemporary terms a signifying agent is never master of the meanings he or she produces. Quintilian's own instructions to the orator reveal the extent to which the

[17] See P. Bourdieu and L. Boltanski, 'La Fétichisme de la langue', *Actes de la recherche en sciences sociales*, 4 (1975), 12.

[18] The rhetorical theorist is thus somewhat like the physiognomist. The former, though, tends to have a more 'therapeutic' gaze as opposed to the diagnostic or declarative approach of the latter. Similarly, physiognomy tends to constitute a science of the other rather than a technique of the self. On physiognomy and the 'decipherment of gender', see Gleason, *Making Men*, 55–81. See also Barton, *Power and Knowledge*, 95–132.

orator will not be able to control fully the readings and rereadings of his bodily meanings. For example, in the following anecdote, Quintilian regulates how and where one may walk. But in the course of this instruction, one realizes that a speaker's stride can and will be read against him.

Stepping forward will be appropriate, but only if opportune, brief, moderate, and infrequent; and one will even at times engage in a certain walking to and fro on account of the unseasonable delays provoked by the audience's applause, although Cicero says that one should do this rarely and not cover much space. But to run around and about and to do that which Domitius Afer said of Manilius Sura, namely, 'to bustle', is totally incompetent. And Flavus Verginius cleverly asked of a certain opposing speaker how many miles he had declaimed. (Quintilian 11. 3. 126)

By seeing himself being seen, the orator hopes to gain possession over himself and his meaning.[19] He installs the self-reflexive in order to attain a sense of mastery: he is not within the gaze; the gaze is his. In response to observation on the part of the world, the orator reacts by observing himself, by being the first and harshest critic of his own body. To this end Quintilian evokes an illustration in which the great Greek orator Demosthenes practises his performance before a mirror in order to see, to know, and to correct the significations produced by his movements (11. 3. 68).

The truths which arise from this auto-theorization are used to posit a subject who is in fact and after all what he sees himself to be. Thus the relationship of self-observation which is installed at the foundation of the relationship to the orator's body is also a relationship which will be used to produce the illusion of a presence and of a valid subject.[20] At the same time, this observation operates as a parody of the function of the gaze. The orator presents an image of himself to an imagined scopic field, photo-graphing his body and movements in this imagined space.

The theatre of the subject, though, is no idyllic scene. Within this private spectacle, the body seen is haunted by spectres which are always in the process of falling away from the light. The desire of the eye which watches over such a theatre is used to constitute a body which meets this

[19] Compare J. Lacan, *The Four Fundamental Concepts of Psycho-Analysis*, trans. A. Sheridan (Norton, New York, 1981), 106 and 79–90.
[20] Compare the prisoner who becomes the principle of his own subjection within the optical apparatus of the panopticon. See M. Foucault, *Discipline and Punish* (Vintage, New York, 1997), 202–3.

desire, a body which is desired both as being the body of a good man and as not being a different body. And, of these two bodies, the good body remains at its core unspeakable (*inenarrabilis*; 11. 3. 177), while the bad body must be spoken of that it may be exiled.

The general situation of observation and self-observation recorded by Quintilian reaches a sort of logical extreme in the case of the analysis of the body.[21] The proliferation of the body parts observed produces more knowledge of the speaking body, but it also leaves that body more liable to the same questions of legitimacy and illegitimacy which have dogged it all along. That is, now the general impression or tenor of a performance is not enough, even the eyebrows must be observed, evaluated, and found acceptable. The more the orator's body is known in detail, the more it is liable to failures and in need of prohibitions and regulations. The expanded analysis of the body is less helpful than it is monitory.

The orator needs to bear in mind that he is watched with more attention than are others. The orator's body is a public object, the object of close public scrutiny. Care must be taken to make sure that appearances are kept up. As far as his clothing is concerned, the orator should keep in mind that 'there is no particular dress for an orator, but in the orator's case it attracts more attention' (11. 3. 137). Quintilian follows these words with a detailed description of personal grooming and its varied significances. But in this introduction to the topic, he points out a crucial dilemma. First, people watch the orator carefully, examining him from head to toe. Accordingly, he ought to look good. But in looking good, he should look like a good man: this is our *vir bonus* again. He must look neither dishevelled nor like a dandy.

In this passage, the orator learns both that he is watched, and then that he is to present himself to be watched. He is to present himself to be watched both as a spectacular or arresting figure but also as a figure which is securely masculine: 'One's dress ought to be spotless and manly, as it should be for all honourable people' (11. 3. 137). The stained, the effeminate, and the dishonourable are the terms which produce the constitutive outside of this portrait. The orator's virility, though, consists neither in a coarse nor in a refined relationship to one's attire and grooming. In short, this attractive virility is an art which conceals itself and which must conceal itself, a discipline which evanesces into a natural appearance. If observation is aggressive, then one ought to offer an

---

[21] For female self-observation in the context of cosmetics, see Wyke, 'Woman in the Mirror'.

appearance which is an essence, one which offers no purchase for the critical eye: how can one find fault with reality?

When a good performance is seen, the body that is presented is mystified. The proper performance and the character it presents, the *vir bonus*, somehow elude simple and positive description. Claims to the potency of a proper performance can only be debunked, positive precepts cannot be offered. So, at any rate, does Quintilian round out his discussion of performance. After giving many and detailed pieces of advice, threats, and behaviours to avoid, Quintilian concludes his precepts with a disavowal of the possibility of a truly positive efficacy for his text. His discussion apparently is valid only in its diagnosis of disease and disorder. The orator is commanded to be seemly and becoming (*decorum, decere*). He is observed for this quality. Indeed, his entire labour tends towards allowing him to project such an air. At the same time, his labour does not secure his goal:

One thing should be added to this. While the becoming (*decorum*) is particularly watched for in performance, often different actions become different speakers. For there is a certain latent and inexpressible logic to performance; and, just as this maxim is true, namely that the principle point of study is to be becoming in whatever you may do, so also is it true that this cannot happen without study nor can the whole of it be transmitted via study. (Quintilian 11. 3. 177)

The oratorical project is always incomplete.[22] The consummate student will only have assured himself that he has a chance of not failing, not that he has actually succeeded. Seemliness remains ever elusive.[23] One cannot make a critique of proper performances because they succeed along the ways indicated by Pierre Bourdieu: the physical bearing in these cases seems to be a gift of the person, a natural and inalienable possession which confirms the legitimacy of the domination of his male gender and high station.

In the same logical moment which promises the socially dominant the sublime status of their own decorum, other lessons are communicated as well. First, this virile decorum can only be secured by study and labour:

---

[22] One can compare Foucault on the care of the self as always incomplete and the production of an existence which is 'a kind of permanent exercise'. M. Foucault, *The History of Sexuality*, iii: *The Care of the Self*, trans. R. Hurley (Vintage, New York, 1988), 49.

[23] There are certain advantages to the mythology of decorum: the common man can never expect a formula or recipe which would allow him to transform himself into a man of substance. Ineffability hence can serve as a guarantor against unregulated social mobility. See Kennedy, *Art of Rhetoric*, 90–5 for the suggestion that the expulsion of the Latin rhetoricians in 92 BCE was partially motivated by the problem of rhetorical training which was too accessible and too easy.

it is not a truly arbitrary trait. The mere fact of having been born does not make a person either properly male or a good speaker.[24] But the orator has also learned a science of unauthorized bodies. The student has been taught to look at the body for the indecorous and the illegitimate, to force the body to answer up in all of its details and divisions to the demand that it not be inappropriate.

Quintilian's detailed discussion of the body of the orator appears in two extended passages. First he describes the face and its elements (11. 3. 72 ff.), and he later moves from the head downwards (11. 3. 82 ff.). In addition to these two sections, the proper use of the hands is a constant bodily theme. It is this last portion of the anatomy that I would like to take up first. The observation due the hands serves as a case study for the regard due all of the body's elements.

The hands are a locus of such keen interest for Quintilian owing to their amazing expressive capacities. 'Truly one can hardly tell how many movements the hands have, the hands without which delivery would be maimed and debilitated, since the hands virtually follow the very wealth of our words' (11. 3. 85). That is, the more invested a site is with meaning or potential meaning, the more knowledge and discipline come to surround it. The supposed eloquence of the hands necessitates special concern and attention. If the hands can all but speak of themselves (11. 3. 85), then the rhetorical theorist is duty bound to speak of and for them, and to speak exhaustively if at all possible.

Quintilian recounts over a dozen specific hand gestures between 11. 3. 92 and 11. 3. 104. Each gesture is defined, delimited, regulated, and often moralized. Knowledge and obligation proceed in tandem.[25] Quintilian is not only defining and delimiting, he is also instructing both performer and audience. The language of the body is being taught and reproduced for both parties alike. And while the language of the body has been described as universal and easily intelligible,[26] it actually finds its reproduction and inculcation in passages such as this.

More than taxonomy is at stake in this detailed examination of the body. A social morality is immediately attached to the speculative project. The moral definition and legislation of these specific and specified gestures can be seen in 11. 3. 103: 'There is that hollow and spread-

---

[24] This is 11. 3. 11 again. This formulation allows for an extension of Sinclair's 'The Sententia in "Rhetorica ad Herennium"': his sociology of rhetorical maxims thereby becomes an analysis relevant to the study of the body as well.

[25] On the relationship between discipline and obligation, compare Foucault, *Discipline and Punish*, 180.

[26] See esp. 11. 3. 65–7.

fingered use of the hand where it is lifted above the height of the shoulder with a certain movement as if it were exhorting: this use of the hands is more accepted by foreign schools, tremulous, and stagy.' This passage, rather than challenging the idea of the universality of gestures, does more to consolidate the notion that foreigners, effeminates, and actors are all the parodic and despised agents whose movements the virile Roman orator specifically does not reproduce.[27] While there is no consistent theory of the use of hands being spelled out in this section, and instead it resembles a laundry-list of gestures, the themes of decorum and boundaries are repeated several times as the hand is given meaning and regulated in the same moment. Quintilian has more to say of the hands than just listing some of their gestures: the hands must be restrained from illicit social allusions.

Furthermore, the hands must be carefully coordinated with the rest of the speech. Indeed all elements of oratory are bound by a law of homology which insists that every part be consonant with the whole. As the body has to be in accord with the text (11. 3. 67), so also should the hands move along with the sense, accompanying the meaning of the verbal aspect of the performance.[28] At the same time, the hand should not be subject to the rigid rule of one gesture per three words.[29] This proposition, called 'too subtle' (*nimia subtilitate*) by Quintilian, is rejected first because it is declared impossible. The three-word rule is, however, well intended as it avoids the two failings of a lazy hand (*otiosa*) or endless movement. The orator needs to observe the 'lurking beats of speech' with his gestures. Such an argument reinstalls gestures into a natural and naturally harmonized role *vis-à-vis* language. The language itself dictates the movements of the hands, and the gesture which follows the sense is actually the one closest to nature.

The orator sets himself to the study and reproduction of signs given by nature. Labour again is a process designed to complement nature and fulfil a teleology latent within it. If the orator lives up to the nature of language, the problem of a lazy or overly busy hand need no longer be

---

[27] On actors, orators, and gestures, see Graf, 'The Gestures of Roman Actors'. The relationship between acting and oratory as well as the morality of acting are topics which cannot be concisely addressed here. See, for example, Gunderson, 'Contested Subjects', 112–51 and Edwards, *Politics of Immorality*, 98–136.

[28] The regulation of the hand also extends to having it perform differently in the different logical sections of a speech. The hand begins a speech one way, and it ends one another. See, for example, 11. 3. 158, 11. 3. 159, and 11. 3. 161–2.

[29] 11. 3. 107. Compare the discussion of Antonius' use of his hands in Cicero, *Brutus* 141: his hands keep to the general tenor of his speech, but they do not express its ideas word for word.

considered. Those who would impose decisive rules will only impose an apparatus divorced from nature and one which will endlessly clash with it. Thus Quintilian's project, while producing and reproducing knowledge and self-knowledge at every turn, pushes the source of its own legitimacy back into an unassailable register. And the apotheosis of the project of submission to Quintilian's dictates is presented not as a mastery of the laws of oratory but as a fulfilment of the dictates of nature. In other words, good gestures have a natural authenticity and efficacy which is put out of reach of critique, revision, and revolution. The consummate student is not only a good man but is a 'natural' one as well.

The rest of the body receives a treatment much akin to that of the hands. As no one element of the body is quite as invested with meaning as the hands are, it is only as an ensemble or collection of prescriptions that the injunctions levelled at the rest of the body fully resemble those given to the hands. None the less, the logic which regulated the hands holds true for the rest of the body, and this body is equally susceptible to ever finer degrees of analysis, description, and prescription.

Quintilian's examination of the orator's body starts with the head: 'The head, just as in the body itself, is of primary importance for performance as well, vital both for that decorum of which I have spoken and also for the conveyance of meaning' (11. 3. 68). From the head, Quintilian moves to the face as the head's dominant feature (11. 3. 72). The face is itself subdivided into the eyes, which are its most important feature (11. 3. 75), the eyebrows (11. 3. 78), and lastly the lips and the nostrils (11. 3. 80). Leaving the face and head, Quintilian continues downwards, discussing the neck (11. 3. 82) and then the shoulders (11. 3. 83). Moving out now rather than continuing down, Quintilian proceeds on to the arms (11. 3. 84) and then gets into the hands in some detail as discussed above. The perusal of the body is thus fairly orderly.

In the course of this survey, Quintilian stops at each feature long enough to describe its potency and its dangers. The face is almost as good as words (11. 3. 72). The spirit shines forth from the eyes (11. 3. 75). Misusing the eyes and showing them filled with pleasure is a failing which is beneath even an idiot (11. 3. 76). The eyebrows must not become comic and dissent from what we say (11. 3. 78). Hardly anything good can come of the lips and nostrils; here restraint is the best course of action (11. 3. 80). The neck ought to be straight, and poor use of the neck lends an impression of servility (11. 3. 82).

Each time Quintilian turns his eyes upon the body it is invested with both significance and risk. The body is first defined as telling, and then it threatens to misspeak and ruin its bearer. The more of the body that is given to be seen, the more labour is required of the student. With each division come new and increased obligations. Clearly the logic of analysis could be taken further, and still more minute elements picked out. The earliest preserved rhetorical handbook in Latin, the *Rhetorica ad Herennium*, makes relatively simple injunctions to the body, and in contemporary editions of the work the *Rhetorica* requires only a couple of pages to makes its survey of performance. On the other hand, the discussion of delivery in an edition of Quintilian today covers scores of pages each of which is filled with the most minute bodily details. By the same token, if the increased knowledge derived from Quintilian is not enough to guarantee security, might not further analysis be in order? The proliferation of body parts has not given more security, but only opened up more prospects for failure, more sites to examine and find wanting, more parts which must be harmonized with a whole, and more telling elements whose tale must be watched. More nature (*natura*), that is, requires more labour (*cura*). And not even Quintilian's massive tome is sufficient to live up either to nature or to discipline.

Not only is the body carefully articulated in its parts, it is also coordinated and organized such that its elements will be orchestrated into a harmonized whole. So the orator's body is first broken into pieces, and then it is reassembled into an ensemble which must give a unified performance. We have already seen how the hands must match up with the passage delivered. This is the harmony of movement and text. But the body should also correspond to itself, its parts moving together and harmoniously. For example, one's torso ought to be in concord with the other gesturing taking place (11. 3. 122). A more elaborate package of movements can be seen in the following: 'A restrained voice, moderate gestures, a toga resting on the shoulder, and a slight motion of the trunk from side to side while the eyes turn to face in the same direction will often be becoming' (11. 3. 161). This whole passage contains collections of other coordinated movements, looks, voices, and gestures: a variety of little scenes have been staged,[30] not only offering examples of good bodies but also consolidating the principle of careful coordination of all of the body's lately discovered parts.

To the carefully orchestrated harmony of this body, Quintilian opposes a variety of bodily failings. At 11. 3. 160, Quintilian enumerates a number of errors of excess. In these instances, the speaker apparently

---

[30] One can also compare 11. 3. 70 which tells how the head should follow the gestures.

seeks to be a good and serious man, but instead comes off as too severe and takes himself too seriously. The stance and face become hardened and harsh. The carefully poised body becomes bent out of its proper shape. The well-placed feet drift apart. These affectations are all intended to make the spectator take the orator and his passions seriously, but they dispel the 'easy' and 'natural' gravity which Quintilian recommends. The ideal oratorical body, a virile body which is taken seriously by an audience, thus conforms to Bourdieu's schema wherein the body is 'something that one is'.[31] This presence should appear neither artificial nor intemperate, neither sterile and contrived nor wild and undisciplined.

On the other hand, many entries are excluded from the orator's bodily lexicon, or if they are allowed, it is with the implied tag 'vulgar' or 'colloquial'. As Bourdieu says of so-called 'popular' language, 'The notion of "popular speech" is one of the products of the application of dualistic taxonomies which structure the social world according to the categories of high and low.'[32] In other words, these vulgar or illegitimate gestures are admitted only so that they may then be made to bear the trace of the principle and structure of domination which excludes them from the register of the proper. One of the primary actions of Quintilian's text is the reinscription of the body as a terrain divided, a space populated by authorized or unauthorized and accordingly abjected sounds and movements.[33] The task of Quintilian's student is to examine his own body after these same principles, to cleanse from his person these unauthorized traces of other and illegitimate selves. This situation produces an obsession with the meaning of the male body as social meaning and concomitantly an obsession with securing one's own body as meaning what it must mean.

Ancient theories of performance train both the body (*actio*) and the voice (*pronuntiatio*). And, as was the case with his body, the orator's voice is likewise a virtual microcosm of the social world.[34] The training of the voice, accordingly, is the disciplining of this aspect of the body such that the voice rings out with the tones of a *vir bonus* and no others. If one

---

[31] See Bourdieu, *Logic of Practice*, 73.

[32] P. Bourdieu, *Language and Symbolic Power*, trans. G. Raymond and M. Adamson (Harvard University Press, Cambridge, Mass., 1991), 93.

[33] For example, we learn that gait reveals station (11. 3. 112); drawing in one's neck is servile (11. 3. 83); the head must not be barbarously inclined (11. 3. 69); and the movements as a whole should seem martial, not taken from the stage (1. 11. 18).

[34] Gleason, *Making Men*, gives an excellent discussion of the sociology of the voice during the Second Sophistic.

plays on the passage cited earlier where the voice rings as it is struck, then the training of the voice contributes to the socially recognized illusion that there is a manly essence striking the vocal chords and lending them its tones.

The care of the voice begins with good eating habits: observing and watching one's diet is important, because one has need of a voice which is 'strong' or *fortis* (11. 3. 23). This voice is going to be the voice of a rugged and hardy performer and not that of a prissy voice professional, a *phonascius*. The *phonascius* has a soft and tender voice, while the orator is a man of hard study and hard labour, a man who toughs it out and breaks a sweat. The voice is *fortis* once again at 11. 3. 64 where it is used in exhortations or calls to action. The function of exhortation is a hegemonic one, and the adjective *fortis* in its more martial or virile associations 'naturally' adheres to the situation. The manliness of the manly voice is hence also always more than mere gender: it implies, in addition to sex, an assumption about the legitimate role of that sex. This role is both martial and authoritative. And, as is implicit in the metaphor, the virility of the rhetorical body is also an aggressive one. One of the first victims of this cruelty, though, is the orator himself, for he is required to attack any signs of failure within his own body. This soldier's task is the production and policing of his own manliness.

Not surprisingly, then, the negative description of the voice is constructed around failures of manliness and authority. Already in 11. 3. 23 we have seen that the *fortis* voice was opposed to a soft and delicate one. This softness is the softness of effeminacy, and *mollis* when applied to another man is intended to be as hostile and unflattering as the use of the term 'fairy' is today.[35] Quintilian concludes in 11. 3. 24, from his arguments of 11. 3. 23, that 'accordingly we should not soften our voice with dainty pleasures nor imbue it with that habitual use which it would desire, but its exercise should be as its use ... It should be made hardy by habitual practice'.[36] This conclusion is practical for being first ethical.

[35] This is not to imply that 'softness' is necessarily isomorphous with any element of contemporary homosexuality. Rather, 'soft' is used in Rome with an aggressivity which resonates with the cruelty and delegitimization deployed by contemporary homophobia. See Edwards, *Politics of Immorality*, 67–8. Edwards also insists upon the pertinence in ancient contexts of the distinction between active and passive sexual pleasure, and the illegitimacy of the latter for a man. See, though, Edwards, *Politics of Immorality*, 96 for the more complex interactions of 'softness' with 'urbanity' in other authors.

[36] As with the parts, so for the whole: the adjective *mollis*, 'soft', again makes an appearance when the sum of performance is discussed: 'One must flee like the plague a *mollis* delivery, such as Cicero says Titius gave, from whence even a certain sort of dance was called the Titius' (11. 3. 128).

The delights which would not be part of the public life of a *vir bonus* are forbidden his voice as well. The orator's practice is precisely as his performance. In other words, he is always in character, even when he is off stage. Moreover, this character is predicated on renunciation, renunciation of pleasure and the feminine. And this renunciation extends not just to his personal habits and practices, but also to his treatment of individual elements of his body.

The voice needs constant protection against the gender troubles which assail it. The orator, in order to ensure the good care of his voice (*vocis bona cura*), needs 'a solid body lest our voice be attenuated to the meagreness of eunuchs, women, and the infirm' (11. 3. 19). And this solid body 'is provided by walks, rub-downs, sexual abstinence, ready digestion, in other words, frugality' (11. 3. 19). The collapse of the voice away from its manly ideal comes with a corresponding corruption of the body. The threat is specifically sexual: castration and effeminacy must be avoided. And then another term is added, illness. Now we can see another trope of authority: the orators are good men and good speakers because they are healthy; they are not defective like women or eunuchs. The path to securing this good health and manliness, though, requires 'frugality'. This observation and modulation of the whole of one's life again has sexuality introduced into it: sexual abstinence secures for the man a manly voice. A regime of discipline is again invoked as a safeguard to a fallible nature. Without discipline, a man may lose even his gender.[37] And this discipline is explicitly predicated on self-denial: pleasure and indulgence threaten one's being, while regulation and abstinence offer by way of pain and refusal the sublime pleasure of being a good man. Sexuality keeps recurring in this scene, but it is always hustled off stage.

The evaluation of performance returns again and again to the trope of deauthorization and silencing. There are legitimate bodies and then those that fall short of the status required to receive a hearing in the political space of Rome. Not surprisingly, the deauthorization of gestures extends to rival authors and orators. Attacks on their teachings are necessarily attacks on the bodies they recommend. And the substance of the attack remains the threat of political impotence produced by a failure to manifest the body borne by those who belong to the hegemonic classes. Even practised hands may go astray (11. 3. 117). Furthermore, the

---

[37] Good pronunciation and the proper use of the voice is described in some detail in 11. 3. 30–2. This passage is a veritable fugue on the sociology of the voice and the sociological dangers which adhere to it.

authority of other handbooks and other authors cannot be trusted: their gestures may be worse than gauche and rustic (11. 3. 117).

Set against these effetes and boors is the man of the city, the good Roman. Yet urbanity is not merely a neutral nor even a positive quality. In these same passages we have been discussing, the use of the term *urbanus* and its derivatives occurs only in hostile contexts. Thus the good man in his charmed circle is also always a man on the attack, actively protecting his exclusive territory. Quintilian's text marks out the space of the urbane as a place where one man assaults another, cutting at his opponents' performance, presence, and authority. Quintilian also urbanely mocks failed rival theoretical texts in this same spirit.

The two occurrences of the adverb *urbane* in Quintilian's discussion of delivery are both found in contexts where Quintilian lauds a witticism of one Roman made at the expense of another.[38] Thus in 11. 3. 126, Verginius Flavus asks an opponent who is moving around too much, how many miles he has declaimed that day. The regulation of the space of the body accordingly finds here its punitive obverse and representation of the cost of failure: too much movement leaves you ridiculous. At the same time, the man who punishes the transgressor and launches the barb that reveals the offence for all to see wins his own title: he is urbane. Similarly in 11. 3. 133 space is violated, a man is ridiculed, and another is praised. The rule of not crossing over towards the opposing counsel's bench is being laid down. Quintilian illustrates his law with an anecdote wherein Cassius Severus urbanely demands that boundary lines be put down on the ground to ward off an opponent's advances. The barb makes the adversary's metaphorical assault on his space into a literal one. It also shows the fellow boorish in that he needs a physical line to point out to him the proper spatial bounding of the Roman orator.

---

[38] M. Winterbottom highlights the adversarial aspect of *urbanitas* in 'Review of Ramage, *Urbanitas: Ancient Sophistication and Refinement*', *Classical Review*, 26 (1976), 59. E. Ramage, 'Cicero on Extra-Roman Speech', *Transactions of the American Philological Association*, 92 (1961), 481–94 recognizes the exclusionary tactics inhering within urbanity. E. Ramage, '*Urbanitas* in Cicero and Quintilian: A Contrast in Attitudes', *American Journal of Philology*, 84 (1963), 390–414 traces the historical variations in the semantic field of *urbanitas* from the period of Cicero to Quintilian. See A. Desmouliez, 'Sur la polémique de Cicéron et des Atticistes', *Revue des études latines*, 30 (1952), 170 for the connection between *urbanitas* and the elitist Attic style. The aggressive side of *urbanitas* is also clear from Quintilian's use of the definition of Domitius Martus at 6. 3. 104 where it is described as 'very well suited to defence or assault'. Quintilian's comment on Domitius' ideas notes that Domitius' full definition of *urbanitas* is virtually identical to Quintilian's own concept of oratory. See the discussion of this passage in E. de Saint-Denis, 'Évolution sémantique de *urbanus—urbanitas*', *Latomus*, 3 (1939), 5–24.

The man of the city is always hostile, sneering and jabbing at his opponents. The *vir bonus* may be socially good, but this goodness is secured via constant aggression. Likewise, Quintilian's own text with its eternal attacks on failed bearing and movement constructs the *vir bonus* via this same aggression. Quintilian assaults his readers' bodies, beating them into manly shape and threatening transgressors with castration and exile: if I speak without following Quintilian's dictates, I might not be urbane or I might appear soft. For the orator the aggression by which he forcibly distinguishes himself from ordinary men always leads back to himself. But the orator is enjoined to turn this same attitude outward in order to confront the rest of the world with it. For example, in the preceding passage, the rules of space that the orator imposes upon himself must also be forced upon everyone else. Those who cross the lines that are invisibly or visibly laid down thereby reveal themselves impotent and illegitimate.

The more the body is discovered, the more footholds there are for this kind of thinking and this kind of assault. The knowledge of the body that is herein produced is a knowledge which is used to provide an orthopaedics and correction. Yet with this correction there comes pruning and excision. The self is taken as the principle of its own domination. The orator's body is invested with a soul and populated with it. But only by strict and rigid disciplining of this same body can the validity of the soul be secured. This body thus becomes the prison of the soul, though this same soul is charged with policing its own prison.[39] We will never get to a first principle by following these logical gyrations. Instead one should note the relationships in general. There is an injunction to more knowledge of the body and closer observation, yet this knowledge produces more insecurity than confidence.

So much, then, for the Roman orator's body. The manual on training has no simple or direct value. After reading Quintilian, one does not walk away a consummate orator, a Cicero or a Demosthenes.[40] A vocabulary of the male body is learned, but this new language is not one of simple analytics and descriptions, nor even a language of precepts aimed at helping an orator be more clear in his movements or his pronunciation of words such that whatever meaning might be conveyed, it is conveyed more effectively. Instead the description and analysis of the body are at

---

[39] Foucault said the same of the prisoner in the panopticon. See Foucault, *Discipline and Punish*, 202–3.

[40] See, for example, Quintilian 1. pr. 18–20, and compare Cicero, *de oratore* 1. 78. The rhetorical handbook claims that its student will not be transformed into a perfect orator.

once and inseparably fused with a gender and a social morality and invested with profound ontological consequences. The gendered social stakes invested in the body result in a body which is always in a state of negotiation. The body cannot be left alone to mean what it may. Instead the body and its relationship to the self and world needs to be constantly thought and rethought: is that speaker a good man? Is he acting like one? Does he have the hands of a good man? Do his words match his gestures? Does his voice or his stance reveal him to be manly and urbane, or is he instead a woman or a rustic? One asks these aggressive questions not only of others but also of oneself: am I a good man?

Quintilian's text relies heavily on the imputation of being to the soul of the good man, and Quintilian uses this soul as the agent which gives form to the unruly mass of the body. Yet Quintilian's own arguments destabilize the centred male subject. By opening up logical paradoxes, the *cura/natura* formulation compromises the vision of a male subject who is the author of his own meanings. Nature requires labour and labour fulfils nature. This is straight out of Aristotle: τέχνη (labour) helps φύσις (nature) achieve itself fully. But labour and labour's observation have a way of producing more or different natures, particularly when illegitimate morphologies are discovered within the orator's own body. The problem of labour makes nature an open and unclosable category. The *vir bonus* can never fully consolidate his being because of the infinite quality of his labour.[41]

Quintilian's panopticism, his observation and discipline, have done nothing to render impossible the bodies and souls he fears. His scopic mechanism acts to reproduce the secure male, but in so doing it also constantly reproduces the possibility of its failure and points out sites of and for contestation. Quintilian's technology of the self and the truth games of the body which he teaches are not decisive ones: there is not an end to study and a good man who thereupon emerges. Instead this whole process is successful only in reproducing itself and its anxieties.[42] This

---

[41] With his arguments on labour, Quintilian points towards Judith Butler's theses on the body. Butler has insisted on a performativity which acts as a process which is necessarily enacted over time (Butler, *Bodies that Matter*, 1–2 and 9). And the performative subject is an accretion formed via these iterations. Furthermore, the possibility and consequences of performative failure are the same for both Butler and Quintilian: the subject's very being is at stake. Quintilian, though, sets himself up as a guardian against the queerness that Butler is glad to see ever waiting in the wings.

[42] Compare here Foucault's insistence that we must ask ourselves why the infinite labour of prisons and criminology is never completed and what the interests are that must be served by this same failure. See Foucault, *Discipline and Punish*, 268–72. Or see Foucault, *The History of Sexuality*, vol. i, for his investigation of sexuality not as a fact or substance but instead as a story which has to be repeatedly and endlessly discovered and told.

analytics becomes the site of a labour designed to secure masculine being, but a labour which is always ready to fail, a labour which can never be completed, and a labour which could always be queered.[43]

Quintilian cannot be read as a simple guide to good voice and gestures. His descriptions always act as prescriptions. In the course of his discussion, Quintilian is creating a body and legislating its bearing and meanings. This technology of the self serves not to describe but to create and control a masculine body and a relationship to that body. The instructions he offers serve to help construct the orator as a certain sort of social agent as set against and above other members of society. The social place of the orator in the Roman world is secured as part of a thoroughgoing corporeal project. With the consolidation of his gender, so also does the orator find in the same moment the sanctity of his station. Moreover the truth of the gendered body cannot be dissociated from these other truths as the station of a man becomes conflated with the virility of station *per se*. The labour of this discovery of the body, accordingly, is more than a theoretical one, it is also immanently practical and has important worldly consequences.

[43] See Butler, *Bodies that Matter*, 108.

8

The Emperor's New Body: Ascension from Rome

MARY BEARD and JOHN HENDERSON

All these supposed methods of reaching heaven are most primitive: they start from the supposition that a *load* has to be lifted up; they hardly imply a separation of body from soul; and they are antecedent to the distinction which philosophers established between different parts of man's being. They are religious survivals of very ancient conceptions which only vulgar minds still interpreted literally. These mechanical means of raising oneself to the starry vault carry us back to an extremely low stage of beliefs.[1]

'Here is an error, Sir; you have made Genius feminine.'—'Palpable, Sir', cried the enthusiast; 'I knew it. But [in a lower tone] it was to pay a compliment to the Duchess of Devonshire, with which her Grace was pleased. She is walking across Coxheath, in the military uniform, and I suppose her to be the genius of Britain.'[2]

> Fly on, my sweet angel, fly on through the sky,
> Fly on, my sweet angel, forever I will be by your side.[3]

IN this chapter, we consider a set of visual representations of imperial 'ascension' within the pagan culture of classical Rome; a series of images—on coins, cameos, and public commemorative sculpture—of that most peculiar journey, which took the latest dead emperor (or his wife or baby) from the funeral pyre to the celestial heaven. We ask how Romans may have seen, imagined, and re-imagined the process that elevated these new divine recruits into the skies. Each and every imperial deification must have entailed a complex series of decisions, affirmations, cosmic realignments, and suspensions of disbelief. What was the relationship between this tricky (cultural) politics of apotheosis and the visual representations of the new deity on his (or her) way to heaven?

---

[1] F. Cumont, *After Life in Roman Paganism* (Yale University Press, New Haven, 1942), 159–60.
[2] T. H. White, *The Age of Scandal* (Penguin, Harmondsworth, 1962), 15.
[3] J. Hendrix, 'Angel', on *The Cry of Love* (Track Record, 1971): as we say, Jimi *lives*.

These images respond to a number of challenges. They must not only find ways to narrate the miracle of metamorphosis, and to capture the new god's wondrous translation from a status that was already endowed with the extremes of imaginable power, to a yet more unlimited existence. They must also carry the paradigmatic significance of the ruler-become-divinity for his successors—as pattern for the past, as dispensation encoding (and legitimizing) the present, and as normative bid to structure the future. The sculptural or engraved glyph, or graphic scene, of apotheosis figured the *permanence* of divine royalty, evoking constant beatification; it was far from the temporary pageantry of the royal funeral, with its purely transitory claims for the ascension of the royal soul from the blazing pyre.

Gender enters the frame, as always, at several levels. It must make a difference to the creation and representation of a new deity, even/ especially in the masculist political culture of the Roman empire. A dead emperor was *the* man among Romans, and is translated to become a (male) god; yet the third apotheosis in the history of the Roman state—or the fourth, if you count the (invented) mythical precedent of the founder-king-god Romulus—honoured a woman, or, rather, a goddess. After the convenient (for his heirs) apotheosis of the murdered dictator Julius Caesar, and after the prototypical consecration of the first emperor Augustus, it was the turn of the crazed emperor Gaius' sister Drusilla to join the gods; and a series of new goddesses followed her—from Augustus' wife Livia (who had to wait more than ten years after her death for grandson Claudius to do the decent thing and send her to join her husband in heaven) to Nero's dead baby daughter.

The rendering of the divine supermale was, in other words, inescapably compromised by the need to define his existence through his affective relations with family and kin, as well as his dominance over subjects and pastoral tutelage of citizens. If the emperor became a god, then did his wife become a goddess? Was the monarch the solitary cynosure of political ascendancy; or did he take the lead in a *domus diuina* (a 'divine *family*')? What was the royal consort to mean, *sub specie aeternitatis*? Dead or alive, how would Rome recognize its empresses? By genuflecting to their conjugality, or by honouring their maternity? As wives? As mothers of emperors? As divine queen-mothers of emperor-gods? Styling an autocracy (divine or not) must always implicate regimes of a potentially endless array of forms of sociality and personhood.

FIG. 8.1   Pedestal of the Column of Antoninus Pius: apotheosis, 161 CE.

The scene in Fig. 8.1 takes us directly to the conjugality of apotheosis.[4] This most glorious of all figurations of transfiguration at Rome shows the emperor Antoninus Pius (died and deified 161 CE) and his wife Faustina (died and deified 141 CE) going to heaven together. The imperial 'we' are shown *enlevants* above a seated Amazonian Rome, clad in manly armour reminiscent of Athene/Minerva, witnessing the miracle along with the semi-nude recumbent male youth opposite. This youth holds for his attribute the great obelisk that was used to cast the shadow across Augustus' massive sundial on the Campus Martius—giving a location to the ascension that definitively soars from the emperor's pyre tradition-ally built there, outside the sacred boundary of the city. But dominating

---

[4] For extended study, see L. Vogel, *The Column of Antoninus Pius* (Harvard University Press, Cambridge, Mass., 1973), 32–55, 125–6 n. 80; cf. D. E. E. Kleiner, *Roman Sculpture* (Yale University Press, New Haven, 1992), 285–8, fig. 253, with D. E. E. Kleiner and F. S. Kleiner, 'The Apotheosis of Antoninus and Faustina', *RendPontAcc*, 51–2 (1978–80), 389–400, and *Lexikon Iconographicum Mythologicae Classicae* (Artemis, Zurich, 1981–   ; hereafter re-ferred to as *LIMC*), i. 403–4, *Aion* 1. We return to this extensively restored relief below.

the scene is the 'angel', hovering in all the glory of gorgeous full frontal nudity, sprawled across the visual field; its spreading wings a jumbo jet fit to ferry an imperial couple to the skies.

It was no doubt scenes such as this that prompted Franz Cumont (in our epigraph) to read the 'mechanics' of apotheosis as the retarded conservation of primitivesque literalism; to scorn the invention of some winged hybrid to transport the imperial body to eternity; to deride such literalism in any representation of 'spritual' ascension. But in so doing he did not face the question of what is to constitute 'literalism' in the representation of imperial ascension; of how any viewer might (or might not) choose to distinguish between the crudest literal-mindedness and the most sophisticated visual metaphor. We shall explore in this chapter how we might read these images against the grain of Cumont's ideological refusal to acknowledge the imagery of the Other, and its complexity. Embedded in the nineteenth-century Western poetics of evolutionary teleology, he was committed to value philosophy over religion, enlightened, superior spirituality over the vulgarity of the body—and at the same time to a stance that must spank *all* iconic representation for falling this side of higher, noumenal abstraction.

At the same time Cumont catches us up in precisely the kinds of metaphor—'heaven' as 'the starry vault'—that once enmeshed antique humanity. Unavoidably so; for the visual representation of apotheosis will always demand that some metaphor of metaphor, some translation of translation, be enlisted to show the impossible-miraculous passage from 'here' to the 'beyond'. Once we valorize, instead of deride, the work of the imagination in devising some rhetoric for making comprehensible, in terms of mundane experience, the strangeness of this process of transcendence, we may appreciate the strategies for the display of sanctification as a vital part of the very power it celebrates.[5] How you get to heaven is one of the most challenging (and silliest) religious questions of all. To make analogies between ascension and other forms of passage that are available to viewers in their lives and in their cultural image-repertoire (while simultaneously estranging the event as beyond human ken) is not to play the savage, but rather to enter the *politics of representation*.[6]

[5] Cf. F. Dupont, 'The Emperor-God's Other Body', in M. Feher, R. Naddaff, and N. Tazi (eds.), *Fragments for a History of the Human Body*, pt. iii (Zone 5, New York, 1989), 397–419, esp. 415.

[6] The enthusiast pioneer here was Mrs Arthur Strong, *Apotheosis and After Life: Three Essays on Certain Phases of Art and Religion in the Roman Empire* (Constable, London, 1915), esp. 30–111, 'Divus Augustus: The Influence of the Imperial Apotheosis on Antique

Climbing, riding, flying, being carried to the sky are, for ever, uncashable metaphors that dead gods must live by. As manifestations of cultural capital, they must be powered, not least, by a discourse of gender. How much triumphalism should be vested in the deceased human? How little control should the god he is becoming, but has not yet become, exert? How should a supernal supermale look? Or is the process itself, i.e. the figural power of the very act of representation, to dominate the view, even to dwarf the commemorated hero? If the subject is to be received as apotheosis, rather than praise of a dead ruler, should the sex of the consecrated make a difference to its dynamics? Should women-heroines-goddesses metamorphose *their way*?

Within the cultural mix of the ancient Mediterranean, Roman viewing always incorporated earlier models of representation—particularly those models mediated through (and lorded over by) Greek cultural poetics. Precedents for imperial apotheosis were, willy-nilly, not lacking among Rome's subject peoples, which by Augustus' day included virtually all the known world and all its histories. Conceptualizing ascension for an emperor could not begin without processing these inherited, alien, schemes for *thinking apotheosis*. The *divus* (that is, the deified emperor) must, but at the same time must not, look like some dominated un-Roman. Divine Herakles reborn offered one way of figuring an imperial exit. The model of the ascetic philosopher paraded another schema of immortality achieved. So too, did the pugnacious princes of the post-classical Greek East. But in such models, imperial divinity inevitably risked, even courted, the extremes of barbaric savagery or of effete decadence. The visual construction of Romanity was, as we shall see, always precariously realized through more or less strenuous moderation of the schemata of such potentially scandalous 'foreign' traditions.

There was a similar set of tensions in native Roman precedents for imperial apotheosis. Almost before history had begun, Rome had been ruled by kings—a previous incarnation of imperial monarchy, in the mythical dynasties that stretched from founder Romulus to the tyranny of (the eventually deposed) Tarquin the Proud. Augustus, so the story went, had refused to take the name Romulus as his new imperial title, despite its convenient political associations with Rome's founding moment. But, like it or not, he found an avatar in Romulus, the founding hero, apotheosed with the brand new divine name 'Quirinus', after the

Design'. She saw a trajectory in the art of pagan Rome toward the centred frontality of Christian design.

king himself had disappeared in a convenient cloud. (An alternative version, not without an eye on the assassination of the divine Julius Caesar, had Romulus taken to the heavens after being stabbed to death by the Roman senators . . .) How could these not be dangerous precedents for imperial deification? Would, and did, Augustus' dynasty collapse just like the mythical kings, with vain Nero standing for Tarquin the Proud? Must a divine father-figure always mask a tyrant, every reformist strong man already a rapist in censor's clothing, all imperial debauchery just Rome reverting to type?

We shall attend here to 'official' images, mostly from within the city of Rome; but we should note that right across the face of the empire there was a continuous pulsation of, and contest in, imperial image-making, with different eyes looking to appropriate royalty for their own advantage and from their own perspectives. Thus provincial representations of ascension constructed Romes of their own. And in the capital itself, small-scale, intimately displayed gems could serve up 'private' engraved images of apotheosis that need not abide by the publicly paraded manners of monumental sculpture. Apotheosis looked, and was, different in different regions, as well as eras, and in different rooms, as well as on different scales. Gender shaped and animated all these differences, always (lodged near) the heart of representation.

As imperial imagery strained toward conveying the mystery of apotheosis, it risked various forms of absurdity, whether at once or when art and ceremony had moved on (for very little such representation—from the Pergamene Altar to the now faded ascension-scene of the last emperor's wife but three—can survive the passing of time without becoming a mockery). Detailed ancient responses to such monuments are in short supply; and we can only guess (helped on our way by such texts as Seneca's *Apocolocyntosis*, or Vespasian's parting squib[7]) at the irreverent mockery of their nonsensical contraptions that have not found their place in the surviving record. But we are convinced that the pomp of consecration constitutively courts provocation; and that a wilful commitment to treat these images (not to mention the whole 'institution' of imperial apotheosis) with gravity misses much of the point. In this spirit we shall allow our rhetoric to deflate the images even as we engage with the logic by which they function. It is far from obvious that a neutral tone and attitude toward the power invested in imperial images is a more proper idiom (or politics) than either celebratory enthusiasm or icono-

---

[7] One of Vespasian's best jokes (as reported by Suetonius, *Vespasian* 23. 4) was his death-bed one-liner: *vae, puto, deus fio* ('Gosh, I get the feeling I'm becoming a god . . .').

clastic sarcasm. For our part, we mean to see how these distorted mutations of power put gender to work; not to respect them.

Before we explore our set of images, we first contextualize in more detail the visual representation of Roman ascension within the political, social, and cultural institutions of the early Empire.

Imperial power at Rome was confirmed through the apotheosis of the dead emperor. The consecration of Julius Caesar in 42 BCE, two years after his assassination, was an important marker in the rise to imperial power of his adopted heir Octavian—the future Caesar Augustus. In the course of the funeral, the emperor's body was witnessed 'going on a journey' up into the sky. The senate duly met to vote formally for consecration and a variety of records and representations attested and blessed the witnessed ascension. Augustus' reign was permanently stamped with the legitimization of this apotheosis—Caesar Augustus (adoptive) 'son of a god'.

Divus Julius (to give Caesar his official divine title) became a god in the chaotic and dislocated circumstances of civil war. But in 14 CE, on the death of Augustus himself, his heir Tiberius (with the combined help of his council of advisers, the praetorian regiment barracked close by Rome, and the senatorial chamber of government) turned those circumstances into an exemplary model for the apotheosis of an emperor. The entire populace of Rome played a role in the fabrication of a tradition for imperial exequies, and the apparatus of coinage, temple dedication and its attendant statuary, together with the proliferation of cult-rites and priesthood, radiated the event across the Roman world. *Divus Augustus* was permanently stamped on the Roman empire.

For each of the succeeding would-be-gods that emerged from the imperial dynasty, the passage from (dead and cremated) human to (immortal) divine was to be negotiated in legible but unique schemata. On the one hand the invented tradition contrived for the first emperor was re-evoked, so that the weight of that tradition could empower the next incumbent seamlessly and beyond challenge; each new *divus* followed in Augustus' tracks, no less divine for coming later. But on the other hand, each imperial heir in orchestrating the deification of his predecessor (in part, at least, to sanction and authorize his own reign) served to diagram the *particularity* of each occasion. Each apotheosis authorized and specified the new reign in, and as, its own, unique, cre(m)ation. Ad hoc improvisation in shaping stone was called for, experimental thinking with metal.[8]

---

[8] The standard account of Roman consecration, assembling a fictitious montage by amalgamating the details we chance to have about the very heterogeneous sequence of

There was, however, more to imperial apotheosis than this. For a start, the death of an emperor more often prompted rather less commemoration than this pageant of apotheosis. Somehow, the senate of Gaius Caesar (= Caligula) contrived not to consecrate Tiberius; on *his* assassination, the senate managed, messily, to spare heaven the pleasure of Gaius' company; Nero elevated Claudius, but his own suicide terminated the dynasty without apotheosis. Consecration, then, was for any emperor, and at any coronation, never automatic, but always, critically, in question. It must always have been the product of a complex process of (tacit, occluded, or open) negotiation about whether to, how to, and (especially) how not to, consecrate particular figures. Those instances of deification for which we have more than the baldest information show up all manner of 'un-Augustan' behaviour, and support no presumption of institutional uniformity with which to fill lacunae in our knowledge.

The construction of legitimate succession (with its twin ritual of coronation/consecration) also involved more players than just the successful claimants themselves. At once, in the first emperor's apotheosis, the position of his widow, Tiberius' mother Livia Augusta, had been controversial; and at her death in 29 CE, fifteen years later, her consecration was mooted in the senate but frowned away by Tiberius, on the grounds that she herself would not have wanted it. If the conveyance of an empress to the heavens—an emperor's wife, an emperor's mother— posed an especially challenging problem for representation, then the reign of Gaius certainly opened the floodgates. Instead of divinizing his predecessor Tiberius, he hugged charisma as close as he could: he promoted, as we have already noted, his tragically deceased favourite sister Drusilla to be the goddess 'Panthea' (literally 'all-goddess'), in a service cloned on the ceremonial for Augustus. Moreover, as if instead of Livia, Gaius (more, or less, officially) divinized his grandmother Antonia—setting the scene for Claudius to send *his* grandmother—Livia—to heaven in 41 CE.

By consecrating his dead baby Claudia, Nero took even further the outline of a family kit, ready for re-assemblage in heaven. Succeeding dynasties kept up these precedents and pressed them onward, further and wider—with the principle becoming ever more clear, in the

instances, is S. R. F. Price, 'From Noble Funerals to Divine Cult: The Consecration of Roman Emperors', in D. Cannadine and S. Price (eds.), *Rituals of Royalty* (Cambridge University Press, Cambridge, 1987), 56–105 (with full bibliographical notes; to which add J. Arce, *Funus Imperatorum: Los funerales de los emperadores romanos* (Alianza, Madrid, 1988)). Such amalgamation is precisely what the present chapter seeks to avoid.

process, that deification enacted the power of deifier rather than deified.

Here is the roll-call: the Flavians consecrated their founder Vespasian, then Titus, Domitilla (Titus' *sister*—or *mother*? Her status is not clear.), Titus' *daughter* Flavia Julia, and Domitian's dead baby *son*.[9] Nerva was deified at the advent of his adoptive heir Trajan (in 98 CE), who later, nevertheless, consecrated both his *natural father* Traianus and his own *sister* Marciana (in 112). Under his successor Hadrian, Trajan was deified (in 117), and then Hadrian's *mother-in-law*, officially dignified as such: *diva Matidia socrus* (in 119: she was Trajan's niece, the daughter of Marciana). Trajan's *wife*, Hadrian's kingmaker Pompeia Plotina, joined her husband in heaven (in 123); Hadrian also divinized his beloved *toyboy* Antinous (in 130), though not, it seems, through official channels of the Roman state, before consecrating (in 137) his own *wife*, Vibia Sabina, grand-niece of Trajan, after nearly forty years of marriage. Hadrian was next himself deified on the accession of his adopted successor Antoninus Pius (in 138), who soon consecrated, as we saw, his *wife* Annia Galeria Faustina (in 141), and was in turn sent to heaven by M. Aurelius Antoninus (in 161). Marcus himself would consecrate his *other half*, the first joint-emperor, Lucius (Aurelius) Verus (in 169), and then *his wife* Faustina II (in 175); he joined her (in 180), but the latest images we shall look at will be creations produced under his aegis, before (that is) his own ascent to the sky.

We may see in this list, in this hastening sequence of familial deifications, a transformation of the fragile institution of imperial apotheosis: from the militaristic brandishing of divine Roman masculinity into the Hellenizing cosmopolitanism of a philosophized ideal of marital concordance.[10] In part, this is a question of increasing stress, as we move through the first into the second century CE, on (divine) imperial wives—with all the debates that that must have raised. Should *every* imperial widow be sent to rejoin her holy husband? Would an emperor's remarriage make a difference to an already deified wife? But it is also a

---

[9] See L. Cresswell, 'AUGUSTA: Images of the Empress and Roman Imperial Power' (Cambridge, Ph.D., 1997), 'The Images and Roles Projected for Women in the Roman Imperial Family from the First to the Third Centuries CE', for the problem of identifying *Diva Domitilla*, and for detailed disaggregation of Roman apotheosis.

[10] For a properly cautious study, cf. S. Dixon, 'The Sentimental Ideal of the Roman Family', in B. Rawson (ed.), *Marriage, Divorce and Children in Ancient Rome* (1991; Oxford University Press, Oxford, 1996), 99–113; for Roman dynastics, cf. M. Corbier, 'Male Power and Legitimacy through Women: The *domus Augusta* under the Julio-Claudians', in R. Hawley and B. Levick (eds.), *Women in Antiquity: New Assessments* (Routledge, London, 1995), 179–93.

question of particular emphasis on divine *conjugality*. Should imperial wives await their husbands in heaven, or must their consecration pend until they could go as a couple? What did deification do to marriage? Consider the answer of Marcus Aurelius, who never really managed to let his (deified) Faustina go: 'By decree of the senate a golden image of Faustina was carried on a chair into the theatre every time he was a spectator, and the effigy placed in the front row from where she watched when alive; with it/her were to sit the most powerful of wives.'[11] However it was debated or orchestrated, though, it is the story of Trajan and Plotina, Hadrian and Sabina, Antoninus Pius and Faustina—Man-God and Wife-Goddess—that dominates the ascensions of the second century CE. The parade of conjugality.

We can trace some of these changes within the visual repertoire of Roman art. Significantly, we have no visual representations for any of the first-century ascensions of imperial women, and nothing to approach a literary narrative of their journey from earth to heaven. A few textual hints let us assume that they were managed on the putative pattern of the emperors' apotheoses.[12] But for male ascension we can mark a clear contrast between the apotheosis of *Divus Julius* on the middle-Augustan Belvedere Altar—where the semi-nude strong man lifts off into the heavens in his triumphal four-horse chariot (Fig. 8.2)[13]—and the conjugal image of Antoninus and Faustina, 150 years later, that we have just overtured.

Nevertheless, any historical narrative of ascension from Rome is as fragile as the 'institution' itself. This change of emphasis from masculinity to conjugality must also be set against a series of factors pulling in quite different directions. On the one hand, the role of the imperial wife had been debated, as we have seen, almost from the very beginning of the story of ascension at Rome. In the mythical prehistory of apotheosis, Romulus wife' Hersilia shortly joined him in heaven to become the goddess Hora;[14] while the second-century narratives of conjugal divinity in some respects replay the story of Augustus and Livia, of Tiberius and Livia, of Claudius and Livia—finding the legitimacy of (invented) tradition in the founding era of the empire.

[11] Dio, *Histories* 71. 31. 1.

[12] See, for example, the references to Drusilla's apotheosis in Seneca, *Apocolocyntosis* 1.

[13] Kleiner, *Roman Sculpture*, 102–3, figs. 85–6; Strong, *Apotheosis*, 65–7, pls. VII–VIII; P. Zanker, *The Power of Images in the Age of Augustus* (Michigan University Press, Ann Arbor, 1988), 220–1; Vogel, *Column of Antoninus*, 46–7, 124 n. 71.

[14] Cf. Ovid, *Metamorphoses* 14. 829–51; T. P. Wiseman, 'The Wife and Children of Romulus', *CQ* 33 (1983), 445–52.

FIG. 8.2   Belvedere Altar: apotheosis of Julius Caesar, 12–2 BCE.

On the other hand, the image of the solitary, divine, male emperor hero (the beneficiary of the coronation/consecration routine) continues right through the period we are discussing. One of the latest images that we may put into our sequence outdoes even the superman take-off we witnessed on the earliest, the Belvedere Altar—as Marcus Aurelius' co-regent Verus boards his one-man module to launch into the skies from the Great Antonine Altar at Ephesus (Fig. 8.3).[15] But the history (and permanence) of representation itself ensures that divine conjugality could never at any period be the only way of thinking apotheosis at

[15] Kleiner, *Roman Sculpture*, 311–12, fig. 211; Strong, *Apotheosis*, 90–2. This schema is at once a reversion to antique tradition, and the reassuring vehicle for a radically avant-garde leap of the imagination, into a bold solar impersonation; a step toward the mystic soldier emperors of the 3rd century, when the empire staggered through a quickfire succession of brigand saviours.

Fig. 8.3　Great Antonine Altar: apotheosis of Lucius Verus.

Rome. The monuments of previous ascensions remained part of the Roman cityscape. Every divine couple, in other words, ascended into heaven against a backdrop of triumphalist masculinity still visible and memorable in the apotheosis-stories of Roman literature and apotheosis-images of the city. By the time of Hadrian the (slightly purged) list of earlier *divi* had been gathered into a confirmed continuity, a quasi-synchronous congregation, of tutelary deities in their cordon of temples about the city—gods in the main (significantly, it must be, new goddesses were not normally honoured with a temple). Hadrianic Rome was no monumentalized museum, but housed a 'meta-dynasty' of all the Augustuses of blessed memory, lined up to power the throne.[16]

Not a simple narrative, then, but a story better plotted, and most likely only plottable, as a *discourse*; here, along the axes of gender.

Apotheosis intrinsically turns on cinematography. Ascension in art *writes movement*: albeit movement through annulled space to represent (ontological) change in status. But, even so, this movement must cope with the cultural values normatively associated with particular modes

[16] See M. T. Boatwright, *Hadrian and the City of Rome* (Princeton University Press, Princeton, 1987), esp. 98.

of bodily transport; however hard it must try, transcendent movement cannot shed those vectors of mundanity. There is always a tension, across any field of any pictured ascension, between insistence on the literal transport of the deity's bodily drive into the sublime, and the injunction on the audience to accept sublation by the image, beyond mere carnal representation. Any viewer may find the representation plummets and shatters if one of these trajectories comes across as in the ascendant. So, for example, if emphasis on the metaphysical intent of the image is carried too far, it will doom the scene to illegibility; the very opacity will prevent the viewer, exactly, from letting themselves get carried away. Instead of uplift, a stalled flight of fancy.

But let us now suppose, to take the other case, that the greatest and best of humans is to be carried aloft by the king of birds. The image will surely collapse if it does not offer some species of corporeal plausibility; yet too much physical realism will hang onto the image like grim death, and fly in the face of any symbolic uplift at all. This is the overriding message in Lévi-Strauss's parabolic account of the play (he claims) he all but wrote, 'The Apotheosis of Augustus':

Augustus then found himself alone, in conversation with an eagle: not the conventional bird, the emblem of divinity, but a wild creature, warm to the touch and foul-smelling. Yet it was Jupiter's eagle, the same eagle which carried off Ganymede, after a bloody fight in which the young boy had struggled in vain. The eagle explained to the incredulous Augustus that the divine nature he was about to acquire would consist precisely in no longer experiencing the feeling of revulsion by which he was now overwhelmed while still a man. Augustus would realize that he had become a god, not by some radiant sensation or the power to work miracles, but by his ability to tolerate the proximity of a wild beast without a sensation of disgust, to put up with its stench and the excrement with which it would cover him. Carrion, decay and organic secretions would appear familiar to him.[17]

This lesson in 'the problem of the relation of nature with society'[18] will be before us constantly throughout this chapter. The point for now is that the programme of ascension demands there has to be a wing as well as a prayer; but what sort of wing—and whose?

Movement implicates notions of agency: is the subject active or passive, moving or being moved? Is the mover self-propelled or baggage? Are they chauffeured or freight? Is attendance the sign of eminence or of

---

[17] C. Lévi-Strauss, *Tristes Tropiques* (Penguin, Harmondsworth, 1976), 491–500, 'The Apotheosis of Augustus', 497.
[18] Ibid. 498.

dependence? Does obvious effort on the part of the new god suggest that his transfiguration was after all precarious? Or does effort connote the higher moral of heroic aspiration? It is here (in the disputed hierarchies of propelled and propeller) that the foundational demarcations of power are *engendered*.

Images of ascension, as we shall see, may hint at ceremonial inertia, at sanctified levitation. Statuesque effortlessness, encoded as superhuman control over subjects/acolytes, pervades the construction of Roman royalty—not least at lift-off into the troposphere. No imperial Romans tread their way to eternity.[19] (Except satire's crippled Claudius, *iter facientem non passibus aequis*, 'making the journey with halting steps'.[20]) Instead, they are driven, or taken for a ride. 'Popemobile'—whether angel or chariot—was more their style than 'walkabout'.

But here we must wonder if divine conjugality trapped the emperor into a denial of his masculinity. A chariot was one thing. But to make the trip to the skies on the back of a languid angel? Such limp conveyancing threatened (as much as it carefully left unruffled) the statufied dignity of the male emperor. If it became a first lady to be carted to the firmament (as prettily as possible), was it the fate of a mighty warrior, on the grandest journey of all, to turn from man of action to god of *in*action?

Somatics always thrust forward the differences embodied by gender. There can be no body movement that eludes coding in terms of gender norms ordained under the particular socio-cultural circumstances of historicality. In the rest of this chapter we shall explore the discourse of gender in a series of images of apotheosis, ending with (and looking in more detail at) the transfiguration of Antoninus and Faustina from which we began.

We shall start with a limit case: the gold coin issued to commemorate the infant death of Domitian's son and heir presents him 'standing on the globe of the earth reaching out to the stars above' *naked* (Fig. 8.4a). The image is otherwise highly under-determined, through a combination of numismatic miniaturism and the struggle to typologize Master

---

[19] It is left to the anti-king, the para-*deus*, Jesus Christ to lower himself to take a stiff climb up a rugged mountain ridge and to accept a firm hand-up from his father's grip as he nears the top. See J. Beckwith, *Early Christian and Byzantine Art* (Yale University Press, New Haven, 1993), 53, fig. 37: the Marys at the sepulchre and the Ascension. Ivory panel. Rome, late 4th or early 5th century (Munich, Bayerisches Nationalmuseum). T. F. Mathews, *The Clash of Gods: A Reinterpretation of Early Christian Art* (Princeton University Press, Princeton, 1993), insists on discontinuity between imperial and Christian schemata.

[20] Seneca, *Apocolocyntosis* 1.

FIG. 8.4*a* (above left)   *Aureus* of Domitian: apotheosis of Domitian's baby son.
FIG. 8.4*b* (above right)   *Aureus* of Hadrian: apotheosis of Sabina.

FIG. 8.4*c* (top left)   *Aureus* of Antoninus Pius: apotheosis of Hadrian.
FIG. 8.4*d* (above right)   *Sestertius* of Antoninus Pius: apotheosis of Faustina I.
FIG. 8.4*e* (lower left)   Medallion: apotheosis of Antoninus Pius.

Universe. Does this baby cosmocrat sprawl and play at batting the circling stars as they pass by? Does he rise up into the aether, flexing leg-muscles for leverage to launch himself 'up' to the firmament, where his splayed hands twinkle along with the other stars he juggles? Are his feet on 'the ground' and his head in the heavens? To find movement in this coin, hold it to read the first words of the legend, *DIVVSCAESAR*, and view the babe supine and gazing 'upwards'; then rotate it to read round toward the final patronymic, *DOMITIANIF* ('son of Domitian') and the boy will leap into action, lunging 'up' toward his right hand, toward the ring of stars, toward the 'central' signifier of power, *IMP* (Imperator=emperor).[21] However this may be, the image stands in our discourse for *apotheosis without ascension*. In terms of gender, nót an exposed, abandoned daughter, but another pancratic baby Jupiter-in-the-making.

The opposite symbolic paradox—*ascension without apotheosis*—marks the jewellery *jeu d'esprit* known as the 'Grand Camée de France', an extravagant piece of courtly luxury, measuring up at roughly 30 by 25 centimetres (Fig. 8.5). There have been centuries of strenuous efforts to 'identify' the figures on this jewel. But let us start from broad outlines: a doublet of would-be ascensions flank a successfully installed imperial divinity ensconced in the skies above the already divinized royal family (the central emperor already in the guise of Jupiter); below ground huddle the subjugated barbarians.[22] The central deity in the topmost register (so all agree) is *Divus Augustus* himself, serenely enthroned with sceptre and clad in the toga of peace—a very unmilitary deity indeed. To the left, a gliding soldier princeling seems to be swimming up to the sky, using his shield for float. Opposite, to the right, a winged cupid guides into heaven a galloping charger with a second laurelled soldier princeling on board. This mount boasts (a pair of) swept-back wings that promise overdrive. Riding this Pegasus risks making a Bellerophon of this prince, so near to, yet so far from, their goal:[23] aptly too, since neither of these Julio-Claudian princes, whichever pair we decide they are, *can* have succeeded in joining Augustus in divinity.[24] Against the serenity of Augustus, they picture *ascension without apotheosis*.

Augustus hovers above his counterpart below, supported by a wafting

---

[21] H. Mattingly saw the baby as 'seated, like a baby Jupiter, on the globe of the earth and stretching out his hands for the stars': *British Museum Coins of the Roman Empire* (British Museum, London, 1923–62; hereafter *BMCRE*), ii, p. lxxxix.

[22] Kleiner, *Roman Sculpture*, 150–1, fig. 126; Vogel, *Column of Antoninus*, 44–5, 123 n. 60, fig. 86. For a convenient table of canvassed identifications, see H. Jucker, 'Der Grosses Pariser Kameo: Eine Huldigung an Agrippina, Claudius und Nero', *JDAI* 91 (1976), 211–50.

[23] Mythic Bellerophon tried to reach Olympus on *his* Pegasus; but Zeus would have nothing of it and blasted him to a nasty fall. Cf. R. Hannah, '*Praevolanti nescio qua ingenti humana specie*... A Reassessment of the Winged Genius on the Base of the Antonine Column', *PBSR* 57 (1989), 90–105. Jucker, 'Der Grosses Pariser Kameo', 228–30 warns us all to rid our minds of Bellerophon.

[24] Suggestions for the Pegasus rider range around most of the deceased under-40s of the Augustan/Tiberian family: Germanicus, Marcellus, Gaius Caesar, Drusus Elder and Younger. For the shield traveller, one of the two Drususes carries most votes. Some of these lads got further than others towards divinity; but none made it, officially.

FIG. 8.5   Grand Cameo of France, *c.*50 CE.

'male personification identified by many as Aion or Eternity in belted tunic and leggings and a cap and carrying an orb in both hands'.[25] This aerodynamically horizontal incarnation of Otherness (best left as a visual operator, rather than pinned to a fabricated title) trails legs behind him to our left, bearing his load of divinity effortlessly and without visible airworthiness: a wingless wonder blown in from the orientalizing Imaginary, complete with Eastern bonnet and leggings. Fixed in place by his

[25] Kleiner, *Roman Sculpture*, 150; cf. Vogel, *Column of Antoninus*, 33–8, 'Winged genius'.

surrounding would-be comrades, and by his accessory status in relation
to the central register's impenetrable antics, the combination of
Augustus and his cosmic flotation would serve well as an independent
group to portray ascension. We would assume that the angel would
gently rise on an up-current, elevating *Divus Augustus* majestically
up, toward top right, into nirvana—except, of course, for his lack of
wings.

On the Grand Camée, this all-male skyscape contrasts with the mixed
populations of infernal subjugation and of the imperial palace, where
familial structure embraces infancy, childhood, parentage, conjugality,
in a parade of clan hierarchized solidarity—alternating female/male.
Whichever sub-section of the Julio-Claudian dynasty this scene represents, it privileges prowess in war as the arduous route to the stars:
howsoever the (so far) incomparable, and strikingly civilian, Augustus
made it there, heaven beckons to arms and men. On terra firma,
the emperor's wife/mother sits beside him, as they regard *their* prime
princeling, arming his manhood for some military crusade for, and
before, his Jupiter-on-earth. Women get their share of the palace mas-
querade, but/so there is no place for them where it counts, among the
Olympian gods.

We have already seen a variety of different transports to the heavens;
and we shall return to 'angels' later—after we have considered two other
Roman conceptualizations of successful ailerons: bird and chariot. Emperors did not grow wings; as Lévi-Strauss reminded us, they used an
eagle. The eagle condensed the military supremacism of the legionary
standards' totem with the symbol of Jupiter's world rule through his
attribute and equivalent among birds; and it cued imperial apotheosis
through the custom of releasing an eagle to rise from the pyre of an
undying emperor.[26] Everywhere in attendance on royal representations,
in all media, the eagle could scarcely be kept out of the picture.[27]

On a (debatably) Julio-Claudian cameo, a prince rides a magnificent
eagle 'side-saddle' as a flying Victory crowns him.[28] The first of many
Roman coins to boast an in-flight royal have 'Sabina, with scarf floating
out behind her, holding sceptre, borne aloft r. by eagle, with head turned

[26] Cf. H. Jucker, 'Auf den Schwingen des Gottervogels', *JBM* 39–40 (1959–60), 266–88; K.
Lehmann-Hartleben, 'L'Arco di Tito', *BCAR* 62 (1934), 89–122, esp. 115–17.

[27] A silver cup from Herculaneum neatly turns Homer into a lookalike Roman emperor,
nonchalantly ascending to Olympus on the back of an eagle, witnessed by the *Iliad* and
Odyssey; G. M. A. Richter, *The Portraits of the Greeks* (Phaidon, London, 1965), 55, fig. (s).

[28] Vogel, *Column of Antoninus*, 44, 123 n. 59, fig. 87: formerly nicknamed 'The Assumption of Nero'.

l., holding sceptre', with the legend *CONSECRATIO* (Fig. 8.4*b*).[29] These Hadrianic *aurei* are very closely matched by others, showing Hadrian on *his* eagle, and bronze coins with Faustina I on hers, all issued under Antoninus Pius; and M. Aurelius was to follow suit.[30] From the time of Faustina II onwards (in 175/6), empresses on coins were regularly re-differentiated from emperors by swapping their Jovian eagles for Junoesque peacocks. Consecration medallions and coins disseminated this neatly absurd difference round the world state for centuries.[31]

Eagles could be useful in more monumental contexts too. Back at the accession of Domitian in 81, he had honoured his brother with the triumphal 'Arch of Titus' to celebrate the despoliation of Judaea. The apex of the vault was chosen for a specially bold, customized, com-memoration of his consecration (Fig. 8.6). Four tiny homunculi (cupids? pixies?) hold a portion of the sky open to afford anyone craning their neck as they pass through the arch a clear view up to heaven: a mighty eagle carries Titus slung on its back overhead, flying out of Rome and into forever.[32] The eagle's talons, legs, and underbelly are on view, while the emperor-god peers straight down his aquiline nose at us, over the beak. Exactly the carnal bird Lévi-Strauss imagined for his *Divus Augustus*.

Myth troubles this (bathetic? perky?) representation of ascension. For at the very moment that this brilliant fantasy calculates how exactly the human body can configure quasi-naturalistically with the eagle, the ma-jestic bird risks instant reversion to a predatory raptor (it really *is* just that). The difference melts away between ascension and abduction, as the schema makes a Ganymede victim of the Roman prince—Zeus' little

---

[29] Ibid. 45. *BMCRE* iii. 362, nos. 955–6 (silver *denarii*, nos. 957–9, pl. 66. 4–5, celebrate the consecration with the eagle minus passenger). For bibliography on the *consecratio* coinage, see O. Brendel, 'Classical "Ariels"', in *The Visible Idea: Interpretations of Classical Art* (Decatur House, Washington, 1980), 49–66, at 64 n. 17.

[30] Vogel, *Column of Antoninus*, 45. Hadrian: *BMCRE* iv. 7, no. 32, pl. 1. 15 (silver *denarii*, showing the eagle only, nos. 33–5; pl. 1. 16–18); Faustina: *BMCRE* iv. 231, nos. 1424–8, pl. 34. 3, 9; Marcus Aurelius: *BMCRE* iv. 763, nos. 394–5, pl. 101. 6. For the numismatic energy thrown into the consecration of Faustina, see *BMCRE* iv. 228–57 (and below, n. 46).

[31] R. Turcan, 'Le Culte impérial au IIIe siècle', *ANRW* II. 16. 2, 'Principat' (Berlin 1978), 996–1084, at 1006; cf. pl. 1 nos. 1–4, 'monnaies de consécration (sesterces) de Paulina . . . de Mariniana'. E. La Rocca, *Rilievi storici Capitolini: Il restauro dei pannelli di Adriano e di Marco Aurelio nel Palazzo dei Conservatori* (De Luca, Rome, 1986), 24–30, 'Esegesi', presents and studies consecration coinage from Sabina to Mariniana and Valerian.

[32] Kleiner, *Roman Sculpture*, 189–90, fig. 157; cf. Vogel, *Column of Antoninus*, 47, 125 n. 78. For the keystone in its surrounds, cf. Lehmann-Hartleben, 'Arco di Tito', 98, fig. 5, and for the visibility of the vault, cf. I. Jenkins and K. Sloan, *Vases & Volcanoes: Sir William Hamilton and his Collection* (British Museum Press, London, 1996), 284–5, fig. 181.

F I G. 8.6   Arch of Titus: vault with apotheosis of Titus, after 81 CE.

toyboy snatched up to heaven by the god himself, conveniently disguised
as an . . . eagle. Nero's Golden House (where Titus too had lived) even
featured a 'Rape of Ganymede' in the central roundel of the ceiling of
one of its grandest rooms, with the boy 'aboard an eagle, glimpsed as if
through a skylight'.[33] Another Roman ceiling even shows a torch- and
jug-bearing Ganymede translated to his astral futurity as Aquarius by a
winged male figure who wears oriental costume reminiscent of the angel
of the Grand Cameo.[34] A man can get taken for a ride on an eagle, heaven

[33] R. Ling, *Roman Painting* (Cambridge University Press, Cambridge, 1991), 90–1.
[34] In the so-called 'Underground Basilica' at the Porta Maggiore; Brendel, 'Ariels', 57, fig.
6, with pp. 59–60: guesses include 'Boreas', 'Polus', 'Polus Borealis' . . . ?

knows; but what happens to the masculist claims of imperial apotheosis if we *think Ganymede* and divine sexual slavery when we catch sight of poor god Titus being snatched up and away?

The chariot might seem a safer bet. Defunct for aeons in (real-life) Graeco-Roman armies, the chariot's triumphal associations conspired with the legacy of Greek representations of strong-man apotheosis to supply a canonical celebration of masculine, warrior, transcendence for imperial consecration. For centuries almost every city frequented by Greeks had carried images of Herakles shipped on Athene's chariot as she ferried him to sit at his Almighty father's right hand. On the same model, Romulus was collected by his father Mars' chariot, before returning to earth for his epiphany as Quirinus.[35] Visual ascensions from Rome follow, and vary, this formula.[36]

On one side of the Belvedere Altar (Fig. 8.2), as we saw, *Divus Julius* takes off in a four-horse chariot, rearing up into the sky figured as the god Caelus with his billowing velification. Here Julius will converge on the orbit of the sun god's chariot, soaring alongside his eagle.[37] In this image, the hulking hero stands steady as a rock, oblivious of the careering of his steeds. His immediate ascendancy is defined by the acclamation his surrounding admirers wave him: a solitary citizen in docile toga to stern, and a group with two boys clinging round a protective 'mother'-figure. Here is the Man-God of Destiny, rising above his people, his family, woman and sons, the dynasty he founds . . .

So Caesar is no one's passenger. But he is in control of only himself; doesn't running a sky-chariot call for rather more than this kind of statue-man? The Great Antonine Altar from Ephesus takes greater care of its emperor, in this respect at least. There the heavily armoured commander Verus steps aboard his chariot, muscular and firm, while Victory helps him join his pair of horses, and a brace of attendants steady their heads: the Sun god and some Amazonian female (Virtue, if you like), whom he oversees. Are we to intuit that Verus here displaces Helios/Sol as the new Sun-King?[38] His unchallenged virility is further

---

[35] Cf. O. Skutsch, *The Annals of Q. Ennius* (Oxford University Press, Oxford, 1985), 205, 260; Horace, *Odes* 3. 3. 16; Ovid, *Fasti* 2. 496.

[36] Four- (and two-)horsed chariots signified apotheosis in simple as well as complex tableaux in Roman culture, e.g. on coins, and atop imperial monuments (Boatwright, *Hadrian*, 175, fig. 37).

[37] For the traces of the eagle, cf. P. Zanker, 'Die Larenaltar im Belvedere des Vatikans', *MDAI(R)* 76 (1969), 205–18, line drawing at 207. On the opposite face of this altar, a solitary Victory hovers down to drop a shield to honour Augustus' virtues.

[38] Cf. F. Eichler, 'Zum Partherdenkmal von Ephesos', *ÖJh* 49 (1971), 102–35. Verus ~ Helios? The matching panel of the relief, with Selene the Moon in her stag-drawn chariot, aided by Evening Star and Night as she drives down to Ocean, argues for no less.

underpinned by the recumbent figure of Earth lying beneath his wheels: this goddess (Tellus) is at his mercy, there to attribute to him the power of a *man*.

Can we not help wondering, however, if he is not rather *over*-provided with assistance? One and all infect the representation with anxiety that the show won't get off the ground. He doesn't look much more than a general; there is nothing to mark him out as a god—except a borrowed chariot.[39]

The imperative to power the chariot-ride of ascension had always run the same gauntlet: if the *divus* just mounts, or freezes in, his gig, the event cannot rise above the mundane celebration of another victory, the latest triumph;[40] yet any display of take-off, too clear a sign that this chariot is on a purposive mission skyward, makes the 'Herakles'-figure look uncomfortably like an abducted heroine in the Greek visual schematization of rape,[41] the prisoner of some outsize hit-and-run charioteer at the reins. The more the apotheosed holds himself statufied like the god he becomes, the more he resembles a stolen bride, or at least a complaisant eloper.[42] Even the supermale Herakles, in the mytho-logic of the Greek visual repertoire, can only clutch his club, cling on to the rail, and try to look dignified, as he takes this ride of rides—the virgin virago Athene his seductress, to whizz him up to the azure.[43] In the supernatural passage beyond the threshold of mortality, female superpower (even in the shape of Athene, the least female of all the unmale deities) is both at the service of and taking control of the extreme of virility.

[39] e.g. Vogel, *Column of Antoninus*, 126–7 n. 87, judges the reliefs 'more likely to be a *profectio* or similar scene'. Apotheosis *is* a similar scene.

[40] Christian ascension often provides the wheels of a 'throne-chariot' beneath the *mandorla* (almond-shaped panel) within which Christs are shown, seated or standing, in various presencing, commanding, imposing, attitudes; pairs or teams of angels take the strain of flying the ensemble up to heaven. Thus Christ may be seen as emblem, as representation of a representation, more statufied than any Roman *diuus*, committed to transvaluation of ascendancy without mundane imperialism. Cf. H. P. L'Orange, *Studies on the Iconography of Cosmic Kingship in the Ancient World* (Aschehoug, Oslo, 1953 = Instituttet for Sammenlignende Kulturforskning Serie A, Forelesninger 23), 124–33, 'The ancient eastern throne in the Christian iconography, a) Throne-chariot and *majestas domini*'; Beckwith, *Christian Art*, 63, fig. 46; 71, fig. 55.

[41] See A. Cohen, 'Portrayals of Abduction in Greek Art', in N. B. Kampen (ed.), *Sexuality in Greek Art* (Cambridge University Press, Cambridge, 1996), 117–35.

[42] Cf. ibid. 129, fig. 54. Mushy red-figure style can make the happy couple look like a marriage made in heaven, e.g. J. Boardman, *Athenian Red Figure Vases: The Classical Period* (Thames & Hudson, London, 1989), fig. 348.

[43] e.g. T. H. Carpenter, *Art and Myth in Ancient Greece* (Thames & Hudson, London, 1991), fig. 230; A. D. Trendall, *Red Figure Vases of South Italy and Sicily* (Thames & Hudson, London, 1989), fig. 50; *LIMC* v, *Herakles* 2927–31, cf. 2916–22.

FIG. 8.7   Arco di Portogallo: apotheosis of Sabina, 136–8 CE.

The avian and the chariot routes are, then, much more precariously gendered than we might have first realized; but their intent is to divinize militarist masculinity. The paean is for god as *man*. Our last three images, from publicly displayed state monuments at Rome and on imperial coins from the second century CE, attempt by contrast to imagine the ascension of empresses from Rome. The designers look to customize other schemata, rather than ape the emperors. The first (Fig. 8.7) is a heavily restored relief of the *Apotheosis of Sabina*, which originally decorated a state monument of 137/8, built to commemorate the uxorious faith of the emperor Hadrian who sits on the right.[44]

It confronts us with a gender inversion of those scenarios for ascension we have already inspected. Whether we compare the royals beneath Augustus' cloud on the Grand Camée de France, or the group of witnesses looking up to Julius Caesar's launch, or Tellus beneath Verus' chariot in Ephesus, we shall see here, uniquely, *women on top*. The (heroized/symbolic) recumbent male plays 'Mother Earth'; the emperor and attendant are the equivalents of the Belvedere Altar's witness plus maternal group of female embracing her boys. Sabina's Amazonian 'angel' is, in fact, very like the squire who is up-front guiding the team for Verus—but she wafts across the sky as bearer of divine royalty in a very close approximation to the aviation of that orientalized male on the Grand Camée (who held Augustus sitting tight on his back and had no wings showing).

It is, however, true that the men putting themselves in their place below are dominant in size. Sabina is awarded no drive at all, all statuesque calm and contemplative gaze into the elsewhere, as if she, like Augustus on the *bijou*, is going nowhere. All the agency is lodged in the powerful sweep of the wings and the massive thrust of the broomstick torch that speed her giant android craft up to approach infinity. The humanesque 'eagle' takes care of her, watching to see she is sitting comfortably, like some tenderized bull with its Europa on board. The sisterly star trek takes Hadrian's wife from him, with never a backward glance, drifting away from mythological and institutional Graeco-Roman prototypes for apotheosis.[45] No monster-slaying; no triumphalism; no manly armour. The image looks instead to fuel the flight of fancy with inspiration from a different iconography.

We find the visual mythography in question exactly where we would least expect to find it. The empress's ascension adjusts the schema dis-

---

[44] Cf. Kleiner, *Roman Sculpture*, 253–5, fig. 222; Vogel, *Column of Antoninus*, 47–8, 125 n. 80; Boatwright, *Hadrian*, 226–9, esp. 227, ill. 54; *LIMC* i. 248, *Aeternitas* no. 71; Strong, *Apotheosis*, 88–9. The head—and index finger—are entirely restored, like that of the comrade tucked behind Hadrian; the body of the torch and probably the blazing pyre. (The restoration is precisely assessed by Rocca, *Rilievi Capitolini*, 24, with colour plates, pls. 7–8; and black-and-white plates, pls. VII–XIV.

[45] The effect is emulated by 'Flaxman's controlled image of the floating and apparently timeless female body', on a 'stele' design, M. Pointon, *Hanging the Head: Portraiture and Social Formation in Eighteenth Century England* (Yale University Press, New Haven, 1993), 202, fig. 237.

played on Augustus' brazen chest, on the body-armour of his most famous statue, from the Villa of Livia at Prima Porta (Fig. 8.8). On this cuirass is imag(in)ed 'cosmic representation of the new ideology of victory'.[46] On Augustus' right breast the Sun god energetically gallops his four-horse chariot up to the sky (sky god Caelus here holds out his canopy)—exactly as Julius Caesar's ascension is envisioned on the Belvedere Altar. To match, the figure of Aurora ('Dawn') wafts across toward our top right, pouring the dawn dew from her jug down onto the iron-ized royal left nipple. She has a passenger, the goddess Luna ('Moon'), who sits with her great torch 'at ease', just the way Herakles carries his club, in the crook of her left arm.[47] Dawn is, latently, another 'eagle' of desire, the slender and evanescent possibility of female rape.[48]

Now, as is well appreciated, this cuirass is co(s)mically encrusted with representations of totalizing power. These are emphatically patterned on gender polarities: Caelus at top, recumbent Tellus ('Earth') at bottom, along the vertical groove up and down the diaphragm that centres the visual field; on the right side of Augustus' torso, Sol ('Sun') above, Apollo below, and Roman generalissimo in the middle; on the left side of this virile body politic, ladies Dawn and Moon above, Apollo's twin Diana below, and the Parthian king, that orientalized, unmanned Other, surrendering in the middle.[49]

In the battle to control this visual field, Sun invades with his onrush the sector of Dawn and Moon. This female team looks back, Moon peeking round behind Dawn's wing, her shield against the glare, for all the world as if they are being chased out of the picture; their gentle floating makes a pacific, passive, foil for the thrash and crash of Sun's charging team. And in the centre, when the submitting un-Roman Parthian proffers the Roman military standard that he duly returns to the vindicated manhood of Augustan Rome, the spread eagle atop the

[46] Zanker, *Power of Images*, 189–92, fig. 148a+b.

[47] Here we follow Zanker: the details are highly controversial, cf. *LIMC* iii. 797–8, *Aurora* 1: Aurora carries Venus, goddess of the morning star; Kleiner, *Roman Sculpture*, 65, 'Aurora riding on the back of a female personification'; for discussion, see J. Elsner, *Art and the Roman Viewer: The Transformation of Art from the Pagan World to Christianity* (Cambridge University Press, Cambridge, 1995), 159–89, ch. 5, 'Reflections on a Roman Revolution: A Transformation in the Image and Conception of the Emperor'.

[48] Cf. R. Osborne, 'Desiring Women on Athenian Pottery', in Kampen, *Sexuality in Art*, 65–80, esp. 67–8; *LIMC* iii. 747–89, *Eos*. In Greek art and myth, Eos is *the* female raptor, who flies off with the pubescents Tithonus or Kephalos.

[49] Here we again follow Zanker: the details are still controversial, cf. Kleiner, *Roman Sculpture*, 65–7.

F I G. 8.8　Augustus, from the Villa of Livia at Prima Porta (detail).

standard carefully comes to rest as the focus of the entire ensemble. This is, truly, a man's, man's, man's male world.

For Sabina, Hadrian's designers bethought themselves of a 'lunar' angel for sky-lift: the Moon's torch blazes a trail for the Amazonian workhorse. The empress is, let's say, *a* moon who is not *the* moon.

Missing, except in the viewing emperor's mind, is her Sun. So in the instant when the empress receives her beatification, solo, the image is recuperated within a repertoire that was precisely contrived to order supernatural signs of power around the emperor's usurpation of the age-old clothes of Herculean, supermale, triumphallicism. *She* flies like a bird in his sky—but she is the kite *he* flies. And it shows: so fly on, his sweet angel.

Only five years later (in 141 CE), amongst the unprecedented and never paralleled profusion of consecration coins minted for the deification of Faustina I, space was found for the ascension of the emperor's wife on the back of the same large-winged female demon, still holding her same great torch athwart (Fig. 8.4d).[50] When her husband joined her, twenty years later, Marcus Aurelius had Antoninus' consecration celebrated with bronze medallions that showed the new *divus* ferried by the warri-or's virility symbol, the eagle, while a reclining half-nude male witnesses below, to match Sabina's (Fig. 8.7).[51] Between them, across a score of years, the two scenarios make as diagrammatically polarized a vision of apotheosis for emperor and empress as the ensemble on Augustus' chest. At the same time, we should bear in mind the disappearance of gender-differentiation in the eagle-borne ascensions given deified Antonines— male and female—on their money (before the diagnostic eagle/peacock recovered the schema for binarist gender stereotyping). As we gave notice at the outset, ascension is a visual discourse, not a cohesive narrative, through history.

The same pious occasion (in 161) that produced M. Aurelius' commemoration of Antoninus marks our return to the image from which we started (Fig. 8.1). Outdoing the column erected by Hadrian to eternalize Trajan, Marcus (and his partner Verus) commissioned yet another miracle of Roman engineering as their predecessor's cenotaph: the Column of Antoninus Pius, whose base alone survives. On opposite sides of this column are carved in relief two versions of military manœuvres by Roman troops, a cavalcade wheeling around squadrons of infantry, presumably on parade for ceremonial duty at the emperor's cremation/apotheosis; one of the other pair of sides bears an elaborate inscription that leaves no room to doubt who consecrated whom; the face opposite presents our apotheosis relief of conjugal deification. Although, as we

---

[50] Vogel, *Column of Antoninus*, 45, 124 n. 68; *BMCRE* iv. 230, 1422–3; cf. Faustina II: *BMCRE* iv. 652, no. 1567, pl. 86. 7.

[51] Vogel, *Column of Antoninus*, 46, fig. 97: noted by J. M. C. Toynbee, *Roman Medallions* (The American Numismatic Society, New York, 1944), 219–20.

have seen, Faustina had already ascended in 141, witnessed by her royal/ loyal husband and their Rome, she is here and now in 161 *re*introduced to eternity along with her freshly divinized man.

We can now see how emphatically the new disposition trades in gender binarism: the youth and his giant prosthetic erection homologous to Antoninus, on their right, as Amazonian Roma is to Faustina, on *our* right. Both monarchs carry sceptres, but Antoninus' is outsize, protruding at both ends through the crook of his right arm, below, over the edge of the 'chariot-rail' of the leading edge of the angel's wing, and, above head height, surmounted by a perched eagle. Faustina just grips her modest knobstick,[52] partially hidden by the angel's locks and tucked in behind her husband's robes, the perfect wife. Just like Sabina, the deified are again dwarfed by the terrestrial beings; all the more so, because they ride on an even more extravagant kite. The new gods are just as statuesque, just as removed from registering any visual contact with their mundane surroundings (us), just as sedately wafted, just as impotently passive.

The massive eagles that flank them further overdetermine the signification of Roman apotheosis. These big birds are Romanized Victories, here to watch the passengers safe in their seats, both his and hers. If Faustina's eagle is distinctly larger, this should draw attention to Antoninus' *pair* of eagles, the outrider in the sky plus the eagle on his sceptre. This imperial divinity (who may originally have worn a cuirass) looks perhaps as gentle as a Herakles in Athene's chariot, but the military hardware of Roma and the eagle *signum* link to the march past of Roman military might on the flanking sides of the pedestal. The whole edifice culminated in a bronze emperor perched on top of the column's Corinthian capital.[53] However pious, he was *not* accompanied to the top of his column by his dear wife; he was, ultimately, up in the clouds, this 'eagle', this charioted *triumphator*, this Jove, to play the generalissimo-warrior-Roman in all his unaccompanied supremacy. Two on a pedestal don't go.

Down below, of course, we never take our eyes off the gorgeous

---

[52] The sceptre she now carries is a modern restoration; but it *can* only have been this size.

[53] For what it is worth, 'a statue, presumably of bronze', perhaps without military uniform, is shown on a coin, L. Richardson, Jr., *A New Topographical Dictionary of Ancient Rome* (Johns Hopkins, Baltimore, 1992), 94, '*Columna Antonini Pii*'; *BMCRE* iv. 528, no. 893, pl. 72. 11: 'a statue of the Emperor with Jupiter's attributes' (R. Bianchi Bandinelli, *Rome the Centre of Power: Roman Art to AD 200* (Thames & Hudson, London, 1970), 286). For Antoninus' cuirass on the base, cf. Vogel, *Column of Antoninus*, 38 and fig. 27.

archangel, a dreamboat built for two.[54] This angel does not tote a torch, unlike Sabina's; but rather, carries a sphere—like Augustus' orientalized mainstay on the Grand Camée de France (though this one is entwined with a fascinated snake). But we shall be ready to complete our investigation of gender in the history of ascension from Rome only if we take our cue from Antoninus' slanting sceptre; if we follow its point—to one of the Vatican's famous fig-leaves.

This fig-leaf covers (and marks) the precise centre of this representation of imperial Rome in its moment of self-immortalization. When the moment came to share divinity between emperor and empress, woman alongside man, the distribution was displayed for all Rome (and Campus Martius) to see. When Antoninus joined Faustina, Sabina's impressive Amazon lost her job, and instead some Belvedere Apollo was conjured up, imposing the loveliest of male bodies on the naked eye. Did the irreverent citizens of Marcus manage not to think of poor Icarus, plummeting in a shower of hot wax and loose plumes, followed, now, by an elderly couple of flightless dummies? However precariously, the image assigned to the imperial couple emblazons the bea(u)tification of *male* bodiliness: angelic manhood is the badge of marital ascension.

Visual play with the historicality of gendered power in imperial Rome has conjured a social construction of the supernatural to raise our viewing selves to heaven; gender and its metaphors may (literally) carry us off to an extremely powerful stage of affective image-theatre. Or we might choose to point up the bathos lodged (for us no less than for the Roman viewer) in the hyperbolic register of this commemorative flight of fancy: see how god is born(e), on automatic pilot—and meet the wife.

---

[54] Vogel, *Column of Antoninus*, 43, for the extra impetus given to this kinesis by the unequal depth of the relief that slants the angel's 'swooping flight up and to the right'.

9

'Ordering the House': On the Domestication of Jewish Bodies

CYNTHIA M. BAKER

'THE geography closest in' is one of many expressions used by poet Adrienne Rich in speaking of the body. She distinguishes this most intimate geography from that of 'a continent or a country or a house', in a phrase that implies both a closeness to, and a distance from, these other, larger geographies.[1] 'The geography closest in' tells us, as Rich's words often do, that bodies not only move through, inhabit, exceed, imagine, and otherwise take up space, but that they are themselves space—and place—overlapping and intertwining with countless others. But 'geography' is also a discipline, a practice of describing and inscribing difference; it is about creating order, and borders, and separations between one place and another, one body and another. It is in all these senses, then, that this phrase serves as an appropriate starting-point for an exploration of ancient Jewish bodies, or rather, one Jewish body in particular: that of the 'wife' as constituted in rabbinic Jewish texts from the third century CE. In their earliest collections of stories and rulings, the rabbis, an emerging class of Jewish authors/authorities in Roman Palestine, imagine the wifely body as precisely 'the geography closest in', as a body that is at once both place and practice, that is at once both 'woman' and 'house'. In this chapter, I shall explore several aspects of this rabbinic construct, not only through examinations of texts in which it is found, but also through consideration of ancient Palestinian domestic architecture and its potential for elucidating the discursive spaces which the wifely body comes to occupy.

I wish to express my gratitude to Donald Polaski, Gail Hamner, Seth Mirsky, H. Aram Veeser, Eric Meyers, Kalman Bland, Daniel Boyarin, Elizabeth Clark, and Miriam Peskowitz, each of whom read drafts of this manuscript at various stages of its development and offered insightful critiques and invaluable suggestions for its improvement. Additional thanks to Eric Meyers for permission to use building plans from the Meiron excavations in this article.

[1] Adrienne Rich, *Blood, Bread, and Poetry* (Norton, New York, 1986), 212.

This body makes one of its earliest appearances in the following Mishnaic dictum:[2]

Seven days before the Day of Atonement they separated the High Priest from his house into the counsellors' apartment, and they made ready for him another priest in his place in case there should befall him some ineligibility. Rabbi Judah says, 'Also another wife they made ready for him in case his own wife were to die, as it is said, "and he shall atone on his own behalf and on behalf of his house", "his house"—that is, his wife'. They said to him, 'If so, there would be no end to the matter!' (*m. Yoma* 1: 1)

This passage, and the preparations for the holiest day of the Jewish calendar which it purports to describe, begins with an act of separation. In order to ensure the cultic purity of the High Priest (a concern made clear later in the same sentence), he must be 'separated from his house'. His house, it seems, occasions the possibility of cultic impurity in a way that the 'counsellors' apartment' in the Temple does not. Why this is so is suggested a few lines later, with the identification ' "his house"—that is, his wife'. However, the Tosefta, the earliest commentary on the Mishnah, makes this identification explicit from the outset: 'Why do they separate the High Priest from his house to the counsellor's chamber? Rabbi Judah b. Paterah says, "Lest his wife come to be in doubt as to whether she is menstruating, and if he has sexual intercourse with her, he will be rendered cultically impure for seven days".'[3] Thus, the separation demanded is at one and the same time spatial and sexual/corporeal; the 'house' from which the High Priest is separated is his wife's (potentially bleeding) body, their shared dwelling, *and* the sexual intimacy that they share.[4]

Rabbi Judah's statement in the Mishnah enlarges on this subject even further. Because Mosaic law stipulates that the High Priest must atone for both himself and his house, it must be determined who or what

---

[2] The Mishnah is a collection of early rabbinic legal discussions, opinions, stories, and brief homilies compiled in Palestine, *c.*220 CE, long after the Temple and its cult (the subject of discussion in the following passage) had ceased to exist. Translations of all rabbinic texts herein are my own and are based on the following Hebrew versions: Hanoch Albeck, *Shisha Sidre Mishnah* (Mosad Bialik, Jerusalem, 1958); M. S. Zuckermandel, *Tosephta* (Bamberger & Wahrmann, Jerusalem, 1937); Saul Liebermann, *The Tosefta* (Jewish Theological Seminary, New York, 1967).

[3] Tosefta *Yoma* 1: 1.

[4] The Babylonian Talmud (BT) and the Palestinian Talmud (PT) both derive the seven-day separation from other biblical commandments as well (BT *Yoma* 2a–b, PT *Yoma* 1: 1). While I will make occasional reference to these later layers of interpretation, my observations in this study are largely confined to the 2nd and 3rd centuries and the rabbinic documents codified prior to 300 CE, namely, Mishnah (*m.*) and Tosefta (*t.*).

constitutes 'his house'. While Judah's interlocutors reject his assertion that another wife must be held in readiness against the possible death of the High Priest's own wife ('If so, there would be no end to the matter!'—i.e. to the number of substitutes required), his identification of 'wife' and 'house' stands as unproblematic—and indeed unquestioned throughout the entire later tradition of rabbinic commentary. In this case, however, the 'house' in question is not so much a walled domicile as the web of relationships better characterized in English by the term 'household'. In the original Hebrew of the Bible and Mishnah, the word is one and the same: *bayit* (and the word *isha* serves for both woman and wife).

How then to understand this rabbinic identification of woman/wife and house? Clearly, the two are conflated—the one made a synonym for the other.[5] Is the identification, therefore, symbolic? connotative? metonymic? While the High Priest is separated from his dwelling as a means of separating him from sexual contact with his wife's body, such a mechanistic rendering of the connection between wife and house is insufficient, for it does not account for all the nuances of the identification. Nor is it sufficient to understand by *bayit* the more abstract and relational term 'household' in all cases—after all, the Mishnah specifies that the High Priest be removed from one concrete location, one place of residence, to another. 'Household' and/or 'wife' signify, but are not entirely coextensive with, dwelling.

In broadest terms, then, we find a general equation of person and place: woman/wife=house/household. Present in this equation are aspects of sex and purity, relationship and responsibility. In fact, from the time of Xenophon's treatise *Oeconomicus* in the fifth century BCE, and earlier, the equation of woman/wife with house/household becomes so familiar in literatures and images throughout the classical and late ancient Mediterranean as to be entirely unremarkable.[6] But the unremarkable becomes remarkable, and the familiar unfamiliar, when the customary 'wife in house' becomes the 'house in wife', as in the following Mishnaic texts:

It is the practice of Jewish women, when they engage in sexual intercourse, to make use of two examination cloths: one for him and one for her; the pious prepare for themselves a third with which to 'set in order the house'. (*m. Niddah* 2: 1)

---

[5] 'The one of his house' (*d'vetehu*) becomes a standard epithet for 'his wife' in the BT.
[6] Xenophon, *Oeconomicus* 7. 20, 22, 30; cf. Plutarch, *Is. et Os.* 75; Plato, *Republic* 9. 579b; Demosthenes, *Contra Neaer.* 59. 122; Philo of Alexandria, *Spec. leg.* 3. 169–75.

The woman who has sexual intercourse and then goes down and immerses [in the ritual bath], and she has not [first] 'cleaned the house', it is as though she has not immersed. (*m. Mikvaoth* 8: 4)

The synonymous or metonymic relationship between woman and house here takes on a cast markedly different from—although closely related to—those formulations considered heretofore. 'House' as euphemism for female body—or, more specifically, female sexual organs—establishes a kind of homology between the two. Woman/wife is not simply the entity in the house; rather, 'house' describes the rabbinic physiology of a wife and at the same time prescribes her relation to that physiology: she is its caretaker. According to these passages, the pious wife will not only 'examine the house' but will have 'the house in order' to receive her husband when he 'comes home' (so to speak); and she will 'clean the house' properly after he does just that.

As with the above passage referring to the wife of the High Priest, the concern in the first of these passages is that her husband not come in contact with a wife's menstrual blood, nor that they have sex while she is menstruating, such that it is incumbent upon a wife to examine herself carefully (with a cloth) for any signs of blood before—and perhaps after—intercourse with him. As for the 'cleaning' or 'setting in order of her house', the mechanics of these activities are not elaborated upon by the Mishnah's authors. Even so, these descriptions of a wife's 'domestic duties' fall squarely within the rabbinic discourse on cultic purity regulations.[7] In this vein, the rabbis go so far as to develop a detailed blueprint of the 'house' in question for the purpose of menstrual-blood identification and classification:

---

[7] See Charlotte Fonrobert, 'Women's Bodies, Women's Blood: The Politics of Gender in Rabbinic Literature' (unpublished dissertation, Graduate Theological Union, 1995), which offers an extended and insightful examination of this discourse—including a brief meditation on the place of the female body as house within it. My own interpretations have been refined and challenged by Fonrobert's work, and I have found my occasional disagreements with her readings as fruitful as my agreements. I am grateful to her for sharing her unpublished work with me. The literature on Jewish purity practices and menstrual taboos is by now quite extensive. Any study of these issues should begin with a reading of the Mishnaic tractate *Niddah*, its biblical antecedents, Mary Douglas's *Purity and Danger* (ARK, New York, 1966), and Howard Eilberg-Schwartz, *The Savage in Judaism* (Indiana University Press, Bloomington, 1990) and should include, as well, Fonrobert's study. One key point which must always be kept in mind when considering Jewish codes of 'purity' is that, in general, in an Israelite or rabbinic context, purity and impurity are cultic categories that bear no relation to moral or hygienic considerations. Most often they determine nothing more than one's ability to engage in particular cultic practices at particular times and places.

The sages offer a metaphor concerning woman: [there is] the room and the antechamber and the upper story; blood in the room is unclean, and if found in the antechamber its condition of doubt is deemed unclean because it is presumed to be from the fountain. (*m. Niddah* 2: 5)[8]

But the conflation of woman/wife and house exceeds this purity discourse and encompasses far more than the proper cleansing of the female body before and after sexual intercourse, or the classification of various genital discharges. In fact, in the *m. Mikvaoth* passage cited above, the expression translated 'has sexual intercourse' reads, literally, 'serves her house'. A full translation would thus read: 'The woman who serves her house and then goes down and immerses [in the ritual bath], and she has not [first] cleaned the house, it is as though she has not immersed' (*m. Mikvaoth* 8: 4). Other Mishnaic passages employ the same phrase:

Twice must she make an examination: in the morning and in the evening. Also when she prepares to serve her house. (*m. Niddah* 1: 7)

If she immerses herself [in the ritual bath] the following day, and then she serves her house, and after that notices [that she has had a genital discharge] . . . (*m. Niddah* 2: 5, *t. Niddah* 9: 19; similarly *m. Niddah* 10: 8)

The context for these statements remains one of regulation of cultic purity, but the language of 'serving her house' is not exclusively tied to purity concerns; it is, rather, a somewhat broader—and gendered— expression for the act of sexual intercourse. The more common (non-gender-specific) expression, and the one that appears in *m. Niddah* 2: 1 (cited above), is simply the verb 'to serve' without an object. But the expression is clearly gendered in the phrase 'serving *her* house', a phrase for which there exists in the Mishnah no masculine construction (i.e. 'he serves his house'), but that none the less poses an apparent contrast to the '*his* house—that is, his wife' formula explored above.

[8] There is a long history of attempts at discerning to which body parts these various chambers correspond: from the Talmud through Maimonides up to doctoral dissertations written within the last ten years. See, for example, Julius Preuss, *Biblical and Talmudic Medicine*, trans. F. Rosner (J. Aronson, Northvale, NJ, 1993 (original German: 1911)), and Tirzah Zechurah Meacham, 'Mishnah Tractate Niddah with Introduction: A Critical Edition with Notes on Variants, Commentary, Redaction and Chapters in Legal History and Realia' (unpublished dissertation, Hebrew University, 1989). The results of such attempts are myriad and often baffling (although most commentaries identify the 'room' with the uterus) and none is entirely compelling. The puzzle of this schema remains unsolved. As for deciphering the distinctions drawn by the rabbis here, they are as follows: blood found in the 'room' is deemed menstrual blood; if it is found in the 'antechamber' it is to be regarded as menstrual blood only if the wife is in doubt as to whether it is or not. If a woman is certain that it is not menstrual blood, it is not regarded as such.

The question then arises: if *she* is *his* 'house', is *he* *her* 'house'? Is there a tidy heterosexual symmetry built into this elaborate literary-cultural construction of domesticity? Could gender ever be so well ordered and egalitarian as that? Not likely. And yet the ambiguity of the phrase 'serving her house' is telling, especially when considered in its other abbreviated form. In *m. Sotah* 1: 2, in a discussion of the ritualized ordeal of a woman accused of adultery, we read:

If he [her husband] said to her before two [witnesses], 'Do not speak with X', and she spoke with him, she is still permitted to her house; . . . if she entered a secluded place with him [the presumed paramour] and she remained with him long enough to become impure, she is forbidden to her house.

A wife who disregards her jealous husband's warning and speaks with a suspected paramour is, according to these rabbis, still permitted 'to her house'. The implied meaning of the phrase is clearly 'to engage in sexual intercourse with her husband' (and only with her husband).[9] But what remains unclear is exactly which part of the implied meaning corresponds to the term 'her house'. If we understand 'her house' to refer to her husband, then by association the phrase 'to serve her house' might be translated 'to serve her husband [sexually]'. This interpretation 'works' to some extent, but poses difficulties when read in light of *m. Niddah* 2: 1 and *m. Mikvaoth* 8: 4, where 'house' unequivocally refers to a woman's body or genitals. The term 'her house' might then be more appropriately interpreted as an abbreviated form of the phrase 'to serve her house', to the effect that 'she sexually serves her body/makes use of her sex'. The inherent ambiguity of the rabbis' phrasing, however, leads to an intriguing confusion of bodies and body parts (is she handling her body or [and?] her husband sexually?).

The Babylonian Talmud (500–600 CE) provides an interesting counterpoint to all this by employing a somewhat different euphemism for a man's engagement in sexual intercourse, namely, 'he serves his bed'. And just as a wife examines 'her house', so too a husband is enjoined to examine 'his bed' for traces of his wife's blood. 'His bed', in this case, apparently refers to his penis (and not to his wife—after all, she is already 'his house').[10] Thus, each member (as it were) of the couple is under-

---

[9] To my knowledge it is only *sex within marriage* that is termed '(serving) her house', the term is not invoked for sexual liaison with a paramour—as the passage above demonstrates in its juxtaposition of the two.

[10] See e.g. BT *Nid.* 16b–17a. The passages in question read, in part, 'the house of Monobaz did three things for which they were honoured: they "served their beds" (had sex) in the daylight, they examined their "beds" with [soft] wool, and they observed the rules of

stood by these Talmudic rabbis to be engaged in 'serving' his or her own body during the act which finds 'his bed' in 'her house'. Even so, 'her house' is not hers alone, for she is 'his house' as well. Ultimately, then, domesticity, or house-ness, characterizes the relation of both husband and wife to her body.

So once again I return to my original query: how to understand the nature and content of rabbinic identifications of woman/wife and house? And, more specifically, what are the implications of that discursive gesture by which women's bodies are not only housed but also 'edified'—that is, the discursive gesture that simultaneously constructs the female body as domestic edifice and institutes a discipline and instruction whereby both men's and women's relationships to the female body are constituted within that framework?[11] What might the housed and edified female body tell us about rabbinically imagined space, and the place of subjects and objects in relation to each other as they occupy and move through it? What might houses, in their material and rabbinic textual manifestations, tell us about genders and bodies in their material and rabbinic textual aspects? What might any of this tell us about women and men, anxiety and desire, relation and separation in the early rabbis' world and in their world-view? The remainder of this study is devoted to an exploration of these questions and their implications through close readings of houses, of bodies, and of the art of domestication that unites the two.

A preliminary note: the term 'house' (*bayit*) is a multipurpose word with dozens of connotations and many forms (much like *oikos* in Greek). In addition to signifying both a domicile and the range of meanings encompassed by the terms 'household' and 'home', *bayit* is found in myriad construct, that is, combination, forms in early rabbinic literature (many of these pre-date the rabbis; some appear for the first time in their

---

purity and impurity in the case of snow. [What is meant by each of these things?] "They 'served their beds' (had sex) in the daylight", read instead "they examined their 'beds' [for blood] in the daylight". And "They examined their 'beds' with [soft] wool", this supports a ruling by Samuel, for he ruled that "the bed" may be examined only with cotton or with soft, white wool . . . "The bed" may not be examined either with a red rag or a black one or with flax' (BT *Nid.* 17a). In the rabbinic system of cultic purity, one uses a rag (as noted above) to examine one's body for signs of blood; one would not need a rag to examine the literal bed upon which one lay. Interestingly, 'he serves his bed' never, to my knowledge, appears in the Mishnah (although the impersonal phrase 'to use/serve *the* bed' does appear), while conversely, 'she serves her house' is not used (except when quoting Mishnah) in the Talmud.

[11] Of course, not only men's and women's relationships but 'man' and 'woman' themselves are also, in part, constituted through this discursive gesture.

writings). These combination words designate everything from nation or *ethnos* (as in *bet Yisrael*, the 'house' or 'people' of Israel), to discipleship circles (as in *bet Shammai* and *bet Hillel*), to institutions and their places of meeting (as in *bet din*, 'law court'; *bet midrash*, 'study house'; and *bet kenesset*, 'synagogue'), to every manner of place or container (as in *bet yad*, 'sleeve'; or *bet ha-sater*, the 'secluded place' of *m. Sotah* 1: 2, cited above), to categories of legal principles (*bet av*). However, while it is no doubt appropriate to consider the entire range of the term's uses when any single one is under scrutiny, the term *bayit* by itself, not combined with another term, specifically signifies a dwelling or household (or wife/woman/female body, as considered in this study). The architectonic elaborations of *m. Niddah* 2: 5 suggest that it is largely on a base of 'house' as dwelling that female body as 'house' is built.

It is thus worth examining closely 'house' as dwelling, in the time and place (second- and third-century Palestine) in which these rabbinic formulations arise. Are there perceptible aspects of the domestic built environment that reflect or participate in—or perhaps undermine—the constructions of gender and bodies also found in rabbinic texts? Is domestic space gendered? What aspects of the ideology and performance of gender might be embodied in domestic building practices current among Jews in Palestine at the time of the Mishnah's development and codification? Or, better, how might domestic building practices play a part in the broader discourses of a society in which rabbinic textual practices, Jewish marriage and burial practices, ritual-purity practices, and so forth also play a part? In recognizing architecture as a system of social practices and a particular genre of cultural expression, and rabbinic literature as another system of social practices and genre of cultural expression, I wish to investigate the ways in which these two systems and genres participate in some of the same wider cultural discourses involved in the negotiation of subjectivity—of social interaction and cultural identity—in a particular geohistorical context. While I am not interested in making claims about 'Jewish' versus 'non-Jewish' houses or building practices, I am interested in exploring building and dwelling practices that create as well as reflect the social environment in which—and by means of which—other, more peculiarly 'Jewish' practices and discourses take place or take shape.

So how does the body as house take shape? And what shape does she take? To begin with, as already noted, it is not simply any woman or female body that is at issue in this construction, but specifically the Jewish wife and the wifely body that is the object of edification. Neither the virginal female body nor the body of the ethnic other is constituted as house.[12] Nor is it specifically the maternal body that is thus constituted; indeed, although the terms 'room' and 'house' are sometimes invoked in describing the location of the foetus in the pregnant body,[13] there is little indication that the homology woman=house belongs to the realm of obstetrical preoccupations, and every indication that it has much to do with sexual activity or 'cohabitation'. That the edified body is not identical with the pregnant or maternal body, however, should not be misconstrued to suggest that it—the edified body—is unrelated to rabbinic concerns about the reproduction of Jewish bodies and rabbinic culture.

The edified female body is always a Jewish body in marital relation, a body constructed around and defined by marital relations and sexual intimacy. As sexuality and cultic purity practices are intimately intertwined in every passage in which this image is invoked, so the edified body is also an object of close regulation, of classification, of 'ordering'. Woman as house is instructed in the examination, purification, and setting in order of that edifice; it is to be her constant occupation and preoccupation. 'The hand that examines often is, in women, praiseworthy', according to *m. Niddah* 2: 1. Hence, the embodying of 'house' is simultaneously the internalizing of a kind of sexual domesticity—the 'house' that inhabits this female body is also a system of habits demanded of it. Sexual intimacy and purity go hand in hand (or hand in house) with regulation and control.

House as dwelling is also always about relation and intimacy, ordering and regulation, purity and control, and this is so in a number of ways. Dwellings house people in relation, whether relation consists of blood, marital, economic, or professional ties, or expedient proximity of some other sort. The building of a dwelling, among Jews and other indigenous peoples of late ancient Palestine, was most likely to occur bit by bit over time (not all at once) and to be intimately bound up with the creation or dissolution of a marital union and the growth or shrinking of a

[12] In fact, the virginal body is constructed with a 'door' (BT *Ketub.* 10a–b) but is not referred to as a 'house', while the wifely body is a 'house' with no 'door'. Cf. Fonrobert's discussion of the 'open door', 'Women's Bodies', 111–13; and from several centuries earlier than the rabbis, Song of Songs 8: 8–10: 'We have a little sister and she has no breasts; what shall we do for our sister on the day she will be spoken for? If she is a wall, we will build upon her a battlement of silver; and if she is a door, we will enclose her with boards of cedar. I am a wall, and my breasts like the towers thereof.'

[13] Cf. BT *Nid.* 31a; BT *Ber.* 61a. The body from which a stillborn foetus emerges is termed 'the grave' in *m. Ohol.* 7: 4.

household.[14] In this sense, 'house' is not some static object that is the context or location of habitation, but, rather, part and parcel with the myriad dimensions of habitation. Timothy Mitchell, in a reading of Pierre Bourdieu, conveys this broader, progressive sense when he remarks of the 'premodern Mediterranean house' that

> the parts of the house are implicated in the life of the household. What exists is this life, in its cycles of birth, growth and death. The house is a process caught up in this life-and-death, not an inert framework that pretends to stand apart . . . there is no mere house, but rather an active housing, engendered in the forming of a household and sustained as an aspect of its vigour, never as a neutral framework. Housing is not an object or container but a charged process.[15]

Needless to say, if house as dwelling is 'a charged process', how much more so the female body as house. Thus, a wife is made in the marrying of her; a female body is rendered 'house' in the same moment and movement in which woman is rendered wife. The consummation of marriage engenders the housing and edification of a wife. A clever little story in the Tosefta about the legitimacy of children echoes this theme:

> Hillel the Elder made an exegesis of ordinary language: When the Alexandrians would betroth a woman, afterward someone else would come along and abduct her from out of the marketplace. Such an incident came before the sages and they considered declaring the children [of the resulting union] illegitimate. Hillel the Elder said to them, 'Show me the marriage contracts of your mothers'. They showed them to him and it was written in them: '*When you will enter into my house, you will become mine* in accord with the law of Moses and Israel [but not before that time].' (*t. Ketuboth* 4: 9, emphasis mine)

Hillel determines that 'entering into [a man's] house', that is, cohabitation, is the act that fully constitutes and legitimizes marriage—an act that had not yet occurred to seal the original betrothal contracts in which it ('entering') was stipulated. But just such housing and cohabiting did occur following the abductions of the betrothed women by other men, who fathered the children in question. The women are therefore judged to be *wives* by virtue of being *housed* and not

---

[14] Cf. e.g. *m. B. Bat.* 6: 4: 'If one got from his neighbour [a plot upon which] to build for himself a marriage-house for his son or a widow-house for his daughter.' Similarly in our own times, homeowners will often add onto or rent out houses or rooms as their households grow or shrink in size.

[15] Timothy Mitchell, *Colonising Egypt* (Cambridge University Press, Cambridge, 1988), 52; a number of my own observations in this vein have become more nuanced through my reading of Mitchell's work. My thanks to H. Aram Veeser for calling Mitchell's book to my attention.

(as customarily understood) by virtue of contract; their children are thus 'legitimate'.[16]

There is, then, a peculiar symmetry to that act by which a woman is housed and edified: she 'enters his house' as wife while he 'enters her house' as husband. But the apparent symmetry has its limitations. For one thing, she 'serves', 'purifies', and 'sets in order' her house; he 'masters' his. That is, while the Hebrew term *ish* ('man') often signifies 'husband' (just as *isha*, as noted, is both 'wife' and 'woman'), the term *baal* ('master') is the more specific term for 'husband', and *baal ha-bayit* signifies 'master of the house' or 'householder'. A husband is charged with mastery over his house, and the master of the house is, in the world-view of Mishnah and Tosefta, the chief economic, political, and legal agent—his household is the basic unit of consumption, production, and reproduction.[17] The mastery involved in husbandry thus characterizes cohabitation as well. *Baal* in its verb form means 'to enter into, take possession, to have sexual intercourse'.[18] Needless to say, the verb is conjugated in the active voice (conjugally speaking) only in the masculine. By 'entering' and/or housing a woman's body, a man renders her 'his house'.[19] Many levels of relation are at once brought into being.

Housing is about other relations and relationships as well. For example, in thinking about domestic space, one might imagine it as standing in juxtaposition to 'society', to social interactions and relations. But this easy division between assumed categories of 'domestic space' and 'social space' (often mapped as 'private' versus 'public' or 'inside' versus 'outside', or even 'female' versus 'male') is, to say the least, highly problematic in a late ancient Palestinian context.[20] Many excavated

[16] Abduction and rape set up the conditions for the story/case, but are of no apparent concern to the discussants or to the outcome. As for 'illegitimacy', the term 'illegitimate' (*mamzer*) refers to a Jew whose birth is the result of a sexual union forbidden according to the Torah, and not simply to any child born out of wedlock.

[17] See Jacob Neusner, *The Economics of the Mishnah* (University of Chicago Press, Chicago, 1990), ch. 4. See also my discussion of these issues in 'Bodies, Boundaries, and Domestic Politics in a Late Ancient Marketplace', *Journal of Medieval and Early Modern Studies*, 26 (1996), 391–418.

[18] Marcus Jastrow, *Dictionary of the Targumim, the Talmud Babli and Yerushalmi, and the Midrashic Literature* (Judaica Press, New York, 1989), 182.

[19] Intercourse is one of three methods by which a man may acquire a woman as wife, according to *m. Qidd.* 1: 1.

[20] The uncritical imposition of the categories 'public' (=social) and 'private' (=non-social) onto built environments throughout the ancient Near East is a widespread, almost universal phenomenon, and one in need of rethinking. See, for example, Leonie Archer, *Her Price is beyond Rubies* (JSOT Press, Sheffield, 1990), 114; Tal Ilan, *Jewish Women in*

domiciles comprise numerous rooms, several of which may contain similar utensils or tools (suggesting similar tasks performed in different rooms of a house and/or various living groups occupying shared space); they may also comprise several courtyards, some fully enclosed by rooms, others communicating with streets, alleyways, or apparently open, undelineated spaces.[21] We assume a great deal if we assume that these domestic compounds or courtyards housed only members of a single—even extended—'family' (a term which, in any case, has no single referent).[22]

Hence, architecturally, many of these excavated houses were 'social', in that they were shared by undetermined numbers of people, of varying relationship to each other, who formed one or more living groups occupying a single courtyard or compound. The social nature of these houses is often masked by historians and excavators with the assertion that 'extended families' were the sole occupants of such complex structures— a claim that can very rarely, if ever, be demonstrated architecturally or archaeologically. On the contrary, many rabbinic texts suggest or assume the presence of otherwise unrelated persons and groups sharing dwelling space within domestic enclosures.[23] Some, like *m. Eruvin* 6: 1–10, consider issues raised by Jews and Gentiles sharing common domestic space or by several living groups sharing a common food stock or dining room. Such evidence suggests that the people occupying these dwellings, whether or not they moved freely in and out of them, or even within them, were, while in their domestic environment, in a fundamentally social environment. Relationships and interaction with others were key elements of 'house' for many, if not most, inhabitants of Palestine's rural and urban domestic landscape in late antiquity. 'House' was rarely a place set aside from society, rarely 'isolated' in the way we tend to

---

Greco-Roman Palestine (J. C. B. Mohr, Tübingen, 1995), 122–9, 176–90; Yizhar Hirschfeld, *The Palestinian Dwelling in the Roman-Byzantine Period* (Franciscan Printing Press, Jerusalem, 1995), 15. While I am not aware of any published work in the field of Jewish antiquity that addresses the need for a reassessment of the appropriateness of these labels, my doctoral dissertation ('Rebuilding the House of Israel: Gendered Bodies and Domestic Politics in Roman Jewish Galilee, *c*.135–300 CE', Duke University, 1997) takes on this issue in a sustained fashion.

[21] Examples of the excavated dwellings described here include those found at Meiron, Capernaum, Chorazim, Katzrin, Sepphoris, Khirbet Kanaf, and many other sites. For perspective drawings and floorplans of many of these see Hirschfeld, *The Palestinian Dwelling*.

[22] See Miriam Peskowitz, ' "Family/ies" in Antiquity: Evidence from Tannaitic Literature and Roman Galilean Architecture', in Shaye J. D. Cohen (ed.), *The Jewish Family in Late Antiquity* (Brown University Press, Providence, RI, 1993).

[23] These include many of the discussions in *m. Nezikin* and *m. Eruvin*, among others.

imagine domestic isolation in its more nineteenth- and twentieth-century, Anglo-American manifestations.

Likewise, house as dwelling was not an entirely closed or self-contained place in this culture. Architectonically, many domiciles, like the larger cities, towns, or villages they comprised, were not separate structures with rigid boundaries, but were, rather, dynamic complexes of access and exclusion, opening and closing, enclosing and disclosing, that shifted and varied with the time of day (and, in Jewish practice at least, the day of the week[24]), the activity undertaken, the season of the year, relations between persons occupying or passing through, mechanisms of exchange and commerce, and so forth.[25]

In part, this fluidity might be expressed in terms of domestic architecture in its relation to domestic and commercial activities. Houses, whether simple or complex, whether occupied by single or multiple groupings of people, rarely encompassed (architecturally) all the activity areas and utilities essential to household functioning. Water, for example, was as likely to be carried daily from a community well, aqueduct, or fountain, or a nearby stream, as to come from a cistern or rain barrel in a courtyard.[26] Similarly, privies and bathing facilities tended to be few and far between, requiring regular trips 'out to the fields' for most people, and occasional trips to the local bathhouse.[27] Ovens, grindstones, and other everyday food-preparation tools, too, might be shared by any number of people—within or outside a household—and require a fair degree of coming and going, giving and taking.[28] Domestic workshops or house-shops were the most common sites of manufacture and commerce in villages or towns, and these were likely be open to traffic during the day but closed off at night; perhaps open to some and denied to others.[29] In addition, the demands of agriculture suggest there were times when most able-bodied people in an area were at work in the fields and at the processing sites for days on end. Other times and seasons were likely to find people engaged in more varied work on the road, in the

---

[24] See *m. Shabbat* 5–6, also *m. Eruvin* ('Sabbath Limits').

[25] Mitchell, citing Roberto Berardi, offers a very similar reading of pre-modern Cairo, *Colonising Egypt,* 56.

[26] This assessment is supported by the extensive aqueduct systems and waterworks found throughout Roman Palestine and by rabbinic references (e.g. *m. Ketub.* 1: 10) to women drawing water from springs. Courtyard cisterns are common in most places as well, as noted by Hirschfeld, *The Palestinian Dwelling,* 278.

[27] Hirschfeld, *The Palestinian Dwelling,* 276 f.

[28] A cause of concern for the purity conscious; see, for example, *m. Tohoroth* 7: 9, *m. Shebi'ith* 5: 9.

[29] On house-shops in Palestine, see Hirschfeld, *The Palestinian Dwelling,* 98 f.

market, in house and courtyard. Courtyards themselves, according to the Mishnah, ranged in type from those that were 'guarded', to those which were locked and unlocked by any number of people, to those that formed a thoroughfare through which strangers might wander freely and unaccosted, to courtyards within courtyards.[30]

Fluidity of boundaries, therefore, seems to be a commonplace. Fluidity does not mean, however, the absence of controls. Houses as dwellings—walls, windows, doors, modes of permission and refusal, patterns of relation—are inevitably involved in the negotiation and control of movement, access, interaction; in this sense they may even be said to participate in a cultural discourse about control. Such discourse may take almost limitless forms; I will focus on a few of the forms it takes here. Dwelling houses in Palestine, throughout the Roman period, were often formed of high walls and accessed by means of narrow entryways set well away from the centre of those walls; they rarely took the form of rows of rooms opening onto a central courtyard or set along a single long hall.[31] Instead, dwellings tended to be extremely asymmetrical in layout, with internal walls effecting separations of space that allowed only very circumscribed movement patterns. Although there is great variety in house layouts, and no single example could properly be called typical, the 'M1 complex' at Meiron from the second–third centuries CE (see Fig. 9.1) provides some sense of these characteristics.[32] One approached this two-storey house from a street or alleyway through narrow corridors. Of the several entrances to the house, most are set near one or other end of a wall, as are the doorways to each room. Doorways on opposing walls are seldom set directly opposite each other so that sight lines rarely pass uninterrupted through more than one room.

Such houses, with their high walls, narrow entries, and asymmetrically set doorways, are mechanisms of control that are not, then, about centralized surveillance, nor about display or spectacle, for example. Sight lines tend to be short and broken; visual access to spaces is limited. If anything, these built structures speak a language of eluding, hiding,

---

[30] *m. Ma'aseroth* 3: 5.

[31] Even the so-called 'central-courtyard' houses of indigenous (as opposed to Roman provincial) design, like those at Chorazim, were frequently built in such a way that very few of the rooms surrounding the open courtyard communicated directly with either the courtyard or the street, and, of those that did, most had openings set well away from the centre of the enclosing wall. On Chorazim, see Ze'ev Yeivin, 'Korazin', in *New Encyclopedia of Archaeological Excavations in the Holy Land* (Simon & Shuster, New York, 1993).

[32] For Meiron see Eric M. Meyers *et al.*, *Excavations at Ancient Meiron, Upper Galilee, Israel 1971–72, 1974–75, 1977* (ASOR, Cambridge, Mass., 1981).

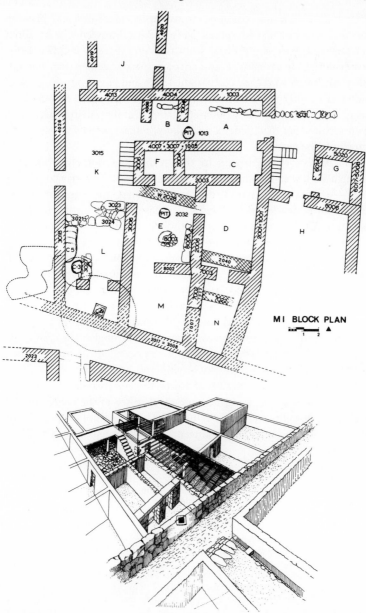

FIG. 9.1   The 'M1 complex' at Meiron, from the second–third centuries CE.

obscuring: of limiting visibility, both within enclosures and between enclosed and unenclosed spaces. This architecture seems to be about not seeing, as well as not being seen from one space to another. Here, people—men or women—may occupy a space together with one another, but rarely may they occupy one space and have immediate visual access to another space and its occupants. No one—man or woman— easily 'keeps an eye on' any other consistently in this environment. This is an architecture that, generally speaking, refuses direct surveillance; it interrupts the gaze.

The pattern that emerges in this reading of domestic buildings throughout Jewish Palestine of this period is one of—if I may coin a new term—'anopticons'. Here I deliberately invert the concept of the 'panopticon', developed by Jeremy Bentham, that so intrigued Michel Foucault. An anopticon is, in some (though not all) respects, the perfect negative of the panopticon. The latter is an architecture of surveillance that induces in the occupant, according to Foucault, 'a state of conscious and permanent visibility that assures the automatic functioning of power'.[33] Ultimately, the occupant or 'inmate' of the panoptic structure 'becomes the principle of his own subjection';[34] whether seen or unseen at any given moment, he carries within himself a sense of perpetual visibility, and begins to monitor himself accordingly. The anopticon functions in parallel fashion such that the occupant of this structure comes to internalize a sense of *invisibility*, and ultimately 'assumes responsibility for the constraints of power' thereby created.[35] The anoptic domestic enclosure is, I suggest, one mechanism of the negotiation of visibility/invisibility and access/refusal that is also part of the negotiation of gender and the body in this ancient Palestinian Jewish culture.[36]

[33] Michel Foucault, 'Panopticism', in *Discipline and Punish: The Birth of the Prison*, trans. Alan Sheridan (Random House, New York, 1977), 201.

[34] Foucault, 'Panopticism', 203. Foucault uses the masculine pronoun throughout his discussion; his observations, however, would apply, in general, to female subjects and objects as well.

[35] Ibid. 202.

[36] I do not understand panopticism and anopticism to be mutually exclusive, although the forms that each takes within a given culture, at a particular historical moment, will be neither consistent nor universal. In addition to negotiation of the gendered body and sexuality we might also ask, in this connection, about negotiation of power balances between Rome and its local Palestinian subjects, or about the uses of surveillance and invisibility in negotiating *urban* life in general. We might then further ask about how these various kinds of negotiations might be related each to the other and be played out in the construction, use, and varied experience of the built environment—and the body. For a consideration of panopticism and the panoptic deity in relation to domestic violence, see Anne Marie Hunter, 'Numbering the Hairs of our Heads: Male Social Control and the All-Seeing Male God', *Journal of Feminist Studies in Religion*, 8 (1992), 7–26.

Masculinity, for example, in the rabbinic texts and the social customs they purport to reflect, is closely entwined with 'husbandry', that is, the mastering of a house. Thus, the measure of a man may be taken, in part, through assessing the skill with which he 'houses' his wife—that is, the means by which he controls her visibility and accessibility to others. This may be seen in a passage from the Tosefta which describes several classes of men through their differing tastes in women (and food):[37] one class of men is represented by Pappos ben Judah, who 'locked the door in his wife's face and went out'. Anopticism in this case takes the form of the locked cell, the prison house that renders its occupant invisible and inaccessible to all but the master who holds the key. In contrast, 'the common man . . . leaves his wife be to converse with her relatives and neighbours'. The implication is that an acceptable balance has been struck between this latter wife's visibility and invisibility: she is accessible to some but not to others, and her husband does not—and need not— overtly police her. Finally, there is the 'evil man', whose wife can be seen by one and all, at home and abroad, in every manner of dress and undress. His wife's visibility is a mark against this man's virtue; because he does not properly 'house' his wife, he is charged to divorce her.

House as viewing mechanism, then, plays a pervasive role in gendering, and in the edification of women in particular.[38] Such an observation is not meant to imply, however, that women were the sole or primary occupants of houses, nor that women were secluded in or restricted to the house.[39] In point of fact, there is very little evidence (rabbinic or architectural) to suggest that any such practices were the case among Jews in late ancient Palestine, and a good deal of evidence to the contrary (see below)—Pappos ben Judah, after all, is singled out and

---

[37] t. Sotah 5: 9.

[38] The phrase 'house as viewing mechanism' follows an expression used by architectural theorist Beatriz Colomina who observes that 'Architecture . . . is a viewing mechanism that produces the subject', in 'The Split Wall: Domestic Voyeurism', in B. Colomina (ed.), Sexuality and Space (Princeton Architectural Press, Princeton, 1992), 83.

[39] A pervasive trope in Greek and Latin literature of antiquity, the domestic seclusion of women is, for the most part, conspicuously absent from the earliest rabbinic literature. On the seclusion of women in Greek and Roman authors and art, see, for example, Averil Cameron and Amélie Kuhrt, Images of Women in Antiquity (Wayne State University Press, Detroit, 1983), 79–106; Sarah B. Pomeroy, Goddesses, Whores, Wives, and Slaves (Schocken Books, New York, 1975), 147 f., 159 f.; Eva C. Keuls, The Reign of the Phallus (Harper, New York, 1985), 98–128; Ann Carson, 'Putting Her in Her Place: Woman, Dirt, and Desire', in David M. Halperin et al. (eds.), Before Sexuality (Princeton University Press, Princeton, 1990), 135–70. It should be noted that archaeologists have had very limited success in identifying 'gendered space' in the remains of any classical Greek houses. See, for example, Michael Jameson, 'Domestic Space in the Greek City-State' in Susan Kent (ed.), Domestic Architecture and the Use of Space (Cambridge University Press, Cambridge, 1990).

differentiated from 'the common man' by his practice of locking up wife and house. Moreover, in the Mishnaic discussions concerning marital rights and obligations, the rabbis insist that a man who attempts to restrict his wife to the house for an extended period of time must release her from the marriage contract and return her marriage settlement to her, 'for he has closed all doors against her'.[40] While these rabbis are willing to grant a husband some control over the movements of his wife, prolonged restriction or seclusion of her are clearly beyond his rights. And the many rabbinic dicta that take for granted (albeit with anxiety) the presence of women—married and unmarried, young and mature— in fields and orchards, markets and streets, at public fountains, wells, baths, and springs, all militate against our imagining widespread domestic seclusion of ancient Jewish women. As for women being the primary occupants of houses, again there is little evidence to support such an assumption. Both rabbinic texts and architectural evidence suggest that the processing, production, and even sale of many kinds of goods were as likely to take place within and around domestic enclosures as away from them. Hence, workers—male or female—would as likely be found working 'at home' (their own or another's) as elsewhere. (Such an assessment must, of course, leave room for regional and seasonal variation, as well as changes over time.[41])

Given these observations, it becomes clear that anopticism is a more complex and generalized phenomenon than can be addressed simply in terms of the domestic seclusion of women, or its lack. Moreover, approaching the issue of anopticism in terms of seclusion obscures more than it reveals. Women do not have to be kept inside houses in this culture (nor men kept outside) for the anoptic qualities of housing to be, none the less, deeply implicated in the gendering of women. 'Invisibility' does not require the physical absence or hiding of the subject any more than visibility requires the physical presence or action of a viewer.[42] It requires only that the subject be disregarded or unperceived *as such*.

---

[40] *m. Ketub.* 7: 4–5.

[41] For a discussion of work in and outside the home (especially textile work) in its relation to the construction of gender, see my 'Bodies, Boundaries, and Domestic Politics'. See also Miriam Peskowitz, *Spinning Fantasies: Gendering the Ordinary in Roman-Period Judaism* (University of California Press, Berkeley and Los Angeles, 1997).

[42] As Foucault notes, Bentham's panopticon 'works' whether or not there is anyone in the central observation post: 'surveillance is permanent in its effects, even if it is discontinuous in its action', Foucault, 'Panopticism', 201. Likewise, one may know oneself to be invisible in socially significant ways or, conversely, may learn to 'look right through' others without 'seeing' them.

Anopticism, then, implies a set of habits, regulations, and practices that constitute a wife's subjectivity through her dis-appearance. A rabbinic maxim found in *t. Qiddushin* 1: 11, for instance, distinguishes between married and unmarried women precisely in terms of their relative visibility when not at home: the latter woman is stared at regardless of how she comports herself, while the former is disregarded—if not invisible:

a woman who has a husband: whether she adorns herself or not, people do not stare at her. And if she does not adorn herself, she will be despised . . . A woman who has no husband: whether she adorns herself or not, everybody stares at her.

The passage is interesting for a number of reasons. First, it is neither an idle nor an appreciative gaze that is directed at the unmarried woman, but, as the wider context confirms, it is the aggressive and policing 'stare' of a crowd that greets her. By what act has she merited this treatment? And to what end is she subjected to it? We know only that she is an unmarried woman. (No accounts tell of unmarried men meeting the same fate.) The married woman, on the other hand, seems somehow protected from such assaults by an aura of non-visibility that attends her marital state. But by what token does 'everybody' discern that the one is married (and therefore unavailable to the common gaze) and the other is not?[43] Clearly, adornment *per se* is not an indicator, despite its significance for keeping one's husband happy. Perhaps some badge or signal marks the one from the other? (Again, no known markers distinguish married from unmarried men.)

Although the actions and codes described in this passage may or may not reflect widespread social custom—we have few other forms of evidence by which to judge—it is likely that the images conveyed are at least consistent with rabbinic constructions of practice. To the extent that this is the case, the married woman's distinguishing mark would probably be her headgear.[44] In fact, 'a hat for her head' is among the clothing items that a husband is enjoined by the rabbis to provide for his wife,[45] and if

---

[43] There is nothing in the passage to suggest that the description applies only to a very small village where everyone is likely to know who is or is not married; hence, some form of signification seems implied.

[44] Regarding hair, heads, genitals, sex, hats, and the like, in the display of gender in Mediterranean antiquity, one of the best studies to date is Molly Meyerowitz Levine, 'The Gendered Grammar of Ancient Mediterranean Hair', in Howard Eilberg-Schwartz and Wendy Doniger (eds.), *Off with her Head! The Denial of Women's Identity in Myth, Religion, and Culture* (University of California Press, Berkeley and Los Angeles, 1995), 76–130, including extensive bibliography in the endnotes.   [45] *m. Ketub.* 5: 8.

he does not, a later commentator adds, others may buy goods from her (even if the profits rightfully belong to her husband) in an amount that would enable her to obtain one.[46] Moreover, wives who 'go out with head uncovered' are threatened with divorce and financial loss,[47] their husbands are reviled as 'evil',[48] and heavy fines are decreed against anyone who would dare remove a woman's hat against her will.[49] A hat, it seems, is what stands between a woman and the stares of the multitudes; a hat decreases or disrupts the common gaze, much as the walls of a house do. And, more to the point, it is precisely when she 'goes out' (presumably from the house) and precisely because she is a wife (that is, a house) that she requires a hat. The matron's hat becomes a technique and device for carrying anopticism beyond the walls of the domestic anopticon.

The habit of donning a hat when leaving the house—a habit reinforced by threats of divorce, ridicule, and aggressive stares—bespeaks precisely the internalization of invisibility by which a woman is trained to participate in her own erasure. It is part of the edification of woman that makes her—and marks her as—'wife'. No similar evidence exists for a corresponding mark of 'husbandry' for males, and distinctive hats to distinguish Jewish men from Gentiles were still centuries away.[50] Needless to say, the wearing of a hat does not in fact render a woman invisible (the practice assumes that women are seen), yet it invests a woman's self-controlling gesture with the power to diffuse the invasive gaze of others. It is a form of display that seems, paradoxically, to signify the opposite of display. In thus marking herself, a wife takes her place in the order of things and thereby ensures that others will keep to their places as well. Her husband's high regard is predicated upon a wife's success in maintaining others' dis-regard for her. In this way, the habit of the hat, like the regimens of ordering, purification, and examination of 'the house', is part of a broader cultural discourse in which woman as wife embodies the practice of 'domesticity', becoming mediator of the boundaries of visibility and invisibility, monitor of access to herself, her 'house', her body, her sexuality. In so partaking in her own domestication a woman becomes—like the work of her hands, the place in which she lives, and

---

[46] *t. Baba Kama* 11: 5.

[47] *m. Ketub.* 7: 6; *t. Ketub.* 7: 6.

[48] *t. Sotah* 5: 9.

[49] *m. Baba Kama* 8: 6.

[50] But see 2 Macc. 4: 12, where the wearing of 'the Greek hat' by Jewish youth in Jerusalem in the 2nd century BCE is reported as a sign of 'extreme Hellenization . . . and wickedness'. Cf. Paul (mid-1st century CE) on the disgrace and inappropriateness of male head-covering in 1 Cor. 11: 4–7.

the children she bears—the domain of her husband, the 'master of the house'.[51]

'The body', notes Susan Bordo, '—what we eat, how we dress, the daily rituals through which we attend to the body—is a medium of culture.'

The body . . . is a powerful symbolic form, a surface on which the central rules, hierarchies, and even metaphysical commitments of a culture are inscribed . . . It is also, as anthropologist Pierre Bourdieu and philosopher Michel Foucault (among others) have argued, a *practical*, direct locus of social control. Banally, through table manners and toilet habits, through seemingly trivial routines, rules, and practices, culture is 'made body'.[52]

The habits of domesticity, inscribed on—and 'in'—the female body in Jewish antiquity, represent one such example of culture made body. But the 'female body as house' of rabbinic discourse pushes even deeper, forcing us to consider not only routines, rules, and habits, but also the spaces and places that give shape to these, and to the bodies that perform them. It moves us away from our accustomed consideration of architecture as simply a context for social practices, and toward an understanding of the built environment as a meaning-laden semiotic system itself intricately bound up with other such systems.

Houses, like all material artefacts, are not simply descriptive—they are discursive. Building and dwelling, like language, are systems of practices with their own proper 'logic' and inherent constraints; but they are also, at the same time, deeply enmeshed in the give and take of social life. Houses signify on many levels, both expressing and creating social relations, and their walls, windows, and doorways may be every bit as actively involved in constituting 'the body' as are rabbinic pronouncements and local customs of dress and address. Indeed, as I have indicated, houses are frequently the very occasion for the construction and negotiation of cultural ideologies of gender and sexuality, intimacy and control.

While this brief study has barely begun to scratch the surface of the 'well-ordered house', it has suggested some of the ways in which that house may participate in the ordering of the lives of women (in particular), of men, and of the wider society responsible for its construction. By unfolding here a handful of the myriad implications of a discourse concerned with the housing and edification of women's bodies, I hope to

[51] On 'the work of her hands' etc. see *m. Ketub.*

[52] Susan R. Bordo, 'The Body and the Reproduction of Femininity: A Feminist Appropriation of Foucault', in Allison M. Jagger and Susan Bordo (eds.), *Gender/Body/Knowledge* (Rutgers University Press, New Brunswick, NJ, 1989), 13.

open a space for further explorations of the ways in which that 'geography closest in' is negotiated through such material and interrelated practices as building and dwelling, dressing and speaking, seeing and being seen. My aim in this endeavour has been to engage a conversation that not only builds on our present understanding of gender and the body in Mediterranean antiquity, but that simultaneously breaks down many of the disciplinary walls that have rendered such conversations so difficult for so long.

10

Playing Roman Soldiers: The Martyred Body, Derek Jarman's *Sebastiane*, and the Representation of Male Homosexuality

In a recent collection of essays entitled *Outlooks: Lesbian and Gay Sexualities and Visual Cultures* (1996), Richard A. Kaye observed that from the late nineteenth century the image of St Sebastian's body pierced by arrows has provided a means of conceiving a male self that encompasses homosexual desire. Kaye's disparate catalogue of representations of the martyred Roman soldier in twentieth-century writing, painting, photography, film, and performance art discloses that in contemporary culture St Sebastian has emerged 'as the very distillation in art of an emotionally and politically fraught homosexual persona'.[1] One such instance Kaye cites is that of the British film *Sebastiane* which was co-directed by Derek Jarman and Paul Humfress and released to mixed critical response in 1976.[2] In his later autobiographical writings, Jarman retrospectively established a specific historical context for and urgent purpose to the making of *Sebastiane*: the film was designed to open to young British men a door into another world, one

I am very grateful to Jonathan Walters for the helpful and enthusiastic suggestions he made when I began my research on St Sebastian. I would also like to express my thanks to Jonathan, Dominic Montserrat, and Helen Morales for their comments on a draft version of this chapter. Helen Morales also kindly drew my attention to the essay by Richard A. Kaye (for which see n. 1) and the book by Joel Black (for which see n. 37). I was able to undertake much of this research thanks to the generosity of the British School at Rome where I held a Balsdon Fellowship in spring 1997.

[1] Richard A. Kaye, 'Losing his Religion: Saint Sebastian as Contemporary Gay Martyr', in Peter Horne and Reina Lewis (eds.), *Outlooks: Lesbian and Gay Sexualities and Visual Cultures* (Routledge, London, 1996), 86.

[2] Although *Sebastiane* was co-directed by Paul Humfress and co-scripted by James Whaley, it has since taken up a place in the analysis of Jarman's *œuvre* as his first feature film. For the purposes of this chapter, which analyses the film in conjunction with Jarman's own writings and his public persona, I shall take the liberty of referring to it hereafter as Jarman's work.

away from their own in which to be a homosexual was frequently to be a social outcast and, until as recently as 1967, a criminal.[3] The other world which Jarman envisaged was that of imperial Rome in the reign of the emperor Diocletian, a place and time at once sexually liberated and oppressive.

Had he lived in ancient Rome, according to Jarman, he could have married a boy,[4] and the film *Sebastiane* accordingly opens with a riotous party held by Diocletian on 25 December 303 CE to celebrate the birth of the sun. Lascivious dancers frantically 'masturbate' huge phalluses as they circle around their chorus-leader who eventually collapses to the floor and, in extreme close-up, exhibits his relish at the ejaculations with which his face is now spattered.[5] However, Sebastian, captain of the palace guard and the emperor's favourite, protests against the subsequent execution of Christians at the imperial party and is therefore banished to a remote outpost of the empire. There he is treated with suspicion by almost all of his fellow-soldiers for his Christian mysticism and renunciation of the flesh and develops a sado-masochistic relationship with his commanding officer that leads to his torture and the death he evidently desires. The sexual liberalism that Jarman perceived in the culture of Graeco-Roman antiquity was for him a revelation, and an inspiration to read between the lines of history, to hunt for forebears who might validate his existence as a homosexual in contemporary Britain, and to pose a question—'was Western civilization Queer'?[6] *Sebastiane* was thus the first of Jarman's cinematic forays into the queering of history.

Understandably an enormous gulf separates the invocations to St Sebastian in modern Christian liturgy from those in Jarman's cinematic and literary works. On the one hand, a prayer card which is currently available for purchase at the Basilica of St Sebastian along the Via Appia Antica explains that in Roman liturgy the martyred soldier is invoked for healing from both physical and spiritual wounds and, in the sample

---

[3] Derek Jarman, *At Your Own Risk: A Saint's Testament*, ed. Michael Christie (Vintage, London, 1993; 1st edn. Hutchinson, 1992), 29.

[4] Ibid. 4.

[5] My description of the sequence follows that of Michael O'Pray, *Derek Jarman: Dreams of England* (British Film Institute, London, 1996), 86–7.

[6] Jarman, *At Your Own Risk*, 46. For Jarman's own use of the term 'queer' see Chris Lippard (ed.), *By Angels Driven: The Films of Derek Jarman* (Flicks Books, Trowbridge, 1996), 9 n. 2. For a more general discussion of its usage, see for example Horne and Lewis (eds.), *Outlooks*, 1–2.

prayer that follows, suppliants ask for Sebastian's spirit of fortitude in order that 'we may learn to bear witness to the Christian Faith and patiently support the sufferings of life'. On the other hand, a hymnic poem composed in Latin by the scholar Jack Welch for the production of *Sebastiane*, and subsequently published in Jarman's public writings about the film, describes nature's empathetic sorrow at the martyrdom of the saint and addresses Sebastian directly (as in the Latin title of the film):

> The fatal arrow has found its mark
> A shadow has fallen across the waters
> The breeze is still
> No birds sing
> Colour has deserted the world.
> Sebastian takes leave of the world
> Like an arrow he flies to the sun
> No night shall ever shroud him
> He leaves the dark hours of the world.
> See the arrows' wounds
> His life blood drips in the sand
> Marigolds spring up spreading their petals in the sun's rays, golden
>   flowers of
> Apollo
> Sebastian
> Sebastian
> Shower kisses on the young god with his golden eyes
> Shower kisses on your beloved
> And in the evening light
> Remember this world of shadows.[7]

This latter invocation appears to heroize the Roman soldier as capable of enduring his cruel earthly torment in order to achieve resplendent erotic union with his god and he is asked, therefore, to remember (and presumably succour) his lonely suppliants left behind in our world of shadows. The purpose of this chapter is, therefore, first to explore the basis on

---

[7] The Latin version, which precedes the English translation given in Derek Jarman, *Dancing Ledge*, ed. Shaun Allen (Quartet Books, London, 1984), 142–3, reads as follows: 'Sagitta funesta acu tetigit | Umbraque tegit aquas | Et aura tacet | Aves non canunt | Deficit ab orbe color. | Sebastianus de mundo discessit | Ad solem modo sagittae advolat | Nox non umquam eum occupabit | Discessit ab horis orbis atris. | Ecce vulnera sagittarum | Sanguis vitae fluit in harena | Calthae solis in radis [*sic*] folia | Explicantes surgunt. | Flores apollinis aureos | Sebastiane | Sebastiane | Da iuveni deo qui luminibus aureis est multa basia | Da amatori multa basia | Et vesperis in luce | Mundum hunc recordare.'

which Jarman's film appropriated the pierced body of St Sebastian from
Christian hagiography in order to refigure it as an emblem of homosexual martyrdom and secondly to map the various readings and
rereadings which have been produced of the Roman soldier's ambivalent
cinematic representation onto the evolution of a male homosexual identity in contemporary Britain. Such an analysis of the film *Sebastiane*
provides an opportunity to explore some of the ways in which classical
bodies have been appropriated as sites on which to configure and to
contest modern sexualities and genders.

Jarman's film *Sebastiane*, both at the time of its release in 1976 and in
subsequent histories of lesbian and gay cinema, has generally been regarded as an innovative work that, unusually for a commercially released
British film of the period, broke with the classical style of film narration
to offer an imagistic, homoerotic celebration of the male body. After the
intricately choreographed, frantic, and orgasmic dance sequence which
opens the film at the court of the emperor Diocletian, a series of relatively
static set-pieces puts on display the erotic beauty of the male nude. As
soon as the film narrative shifts to the remote imperial outpost, day
dawns over Sebastian who washes himself in the courtyard of the barracks watched at a distance by his commander Severus. Repeatedly the
commander's lustful gaze is counter-cut with slowed-down shots in
extreme close-up of Sebastian's naked body, so that its fragmented parts
move in a languorous and sensual slow motion in the eye of the film's
internal (and, by extension, external) beholder.[8] The English subtitles,
which at this point overlay Sebastian's glistening body on screen and
translate his voiced-over Latin hymn to the god of the sun, detail nature's
amorous response to the god's awakening and thus suggest an identification between the latter's stimulating beauty and that of the awakened
Sebastian: 'Hail, messenger of dawn. The young God has arisen . . . The
reeds sigh when the young God rises. The waters sing when the young
God rises. Mankind awakens from sleep. The scarlet cock struts when the
young God rises.' A central, extended sequence of the film depicts two of
Sebastian's fellow-soldiers, the lovers Antony and Adrian, stroking and
kissing each other by the seashore. According to the approving description of this scene of 'untrammelled eros' in Richard Dyer's discussion of
lesbian and gay cinema, 'slow-motion photography caresses their limbs
and in the pool shows mesmerising streams of waterdrops glancing off

---

[8] As O'Pray, *Derek Jarman*, 87.

and haloing their bodies'.[9] Again, in a later sequence set in the bathhouse of the barracks, the camera in close-up moves smoothly over the naked bodies of the Roman soldiers as they wash and then scrape their oiled skin with strigils.[10] And, in the final culminating moments of the film, after Sebastian's comrades have tied his body to a stake, according to the contemptuous review of the *Evening News* for 5 November 1976, they proceed to 'zing those arrows into him—in the same kind of slow, tender motion that is used to show the centurions sodomising each other'.[11]

For Jarman, the source and validation of his eroticized depiction of St Sebastian's martyrdom lies not in the archaeological, historiographic, or hagiographic tradition of the early Christian Church but in the regular appropriation and frequent deployment of this sacred subject by artists from the Renaissance to the present day:

As one stands in the catacomb in front of his tomb, one can dream of the artists who have rescued him from the darkness. To Bernini, whose sculpture is in the catacomb, he is a hero who gazes into the sunlight next to him. Georgetti [whose sculpture is in the basilica above Sebastian's crypt] has sculpted him as a youth captured in the ecstasy of death. But through all these and many other interpretations one thought is shared. The arrows are laid on Sebastian as lightly as a caress.[12]

The martyred body of St Sebastian is certainly shrouded in darkness where the historical record is concerned.[13] The most ancient reference to the saint appears in the *Depositio martyrum*, the calendar of the Roman Church dated to 354 CE: *XIII Kal. feb. Fabiani in Callisti et Sebastiani in Catacombas*. Registering the annual commemoration that the Christian community at Rome celebrated on 20 January over the tombs of the two

---

[9] Richard Dyer, *Now You See It: Studies on Lesbian and Gay Film* (Routledge, London, 1990), 169. Cf. O'Pray, *Derek Jarman*, 89 and Jarman's own comments in *At Your Own Risk*, 83–4.

[10] As O'Pray, *Derek Jarman*, 89 and cf. Jarman's account of the erotic charge attached to the Roman strigil by the actor Ken Hicks in *Dancing Ledge*, 143.

[11] On the erotic symbolism of this last scene, see Kaye, 'Losing his Religion', 98.

[12] In item 3 of the production documents on *Sebastiane* in the British Film Institute's Derek Jarman Collection. Cf. the similar press release put out by Jarman's production company Megalovision at the time of the film's initial screenings.

[13] As Sylvie Forestier observes in the exhibition catalogue *Saint Sébastien: Rituels et figures* (Musée National des Arts et Traditions Populaires, Éditions de la Réunion des Musées Nationaux, Paris, 1983), 27. St Sebastian's historical record and early legend is conveniently catalogued in the *Bibliotheca Hagiographica Latina Antiquae et Mediae Aetatis* (=*BHL*), ed. Socii Bollandiani (Brussels, 1900–1) and presented in greater detail in *Acta Sanctorum* (=*AA.SS*), Ianuarii vol. ii, ed. Johannes Bollandus (Venice, 1734), 257–96.

martyrs Fabian and Sebastian at the cemeteries along the Via Appia, the liturgical calendar briefly lists only their anniversary day, names, and places of veneration. Adding to the *Depositio martyrum* only a place of origin, Psalm 118 of St Ambrose (dated towards the end of the fourth century) exhorts the faithful of Milan to imitate the example of the martyr who is called their fellow-citizen: 'utamur exemplo Sebastiani martyris, cuius hodie natalis est; hic Mediolanensis oriundus erat.' Ambrose does not provide a precise date for Sebastian's death but suggests that, learning of a religious persecution raging in Rome, he took himself there to seek the crown of martyrdom.[14] So meagre is the ancient historical evidence concerning Sebastian that it has led some scholars to question whether he ever existed.[15]

Scholars of the early Church are in general agreement that all subsequent record for Sebastian is entirely unhistorical, for the saint possesses no 'authentic' *Acts*. The initial, foundational hagiographic recital of St Sebastian's deeds and death is the anonymous *Passio S. Sebastiani* whose composition is attributed to the period 432–40 CE. It consists of a muddled and romantic narrative obedient to the rules for the production of legendary Roman hagiographies as laid out earlier this century by Hippolyte Delehaye. Although full of precise details, the *Passiones* characteristically group around their central heroic protagonist a series of subordinate martyrs whose relation to the hero has little or no historical basis. Such texts imagine a grandiose and dramatic struggle between the early Christians and their imperial persecutors. Replete with mass conversions, baptisms, cures, and visions, interrupted by long doctrinal homilies, they recount how the subsidiary martyrs are imprisoned, judged, tortured, and immolated one after the other until the recital culminates in the glorious death of the principal character.[16]

The *Passio* of Sebastian belongs among such fictions and constitutes the ultimate source for all the successive versions of his martyrdom.[17]

---

[14] See further Hippolyte Delehaye, *Cinq leçons sur la méthode hagiographique*, Subsidia Hagiographica 21 (Société des Bollandistes, Brussels, 1934), 33; P. Benedetto Pesci, 'Il culto di san Sebastiano a Roma nell'antichità e nel medioevo', *Antonianum*, 20 (1945), 177–9; Forestier, *Saint Sébastien*, 27; Antonio Ferrua, *La basilica e la catacomba di S. Sebastiano* (Pontificia Commissione di Archeologia Sacra, Città del Vaticano, 1990), 33; Lucia Giubelli, *Sebastian: Roman Martyr* (Co. Graf and ATS Italia, Milan, 1992), 2–3.

[15] See e.g. Pesci (on the doubts of S. Minocchi), 'Il culto di san Sebastiano', 178 n. 1.

[16] Delehaye, *Cinq leçons*, 33–7.

[17] For the Latin text of the *Passio S. Sebastiani*, see *BHL* no. 7543; *AA.SS* Ian. ii. 265–78; *Patrologia Latina* (=*PL*), ed. J. P. Migne, vol. xvii (1845), col. 1021–58. An approximate English summary can be found in Revd S. Baring-Gould, *The Lives of the Saints*, January, vol. i (John Grant, Edinburgh, 1914; 1st edn. 1872), 300–5. For discussion of the *Passio*, see

According to it, Sebastian was a most Christian man of outstanding virtue—prudent, truthful, just, prescient, faithful, and rigorous—who was so greatly regarded by Diocletian and Maximian that he was elevated to the command of the first cohort. He was revered like a father by the soldiers and held in dearest affection by all, since he was a true venerator of God and, therefore, necessarily lovable. At Rome, thanks to his encouragement, two imprisoned brothers reaffirm their faith and learn the bravery of Christ's soldiers. Sebastian variously encourages, cures, and converts until he is denounced to the emperor. Faced with the soldier's claim that succour can only come from the one God of heaven, Diocletian orders him to be taken into a field and shot with arrows. Despite his ensuing resemblance to a hedgehog, so riddled is he with arrows, Sebastian does not die but is taken into the care of a widow. Once healed of his wounds, he seeks out Diocletian in order to bear witness against the persecutor of the Christians and is accordingly transferred to the Palatine where he is clubbed to death. The saint now appears to a matron in a dream and orders her to find his body (which has been tossed in a Roman sewer) and to bury it in the Catacombs. A church is soon built there over his relics.

Except for brief references to the regard, affection, and love in which the Roman soldier was universally held, the legend of St Sebastian—as Jarman himself intimates—does not provide promising ground on which to build a homosexual martyrdom.[18] The *Passio* belongs rather to the theatre of militant Christianity of the fifth to ninth centuries, when such texts were regularly read out by clerics on a saint's feast-day as a privileged means to evangelize. In his suffering body, the martyr bore tangible witness to the truth of the Christian faith when confronted by persecution. Sustaining the courage of the faithful and earning their veneration, the martyrdom of a Roman soldier in particular demonstrated the victory of faith in Christ and his Church over a citizen-soldier's loyalty to his emperor.[19] Sebastian became an immensely popular figure for devotion in the medieval cult of the saints as a result not only of the wide diffusion of his *Passio* but also of the power

---

Delehaye, *Cinq leçons*, 33–7; Pesci, 'Il culto di san Sebastiano', 179–85; Forestier, *Saint Sébastien*, 30–3; Ferrua, *La basilica e la catacomba*, 33; Giubelli, *Sebastian*, 7–16. The text subsequently referred to here is that in *PL*.

[18] Cf. Kaye, 'Losing his Religion', 89. The Latin text reads: 'Hunc milites ac si patrem venerabantur; hunc universi, qui praeerant palatio, charissimo venerabantur affectu: erat enim verus Dei cultor, et necesse erat ut, quem Dei perfuderat gratia, ab omnibus amaretur' (=*PL* col. 1021, 1. 1).

[19] See Forestier, *Saint Sébastien*, 27–33.

attributed to him of hindering the plague which regularly decimated Europe until the eighteenth century. The *Historia Longobardorum* details his miraculous intervention against one such plague which desolated Rome in 680 CE and the story is repeated in the *Golden Legend*, a collection of such miracles of the saints which achieved immense popularity in the thirteenth century and was translated into most European languages. From these accounts arose Sebastian's fame as a thaumaturge. Seeing in the wounded body of the saint a symbol of their own sick bodies, sufferers from the plague took up Sebastian as their patron and assumed that he could combat its 'arrows' because, although himself severely wounded, he had been healed. Devotion extended to the veneration of Sebastian's relics (for fragments of which churches competed), the establishment of fraternities, the foundation of churches (including eventually the dedication to his name of the church above Sebastian's crypt), pilgrimages to his tomb, performances of mysteries, and the production of many votive depictions.[20] A seventh-century mosaic designed to adorn an altar erected to St Sebastian in S. Pietro in Vincoli at Rome (in commemoration of his assistance against the plague there) displays the iconographic type first developed to suit the saint's status as both militant soldier of Christ and thaumaturge: as befits the significance of his name ('venerable') and in accordance with the description in his *Passio*, St Sebastian appears as a pastor, elderly, bearded, and severe, dressed in a tunic under which can be glimpsed golden armour, and grasping in his hand the crown of martyrdom (Fig. 10.1).[21]

From the thirteenth century, given St Sebastian's continuing function as interceder against the plague, Christian iconography began more regularly to privilege his sagittation. Little or no artistic attention was paid to other aspects of his legend, especially his second martyrdom, clubbed to death on the Palatine. And, rather than depict the Roman soldier conventionally, holding the instruments or the result of martyrdom in his hand, artists represented him at the very moment of his torment, bound and pierced by arrows. His body, having triumphed over

---

[20] On the veneration of St Sebastian, see Victor Kraehling, *Saint Sébastien dans l'art* (Éditions Alsatia, Paris, 1938), 10–16; Pesci, 'Il culto di san Sebastiano'; Louis Réau, *Iconographie de l'art chrétien*, vol. iii. 2 (Presses Universitaires de France, Paris, 1959), 1191–2; Patrick J. Geary, *Furta Sacra: Thefts of Relics in the Central Middle Ages* (Princeton University Press, Princeton, 1978), 45–8; Forestier, *Saint Sébastien, passim*; Ferrua, *La basilica e la catacomba*, 23–7 and 34–8; Giubelli, *Sebastian*, 18–28.

[21] On the earliest iconography, see Kraehling, *Saint Sébastien*, 9; Pesci, 'Il culto di san Sebastiano', 191–5; Réau, *Iconographie*, 1192–3; Forestier, *Saint Sébastien*, 17, 34, 40 no. 14, 50; Ferrua, *La basilica e la catacomba*, 34; Giubelli, *Sebastian*, 28.

FIG. 10.1   St Sebastian. Seventh-century CE mosaic.

the arrows' bite, was rendered beautifully intact. Exhibiting scarcely any diminution of its perfection, undergoing no physical degradation, it became an index of Sebastian's incorruptible saintliness and, for the faithful, an invitation to patience and the hope of victory over their own suffering.[22] So in Andrea Mantegna's *St Sebastian*, an altarpiece commissioned for Sainte-Chapelle at Aigueperse and dated to the period 1481–8, the saint appears bound to the ruins of a delicately carved imperial arch and a fluted Corinthian column, his lined and careworn features expressing the pain of sagittation which his heavily muscular, manly body

[22] Réau, *Iconographie*, 1194; Forestier, *Saint Sébastien*, 66–7.

endures. He displays the robustness appropriate to a Roman soldier, but one who is now learning the better fortitude of martyrdom. More noble in appearance than his plebeian executioners who are partially visible in the painting's bottom right-hand frame, classically statuesque, perfectly chiselled, and more complete than the monumental ruins around him, Sebastian's body here bears witness to the triumph of Christianity and the decline of brutal empire.[23]

Historians of Christian iconography, however, have observed that from the fifteenth century the Italian Renaissance more commonly rejected the depiction of St Sebastian in terms of a muscular and mature masculinity in favour of the alignments of an exquisite youth. The Roman soldier becomes a beardless adolescent of Apollonian beauty, a naked ephebe. The most frequently deployed explanation for this development grounds it in aesthetics: the representation of St Sebastian's martyrdom provides an opportunity to imitate and to challenge antiquity in the glorification of the beauty of the male nude. Painters 'sculpted' saints inspired by the discovery of antique statues such as the Apollo Belvedere.[24] Margaret Walters, among others, has added a further explanation in her study *The Nude Male: A New Perspective* (1979): 'The martyr is often no more than an excuse to paint a luscious classic nude; he also provides an outlet for usually suppressed homosexual fantasies. The arrows signify pleasure *and* punishment, the nude saint is a focus for growing delight in the flesh, *and* for guilt at being seduced by the grace of the body.'[25] Appropriations of the classical male nude for the representation of martyrdom provided the painters of the Italian Renaissance with an opportunity to subvert the puritanism of traditional Christian iconography, for such nudes carried the charge of a culture in which the male body appeared to be freely admired as an object of beauty and of sexual desire.[26] In particular, the martyred body of St Sebastian provided a ready site on which to convey a classicizing male *eros*. As Derek Jarman

[23] On Mantegna's painting, see Kraehling, *Saint Sébastien*, 29 and pl. 12; Margaret Walters, *The Nude Male: A New Perspective* (Penguin Books, Harmondsworth, 1979; 1st pub. 1978), 97–8; Ronald Lightbown, *Mantegna* (Phaidon, Christie's Ltd., Oxford, 1986), 134–6, 420–1, and catalogue no. 22.

[24] Kraehling, *Saint Sébastien*, 25–35; Réau, *Iconographie*, 1192–3; Ferrua, *La basilica e la catacomba*, 34; Giubelli, *Sebastian*, 30–3. Cf. Walters, *The Nude Male*, 78–9, 94, and 96; Emmanuel Cooper, *The Sexual Perspective: Homosexuality and Art in the Last 100 Years in the West* (Routledge, London, 1994: 1st edn. 1986), 1.

[25] Walters, *The Nude Male*, 82 (the emphasis is hers). Cf. Richard Dyer, *The Matter of Images: Essays on Representations* (Routledge, London, 1993), 43–4; Cooper, *The Sexual Perspective*, pp. xvii and 1; Kaye, 'Losing his Religion', 88–9.

[26] Walters, *The Nude Male*, 99; Cooper, *The Sexual Perspective*, 2.

himself observed, 'the arrows which pierce the passive adolescent are as overt a symbol as any Freudian could wish for'.[27]

Play with the signs of gender could further mark Sebastian's sagittation as the tacit delineation of a forbidden sexual act. *The Martyrdom of St Sebastian*, attributed to a collaboration between the brothers Antonio and Piero Pollaiuolo and dated to 1475, exhibits a carefully balanced composition (Fig. 10.2). The viewer who looks up at the painting, originally designed as an altarpiece for the Pucci Chapel at S. Sebastiano dei Servi, observes in the centre a young and nude Sebastian tied high up on a tree-trunk below and around whom six archers are grouped in a contrapuntal arrangement of poises. Together the six executioners provide a complete record, in fine anatomical detail, of the strenuous actions an archer must perform. The veins and muscles in the archers' arms and legs swell in brutal and manly activity, while they stretch bows, take aim, and release arrows. Against these tough and vigorous athletes Sebastian performs a passive, feminine role. Young, gracefully nude, soft of flesh, and beautifully fragile, the martyr submits to his suffering with seeming resignation.[28] So gendered, the act of penetration is also sexualized. As Richard Dyer notes in *The Matter of Images: Essays on Representation* (1993), sexuality (which has no equivalents to the biological markers of sex and race) is often conflated with gender roles in acts of representation in order to make the invisible visible. In the iconography of the Italian Renaissance, therefore, the nude body of Sebastian is regularly configured as in some sense feminine— passive, submissive, and receptive to penetration by brute, masculine force.[29]

Furthermore, masculine penetrators do not need to be present in a painting for Sebastian's martyrdom to be rendered sexually suggestive and homoerotic. In many examples, such as the multiple versions produced by Pietro Perugino towards the end of the fifteenth century or that of Guido Reni at the beginning of the seventeenth, Sebastian appears as an isolated languorous ephebe. Nonchalantly posed, nude, fragile, and

---

[27] In item 2b of the production documents on *Sebastiane* in the British Film Institute's Derek Jarman Collection. Cf. Kaye, 'Losing his Religion', 88–9.

[28] On the painting by the Pollaiuolo brothers, see further Kraehling, *Saint Sébastien*, 28–9 and pl. 15; Leopold D. Ettlinger, *Antonio and Piero Pollaiuolo* (Phaidon Press, Oxford, 1978), 49–50, 139–40 and pls. 83–9; Walters, *The Nude Male*, 102 and 113–14. Cf. Jarman's comments on this painting in item 2b of the production documents on *Sebastiane* in the British Film Institute's Derek Jarman Collection.

[29] Dyer, *The Matter of Images*, 19–25 and 42–4. On the gendered iconography of male martyrs in the Italian Renaissance, cf. also Walters, *The Nude Male*, 10; Cooper, *The Sexual Perspective*, 6–9; Kaye, 'Losing his Religion', 88–9.

F I G. 10.2   *The Martyrdom of St Sebastian* by the Pollaiuolo brothers, *c.*1475.

alone, bound to his post and delicately pierced by a few arrows, his uplifted face is transfixed by an ecstasy that speaks of loss of self, erotic abandon, the *desire* to be penetrated.[30] Here, and in the blatantly sensual seventeenth-century sculptures by Bernini and Georgetti which Jarman was able to see at the Catacomb of St Sebastian, the bodily metaphors of passion which had earlier been deployed by mystics to express the soul's joyful ravishment by and ecstatic union with God regain their literalism and materiality as Sebastian takes orgasmic delight in his suffering.[31] The isolation of Sebastian also opens up a greater space for the viewer both to identify with and to desire the pierced, beautiful body on display.[32]

Richard A. Kaye, in his essay cited at the opening of this chapter, suggests that the representation of Sebastian's self-absorbed detachment which had been developed in the Renaissance possessed a particular utility towards the end of the nineteenth century:

The crux of the saint's mythic power for writers and artists of the last century comprises an evolving dynamic of the self in isolation, in which a young, accomplished soldier announces a 'true' self and is therefore punished for his self-incriminating candour. Sebastian thus could stand for homosexual self-revelation as opposed to homosexual affection, and as such he was a splendid vehicle for a new conception of same-sex desire, which, as numerous historians of sexuality have suggested, encompassed a shift from a stress on homosexual *acts* to an emphasis on homosexual *identity*.[33]

This new suggestiveness for St Sebastian partially accounts for the virulence with which the Catholic Church condemned a performance of *Le Martyre de Saint Sébastien* staged in Paris in 1911. A 'mystery' in five acts composed by the poet Gabriele d'Annunzio and set to the music of Claude Debussy, it starred the famed Russian dancer Ida Rubinstein in the lead role crying 'Encore! Encore!' during her execution by arrows.[34] The apparent perversity of allotting the martyr's role to a woman, of rendering Sebastian a decadent, androgynous icon, may have been

---

[30] On representations of Sebastian's serenity or erotic ecstasy, see Kraehling, *Saint Sébastien*, 29 and pls. 17, 39, and 40; Réau, *Iconographie*, 1194; Carlo Castellaneta and Ettore Camesasca, *L'opera completa del Perugino* (Rizzoli Editore, Milan, 1969), 6; Walters, *The Nude Male*, 82; Kaye, 'Losing his Religion', 88–9.

[31] Kraehling, *Saint Sébastien*, 37 and 41; Walters, *The Nude Male*, 177–9 and 183–7.

[32] See, for example, the speculation of the writer Michel del Castillo on the appeal of Sebastian's representation to generations of young men quoted in Dyer, *The Matter of Images*, 90–1 n. 3 and Kaye, 'Losing his Religion', 88.

[33] Kaye, 'Losing his Religion', 91. The emphasis is his.

[34] On the production, see Forestier, *Saint Sébastien*, 156–63; Kaye, 'Losing his Religion', 88.

exacerbated by the current medicalization of homosexuality as a congenital abnormality, a distinctly feminine illness, which lead to a widely circulated definition of the homosexual as *anima muliebris virili corpore inclusa* ('a female mind trapped in a male body').[35]

During the course of the twentieth century, St Sebastian came to represent the formation and self-formation of the modern male homosexual in quite explicit terms. Thus a *St Sebastian* of 1934 by Albert Courmes playfully transfers the martyr to the modern setting of a French harbour and converts him from soldier to camp sailor. Posed with his hands placed lightly behind his head, Sebastian's profile appears before a partially glimpsed full moon that stands in for a sanctifying halo. Dressed in a sailor's costume only from head to waist, he displays that part of his body which was conventionally hidden in Renaissance iconography. The arrows pierce his skin only from calf to waist and in directions which lead the viewer's eye directly upward to his genitals provocatively on display centre-frame.[36] The Japanese writer Yukio Mishima even configured his own erotic awakening and his very body in terms of the martyrdom of St Sebastian.[37] He gave an initiatory significance to his discovery as a boy of a reproduction of the painting by Guido Reni in one of his father's art books, claiming that it stimulated his first ejaculation. The martyr came to dominate Mishima's narrative of adolescent homosexual self-awakening. In his autobiographical *Confessions of a Mask* published in Japan in 1949, the narrator describes his intense fascination with St Sebastian's apparently fatal eroticism and finds himself adopting the saint's gestures as they had been represented in Reni's painted version:

Ever since becoming obsessed with the picture of St Sebastian, I had acquired the unconscious habit of crossing my hands over my head whenever I happened to be undressed. Mine was a frail body, without so much as a pale shadow of

---

[35] See Kaye, 'Losing his Religion', 87 and 89, for the relationship between Sebastian's modern representations and the medicalization of homosexuality. On the latter, more generally, see Jeffrey Weeks, *Coming Out: Homosexual Politics in Britain, from the Nineteenth Century to the Present* (Quartet Books, London, 1977), esp. 26–7; Kenneth Plummer, 'Homosexual categories: Some Research Problems in the Labelling Perspective of Homosexuality', in K. Plummer (ed.), *The Making of the Modern Homosexual* (Hutchinson, London, 1981), 53–75; John Marshall, 'Pansies, Perverts and Macho Men: Changing Conceptions of Male Homosexuality', in Plummer (ed.), *The Making of the Modern Homosexual*, 142–5.

[36] For the painting, see Kaye, 'Losing his Religion', 87 and Dyer, *The Matter of Images*, fig. 6.5.

[37] For Mishima's use of St Sebastian, see Joel Black, *The Aesthetics of Murder: A Study in Romantic Literature and Contemporary Culture* (Johns Hopkins University Press, Baltimore, 1991), 200–1 and 206–7; Kaye, 'Losing his Religion', 91, 93–4, and 101.

Sebastian's abundant beauty. But now once more I spontaneously fell into the pose. As I did so my eyes went to my armpits. And a mysterious sexual desire boiled up within me . . .[38]

In gruesome anticipation of his own suicide by seppuku in 1970, Mishima posed four years earlier for a series of photographs taken by Kishin Shinoyama entitled 'Death of a Man'. One such scene comprised a recreation of St Sebastian's martyrdom, where Mishima is seen to copy closely the attire and gestures of Reni's depiction, down to the location of the three arrows which pierce the flesh.[39] Reading the iconography of the martyr's sagittation as an image of an intense erotic pleasure in excruciating death (although in the legend of the saint death occurs at a later occasion), Mishima drew on St Sebastian as an aesthetic embodiment of extreme sado-masochistic eroticism that required duplication completely.

In the literature of the Catholic Church and its defenders reference to St Sebastian's *Nachleben* as homosexual icon is almost completely elided. For example, two of the reference works available for purchase at present in the souvenir shop at St Sebastian's Catacomb along the Via Appia Antica, Antonio Ferrua's *La basilica e la catacoma di S. Sebastiano* (1990) and Lucia Giubelli's *Sebastian: Roman Martyr* (1992), fail to refer to this rich tradition even though their illustrations contain examples of it. Similarly, the prayer card which is also available from the shop carries on its obverse the reproduction of an early sixteenth-century depiction of an Apollonian Sebastian by Giovanni Antonio Bazzi whose notorious behaviour had earned him in his lifetime the nickname 'Il Sodoma'.[40] The card does not name the originator of the painting and the omission is, of course, scarcely surprising. The 'official' version of Sebastian's martyrdom concerns only militancy, fortitude, faith, suffering, and healing. In *Dancing Ledge* (1984), however, Derek Jarman acknowledges the full range of Sebastian's tradition:

Sebastian. Renaissance. Pretty boy smiles through the arrows on a thousand altar pieces—plague. Saint. Captain of Diocletian's guard. Converted, stoned, and thrown into the sewers. Rescued by a Holy Woman. Androgyne icon banned by

---

[38] Quoted in Kaye, 'Losing his Religion', 94. The ellipses are introduced by Mishima.

[39] In *The Aesthetics of Murder* Black helpfully juxtaposes a reproduction of Reni's painting with Mishima's enactment of it.

[40] For the nickname see Cooper, *The Sexual Perspective*, 12–15 on the account given by Vasari.

the bishop of Paris. Danced by Ida Rubinstein. Impersonated by Mishima. In love with his martyrdom.[41]

Sebastiane itself is a painterly film that contains numerous references to the martyr's homoerotic iconography. Jarman's cinematic style here has been well documented: slow-motion techniques foreground the static, pictorial quality of the film's compositions; the frequently frontal orientation of those compositions slides into lingering tableaux vivants; the absence of significant character development and the employment of only brief amounts of dialogue delivered in Latin draw the attention of spectators both away from the film's narrative drive and toward its presentation of spectacle.[42] In particular, Sebastian's invocations of and identifications with the god of the sun—the beautiful and beloved Apollo—during the course of the film and the composition of his final martyrdom evoke the multiple Apollonian Sebastians of the Italian Renaissance (Fig. 10.3). The arrangement of the six executioners around the martyr in the closing sequence of *Sebastiane* recalls that in the paint-ing by the Pollaiuolo brothers. The actor who plays the Roman soldier, Leonardo Treviglio, is posed with both hands tied above his head and with one arrow in his armpit in imitation of the Reni Sebastian which so possessed Mishima, while the arrow piercing his neck and his uplifted expression of ecstatic agony are suggestive of works by 'Il Sodoma' and Perugino respectively.[43] It is precisely through such evocations that Jarman's cinematic representation of St Sebastian as a homosexual martyr gains a feeling of credibility and much of its aesthetic effectiveness.

At the time of the release of *Sebastiane* in 1976 its celebration of the male body from a distinctly homoerotic perspective made the film a *cause célèbre* in Britain and elsewhere.[44] Responses varied wildly from expres-

---

[41] Jarman, *Dancing Ledge*, 142. Cf. Jarman's detailing of Sebastian's *Nachleben* in the various production documents for *Sebastiane* in the British Film Institute's Derek Jarman collection.

[42] See further, Mark Nash, 'Innocence and Experience', *Afterimage*, 12 (1985), 31–2; Dyer, *Now You See It*, 168; Chris Lippard and Guy Johnson, 'Private Practice, Public Health: The Politics of Sickness and the Films of Derek Jarman', in Lester Friedman (ed.), *Fires were Started: British Cinema and Thatcherism* (University of Minnesota Press, Minneapolis, 1993), 282; Tracy Biga, 'The Principle of Non-narration in the Films of Derek Jarman', in Lippard (ed.), *By Angels Driven*, 23; David Hawkes, '"The Shadow of this Time": The Renaissance Cinema of Derek Jarman', in Lippard (ed.), *By Angels Driven*, 105 and 108; O'Pray, *Derek Jarman*, 9–10, 67, and 82.

[43] Cf. on this final scene, Nash, 'Innocence and Experience', 31; Dyer, *Now You See It*, 169.   [44] O'Pray, *Derek Jarman*, 8.

FIG. 10.3   The martyrdom of Sebastian, from Derek Jarman's *Sebastiane* (1976).

sions of discomfort or condemnation to unqualified praise. When first screened at the Locarno film festival in June 1976 it was barracked by the audience, whereas it gained record attendances when later premiered in London at the Gate, Notting Hill.[45] Many of the reviews in mainstream British newspapers suggested that the film could be of no interest to a heterosexual spectator: 'It is, however, more geared to attract chaps who

[45] See the comments of Jarman in *Dancing Ledge*, 156 and 159.

like chaps, lying and stretching and fainting in tormented, bronzed coils, than your family audience . . . The film positively encourages the restive hetero to resist it.'[46] Yet it was the commercial release of *Sebastiane* and its correspondingly wide distribution that constituted one of the film's distinctions. As Jarman himself later recalled,

Sebastian [*sic*] didn't present homosexuality as a problem and this was what made it different from all the British films that had preceded it. It was also homoerotic. The film was historically important; no feature film had ventured here. There had been underground films, *Un Chant d'Amour* and *Fireworks*, but *Sebastian* was in a public space. Although it is flawed and lacks any of the finesse of professional film-making, it altered people's lives.[47]

Both Jarman and historians of cinema have read *Sebastiane* as a contribution made to the British politics of gay liberation—a movement stressing openness, defiance, pride, and identity—that had developed rapidly after the partial decriminalization of homosexual practices in 1967.[48] Part of the film's polemical value was seen to lie in its public revelry in what had, until the successful passage of Leo Abse's Sexual Offences Bill, been both private and illegal. And for this it was warmly embraced by the gay community, as a review of the period in *Gay News* suggests: 'Very occasionally there appears a film of such power and authority that one emerges from the cinema feeling somewhat shaken and disoriented . . . *Sebastiane* is a very special, and indeed, a quite remarkable film that represents a milestone in the history of gay cinema.'[49] 'A gorgeously evangelistic vision of homosexuality',[50] *Sebastiane*, in terms of its narrative structure, also constituted a critique of the British society in which that homosexuality need assert its existence.[51] The filmic representation of the torment and martyrdom of St Sebastian comprised an indictment of both the long-standing oppression of male homosexuals in this

---

[46] *New Statesman*, 29 Oct. 1976. Cf. the review in the *Sunday Times* for 31 Oct. 1976 which contains the statement 'I had been given the wrong menu.'

[47] Jarman, *At Your Own Risk*, 83. Cf., with only slight qualification of Jarman's claims, Dyer, *Now You See It*, 168; O'Pray, *Derek Jarman*, 11 and 83.

[48] For the development in Britain of the gay liberation movement after 1967, see Weeks, *Coming Out*, 185–237, and Jarman's own account which forms a constant thread through *At Your Own Risk*. Weeks's book was published only a year after the release of *Sebastiane*, suggesting that as the tenth anniversary of decriminalization approached the achievements (and the future) of the gay liberation movement were undergoing significant scrutiny.

[49] Quoted in O'Pray, *Derek Jarman*, 83. Cf. James Cary Parkes, 'Et in Arcadia . . . Homo: Sexuality and the Gay Sensibility in the Art of Derek Jarman', in Roger Wollen (ed.), *Derek Jarman: A Portrait* (Thames & Hudson, London, 1996), 143–4; Lippard, *By Angels Driven*, 3.

[50] According to the *Financial Times* for 29 Oct. 1976.

[51] As, for example, O'Pray, *Derek Jarman*, 92.

country and the fixity of notions of gender which had accompanied it. Designed for the public pleasure of the gay community, *Sebastiane* also offered a challenge to what Jarman customarily labelled the dominant culture of 'Heterosoc'.[52]

In his cinematic rereadings of history, Jarman constantly used the past to colour polemical examinations of contemporary British society.[53] In this respect, as Jarman himself makes clear, his exploration of imperial Rome in the time of Diocletian was no different: 'One of the things that most fascinates me about film-making is recreating the past in terms of the present. Therefore, as in the first scene of *Sebastiane*, modern London can become ancient Rome.'[54] Exhibiting a gallery of faces familiar from the London 'counter-cultural' scene of the 1960s and early 1970s—the painter Robert Medley as Diocletian, Lindsay Kemp and Troupe as court dancers, the punk figure Jordan as party guest in modern dress—the opening of *Sebastiane* draws explicit attention to its presentist interests. Throughout the film humorous contemporary references abound transposed into Latin dialogue, from self-reflexive comments on the earlier cinematic depictions of ancient Rome directed by Cecil B. DeMille and Federico Fellini, to the categorization of Mary Whitehouse (in the guise of Maria Domus Alba) as 'the terror of civilization'.[55] This latter reference discloses the film's central narrative concern with British assaults on the expression of homosexual desire, here epitomized by the right-wing evangelical Festival of Light which, in the era of gay liberation, had been set up by Mary Whitehouse to campaign against precisely such 'permissiveness' as well as against pornography.[56]

The motif of martyrdom has had a long-standing history in Britain as a means of expressing the male homosexual's painful experience of institutional victimization. After his notorious trial and imprisonment, Oscar Wilde wrote during the 1890s: 'I have no doubt we shall win but the road is long, and red with monstrous martyrdoms.'[57] In Jarman's film, the execution of St Sebastian is thus available to be read as an angry indictment of the repressive apparatus of Heterosoc's economy, his torture

---

[52] For Jarman's notion of Heterosoc, see Martin Quinn-Meyler, 'Opposing "Heterosoc": Derek Jarman's Counterhegemonic Activism', in Lippard (ed.), *By Angels Driven*, 117–34.
[53] As O'Pray, *Derek Jarman*, 7–8; Parkes, 'Et in Arcadia', 141–3.
[54] Megalovision press release for *Sebastiane*, 1976.
[55] Tony Rayns, 'Sebastiane', *Monthly Film Bulletin*, 43.514 (1976), 236; David Gardner, 'Perverse Law: Jarman as Gay Criminal Hero', in Lippard (ed.), *By Angels Driven*, 55–6; O'Pray, *Derek Jarman*, 86.
[56] Weeks, *Coming Out*, 205; O'Pray, *Derek Jarman*, 54.
[57] Quoted in Weeks, *Coming Out*, 115.

Maria Wyke

and death at the orders of his military commander a hyperbolic articulation of the violence with which the British state regularly treated those citizens deemed not to conform to its regimes of the sexual.[58] Displacing the narrative of Sebastian's martyrdom to a lonely outpost of the Roman empire, the film establishes a self-contained, entirely male community, where Sebastian embodies a challenge to the authority of the soldiers' world expressed frequently in terms of a transgression of gender. The sexually voracious soldier Max acts as a brutal and hypocritical guardian of the community's heterosexual morals. His constant condemnation of homosexuality as a perverse decline into the feminine adheres to the traditional deployment in this century of gender, rather than sexual orientation, to define homosexual identity,[59] while his obsessive concern to perform and to enstate in others an aggressive masculinity at the same time as he involves himself in violent sexual horseplay suggests the fragility of that definition and the moral bankruptcy of its proponents. For Max, the commander's desire for his subordinate Sebastian represents a potential breakdown of the community's order and its source therefore requires violent elimination.[60]

According to this reading of *Sebastiane* as a reflection on homosexual experience in Britain prior to and after the possibilities afforded by gay liberation, the Roman soldier's martyrdom is characterized ambivalently as simultaneously heroic and unnecessary.[61] Sebastian displays a guilt over his desire for the earthly Apollonian commander Severus which is understandably stifled and displaced, as a result of his sadistic persecution and developing Christian mysticism, onto an idealized unworldly love object—his beloved god of the sun. As a homosexual under a state of siege, Sebastian is sympathetically portrayed despite the feminine religious passivity into which he retreats when confronted by masculine military aggression.[62] The spectator is offered several opportunities, for

---

[58] As Parkes, 'Et in Arcadia', 138–40.

[59] For which see Weeks, *Coming Out*; Marshall, 'Pansies, Perverts and Macho Men'; Dyer, *The Matter of Images, passim*.

[60] For this reading of the role of Max, see esp. Dyer, *Now You See It*, 168–9 and O'Pray, *Derek Jarman*, 85–92.

[61] The film's ambivalent characterization of Sebastian was recognized by Jarman himself in a Megalovision press release, and in some contemporary newspaper reviews, as well as in later critical accounts.

[62] Michael O'Pray, 'Derek Jarman's Cinema: Eros and Thanatos', *Afterimage*, 12 (1985), 12–14; O'Pray, *Derek Jarman*, 84–5. Cf. Parkes, 'Et in Arcadia', 142–3, for a similar reading of the besieged homosexual in other films directed by Jarman, and Dyer, *The Matter of Images*, 84 and 89 on the typology of 'the sad young man' (popular in the 1940s to 1960s) as a means to express the melancholy of gay existence under oppression.

example, to identify with Sebastian's bodily suffering. When he is staked out in the hot sun the camera looks up into its glare as seen from the martyr's point of view and, in the last lingering shot of the whole film, a wide-angled lens is employed to distort the image into a curving horizon filled with six executioners who face *us*—a perspective never depicted in Sebastian's Renaissance iconography.[63] Yet *Sebastiane* also characterizes the martyr's renunciation of the flesh as perverse by elaborating within the community of Roman soldiers an entire taxonomy of male *eros* which allocates significant space to a desire classified as neither aggressively masculine nor defensively feminine.[64] No rigid gender categorizations are affixed to the lovers Antony and Adrian whose sensual love-making is allocated a central and extended place in the film and was later described by Jarman himself as 'ecstatic'.[65] The Renaissance iconography of Sebastian's homoerotic, mystical self-absorption is here ousted by the mutual, fleshly embrace of a pair (whose names are perhaps designed to recall another ancient Roman precedent for homosexual desire—the lovers Hadrian and Antinous) (Fig. 10.4).[66] The centrality of this sequence in *Sebastiane* would appear to argue that, in the post-liberation climate of mid-1970s Britain, there should be no further need for homosexual martyrs. Or, as Jarman put it more vigorously in a later reflection on his film: 'Sebastian, the doolally Christian who refused a good fuck, gets the arrows he deserved. Can one feel sorry for this Latin closet case?'[67]

Since 1976, however, several significant developments in the politics of British homosexuality have seemed to call for yet further revisions of the martyrdom of St Sebastian and Jarman's cinematic representation of it. In conclusion, I will concern myself briefly with two of them, namely the debates that have arisen since the late 1970s concerning the value of sado-masochistic practices and the renewed gay activism of the late 1980s and 1990s necessitated by the AIDS epidemic. In an analysis of how film critics have come to interpret the sado-masochistic representation of homosexuality in Jean Genet's *Un chant d'amour*, Richard Dyer has

---

[63] Cf. the analysis by Lippard and Johnson, 'Private Practice', 282, of a sequence in the film which interconnects the savage hunting and killing of a pig with the torture and death of Sebastian.

[64] Cf. Rayns, 'Sebastiane', 236; O'Pray, *Derek Jarman*, 92.

[65] Jarman, *At Your Own Risk*, 84. Some contemporary reviewers and subsequent critics have been less generous.

[66] For this reading, see esp. Dyer, *Now You See It*, 168–9.

[67] Jarman, *At Your Own Risk*, 83. On this comment, cf. O'Pray, *Derek Jarman*, 84 and, more generally, Kaye, 'Losing his Religion', 87.

FIG. 10.4   Antony and Adrian make love, from Derek Jarman's *Sebastiane*
(1976).

noted that under the influence of the writings of Michel Foucault it has
no longer been understood as an allegory for, or evidence of, the distaste-
ful state oppression of gay men but as a discourse on the rituals of sexual
pleasure. According to this account, through the dynamic play of domination and submission and the allocation of heavily marked gender roles
to the penetrator and penetrated, sado-masochism can explore and interrogate the social relations of power that are the essence of sexuality
and thus dismantle utopian visions of caring, romantic intimacies. Gay
male sado-masochism can thus both reclaim conventional masculinity

and, perhaps more importantly, empower and render appealing the passivity and self-renunciation traditionally marked as both feminine and demeaning.[68] Those critics, like Michael O'Pray, who have in turn interpreted the associations of sex and ritual violence in *Sebastiane* as a covert discourse on sado-masochism's pleasures have accordingly reread the depiction of Adrian and Antony's love-making as 'stylised, idealised and ultimately unworldly and unconsummated'[69] and sensed in the film a certain admiration for Max as a character 'who recognises lust for what it is and refuses to sublimate or idealise it',[70] but have yet to redeem the martyrdom of Sebastian as a dramatization through pain of the potential erotic ecstasy of self-renunciation. And this despite Derek Jarman's own repeatedly published statement on the question of his attitude to masculinity: 'Until I'd enjoyed being fucked I had not reached balanced manhood. When you overcome your fear you understand that gender has its own prison. When I meet heterosexual men I know they have experienced only half of love.'[71]

Richard A. Kaye details, in his essay on the contemporary image of St Sebastian with which I began this chapter, how the symbolic importance of the martyr has undergone a transformation and taken on greater intensity in the late 1980s and 1990s. In the time of AIDS, his legend as a thaumaturge able to ward off the 'arrows' of plague has been revived as of consoling value, and his status as a Roman soldier who none the less resists the state has been appropriated as emblematic of the militant, politicized homosexual who must combat government neglect and social persecution.[72] Given that from the early 1980s Derek Jarman emerged centre-stage in Britain as a persistent defender of gay rights, as an HIV positive activist engaged in the politics of ACT UP, Queer Nation, and Outrage!, it is perhaps no surprise that in the title of his 1992 autobiography *At Your Own Risk: A Saint's Testament*, in his public account of his canonization by the Sisters of Perpetual Indulgence, and in the obituaries published on his death from AIDS in February 1994, the metaphor of martyrdom was appropriated for the director himself.[73] But here

---

[68] Dyer, *Now You See It*, 70–99. See further Leo Bersani, *Homos* (Harvard University Press, Cambridge, Mass., 1995), 77–112, who expresses some reservations concerning Foucault's enthusiastic advocacy of sado-masochistic sex.

[69] O'Pray, *Derek Jarman*, 89.

[70] Ibid. 93.

[71] See, for example, Jarman, *At Your Own Risk*, 32.

[72] Kaye, 'Losing his Religion', 86–7, 98, and 101–2.

[73] For Jarman's involvement in gay political activism in the 1980s and 1990s, see *At Your Own Risk*, passim; Parkes, 'Et in Arcadia', 137–40; O'Pray, *Derek Jarman*, 7–15 and 174–207. See also the substantial obituary by Colin MacCabe in the *Independent* for 21 Feb. 1994.

martyrdom regained the significance it had had at the turn of the century when, for example, the sexologist Havelock Ellis had talked of the perilous attempt to change public attitudes to homosexuality as 'the pursuit of the martyr's crown'.[74]

---

[74] Quoted in Weeks, *Coming Out*, 65. On martyrdom as metaphor for Jarman's political activism, cf. Gardner, 'Perverse Law', 40–1.

11

Sowing the Seeds of Violence:
Rape, Women, and the Land

CAROL DOUGHERTY

> But Romulus himself went around . . . and told them [the Sabine women] that they would be married and would share in all the possessions of the Romans—their city, and the thing most dear to all, their children. (Livy 1. 9. 14)

> And while they were doing it, they said I was going to have a baby by them and that it'd be an honor for a Muslim woman to give birth to a Serbian kid. (Ifeta, a 26-year-old woman from a village near the northern Bosnian village of Doboj)

HELKE SANDERS opens *Mass Rape: The War against Women in Bosnia-Herzegovina* (1994), a collection of essays on rape as part of ethnic hostilities in the former Yugoslavia, with a letter to Lysistrata. Since Lysistrata successfully led the women of Athens and Sparta in a sex strike in order to put an end to the Peloponnesian War, Helke Sanders wants to know if her strategy 'would make any sense today in the war zone of the former Yugoslavia'.[1] Her letter proceeds then to lay out the issues and problems particular to what she sees as a similar coincidence of violence, war, and sexuality played out on the bodies of women in the current ethnic and political conflict between Serbs, Croats, and Bosnians.

I found this opening rhetorical gesture interesting, not because I thought Lysistrata would have the answers to the questions posed by Sanders and the others in the volume, but both because the appeal to antiquity underscores the historical longevity of this phenomenon—war and rape have long coexisted—and because it highlights the influential and insidious relationship between representation and reality. Lysistrata, of course, was not a real Athenian woman—rather a male playwright's representation of such a woman, a fantasy of how she should or would

---

[1] Helke Sanders, 'Prologue', in Alexandra Stiglmayer (ed.), *Mass Rape: The War against Women in Bosnia-Herzegovina* (University of Nebraska Press, Lincoln, 1994), p. xvii.

act. Yet clearly her fictional existence continues to wield real influence upon how we understand gender politics in ancient Athens and elsewhere. Far more insidious than the confusion between real and fictional characters in Athens, however, is the slippage between myth and reality in the former Yugoslavia as different ethnic groups contest their rights to land. Territorial conquest has long been represented metaphorically in art, literature, and mythology as a kind of rape. And now, as the rape camps in Bosnia-Herzegovina have shown all too clearly, rape is not just a metaphor—these symbolic representations have had a devastatingly powerful effect on how real women experience political and ethnic violence.

If we are going to look to the past for help in understanding rape as a weapon of war, instead of writing to Lysistrata for advice, I propose that we view the rape camps in Bosnia through the eyes of the Sabine women to restore the symbolic significance to what has rightly been recognized as a war crime. The rapes of Bosnian women prefigure and represent Serbian conquest of Bosnian land. At the same time, however, recent events in Bosnia (and elsewhere) suggest that we recognize the possibilities for real violence against women in our discussions of political conquest in the ancient world whether that be Greek colonial expeditions, early Roman state formation, or later imperial expansion. This chapter sets out to read first-hand testimony from Bosnian women together with mythical accounts about the Sabines to explore the dynamic relationship between the historical experience of rape and its metaphorical role in representing ethnic conflict and territorial conquest.

Let's start with the Sabine women. Livy recounts the rape of the Sabines in the first book of his history of the founding of Rome. He explains that because of a shortage of women, the future of the newly founded city was at risk. In an attempt to rectify the situation, Romulus consulted the neighbouring tribes to ask for the rights of intermarriage, explaining that they would be lucky to mix with Roman stock, but none agreed. They were all afraid that Rome would gain too much power. And so, Livy says, the matter seemed certain to end in violence: 'haud dubie ad vim spectare res coepit' (1. 9. 6). Romulus then contrived a plan to take place during the Consualia games, which the Sabines would attend with their children and wives. At a designated signal, each Roman youth grabbed a Sabine girl: 'signoque dato iuventus Romana ad rapiendas virgines discurrit' (1. 9. 10). The Sabines were furious at this attack on their daughters, but Romulus explained to the girls that they were to be married and thus would become partners in the possessions— citizenship and children—of the Romans, and the Sabine girls were soon reconciled (so Livy says) to their new status as Roman wives. The hostile act of violence that begins the story is immediately subsumed into the marriage ritual and thus transformed into an act of civilization or culture. Moreover, the women, too, are transformed in the process—once Sabine girls, now Roman wives, their native ethnic or national identity has been erased and replaced by that of their conquerors.

Livy's account of the rape of the Sabines draws upon a well-established rhetorical tradition in the ancient world that includes rape within the cultural and ideological concept of marriage. Not just a celebration of the progress from primitive wildness to a state of greater civilization, marriage entails an expression of sexual violence, and myths of rape, both within and without marriage, reflect the destructive nature of erotic power. A girl's virginity is a highly prized commodity, one not easily nor willingly relinquished, and this fact is also reflected in aspects of the marriage ceremony. In addition to separating the bride from her family and home, marriage includes the very real physical violence of defloration. Although marriage and the production of children may define a woman's adult existence, her transition to that status is marked with great reluctance and ambivalence. Thus in myth and art, marriage is represented both as a manifestation of culture and as an expression of violent nature.

While, on one level, Livy's account of rape and marriage certainly reflects these views of sexuality and gender roles, the theme of sexual violence in his account of the Sabines is clearly symbolic of larger cultural and political issues as well. As others have already noted, tales of rape figure prominently and programmatically in Livy's history of Rome's early days to recount a view of the city's origins that will help celebrate and confirm its rebirth as an imperial power under Augustus.[2] Indeed, within the context of foreign conquest and overseas settlement, the discourse of rape and the institution of marriage provide models for representing the complicated relationships which must be forged between the conquerers/colonizers and native populations upon annexing foreign territory.[3] Greek and Roman literature is full of tales of young nymphs or

---

[2] Cf. Sandra Joshel, 'The Body Female and the Body Politic: Livy's Lucretia and Verginia', in Amy Richlin (ed.), *Pornography and Representation in Greece and Rome* (Oxford University Press, New York, 1992), 112–30; Ian Donaldson, *The Rapes of Lucretia* (Oxford University Press, Oxford, 1982). On the connections between the rhetoric of rape and politics more broadly construed, cf. Froma Zeitlin, 'Configurations of Rape in Greek Myths', in S. Tomaselli and R. Porter (eds.), *Rape* (Blackwell, Oxford, 1986), 122–51; Edith Hall, 'Asia Unmanned: Images of Victory in Classical Athens', in John Rich and Graham Shipley (eds.), *War and Society in the Greek World* (Routledge, London, 1993), 108–33.

[3] Cf. Carol Dougherty, *The Poetics of Colonization* (Oxford University Press, New York, 1993), 61–80, for a discussion of the role that rape plays in myths of colonization.

mythological heroines raped by Olympian gods such as Zeus, Apollo, or Poseidon, who then give their name (or the name of their offspring) to the new territory.

Pindar's *Pythian* 9, to take just one example, recounts the founding of the Greek colony of Cyrene as the rape and marriage of a nymph, Cyrene, by Apollo. Pindar paraphrases the myth right at the beginning of the ode as he praises Cyrene, 'whom the long-haired son of Leto once took from the valleys of Pelion which echo in the wind, and he brought the wild maiden in a golden chariot and made her mistress there and caused her to live in the lovely flourishing third continent of the many-flocked and much-fruited land' (*Pyth.* 9. 5–9). As part of this narrative that describes the political foundation of a new city as the transformation of a wild girl into a fertile and flourishing landscape, Pindar uses rather graphic agricultural imagery. In the passage where Apollo asks Cheiron, the centaur, if he can have intercourse with the nymph, he first asks who her family is: 'From what stock was she torn?' (*Pyth.* 9. 33) and then continues, 'is it permitted to lay my famous hand on her and to cut down the honeyed flower from her bed?' (*Pyth.* 9. 36–7). The violence of marriage, as represented through this harsh agricultural image, evokes the violence of colonization as well—violence to the landscape and to the native populations. The poem equates the body of Cyrene, the nymph, with the land that takes her name, and her sexual deflowering thus represents the greater civilizing project of establishing a Greek city on foreign soil.[4] In much the same way, the rape of the Sabine women by Romulus and his men symbolizes Rome's political conquest of the Sabine people. Furthermore, the power imbalance between husband and wife inherent in the marital partnership comes to represent the similarly asymmetrical political relationship of Romans and Sabines, Greeks and Libyans.[5]

In these stories, the bodies of the eponymous nymph or indigenous women symbolize both the physical land and its occupants; their sexual conquest thus represents both the agricultural domestication of a terri-tory *and* the political domination of a people. The female body is often

---

[4] For a more detailed discussion of rape as a colonial theme in this poem, see Dougherty, *Poetics of Colonization*, 136–56.

[5] Although marriage may be, as Plutarch says (*Mor.* 140e–f), a unified partnership, it is not an equal one, and part of what the rhetoric of acculturation does is to establish the terms of the relationship between husband and wife. The husband is the one with the plough; he brings order and culture to the feminine land; he has the power and control. In Plutarch's view (*Mor.* 139d), the ideal marriage is one where husband and wife are in agreement, but one in which the husband's leadership is evident.

characterized in classical literature as a fertile field, ready to be ploughed and sown with seeds.[6] The ultimate purpose of marriage is to produce legitimate children, and this goal too is conceived in agricultural terms. When the father of the Greek bride hands his daughter over to her future husband, he utters the following formula: 'I give her to you for the cultivation (ploughing) of legitimate children.'[7] 'The fact is', as Jean-Pierre Vernant bluntly puts it, 'for the Greeks marriage is a form of ploughing, with the woman as the furrow and the husband as the labourer.'[8] The poetry of Catullus shows that this imagery is at work in the Roman world as well. In a wedding hymn, Catullus uses agricultural imagery to represent both the civilizing force and the violence of marriage.[9] First, from the feminine perspective, an unmarried girl is compared to a flower thriving in a walled garden—as long as she is untouched by the plough, many desire her. But as soon as she is picked, she is no longer attractive to anyone. In the responding strophe, however, the boys challenge this view with a song in praise of the productive benefits of agriculture. Untended, they say, the unmarried vine wastes its fruit on the ground, but if it should be 'married' to an elm tree, it will flourish productively. Catullus makes the connection quite clear: untouched (*intacta*) is the equivalent of uncultivated (*inculta*), and it is only as a cultivated vine, 'married' to an elm, that a young girl will be either desirable or useful.

The social mechanism for transforming a virgin girl to a fruitful mother is marriage, and it follows then that images from the realm of agriculture—the means for making unworked land productive—play an important role in marriage ideology. This impulse to feminize the land also reflects a belief in the similarities between a woman's power to reproduce and the annual agricultural cycles of the earth and may be especially potent in predominantly agricultural societies. As the myth of Demeter and Persephone and the ritual of the Thesmophoria also suggest, female reproduction is coincident with the fruit which mother earth

[6] Cf. J. Henderson, *The Maculate Muse* (1975; Yale University Press, New Haven, 1991), 134–6, 166–9; cf. Page DuBois, *Sowing the Body: Psychoanalysis and Ancient Representations of Women* (Chicago University Press, Chicago, 1988), 39–85 for further examples of agricultural imagery used to describe sexual intercourse.

[7] Menander, *Perikeiromene* 1013–14. Similarly Plutarch (*Mor.* 144b) remarks that the Athenians observe three sacred ploughings, and the most sacred of all is the 'marital sowing and ploughing for the procreation of children'.

[8] J.-P. Vernant, 'Introduction', in Marcel Detienne, *The Gardens of Adonis: Spices in Greek Mythology*, trans. J. Lloyd (Humanities Press, Atlantic Highlands, NJ, 1977), p. ix.

[9] Catullus 62.

produces each spring.[10] The bodies of women, like the unworked land itself, are in need of men and the tools of civilization in order to bear fruit.

As a literary or artistic motif, rape powerfully and persuasively represents military and political domination as erotic conquest, with women's bodies as symbol for a land and its people, and this motif is not at all restricted to ancient Greece and Rome.[11] We have already seen how Livy retells the story of the rape of the Sabine women within an Augustan context of imperial expansion, and the tale continues to represent political conquest long after the fall of Rome. Margaret Carroll has shown how Giovanni da Bologna's sculptural group *Rape of the Sabine Women*, located in the Loggia dei Lanzi in Florence's Piazza della Signoria in 1583, appears 'to commemorate the success of the Medici dukes in wresting control of Florence away from rival factions over the course of the sixteenth century' (Fig. 11.1).[12] Although the sculptor apparently composed the group without any specific story in mind, its meaning as a generic rape scene is clear—that of a victory monument over neighbouring territories—and this generic theme resonates clearly within the political negotiations of sixteenth-century Florence. The sculpture has three figures, and the central male figure (representing the Romans) stands triumphantly over a crouched and subservient male figure as he carries off the Sabine woman. Her struggling body, held triumphantly aloft, is only partially visible from the front and appears as an extension of the male figure, an attribute of his identity rather than a figure in her own right. The third figure cowers at the base of the sculpture, and as Carroll points out, 'the inclusion of a defeated rival in the group suggests that the young man's triumph is not only over the woman but also over the man at his feet'.[13] Thus the sculpture links the rape of one woman not

[10] Froma I. Zeitlin, 'Cultic Models of the Female: Rites of Dionysus and Demeter', *Arethusa*, 15 (1982), 141 observes that in myth and ritual women are more often associated with cosmic phenomena and cycles than with historical time-frames or events. See also Detienne, *Gardens of Adonis*, 116.

[11] See e.g. A. Kolodny, *The Lay of the Land: Metaphor as Experience and History in American Life and Letters* (University of North Carolina Press, Chapel Hill, 1974); Ruth Harris, 'The "Child of the Barbarian": Rape, Race, and Nationalism in France during the First World War', *Past and Present*, 141 (1993), 170–206; Margaret Carroll, 'The Erotics of Absolutism: Rubens and the Mystification of Sexual Violence', *Representations*, 25 (1989), 3–30; Patricia Parker, *Literary Fat Ladies: Rhetoric, Gender, Property* (Methuen, London, 1987), 126–54; Hall, 'Asia Unmanned'.

[12] Carroll, 'Erotics of Absolutism', 7.

[13] Ibid. 7. She quotes a line from a contemporary poem about the sculpture that compares Florence to the Sabine woman, praising Francesco dei Medici ('who with such valor, with such wisdom possesses her'), 7–8 n. 25.

FIG. 11.1 *Rape of the Sabine Women* by Giovanni da Bologna.

just with the subjugation of all Sabine women, but with the conquest of the Sabine land and people as well. Sexual violence against the bodies of the Sabine women represents political violence against the body politic. Moreover, the use of this Roman tale within a Renaissance Italian context to represent Florentine supremacy shows that it has mythic or rhetorical force that transcends the specific historical context from which it first emerged.

Rape is an act of violence, but as an act of violence perpetrated on women, it has important consequences that transcend the act itself. As the imagery that connects rape and marriage to the agricultural realm makes clear, the birth of children that follows rape is an important part of this discursive strategy. If we return to Livy, we notice that his account of the rape of the Sabine women does not end with the rape itself as an expression of political conquest. The story concludes with the subsequent attack by the Sabines upon Rome in which the now-Roman wives, with loosened hair and torn garments, rush out into the middle of the fray—between fathers and husbands—to call for peace on the strength of the marriage tie lest there be impious bloodshed as fathers kill children and vice versa. Livy explains that, in response to this demonstration, the leaders called a truce and thus made one city out of two: 'sed civitatem nam ex duabus faciunt' (1. 13. 4). And so it is clear that Romans marrying Sabines is only the first chapter of this programmatic tale; it sets the stage for what is truly significant—the establishment of a political relationship between Romans and Sabines. Rape, an act of violence, contains the seeds of its own transformation into an act of culture. The transfer of women from (Sabine) fathers to (Roman) husbands together with the ensuing Roman children establishes a familial connection that erases cultural difference and ultimately determines future political relationships. Sabine women take on new identities as Roman wives just as Sabine territory is renamed Roman. One city remains where once there were two.

Ovid tells a slightly different story of the Sabine women in the *Art of Love*, and his account begins to remind us that the original act of violence against women is not just metaphorical and should remain a focal part of the story. As part of his advice to men about where to find women eager for love, Ovid suggests going to the theatre since it has been a fertile hunting ground as far back as the time of Romulus:

> The king gave the awaited sign for booty to the people.
> They sprang up immediately, voicing their enthusiasm,
>   and threw eager hands upon the girls;

like the most timid flock of doves flees hawks
   and like the newborn lamb flees the hated wolf,
so these girls feared the men rushing at them without legal right
   and they all lost their previous colour.
For although fear was unanimous, it took different appearances;
   some tore their hair, some stood still in shock;
others kept silent in grief, others called in vain upon their mothers;
   one complained, another was silent; one stayed still; another fled.
The raped girls were led, like marriage booty, and fear itself
   caused many to look becoming.
If any one fought back too much or denied her partner,
   her husband picked her up and carried her off in desire
Saying, 'why do you ruin your sweet eyes with tears? What
   your father is to your mother, I will be to you', he said.

(*Ars Amat.* 1. 114–30; my translation)

Mythical accounts like this of rape appear quite frequently in Ovid's works, and it is never easy to know what to make of them.[14] A light-hearted sense of parody mixes uncomfortably with accounts of sexual violence as in this passage where, not very far beneath the surface of Ovid's quite witty and cynical telling of what had become a cornerstone of Roman historical memory, lie clear signals of sexual aggression. While Livy moves quickly past the act of rape in his account, focusing more on the power of marriage to transform girls into mothers and Sabines into Romans, Ovid restores a glimpse of the real violence that may lie behind this rhetorical strategy. The poignant similes that compare the raped Sabine girls to fluttering flocks of doves or newborn lambs running from animals of prey convey a sense of real fear and potential brutality. The girls themselves are described as war booty (*praeda*), and the catalogue of their terrified responses to the hostile advances of Roman men reinforces a sense of foreboding in spite of Ovid's flippant tone. Although this poem is far from first-hand testimony from real rape victims, Ovid's narrative does shift the focus away from the men enacting the violence and onto the women who experience it, and therein, I suspect, lies much of our discomfort with Ovid's account. Ovid eroticizes the girls' fear, and this conflation of sexuality and violence provides the framework for rape as a military weapon in ancient Rome and, as we will see, in modern Bosnia as well.

[14] On rape in Ovid, see Leo C. Curran, 'Rape and Rape Victims in the *Metamorphoses*', in John Peradotto and J. P. Sullivan (eds.), *Women in the Ancient World: The Arethusa Papers* (State University of New York Press, Albany, NY, 1984), 263–86; Amy Richlin, 'Reading Ovid's Rapes', in Richlin (ed.), *Pornography and Representation in Greece and Rome*, 158–79.

Like so many tales from antiquity, 'The Rape of the Sabine Women' tends to take on an air of mythical unreality; read sometimes as fiction, sometimes as history, the episode is easily trivialized as a kind of party game whereby Roman boys get matched up with Sabine girls, and everyone lives happily every after, and (by the way) the future of the Roman Empire is now secure. Rereading this story in light of Renaissance politics and the recent war in Bosnia, however, suggests that we rethink our understanding of the rape of the Sabine women and what it tells us about early Roman history. The hostilities in Bosnia have shown how powerful ethnic identities remain in spite of attempts, military and political, to replace them with a broader national identity. This tenuous coexistence of ethnic and national identities lies at the heart of Livy's account of the incorporation of Sabines into the Roman state as well. As the Romans attempted to consolidate their position and unify all of Italy under their control, they waged a series of territorial wars against neighbouring peoples, including the Sabines. It is quite possible that the historical conflict between Romans and Sabines included real acts of sexual aggression against women that then became incorporated into the city's founding mythology. Obviously, this tale then takes on renewed currency in Augustan times as a way to represent a new period of conquest and the consolidation of Roman expansion and thus is retold in the works of Livy and Ovid. My point, however, is that the later use of the myth of the Sabine women to represent Augustan expansion does not rule out the possibility of real violence—both at the founding of Rome and in later imperial conquests. Some comparative evidence will help elaborate this point.

What the recent events in Bosnia have graphically shown us is that rape is not just an ancient metaphor for political conquest. As part of their conquest of Bosnia in the spring of 1992, the Serbs systematically raped tens of thousands of Bosnian women of Muslim or Croat origin.[15] In an eighty-two-page essay, Alexandra Stiglmayer relentlessly presents the testimony of women from Bosnia, Croatia, and Serbia who were raped as part of the recent hostilities. One woman struggles with how to tell the story of what happened to her, and her testimony shows all too clearly how sexual and military tools merge into one powerful weapon:

[15] As of March 1993, data gathered by the State Commission in Bosnia showed estimates of 25,000–30,000 women, girls, and underage girls raped. 'State Commission for Gathering Facts on War Crimes in the Republic of Bosnia and Herzegovina', *War Crimes in B-H: Bulletin 3–1.0, 3–1.1,* http://www.intac.com/PubService/human_rights/balkans/hr/boscom3.html (23 June 1996).

'They pushed bottles into our sex, they even stuck shattered, broken bottles into some women . . . Guns, too. And then you don't know if he's going to fire, you're scared to death, everything else, the rape, becomes less important, even the rape doesn't seem so terrible anymore.'[16] Another woman describes her rapists: 'Each one of them weighed at least 220 pounds. They were horses, beasts . . . They played with their knives and said they were going to butcher my kids.'[17] Thirty-nine-year-old Fatima recounts the threats that accompanied her rape and that of her daughter, '"we'll knock out all your teeth, we'll butcher your kids, hack them to pieces, and make you watch."'[18] This and other painfully graphic testimony of first-hand experience makes it clear that real women are suffering real violence as part of ethnic hostilities—this is no party game.

Yet this horrific violence stems from a particular context—these are not random acts of male agression. These rapes comprise a wartime strategy not unlike Romulus' command to rape the Sabine women as part of a strategy to preserve the Roman state. One 40-year old woman, Kadira, is convinced that the rapes at the camp in Doboj were happening on military orders: 'How could it be anything else? 'Cause I'm sure our Serbs wouldn't have done that to us on their own, not our neighbours . . . We were good friends; we watched out for each other and helped each other out . . . The orders came from Serbia, those were Serbian directives.'[19] Another woman thinks that 'ethnic cleansing' was the reason for the rapes: 'They said they wanted to drive us out, that there shouldn't be any more Muslims in Europe.'[20] Testimony shows that, over and over, Serbian soldiers boasted of the ethnic imperialism they were waging upon the bodies of women. Kadira tells about how she and other women had to dance naked for the Serbian guards and sing Serbian songs. She has forgotten how many times she was raped.[21] Serbian women were raped too and were subjected to similar nationalistic treatment. Similja recounts being raped by her Croatian neighbours: 'There were eight of them. While they were raping me they sang anti-Chetnik songs.'[22] This first-hand testimony incontrovertibly shows the political and ethnic ideology that drives these very real, and coldly calculated, acts of violence.

[16] Cited in Alexandra Stiglmayer, 'The Rapes in Bosnia-Herzegovina', in Stiglmayer (ed.), *Mass Rape*, 118.
[17] Cited ibid. 106.
[18] Cited ibid. 105.
[19] Cited ibid. 120.
[20] Cited ibid. 121.
[21] Ibid. 119.
[22] Cited ibid. 141. 'Chetnik' is a slang term for Serbian.

Moreover, from Stiglmayer's interviews, we recognize some of the same underlying themes at work in the rhetoric of symbolic violence in ancient Greek and Roman culture. Testimony from Ifeta, a former sales clerk, poignantly reveals the powerfully persuasive association between women's bodies and the world of agriculture that makes these rapes make a kind of ideological sense. About Serbs and rape camps, she says: 'For them the camp was like a fruit stand . . . or to put it better, a livestock stand. Anyone could pass by and just take whatever he wanted, just do whatever he wanted. The Serbs had the power.'[23] Ifeta's choice of imagery (women as fruit or domesticated animal) reinforces the equation of women with the world of nature in need of being tamed, vulnerable to men and their powerful tools of culture.[24]

In an essay on the rapes in Bosnia, Catharine MacKinnon provides chilling testimony given by Haris, a Bosnian soldier who observed a gang rape in a village in Serbian-occupied Croatia. This account shows yet again how the association between women's bodies and the land continues to precipitate violence against women as a way to represent political dominance. While the soldiers raped the woman, who was tied to four stakes driven into the ground, they said that Yugoslavia was theirs since they had fought for it in the Second World War and had given everything for Yugoslavia. Later Haris reports that the superior officer who was ordering the rape said: 'She has to know that we are Chetniks. She has to know this is our land. She has to know that we're commanding, that this is our Greater Serbia, that it'll be like this for everyone who doesn't listen.'[25] Staked into the ground, the woman's body literally becomes inseparable from the land that the soldiers are fighting each other to control. By raping her they are sowing seeds of political as well as sexual conquest. This act and their accompanying boasts ('she has to know this is our land') shows how quickly metaphor and reality converge and collapse here, how difficult it is to separate the strands of physical and symbolic violence.

Furthermore, as in the case of the Sabine women, rape as part of a political strategy in Bosnia is only half the story. Bosnian and Croatian women are raped so that they will give birth to Serbian children, and these children complicate and threaten the native political, ethnic, and religious identity of their mothers as well. The act of rape attempts to

---

[23] Cited in Stiglmayer, 'Rapes in Bosnia', 118.
[24] Cf. for example, Sappho, frr. 105a and c Loebel-Page; Pind. *Pyth.* 9.
[25] Catharine A. MacKinnon, 'Turning Rape into Pornography: Postmodern Genocide', in Stiglmayer (ed.), *Mass Rape*, 79.

replace Bosnians with Serbs. Fatima, who used to work as a cleaning woman and who now lives in a refugee camp in central Bosnia, says, 'they used to get together and sing "o beautiful bula, a Chetnik's beard will scratch you", or about how Muslim women would give birth to Serbian children'.[26] Ifeta was raped by a group of Serbian soldiers, and says that 'while they were doing it, they said I was going to have a baby by them and that it'd be an honor for a Muslim woman to give birth to a Serbian kid'.[27] Hatiza was taken to a concentration camp and told, 'the next time we meet, you'll have one of our kids in your belly'.[28] Mirsada says, 'they told us we were going to give birth to Serbian children and they would do everything they could so we wouldn't even dare think of coming back again'.[29] In Livy's account, the Sabine women were transformed into Roman wives as a representation of Rome's political conquest of the Sabines, and it was the birth of Roman children that articulated and reinforced this new identity. Here, too, giving birth to Serbian babies is meant to redefine the ethnic identities and loyalties of the Bosnian women.

A careful reading of just some of the testimony from women raped as part of ethnic hostilities in the former Yugoslavia provides strong evidence of the same ideology of territorial and ethnic conquest that we can sometimes see more easily in the distant myths of ancient Greece or Rome. These are not isolated acts of wartime violence—they are part of a larger discursive framework that unites women's bodies and the land to express political domination of the latter as sexual conquest of the former. As Lance Morrow observed in a 1993 article on the role that rape has played in these fierce ethnic battles in the former Yugoslavia, 'Serbs are undoubtedly committing most of the rapes at the moment; they have also seized most of the land.'[30] Unfortunately, since so many literary and artistic traditions use rape as a pervasive metaphor to represent acts of political foundation, this correlation of rape and territorial imperialism should come as no shock.

But the story cuts both ways, and this may be the real surprise. Not only does the classical theme of foundation rape contextualize and clarify individual acts of violence in modern Bosnia, but the brutal mass rapes today provide a fuller, more realistic political framework for interpreting

---

[26] Cited in Stiglmayer, 'Rapes in Bosnia', 104.
[27] Cited ibid. 117–18.
[28] Cited ibid. 92.
[29] Cited ibid. 109.
[30] *Newsweek*, 2 Feb. 1993.

myths of the past. Unlike those of previous wars, the rapes in Bosnia have been documented by women's organizations in an attempt to redefine human rights in favour of women. As a result, we have an unparalleled amount of first-hand testimony from the women themselves about their experiences. These women tell their own stories of being raped, tortured, and subjected to all kinds of violence in the name of ethnic superiority. It is worth considering whether similar acts of real violence against women were not also part of the Roman subjugation of the Sabines or the Greek colonization of Cyrene.

The symbolic violence of rape depends on the intersection of rhetoric and social practice, and we need to keep both aspects in play as we try to understand the twofold role that rape plays in wars of conquest and in representing them. Ruth Harris's discussion of First World War France shows just how permeable and reciprocal the boundaries between real and metaphorical rape can be. In the case of the Sabine women, the story of rape is told by those with the power as part of a celebration of victory over a neighbouring people. In fact, Livy and Ovid's retelling of this foundation myth in an Augustan context gives the tale a double significance—it functions as a representation both of Rome's original foundation and of its later imperial expansion. But the symbolic representation of conquest as rape functions within the rhetoric of the conquered as well. In the early weeks of the First World War, hundreds of French women were brutally raped by German soldiers. Ruth Harris has written about how 'the actual victimization of women was transformed into a representation of a violated, but innocent, female nation resisting the assaults of a brutal male assailant'.[31] Harris is concerned with investigating how real crimes against women became part of the symbolic rhetoric of national propaganda, and her evidence helps us see how mutually embedded the relationship is between reality and rhetoric.

Indeed, one of the propaganda posters she discusses operates within a very familiar discursive framework. The poster bears the caption 'Germany treacherously attacked peace-loving France in August 1914' (Fig. 11.2). France is represented as Marianne, a young woman dressed as Ceres with an armful of wheat and a liberty cap. Standing innocently in a wheat field, she is threatened by a German soldier with a gun in one hand and a knife in the other. The agriculturally fertile Ceres thus merges with her raped daughter Persephone to present an image of domesticated fertility combined with natural innocence, both threatened

---

[31] Harris, ' "Child of the Barbarian" ', 170.

L'ALLEMAGNE A TRAÎTREUSEMENT ATTAQUÉ LA FRANCE PACIFIQUE EN AOÛT 1914

F I G. 11.2   First World War propaganda poster.

by barbarian male force. Harris argues for a relationship between the real experience of French women raped by German soldiers and this symbolic representation of it: 'Individual women victimized by the marauders were thus often transformed into a representation of a feminized

nation, *la France civilatrice*, fighting a war of liberation against a plunder-
ing, overarmoured brute.'[32]

What the evidence provided by accounts of the Sabine women, contemporary Bosnia, and First World War France (to take just a few examples) can give us is a framework for recognizing the reciprocity of the
relationship between real and symbolic violence against women. Approaching the rape camps in Bosnia through myths like that of the
Sabine women can restore symbolic significance to what has been rightly
recognized as a war crime against real women. In the former Yugoslavia,
a country torn by ethnic conflict, where territory continues to be fiercely
contested and political identity is very much at stake, rape remains the
ultimate manifestation of territorial imperialism. By literally sowing
their seed in the bodies of Muslim women and girls, the Serbs lay claim,
physically and metaphorically, to the land that women's bodies so often
symbolically represent. Yet not only does the classical theme of foundation rape help clarify individual acts of violence in modern Bosnia, but
the events in Bosnia have shown us all too chillingly that rape is not just
a metaphor for political conquest. First-hand testimony (something
classicists never have) from Bosnian women suggests that we must revisit
and revise our often overly sanitized or theoretical readings of rape in the
ancient world to include the very real possibilities of violent conflict
and actual violence against women.[33] I am not suggesting that events
in Bosnia or First World War France provide evidence for real violence
against women in Rome—rather that all three situations reflect a similar
practice of both real and symbolic violence against women, each inform-
ing the other. In other words, a symbolic reading of the rape of the
Sabine women need not preclude but rather might suggest traces of real
violence against women as part of a larger territorial conflict both at
Rome's founding and at moments of later expansion. While the Sabine
and Serb accounts celebrate rape as a manifestation of victory of one
people over another, Harris's discussion of rape in early First World War
France shows how real rapes can take on larger symbolic value for a
conquered people as well.

[32] Harris, ' "Child of the Barbarian" ', 179–80.
[33] For an argument against reading rape in classical myth in connection with the violent
treatment of women, see Mary R. Lefkowitz, 'Seduction and Rape in Greek Myth', in
Angeliki E. Laiou (ed.), *Consent and Coercion to Sex and Marriage in Ancient and Medieval
Societies* (Dunbarton Oaks, Washington, 1993), 17–37. Even readings that do address myths
of rape as expressions of symbolic violence often fail to consider the potential connections
with actual violence against women as well. See e.g. Zeitlin, 'Configurations of Rape'; Hall,
'Asia Unmanned'.

Real violence against women is part of a discursive framework that aims to express or represent political violence against a people. Women—Cyrene, Sabines, Marianne, Bosnians—function as metaphors for the land. At the same time, this physical land or territory often stands metonymically for all the people who inhabit it. Therefore, by a kind of transitive dynamic, women come to stand for the larger political entity. One way to dominate the larger political group is through acts of violence against particular women. There is little to gain in trying to decide whether these rapes are primarily crimes against women or ethnic crimes—they are both. The metaphorical alliance of woman and the land deliberately mystifies and obfuscates the distinctions between the two. Rape is an all too common part of wars of territorial conquest and ethnic conflict, and it operates simultaneously at the level of real violence against real women and at the symbolic level to express power over another land or people.

If, as often, the aim of war is to destroy a culture and/or to acquire its territory, women are prime targets as symbols both of the land and its culture. As Ruth Seifert reiterates, the 'female body functions as a symbolic representation of the body politic'.[34] Her rape stands for the violation and domination of a culture and its community at large. The material from the First World War and Bosnia suggests that real experience and rhetorical uses of rape criss-cross and intersect to create a rhetoric of violence that is itself capable of doing violence. As Teresa de Lauretis has argued,

the very notion of a 'rhetoric of violence' . . . presupposes that some order of language, some kind of discursive representation is at work not only in the concept of 'violence' but in the social practices of violence as well. The (semiotic) relation of the social to the discursive is thus posed from the start. But once that relation is instated, once a connection is assumed between violence and rhetoric, the two terms begin to slide, and, soon enough, the connection will appear to be reversible.[35]

De Lauretis goes on to contend that the representation of violence is inseparable from the notion of gender—the subject of violence is always male while the object is female.[36] Furthermore, even though we may

[34] Ruth Seifert, 'War and Rape: A Preliminary Analysis', in Stiglmayer (ed.), *Mass Rape*, 63.
[35] Teresa de Lauretis, *Technologies of Gender: Essays on Theory, Film, and Fiction* (Indiana University Press, Bloomington, 1987), 32–3.
[36] Cf. ibid. 43: 'For the subject of the violence is always, by definition, masculine; "man" is by definition the subject of culture and of any social act.'

agree that gender is socially constructed, the experiences that follow from its construction are very real. Thus, while rape may function rhetorically as a representation of political power, the object of that rape, both symbolically and, more importantly, in practice, will always be female.[37] Alexandra Stiglmayer hits upon the significance of this slippage between rhetoric and reality when she observes that 'in Bosnia-Herzegovina a war is being waged against women. Not because they are women, but because they are Muslim, Croatian, or Serbian women. Yet because they are women, men are using against them their most effective weapon: rape.'[38] The challenge is to see both the particularity of these crimes and their generic force, focusing on the dynamic interactions between them.

[37] Or, as in cases of male rape, the victims will be feminized.
[38] Stiglmayer, 'Rapes in Bosnia', 84.

Index